Key Learning Skills

for Children with Autism Spectrum Disorders

Thomas L. Whitman and Nicole DeWitt

Key Learning Skills

for Children with
Autism Spectrum
Disorders

A Blueprint for Life

Jessica Kingsley *Publishers*
London and Philadelphia

First published in 2011
by Jessica Kingsley Publishers
116 Pentonville Road
London N1 9JB, UK
and
400 Market Street, Suite 400
Philadelphia, PA 19106, USA

www.jkp.com

Library of Congress Cataloging in Publication Data
Whitman, Thomas L.
 Key learning skills for children with autism spectrum disorders : a blueprint for life / Thomas L. Whitman and Nicole DeWitt.
   p. cm.
 Includes bibliographical references and index.
 ISBN 978-1-84905-864-3 (alk. paper)
 1. Autistic children--Education. 2. Autistic children--Behavior modification. I. DeWitt, Nicole. II. Title.
 LC4717.W45 2011
 371.94--dc22
                                        2010053636

British Library Cataloguing in Publication Data
A CIP catalogue record for this book is available from the British Library

ISBN 978 1 84905 864 3

Printed and bound in the United States

Contents

For the many students who have taken our courses, participated in home and school-based intervention programs for children with autism and been part of our research groups. Thank you for your support, service to families, and stimulation.

Preface

Autism spectrum disorders (ASD) are characterized by a diverse set of symptoms that vary in the way they are manifested across individuals. In addition to the social interaction deficiencies, language/communication delays, and repetitive, restricted, and stereotyped behavior patterns that diagnostically characterize these disorders, a variety of sensory, motor, emotional, and behavioral problems frequently co-occur. Because of the complexity of ASD, a broad range of intervention approaches have evolved. Such interventions have varied considerably in their focus, structure, and comprehensiveness.

Parents and professionals who must make decisions about intervention programs for children with autism spectrum disorders are confronted with a major challenge because of the multitude of interventions available and a lack of consensus about which are most appropriate. This lack of consensus has arisen in part because the causes and exact nature of autism have not yet been clearly delineated. Controversy has also been generated because many interventions have been developed outside of a scientific framework. Such interventions often do not have a standardized protocol; as a consequence they are difficult to replicate for either empirical or clinical purposes. These interventions have typically been designed by individuals who have not known how or thought it unnecessary to evaluate their effectiveness. Sometimes parents and professionals searching for appropriate interventions feel they are being forced into making a decision between doing nothing, which is unacceptable, or adopting untested interventions.

The present book presents an intervention program for teaching children with ASD that is comprehensive in scope and consists of techniques that are evidence-based. These techniques have been derived from extensive basic research that has uncovered fundamental principles guiding behavioral, cognitive, and emotional development. Applied research in turn has developed, based on these principles, educational procedures that have been employed and evaluated with both neurotypical and atypical children and adults.

The purpose of this book is to present a blueprint for developing a comprehensive intervention program for children with autism spectrum disorders. This book is directed at parents as well as professionals from various disciplines, including education, clinical psychology, speech therapy, occupational therapy, physical therapy, and medicine, who are searching for a better way to address the needs of children with ASD. In addition, this book is appropriate for college courses in autism that have a practicum component.

In Chapter 1, the assumptions and general principles that guided the formulation of this comprehensive intervention program are examined, followed by a discussion of characteristics considered critical for such a program to be successful. Chapter 2 describes evidence-based techniques for promoting adaptive behavior development, behavior maintenance, and behavior generalization, as well as techniques for dealing with behavior problems associated with autism spectrum disorders. From a theoretical perspective, these techniques are derived from ecological, classical conditioning, operant, social, and cognitive-behavioral learning theories. All of these theories emphasize the important role that the environment plays in human development. For purposes of discussion, the techniques are grouped into several categories: ecologically focused, behavior-oriented, emotion-focused, cognitively oriented, and behavior reduction. The effectiveness of these techniques have been empirically established for use with a wide range of behaviors and clinical populations, including children with ASD.

Chapters 3 to 10 describe interventions for addressing deficiencies and delays and developing competencies in core learning skills and emotional, sensory, motor, language, cognitive, social, and self-regulatory functioning. The structure of these chapters is similar. Each chapter begins by examining basic symptoms, delays, and deficiencies associated with autism spectrum disorders as well as the causes of these problems, their impact on development, and behaviors that need to be targeted for intervention. Then basic strategies for creating behavior change are described. Finally, examples of specific intervention programs are presented.

Chapter 3 describes intervention programs for establishing core skills, behaviors that provide a basic foundation for learning and development. The core skills discussed include: attention, joint attention, and social referencing, imitation, request-making, labeling, instruction-following, matching, and sequencing. In Chapter 4, skills necessary for developing emotional competence, specifically emotion awareness, emotion expression, and emotion regulation, are described. In addition, emotion-based problems, including hyperarousal, hypoarousal, anxiety/fear, and anger, are discussed. Chapter 5 examines sensory problems commonly displayed by children with autism, specifically hypersensitivity, sensory overload, hyposensitivity, and sensory integration deficiencies. Chapter 6 focuses on sensorimotor impairments, including delays and deficiencies in gross and fine motor skills, which affect personal, academic, and community functioning.

In Chapter 7, language behaviors that are critical for communication competency are discussed, ranging from simple gestural responses and sound production to conversational speech. Chapter 8 examines key cognitive processes that need to be targeted for intervention, including holistic processing, memory, abstract thinking, and pretend play as well as the use of these processes in academic situations. The importance of intervention programs building on cognitive strengths is also emphasized. In Chapter 9, social behaviors are discussed, including the importance of developing social play, friendships, theory of mind, empathy, rule-governed behavior (e.g. following social protocols), and community engagement skills. Chapter 10 looks at the relationship between self-regulation deficiencies and stereotyped, repetitive, and restricted behaviors. Components of executive-functioning processes, that are critical for the development of self-regulation and independent functioning are examined, including impulse control, self and other awareness, flexible action, verbal control of behavior, and problem-solving.

Finally, Chapter 11 begins with a discussion of common co-morbid symptoms diagnosed in children with autism, including attention deficit hyperactivity, anxiety, and depressive symptoms. It also describes an array of other behavioral and developmental problems that frequently occur in this population, specifically repetitive, restricted and stereotyped behaviors, self-injurious behaviors, noncompliance, temper tantrums, aggression, self-toileting delays, eating problems, and sleeping problems. For each of these problems, intervention strategies are discussed. The chapter then examines the relationship between medical problems and autism and the various ways that biological and environmental factors might influence this relationship. This chapter also concludes with the presentation of specific intervention examples.

Although considerable information is presented in this book concerning how the goals and techniques of this comprehensive intervention program should be structured and implemented, we recommend that the actual implementation of this program be coordinated with qualified professionals who have appropriate educational credentials and professional certifications. With a few exceptions, the book does not discuss biological treatments, but rather emphasizes, because of the absence of curative medical treatments for ASD, the critical importance of educational interventions for developing adaptive behavior.

A number of people have been very helpful in preparing this book. In particular, we owe a debt of gratitude to Kristin Wier who generously shared her clinical expertize and experience with us throughout the writing of this book. Special thanks are also due to Judy Stewart for her considerable assistance in the preparation of this manuscript. Finally, we would like to thank our students, past and present, and the many families who have taught us so much about teaching and supporting the development of children with autism. In recognition of their contributions to this book, all royalties will be used to support intervention programs provided by the Sonia Ansari Regional Autism Center at Logan in South Bend, Indiana.

Chapter 1

Selection of Appropriate Interventions

Parents raising a child with an autism spectrum disorder are confronted with a variety of personal, familial, vocational, and financial challenges. After a diagnosis of autism is given to their child, they struggle to understand the implications of this event for themselves and their family (Milshtein, Yirmiya, Oppenheim, Koren-Karie, & Levi, 2010). They search for information about autism and its complex and mysterious symptomatology as well as for appropriate intervention programs for their children. The search for services is particularly time-consuming and often frustrating. Due to the wide variety of interventions available, parents wonder which would be best for their child (Whitman, 2004).

The different schools of thought regarding intervention programs for children with autism spectrum disorders (ASD) often engenders passionate discussion and disagreement among both service providers and parents regarding best practices. As parents search for appropriate programs, they are confronted with the myriad of choices, sales pitches, and testimonials from therapists and satisfied consumers. As a consequence, it is not uncommon for them to become hopelessly confused. Rationales are provided by service providers to convince parents of the validity of a particular approach or approaches, sometimes accompanied by arguments as to why other interventions are ineffective and to be avoided. Not surprisingly, parents are often drawn to interventions that are intuitively appealing, easy to administer, emotionally satisfying, "natural," and promise cures.

In response to the increasing diversification of treatments, a call for a new approach has been put forth by the scientific community, emphasizing the development of an evidence-based approach and a merging of programs from various disciplines, such as psychology, speech pathology, occupational therapy and education (Feinberg & Vacca, 2000). However, for such an integration to be successful and to avoid being arbitrary and chaotic, it needs to be formulated in a manner that makes theoretical, empirical, and practical sense.

The present book describes an educational intervention program that is designed to be both comprehensive in scope and integrative in its approach. In this chapter assumptions that guided the formulation of this intervention program are discussed, followed by a description of characteristics considered to be critical for such a program to be successful. Subsequent chapters will describe the specific goals of this intervention program, the rationales for pursuing these objectives, along with specific techniques for accomplishing these goals.

Program assumptions

Autism is a developmental disorder

The examination of autism within a developmental context makes sense because it emerges early in life, with symptoms gradually unfolding as development occurs.

Formally, autism is classified as a developmental disability (Whitman, 2004). Although developmental psychologists conceptualize development as a process that occurs across the lifespan, the term developmental disability typically refers to a dysfunction that emerges during the early portion of the lifespan. The Developmental Disabilities Assistance and Bill of Rights Act of 1990 defines a developmental disability as a severe, chronic disability that: 1) is attributable to a mental or physical impairment, or a combination of mental and physical impairments; 2) is manifest before 22 years of age and is likely to continue indefinitely; 3) results in substantial functional limitations in three or more of areas of major life activities, including self-care, receptive and expressive language, learning, mobility, self-direction, capacity for independent living and economic self-sufficiency; and 4) reflects the person's need for a combination of individualized and coordinated services that are of lifelong or extended duration. This definition originated as part of an effort by the federal government in the United States to identify and assist people in need of support services through federal legislation.

Using this definition, most individuals with an autistic disorder would be defined as having a developmental disability; certainly early in their life, and often later as well. Because persons labeled as autistic have deficiencies in the areas of language and social interaction, they usually experience problems in other areas, such as academic and vocational functioning and independent living, all of which are central to the definition of developmental disabilities. Viewing autism from a developmental perspective has important intervention implications. Three of these implications, relating to the importance of the social environment, the timing of intervention, and the multidimensional and dynamic nature of autism, are briefly discussed in the following sections.

The impact of the environment is substantial

Figure 1.1 shows the relationship between biological and environmental factors and their influences on the development of autism. As shown in this figure, one pathway of influence is from genes, which affect the development of the neurobiological substrate, which in turn influences the emergence of behaviors associated with autism. Other (non-autism) genes influence through this same general pathway neurotypical characteristics of the child, such as temperament and personality.

Figure 1.1 also shows two important pathways from the environment. In one pathway the environment influences the development of the behavioral phenotype of children with ASD, including behaviors diagnostically associated with autism spectrum disorders (e.g. language delays), other related autism symptoms (e.g. motor delays), behavior problems (e.g. temper tantrums, aggression, eating and sleeping problems), and other non-autistic more normative characteristics. In the other pathway the environment (e.g. prenatal) influences the neurobiological substrate underlying these behaviors, including how brain connections develop. Some of the changes in the biological substrate are also mediated by changes in behavior produced by the environment. The social and physical factors that make up this environment are quite diverse. They include the influence of parents, family, teachers, specific educational interventions, environmental stressors, the restrictive environments that children with autism create for themselves, the prenatal environment, and toxic substances in the air, water, and soil.

Other interesting pathways, from genes to environment and environment to genes, are also shown in Figure 1.1. For example, the genes of both children and their parents may affect how they interact with one another; for example there is a genetic foundation for parenting style and child activity level. Moreover, the physical environment may under certain circumstances influence the child at the genetic level, through agents, such as x-rays, which can cause gene mutation. Finally, the physical environment, through its impact on the underlying biochemical substrate, can influence which genes are turned on, that is expressed and become operational, and which genes turn off. More generally, what Figure 1.1 shows is that there is a complex and interactive relationship between the environment, biological factors and the development of children with autism. Educational interventions that focus on changing the physical and social environments of children with autism can and do have profound influences on the child's biological and behavioral development.

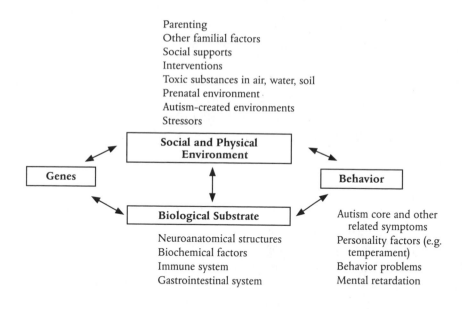

Figure 1.1 Reciprocal interaction of biological, environmental, and behavioral factors

Although the specific defects that produce autism have yet to be identified, research within the last decade has provided initial insights into their general genetic and neurobiological foundation. In contrast, less is known about how the social and physical environment influences the emergence of autism and molds its underlying biological substrate. It is likely that research examining the impact of the social environment and parenting on autism has been inhibited by the vigorous rejection by the professional community of early theories suggesting that autism is caused by aloof and affectively disengaged parenting styles as well as the growing realization that autism is a genetically based disorder. However, even though autism has genetic origins and is not caused by poor parenting, it does not follow that the social environment has no influence on the trajectory of this disorder.

As autism emerges, parents are confronted with children whose characteristics are peculiar and confusing. At least initially, they have little insight into why their children act as they do and what they as parents should do to help their children. For example, they are often bewildered by their children who are hypersensitive, motorically challenged, fearful, socially avoidant, linguistically and cognitively delayed, and prone to engage in unusual stereotyped and ritualistic behaviors. As a consequence parents experience stress and, not infrequently, a sense of helplessness.

In order to assist parents, appropriate social and emotional supports must be provided to them. Intervention programs need to help parents to create social environments for their children with ASD that are safe, predictable, and growth enhancing and to deter their children from developing and utilizing maladaptive coping mechanisms that disengage them from the social environment. From a neurological perspective, the brain of the child with ASD will get wired; it is just a question of how and by whom, either by the restricted environments created and controlled by the atypical behaviors of the child with autism or by a stimulating and educational environment created by parents and other significant socialization figures.

A variety of recent research points out the importance of the parent–child interaction. For example, Stiller and Sigman (2002) found that parents of children with autism vary in the degree to which they are able to synchronize their behaviors with their children and that their level of synchronization is related to the children's joint attention and language skills. Similarly, Baker, Messinger, Lyons, and Grantz (2010) found that maternal sensitivity was associated with language growth in young children with ASD. Moreover, results by Brigham, Yoder, Jarzynka, and Tapp (2010) indicated that more extensive parental cuing behaviors supported sustained object attention in children with autism. It appears that parents who learn how to synchronize and respond to the needs of their children in a more sensitive and contingent fashion are more successful teachers. Overall, the results of these types of research, as well as early intervention studies (Remington et al., 2007), suggest that parents and primary caretakers of children with autism, like parents of neurotypical children, can have a substantial and positive impact on their children's cognitive, language, and behavior development.

Early intervention is important

From a biological perspective, it is known that during early infancy, brain development has already proceeded to a point where billions of neurons, the basic building blocks of the brain, have been formed. The process of interconnecting these neurons, however, has only begun. During the early years of a child's life, trillions of connections between neurons are formed. Many of the connections are later eliminated with the passage of time. The early experiences of the child with an autism spectrum disorder play a critical role in determining which connections between neurons are developed and sustained and which ones disappear. Although genes play a vital role in developing the building blocks of the brain, the environment is the vital force determining how these blocks will be specifically organized, or to use another metaphor, how the brain is wired.

Basic processes, including sensory, motor, perceptual, cognitive, and linguistic, are profoundly influenced by the environments in which children with autism live. These processes become integrated with one another through experience. Cognitive processes emerge out of this vast pattern of connections. Body and person recognition develop. Thoughts become linked to emotions. Inhibitory pathways are formed that allow emotions to be controlled as social rules are learned.

Fox, Levitt, and Nelson (2010) point out that early life events exert a powerful influence on both brain and behavioral development. This extremely complex developmental process is disrupted when autism occurs. What exactly produces this disruption is not well understood, nor are all the specific effects of this disruption on later development. Genes undoubtedly play a role through influencing how basic brain biochemistry and structures evolve, as well as by placing restrictions on the way environments influence the wiring of the brain. Nevertheless, the environment has a substantial influence on the development of children with autism. Depending on how this environment is structured, the trajectory of their development may be positive and growth facilitating or negative and growth inhibiting.

Although the brain is extremely malleable, there are limits. There are most likely windows of opportunity for the wiring of emotional, motor, sensory, cognitive, and language processes (Fox & Rutter, 2010; Fox, Levitt, & Nelson, 2010). If, due to restrictions in the environment, proper stimulation of these processes does not occur within a certain time frame, development may be inhibited and delays may occur. Although such delays can be, at least partially, remediated through intervention programs, learning becomes more difficult if it occurs outside of these windows of opportunity. More basic processes, including sensory, motor, and emotion, appear to be wired earlier than language and social processes.

Because all of these processes are interwoven in the brain, it is important to address any emerging delays and deficiencies as soon as possible (Whitman, 2004). Intervention programs for children with autism need to be directed, not only at establishing patterns of adaptive behavior, but also at preventing the formation of maladaptive behaviors and the restrictive behaviors associated with autism. Maladaptive behaviors that are established early can become habitual. The more established these habits become, the more difficult they are to break. Such habits in turn make the learning of adaptive behaviors more difficult. To the extent that the initiation of intervention programs is delayed, the establishment of adaptive habits takes longer, and complex behaviors, like language, become much more difficult to teach.

Although it cannot be stated with any precision how soon early intervention programs should begin for children with ASD, a general rule of thumb is to initiate early intervention programs as soon as possible, with the focus and structure of these programs dictated by the child's age and developmental level. Even if a formal diagnosis of autism has not been confirmed, but only suspected, it is appropriate to put interventions in place to address any significant developmental problems that are occurring. In summary, the rationale for early intervention programs, which is based on both basic and applied research as well as developmental theory, is compelling.

Deficits are multidimensional and interactive

Autism has been likened to a complex puzzle, with many pieces that can be put together in various ways to form different pictures of autism and how it emerges. Given the multiplicity of symptoms associated with autism, a critical question arises concerning which of these symptoms should be the prime focus of intervention programs. From a developmental perspective, Whitman and Ekas (2008) suggest that autism should be viewed as evolving through an interaction of a number of characteristics/processes, with the relationship between these characteristics/processes changing over time. Figure 1.2 depicts how this emergence might occur, along with the processes that need to be considered in order to understand the development of autism in its diverse manifestations.

The conceptual model in Figure 1.2 includes three symptoms/processes referred to in the *DSM-IV-TR* (American Psychiatric Association, 2000) definition of autism—social interaction deficiencies, communication/language deficiencies, and repetitive, restricted, and stereotyped responses, as well as four other symptoms/processes: arousal/emotion, sensory, motor, and cognitive—that are not a formal part of this definition. The self-regulation construct in Figure 1.2 refers to the unique coping processes employed by individuals with autism; specifically the stereotyped, restrictive and repetitive behaviors displayed by individuals with autism are reflective of a poorly developed self-regulatory system that evolves because more mature forms of self-regulation are not learned.

Whitman and Ekas (2008) suggest that the immature self-regulatory system of individuals with autism is shaped by their cognitive, language, and social deficiencies as well as their emotional, sensory, and motor problems. Effective self-regulation requires an optimal level of arousal, with both hyperarousal and hypoarousal associated with diminished functioning. The sensory system is critical for self-regulation because it provides information about the environment and a person's behavior. The motor system enables children to engage in rudimentary self-regulation acts when distressed, such as sucking, as well as provides a structural foundation for the development of more complex cognitive, linguistic, and social forms of self-regulation. The cognitive, language, and social interaction systems provide children with the advanced tools (e.g. executive functioning, self-instruction, and information-seeking) that are needed to strategically guide their behavior. Because each of six processes described in Figure 1.2 are frequently compromised in children with autism, an immature self-regulatory system emerges.

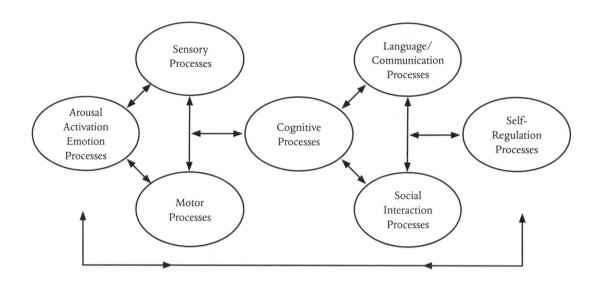

Figure 1.2 The role of emotion, sensory, motor, cognitive, language/communication, social, and self-regulation processes in the emergence of autism

All of the processes in Figure 1.2 can be considered, either directly or indirectly, as "causes" that exert influence across time on the other processes; thereby constituting a complex chain of "causality" that results in the emergence of the symptoms of autism; the system as a whole is in a constant state of reorganization.

Although all of the processes exert influence, either directly or indirectly, on the other processes, the three processes on the left side of Figure 1.2 (arousal/activation/emotion, sensory, and motor processes) mature earlier developmentally than the other processes (cognition, language/communication, and social interaction) and for that reason are likely to play a critical early role in the emergence of autism. For example, children with autism appear to be especially vulnerable to emotional stress because their early environment is chaotic and challenging. If early stress is not managed, the development of their cognitive, language, social interaction, and self-regulatory systems is likely placed at risk for delays. Thus the theory allows for the possibility that these early occurring processes may play a major role in the development of different symptom patterns for children on the autism spectrum, with the role of these early emerging processes diminishing as the cognitive, communication, and social systems mature.

In summary, the theory outlined in Figure 1.2 not only describes the processes that appear to be involved in the development of autism, but also provides a general blueprint for designing a comprehensive and multidimensional intervention for altering this disorder. This perspective suggests that during early development particular attention should be given to emotional, motor, and sensory processes and that as development proceeds during the second year of life increasing focus should be placed on cognitive, language, social, and self-regulatory processes. From a causal standpoint, because each of the aforementioned processes are postulated to influence one another in a reciprocal fashion, it follows that intervention in one domain (e.g. language) often influences functioning in the other domains. As each of the processes presented in Figure 1.2 is discussed in future chapters, research describing the dynamic linkages between these processes will be summarized.

Program characteristics

Now that the need for early intervention programs and the processes to be focused on in these programs have been discussed, some of the key characteristics of a comprehensive early intervention program will be described. These characteristics emphasize the importance of: a comprehensive developmental assessment, individualized goals and interventions, clear specification of program goals and intervention procedures, program structure, motivational components, active supports, maintenance and generalization components, systematic program evaluation, use of evidence-based interventions, and parent/teacher training.

A comprehensive developmental assessment is critical

In order to obtain information about program goals, a developmental assessment is critical. This assessment should evaluate functioning in each of the domains (emotion, sensory, motor, cognitive, language, social interaction, and self-regulation) described in Figure 1.2. In contrast to ability and achievement assessments which evaluate a child's performance compared to a norm group (e.g. comparing children with ASD to neurotypical children), developmental assessments focus on evaluating a child's performance along a continuum of skill acquisition that occurs during normal development.

This type of assessment reveals what a child with autism can do currently in various developmental areas and what he or she needs to do next in order to grow in competency. For example, when examining expressive and receptive language, an evaluation may reveal that a child can label an object when presented alone, but not when the object is placed in a group with other objects, or that a child may be able to respond to simple instructions involving a single motor response, but has difficulty with more complex instructions, requiring multiple, sequentially ordered responses. In addition to evaluating development and deficiencies in the various aforementioned domains (see Figure 1.2), the presence of problems such as anxiety, hypersensitivity, aggression, and sleep disorders, should be monitored.

A good developmental assessment has direct implications for developing a curriculum. It specifies which skills, concepts, and behaviors need to be taught and the sequence in which they should be taught. Ideally, developmental assessments should be conducted through direct observation of a child's performance in specific task situations (Carlson, Hagiwara, & Quinn, 1998). An alternative, albeit less desirable, approach to assessment relies on the self-report of persons who know the child well. Information about the child is most often based on the parents' or teachers' perception of what they think the child can do. Many of the critical target skills and behavior problems that should be evaluated are described in Chapters 3 to 11. For further information on developmental assessments the reader is referred to books by Handleman and Delmolino (2005) and Partington and Sundberg (1998).

Program goals and interventions should be individualized

The process of selecting target behaviors to be taught in an intervention program should be guided by several criteria. Most importantly, they should, as just discussed, be developmentally appropriate, focusing on the child's existing pattern of skills and limitations. Intervention programs should build on existing achievements while addressing deficiencies. Because the developmental profiles of achievements differ across children, each intervention program of necessity needs to be individualized in its curriculum.

In addition, specific interventions should be tailored to the individual, not only in terms of goal selection, but also in their mode of delivery. For example, specific interventions may vary in the settings in which they are delivered, motivational procedures and instructional supports employed, and sensory modalities (e.g. visual and/or auditory) utilized for teaching. Instructional programs delivered by parents in a home setting may also have to be adapted to the family culture and personality. Relatedly, programs may need to be introduced to assist families experiencing stress, depression, isolation, marital problems, and financial concerns.

Intervention goals and procedures should be clearly specified

Many therapeutic and educational programs fail to clearly specify the goals to be pursued. Goals are articulated in a global, vague or ambiguous fashion. Before beginning an intervention program, it is critical that the target behaviors be clearly defined so that the training procedures can be consistently applied and changes in the target behaviors can be reliably evaluated. Precise definitions specify the observable characteristics of the behaviors to be taught and provide concrete examples of behaviors that meet the definition's requirements.

In education programs for children with ASD, a myriad of target behaviors are taught, such as those directed at developing self-help, social, communication, and academic skills; for example in the self-help area children typically need to be taught oral hygiene, bathing, and toileting skills. Each of these skills involves complex response sequences that need to be carefully defined so that they can be systematically taught. The target behaviors to be taught should be part of what educators refer to as their "individualized education program" or IEP. This IEP should be reviewed, at least monthly, more frequently if the child is a rapid learner, and revised as necessary, depending on whether goals have been reached. In instances where no or minimal progress is occurring, the program goals and/or training procedures often need to be modified.

In addition to clearly articulating program goals, the intervention procedures to be employed in helping a child reach these goals also need to be specified. If the treatment program protocol is not clearly articulated, it becomes virtually impossible to apply the program with any consistency, to transfer that protocol to others wishing to use it, and to monitor treatment fidelity, that is whether the treatment protocol is applied correctly by a therapist, teacher, or parent. Moreover, without clear specification of the instructional goals and therapeutic/educational protocols, research cannot be conducted to determine whether changes in behavior occurred and most importantly whether the intervention programs were responsible for the changes that did occur.

Program structure is important

In order for any child to learn, an educational environment must be structured so as to have order and predictability. Children with ASD are in particular need of structure in their educational programs. They are easily stressed when confronted with environments that are in flux because they have fewer cognitive, language, and social resources for coping with change than neurotypical children; as a consequence, they often disengage attentionally from the social environment and may try to physically escape. Many of the stereotyped, repetitive and restricted behavioral symptoms of children with ASD, including their obsessions with certain stimuli and compulsive adherence to certain routines, appear to be their way of controlling environments that are chaotic and overwhelming. For these reasons, structured intervention programs that are stable and follow set routines are advantageous to children with autism. Structure helps keep children from getting anxious and frees them up cognitively to benefit from educational and training experiences.

A structured program should not only have, as already discussed, clearly defined goals and intervention procedures, but also specify the educational materials to be employed and the type of physical environment (e.g. room characteristics) in which the program will be delivered. Initially, the educational environment should be free of extraneous auditory, visual and other sensory distractions, containing only a table and chair, a floor play/work area, and educational materials to be used during a session. Children should be given information verbally and through visual schedules about the exact nature of their daily program schedule. Change, when it needs to occur, should be introduced in a slow and orderly fashion. As children with autism acquire new adaptive behaviors and coping skills, they should be able to tolerate change more easily. A well-structured intervention also specifies how a child's newly acquired skills and behaviors will be generalized into everyday living environments. In formulating structured programs, the child's developmental level, pattern of strengths and limitations, interests, choices, and motivational level should be considered.

Some therapists, particularly advocates of play therapy, suggest that intervention programs for children with ASD should occur in everyday living environments, specifically because this is where neurotypical children's major learning experiences occur and because such settings are more likely to motivate a child to learn. However, this approach for children with ASD is questionable, given the unpredictable nature of everyday environments, the sensory and attentional problems of these children, and their motivational orientation, which is often directed at isolating and protecting themselves from environments that are in constant flux. It should be pointed out, however, that after children with ASD have developed core skills (see Chapter 3), programs can and should be gradually introduced into everyday settings. This type of "naturalistic" program should build on structured programs, the children's learning experiences, their interests, and their everyday encounters with the environment.

In such a naturalistic teaching program, the setting is less controlled, activities are more varied, and children are allowed to initiate entrance into activities that interest them. Nevertheless, there is a structure to such programs. Through a variety of shaping and prompting procedures (see Chapter 2), the children's adaptive response repertoire is gradually expanded. Naturalistic teaching programs can be introduced into play situations, as well as daily activities and routines. Some programs, for example those focused on teaching self-help, language and social skills, are often more easily taught in everyday living environments. Moreover, programs for younger children, especially for children age three or younger, are often best delivered in such environments.

Proponents of less structured play therapies often emphasize that what children learn in structured programs, while potentially important, is often not generalized into everyday living settings. Two points in response to this criticism need to be made. First, as suggested earlier, the reason why children with autism are often taught in structured educational environments or controlled natural settings is to create a simple and predictable environment where the child is comfortable and where painful, distracting and educationally unimportant stimuli are reduced to a minimum. Because children with autism have difficulty distinguishing signal (important information) from noise (unimportant information), simpler structured environments help them focus their attention on what is instructionally important. Before children with autism can generalize what they learn to other environments, they have to learn first. Once foundation language and other core skills are acquired, generalization programs of different types can be introduced. Strategies for facilitating generalization are discussed later in this chapter and in Chapter 2.

Second, the generalization problem just discussed, getting children to utilize or transfer what they have learned in more formal and structured educational environments into other environments, including everyday living settings, is a problem that educators have been struggling with for a long time. Both neurotypical children as well as children with ASD have difficulties applying and using what they have learned in educational settings. Children with ASD have a particular problem in this regard because of a poorly developed self-regulatory system. Fortunately, educators have made significant strides in helping both neurotypical children and children with autism develop their self-regulatory system and generalize what they have learned. This issue will be discussed at length in Chapter 10. The major point to be made is that the educational process does not end once a child is taught a cognitive or behavioral skill. The most important part of an education program is getting children to apply dynamically what they have learned.

Interventions need to motivate a child to learn

Typically developing children seem to learn spontaneously because of their natural curiosity about the world. They learn through observation, exploration, experimentation, and the socialization/parenting process. In contrast, early in development, children with ASD appear to be overwhelmed by the world and its sensory input. Both attentionally and behaviorally they restrict the world in which they live in order to cope with environments that are chaotic and sometimes painful.

Some approaches to teaching children with autism emphasize that the therapist should follow a child's lead and interests. However, this approach only works if the therapist gradually leads or shapes the child's interest in a direction that is developmentally and socially appropriate.

Whereas typically developing children learn more spontaneously through play and everyday social interactions, children with autism, if left to their own devices, withdraw from many routine social encounters, opting instead to engage in repetitive and stereotyped routines. Their intrinsic motivational system leads them to protect themselves, not to explore. They need to be motivated to leave the safe world they have created for themselves. For this reason and more generally, because children with ASD do not learn like other children, special extrinsic methods of motivating often need to be put into place. These methods employ what behaviorists refer to as reinforcers, which involve tangible rewards, physical affection, and praise. However, to be effective reinforcement procedures need to be developed that are individualized, desirable and as naturalistic as possible. These procedures are discussed in Chapter 2.

The process of learning and skill acquisition needs to be actively supported

During an intervention program, it is critical not only to motivate the child with ASD but also to support their learning endeavor. Developmental psychologists frequently emphasize the importance of creating a scaffold to assist children in their attempts to learn new skills. This scaffold consists of a range of techniques that vary from: providing no assistance and letting the child proceed in a trial and error fashion, providing some assistance, for example by telling or showing (modeling) the child what to do, to providing a great deal of assistance, for example, by physically helping the child make a response. Two other techniques used to assist learning are shaping, which involves reinforcing a child for making increasingly better approximations to a correct response, and chaining, which involves rewarding a child for completing an increasing number of steps of a complex response, such as toothbrushing. Educationally, it is best to provide only the minimal amount of assistance necessary for the student to learn. However, in contrast to neurotypical children, children with autism, require a more elaborate scaffold to support learning. Once learning occurs, the scaffold of prompts is gradually removed so that the child can learn to act independently.

Maintenance and generalization of learning must be programmed

Children with ASD are able to learn a range of new skills. However, as discussed earlier, they frequently fail to maintain and generalize what they have learned. In order to ensure that new skills are maintained over time and generalized to situations in which they are appropriate, intervention programs need to incorporate additional instructional strategies. Many of these strategies were initially outlined by Stokes and Baer (1977). Some of these strategies include: teaching behaviors that have a high probability of being reinforced in the natural environment, employing "natural" reinforcers, using intermittent reinforcement, gradually fading out prompts, modifying natural environments to ensure that appropriate behaviors are reinforced, teaching children to actively solicit positive feedback for their appropriate behavior, showing children the relevance of a response in other situations, varying the nature of the environment in which training occurs, and teaching children verbal rules that specify when a response is appropriate.

Undoubtedly one of the most powerful vehicles for effecting change that is maintained and generalized involves teaching a child to self-regulate (Whitman,

2004). Self-regulation creates both short-term and long-term benefits for the child. Self-regulation refers to an individual's ability to control and change his/her behavior, inhibiting responses that are not useful, anticipating effects that result from one's actions and initiating behavior in a planful and organized manner. Complex forms of self-regulation involve self-monitoring, self-instruction, self-evaluation, and self-reinforcement as well as higher order metacognitive and executive-functioning skills. Because children with ASD lack many of these skills, autism has been described as a self-regulatory disorder (Whitman, 2004).

Due to their inability to self-regulate their behavior, children with ASD often depend on others for guidance or utilize a variety of self-regulatory behaviors that are not adaptive, behaviors that are symptomatic of their disorder. In order to assist children with ASD in more appropriately regulating their behavior, a wide range of techniques, developed through psychological and educational research, have been employed, many of which are cognitively focused. These and other techniques for promoting maintenance and generalization are discussed in future chapters and at length in Chapters 2 and 10.

Program efficacy needs to be evaluated

Whatever therapeutic techniques are used in an intervention program, a child's progress needs to be evaluated. Baseline data should be taken, examining the functioning level of the child before an intervention program is initiated; then progress or lack thereof should be monitored during an intervention, including whether skills learned are maintained over time and generalized to everyday living environments. It is critical to monitor progress during an intervention program in order to determine whether the program needs to be modified or completely revamped. Moreover, evaluating generalization of behavior provides valuable information to the therapist regarding whether intervention programs need to be extended into new settings. In short, interventions need to be flexible, modified as necessary based on information received from these evaluations.

Periodically, at least once or twice a year, developmental evaluations assessing the general functioning level and overall achievements of the child should also be conducted. Such evaluations can be used not only to document overall gains in areas targeted by intervention, but also gains in areas not directly targeted by the intervention. For further information on procedures for evaluating program efficacy, the reader is referred to books by Alberto and Troutman (2006) and Cooper, Heron, and Heward (2007).

Where possible evidence-based intervention should be employed

With the exception of applied behavior analysis (ABA), behavior therapy and related programs, such as precision teaching, incidental learning, and cognitive behavior therapy, most intervention programs employed with children with autism have not been subjected to rigorous empirical scrutiny. Some programs, like TEACHH (Treatment and Education of Autistic and Related Communication Handicapped Children), are difficult to evaluate because it is a multidimensional lifespan intervention that integrates a variety of treatments (best practices) that change over time. The intervention protocols and goals of many other programs, such as Floor-time and Option, have often not been articulated sufficiently to establish whether they have been applied correctly and whether behavior change occurs. Without clear specification of intervention protocols and program goals, functional (causal) connections between intervention application and behavior changes are not able to be systematically evaluated.

There are many reasons for using evidence-based interventions (Whitman, 2004). The major reason is that there is objective evidence for their efficacy. Based on research, a variety of other types of information is also available about the intervention, such as the specific characteristics of the participants for whom the intervention has been found effective, treatment side effects, therapist training and experience required to apply the intervention, and information about the specific structure of the intervention utilized. In other words, the specific conditions under which the intervention has been found to be effective is clearly specified.

When alternative interventions are employed that have not been empirically validated, evidence for their efficacy is typically based on the subjective evaluation of the originator of the treatment, the therapists employing it, and/or consumers, such as parents, who have utilized the treatment. Self-report data from these sources is notoriously unreliable, influenced by the biases, hopes and expectations of the observer. Moreover, without systematic research, it is not possible, even if an individual appears to change during the implementation of an intervention, to determine whether the intervention was actually responsible for the changes that occurred or whether the changes were due to other factors unrelated to the intervention, such as other educational programs or the biological maturation of the child.

The reasons that families choose alternative interventions that have not been empirically evaluated vary widely. For example, evidence-based interventions may not be available in the family's geographical area; such interventions may be too costly; or these interventions may be too time-consuming, given other demands on the family. Some consumers of alternative therapies are looking for a magic bullet for their children's autism and adopt alternative procedures out of hope and sometimes desperation, not always considering the financial costs and potentially serious side effects. Perhaps the greatest problem associated with the use of alternative therapies occurs when they are used in place of procedures that have been empirically established as effective and are readily available.

Some families also receive misinformation about evidence-based interventions and/or are subjected to propaganda from uninformed and/or poorly trained therapists. Alternative treatments for autism are sometimes adopted by consumers because they have gained notoriety based on the testimonial evidence and the charismatic presentations of those who developed the treatments and/or financially profit from their employment. It is not uncommon for some therapists who utilize alternative interventions to become "certified" after attending a few workshops. They may not have received any formal, academically based, clinical training from a recognized graduate program, had exposure to evidence-based treatments, or been certified by a reputable national professional organization. Moreover, therapists who employ alternative therapies typically do not attempt to evaluate formally, through objective measurement, the efficacy of the interventions that they administer with their clients; often because they lack the appropriate training and assessment skills to conduct such an evaluation.

Families who use alternative interventions should do so cautiously. They should check out carefully the credentials of the therapist and recognize that the money and time they invest in such programs might not help their child. Because most families have limited resources, they need to consider all of the intervention options available to them. In this book most of the techniques recommended, and the theories on which they are based, have been developed and validated through extensive basic and applied research with both typically developing and developmentally delayed populations, including children with autism.

Parent/teacher training is critical

Because children with ASD are unique in the way they learn and do not develop like other children, interventions need to be tailored to the specific characteristics of this population. Parents, teachers and other professionals often need to change the way they interact with and teach children with ASD. For this reason, interventions should focus, not only on the child with autism, but also on parents, classroom teachers and teacher assistants, therapists, and volunteers, providing them with new ways of teaching and interacting. Well-designed autism intervention programs are developed to be transferred to these individuals so that they can act in a coordinated and consistent fashion. Unfortunately, programs for children with ASD are often delivered by a variety of professionals with divergent approaches, who have no or minimal communication with each other.

Final thoughts

In an emerging area like autism, where questions are often more numerous than good answers, there is considerable speculation by parents about which of the many intervention approaches available are best for their children. Some interventions are quite controversial, and many of them have not been empirically evaluated. Sometimes, a treatment is selected based exclusively on the testimonials of either the person who developed the treatment and/or other parents who believed that their children were helped by the treatment. Even though some of these treatments are very expensive, parents may feel guilty if they do not give their children every chance to get better. Some parents are continually shopping for new treatments that might help their children recover from their autism. Some parents tend to jump on one treatment bandwagon after another, hoping to help their children. They hope that the next treatment that is tried will be the one that will bring their children out of their autistic world. Their hopes may be encouraged by other parents' stories or by the times when their own children showed unexpected competencies; brief snapshots of the children they thought they would have before the symptoms of autism became apparent.

What is the likelihood of a miracle treatment being developed that will cure autism? Based on our present state of knowledge, parents are well advised to temper such hopes. Although major advances are being made in the search for the causes of autism, the advent of "curative" types of treatment awaits the isolation of specific genes and environmental triggers, as well as the biochemical processes they control. This search will take time, particularly because of the polygenetic (more than one gene) nature of autism.

If a miracle cure is not likely to be found soon, what should parents do? Most importantly, they should be optimistic about the future. Currently, there are numerous research programs directed at isolating the genetic, other biological, and environmental mechanisms that produce autism. Some of these projects are starting to provide insights into the mechanisms underlying autism. In their advocacy role, parents should encourage their political representatives to support funding for basic research on autism. Even though primary prevention, which involves a cure for autism, is not yet possible, researchers are gradually coming to better understand how autism unfolds. With such knowledge, secondary prevention and treatment programs are being designed that can alter, sometimes dramatically, the developmental trajectory of children with ASD, thus moderating the severity of this disorder.

The "faces" of autism are already changing. Currently, many children with ASD do not display the classical characteristics of this disorder. For example, they frequently form strong bonds with their parents and are affectionate, socially attentive, and quick learners. As new evidence-based therapeutic and educational programs evolve and are put in place, this positive trend is likely to continue. Until definitive cures for autism are discovered, parents should initiate as early as possible intervention programs that have been shown to be effective. Conversely, they should be very cautious about spending their time and money on unproven "quick cure" treatments that have a low probability of success, and may even adversely affect their children's development.

Making prudent treatment decisions for individuals with autism is a difficult enterprise. One approach to making these decisions is to think scientifically (Whitman, 2004). Thinking scientifically involves considering treatment decisions as objectively and dispassionately as possible. The need for parents to help their children can generate intense emotions, which in turn can endanger the unbiased analysis needed to evaluate a treatment. Parents should also be aware that some therapists may recommend interventions based solely on their own informal observations and opinions and the anecdotal reports of their clients. Because such therapists are often not well trained in the use of scientific methods, they are subject to the same logical fallacies and emotional influences as parents. Although therapists are invested, like parents, in wanting to help children and wanting to believe that what they are doing is useful, they may also be ego-invested because they know that their reputation as a therapist is in large part a function of how successful they are perceived as being.

The following questions and guidelines may be helpful in guiding parents and therapists in their decision-making. Has the intervention been developed within the framework of a formal academic discipline like education, psychology, occupational therapy, speech therapy, or medicine? Has the intervention been empirically shown to be useful with individuals with ASD and/or a similar disability? Is there a standardized intervention protocol? Is the process by which the intervention exerts its effects understood? Is there any evidence of undesirable side effects associated with the delivery of the intervention? In instances where the precise nature of the intervention is unclear and where reputable empirical research evaluating the intervention is either absent or does not yield convincing evidence of its efficacy, parents should exercise extreme caution as they make intervention decisions for their children. In general, parents and therapists should feel more secure in their choice of an intervention to the extent that it has been developed within the framework of a formal academic discipline, is standardized, and has been empirically evaluated as effective when employed with individuals with ASD or related developmental disabilities. Specific techniques that are recommended as a part of a comprehensive intervention program are described in Chapter 2.

Organization of book

In the next chapter, an overview of evidence-based techniques derived from basic and applied research on how people learn is presented. These techniques have been used in intervention programs with both neurotypical children and children with developmental disabilities, including children with ASD. Specific procedures for promoting behavior development, behavior maintenance, and behavior generalization are summarized. In addition, techniques for reducing undesirable behaviors and dealing with behavior problems are discussed. In Chapters 3 to 11, basic processes and behaviors that need to be addressed as part of a comprehensive intervention program are examined. Each chapter begins with an overview of these processes and behaviors along with a discussion of how they impact the overall development of children with autism. Then critical skills that need to be targeted for intervention in each area are discussed along with intervention strategies for developing these skills. At the end of each chapter specific examples of intervention programs are provided. The specific processes and behaviors discussed are: core skills (Chapter 3), emotional behaviors (Chapter 4), sensory processing (Chapter 5), sensorimotor functioning (Chapter 6), language and communication (Chapter 7), cognitive processes (Chapter 8), social interaction (Chapter 9), self-regulation (Chapter 10), and behavior problems (Chapter 11).

References

Alberto, P. A. & Troutman, A. C. (2006). *Applied behavior analysis for teachers* (7th ed.). Upper Saddle River: Pearson/Merrill Prentice Hall.

American Psychiatric Association (2000). *Diagnostic and Statistical Manual of Mental Disorders* (4th ed.). Washington, DC: American Psychiatric Association.

Baker, J. K., Messinger, D. S., Lyons, K. K., & Grantz, C. J. (2010). A pilot study of maternal sensitivity in the context of emergent autism. *Journal of Autism and Developmental Disorders, 40,* 988–999.

Brigham, N. B., Yoder, P. J., Jarzynka, M. A., & Tapp, J. (2010). The sequential relationship between parent attentional cues and sustained attention to objects in young children with autism. *Journal of Autism and Developmental Disorders, 40,* 200–208.

Carlson, J. K., Hagiwara, T., & Quinn, C. (1998). "Assessment of students with autism." In R. L. Simpson & B. S. Myles (Eds.), *Educating Children and Youth with Autism* (pp. 25–53). Austin, TX: Pro-Ed.

Cooper, J. O., Heron, T. E., & Heward, W. L. (2007). *Applied behavior analysis* (2nd ed.). Upper Saddle River, NJ: Pearson/Merrill Prentice Hall.

Feinberg, E. & Vacca, J. (2000). The drama and trauma of creating policies on autism. Critical issues to consider in the new millennium. *Focus on autism and other developmental disabilities, 15,* 130–137.

Fox, N. A. & Rutter, M. (2010). Introduction to special section on the effect of early experience on development. *Child Development, 81,* 23–27.

Fox, S. E., Levitt, P., & Nelson III, C. A. (2010). How the timing and quality of early experiences influence the development of brain architecture. *Child Development, 81,* 28–40.

Handleman, J. S. & Delmolino, L. M. (2005). "Assessment of children with autism." In D. Zager (Ed.), *Autism spectrum disorders: Identification, education and treatment* (3rd ed.) (pp. 269–294). Mahwah, NJ: Erlbaum.

Milshtein, S., Yirmiya, N., Oppenheim, D., Koren-Karie, N., & Levi, S. (2010). Resolution of the diagnosis among parents of children with autism spectrum disorder: Association with child and parent characteristics. *Journal of Autism and Developmental Disorders, 40,* 89–99.

Partington, J. W. & Sundberg, M. L. (1998). *The assessment of basic language and learning skills.* Pleasant Hill, CA: Behavior Analysts Inc.

Remington, B., Hastings, R. P., Kovshoff, H., degli Espinosa, F., Jahr, E., Brown, T., Alsford, P., Lemaic, M., & Ward, N. (2007). Early intensive behavioral intervention: Outcomes for children with autism and their parents after two years. *American Journal on Mental Retardation, 112,* 418–438.

Stiller, M. & Sigman, M. (2002). The behaviors of parents of children with autism predict the subsequent development of their children's communication. *Journal of Autism and Developmental Disorders, 32,* 77–89.

Stokes, T. & Baer, D. (1977). An implicit technology of generalization. *Journal of Applied Behavior Analysis, 10,* 349–367.

Whitman, T. L. (2004). *The development of autism: A self-regulatory perspective.* London: Jessica Kingsley Publishers.

Whitman, T. L. & Ekas, N. (2008). Theory and research on autism. Do we need a new approach to thinking about and studying this disorder? *International Review of Research in Mental Retardation, 35,* 31–41.

Further readings

Prizant, B. & Rubin, E. (1999). Contemporary issues in interventions for autism spectrum disorders: A commentary. *Journal of Association for the Severely Handicapped, 24,* 199–208.

Ruble, L. (2001). Analysis of social interactions as goal-directed behaviors in children with autism. *Journal of Autism and Developmental Disorders, 31,* 471–482.

Chapter 2

Interventions

In this chapter, a diverse, but theoretically integrated, set of educational intervention techniques are described for developing adaptive behaviors and addressing the various delays, deficiencies, and problems that are associated with autism spectrum disorders. These techniques are based on research and principles derived from ecological, operant, classical conditioning, social and cognitive learning theories. All of these theories stress the important role that the social and physical environment plays in cognitive, emotional, and behavior development.

Although somewhat arbitrary, we group the techniques into the following categories for purposes of discussion: ecologically focused, behavior-oriented, emotion-focused, cognitive-behavioral and self-regulation, and behavior-reduction (see Table 2.1). With the exception of the ecological approach, the effectiveness of these techniques has been empirically established for use with a wide range of behaviors and clinical populations, including children with autism spectrum disorders and other developmental disabilities. For each of these categories of techniques we begin with a general description, then discuss areas in which these techniques can be employed along with examples of how they might be applied in a specific situation. For further information regarding the theories and techniques described in this chapter, recommended books on learning theory-based interventions are presented at the end of this chapter.

Ecologically focused interventions

The ecological approach examines how various aspects of the physical and social environment are related to human adjustment and achievement and can be systematically arranged so as to promote behavior change. This approach recognizes that the environments in which children live and learn vary considerably in their overall structure, complexity, and organization, as well as in the extent to which they change over time.

For many children, the world is a wondrous place to behold, full of interesting sights, sounds, smells, tastes, and things to feel. For other children, including many children with ASD, the world is sometimes too bright, too loud, abrasive, stinky, and/or distasteful. Parents and teachers are constantly creating environments that affect the behaviors of children whether they recognize it or not. Unfortunately,

Table 2.1 Environmentally based interventions for teaching children with ASD

Ecological

Behavior-oriented
    Reinforcement
    Response induction and prompting
    Discrimination training
    Maintenance and generalization

Emotion-focused
    Full exposure
    Gradual exposure
    In-vivo, pictorial, and imagined exposure
    Reciprocal inhibition
    Vicarious extinction
    Habituation

Cognitive-behavioral and self-regulation
    Modeling
    Pictorial instruction
    Verbal instruction
    Correspondence training
    Self-instruction
    Executive functioning and metastrategic interventions

Behavior reduction
    Extinction
    Differential reinforcement
    Response cost and time-out
    Aversive stimulation
    Overcorrection

relatively little attention has been given to evaluating how different environments influence the ability of children with ASD to learn and adapt. Increasingly, however both educators and clinicians have come to recognize that the contexts in which interventions occur can have a profound effect on learning. For example, both children's adaptive and maladaptive behavior can be influenced by such diverse environmental factors as the difficulty of tasks taught, the order in which tasks are taught, the length of an instructional period, changes in schedules, classroom seating arrangements, class size, room size, color and brightness, noise levels, temperature, humidity, recreational schedules, time of day, and time of year.

Behaviorally oriented therapists have made a number of general assumptions about how these environments should be structured when teaching children with

ASD. One assumption is that these environments should be simple in their structure and relatively unchanging when intervention programs are first initiated. Sensory distractions are kept to a minimum. When teaching environments have extraneous visual and auditory stimuli intruding, children with ASD seem to have greater difficulty focusing their attention on the instructional message. They also have more difficulty processing information when greater amounts of information are presented and/or information is rapidly presented. Children with ASD appear to have a particular problem attending and learning when their instructors speak in a rapid fashion, frequently change facial expressions and gesticulate actively with their hands and body. Conversely, many children with ASD seem to learn more quickly and with greater enjoyment when information is presented via a computer, perhaps because computer programs operate in a systematic, predictable, and less variable fashion.

Thus, during the early stages of an intervention program for children with autism, environmental arrangements should be simple and predictable. However, over time the structure of the environments should be changed to approximate those in which neurotypical children learn and live. Educators and therapists suggest that this environmental transition should be gradual in order to allow the child to accommodate to the change as well as to promote generalization of behaviors from highly structured learning environments to everyday learning environments.

Although ecologically oriented research has examined a variety of relationships between environmental arrangements and human behavior, more research is needed to validate the aforementioned assumptions regarding the ideal teaching environments for children with ASD. To date these assumptions are based more on clinical intuition than on hard evidence. In contrast, the other intervention approaches to be described in this chapter have been the focus of extensive empirical research. This is particularly true of behavior-oriented programs.

Behavior-oriented programs

Probably the most commonly employed intervention programs for children with autism are behaviorally oriented. These programs are often initially delivered in highly structured and simple environments in order to minimize extraneous visual, auditory, and other sensory stimuli that may distract the child's attention during the teaching process. In the early stages, this type of intervention program typically involves a one-to-one interaction with a teacher/parent rather than group instruction.

The techniques employed in these programs are based on operant principles of learning. These principles have been established through extensive basic research that has been conducted over the past century. The intervention techniques derived from these principles have also been extensively evaluated with both typically developing and clinical populations, including with children with ASD and other developmental disabilities. Although applied behavior analysis (ABA) is the most commonly recognized behavior training program, there are many variants of this approach, such as discrete trial training, precision teaching, contingency management, gentle teaching, incidental learning, and token economies, that bear considerable similarity to each other in the techniques employed.

In this section, the basic components of the behavioral intervention approach will be described, including: 1) goal selection and specification, 2) the motivational component, reinforcement, 3) response induction and the use of supportive prompts, 4) discrimination training and the establishment of stimulus control, and 5) maintenance and generalization of what is learned to everyday living environments.

Goal selection and specification: what should be taught?

The first step in any intervention program involves making a decision about what the goals of the program should be. Behavioral programming also requires careful specification of the educational objectives so that intervention procedures can be consistently implemented and their effects carefully assessed.

GOAL SELECTION

At first glance the selection of appropriate target behaviors would seem to be a somewhat mundane and simple task. However, one of the most perplexing issues confronting teachers, therapists and parents, who make decisions regarding educational goals for a particular child with ASD, is determining what constitutes an appropriate goal. In making this type of determination, numerous questions must be posed and answered. For example, from a pragmatic perspective, if certain behavioral objectives were achieved, would these behaviors be useful to the child in his/her everyday living environment? Would the achievement of the program objectives help the child live more normally?

In addition to considering the utility of what is to be taught, a developmental perspective can also be very helpful in making decisions about appropriate goals. A determination is made concerning the developmental level at which a child is operating and whether a proposed educational objective represents the next logical step along a developmental continuum. Following a developmental model makes good sense from a learning perspective, specifically because each response taught involves building on the behaviors that precede it. For example, in teaching children how to feed themselves, it is first necessary to teach them how to grasp objects, including food and eating utensils, appropriately. If a behavioral goal is selected for which a child is not developmentally ready, program failure is more likely. For this reason, children with ASD should be given a comprehensive developmental assessment before an intervention program is initiated. The importance of using developmental assessments in intervention planning and evaluation is discussed in Chapter 1.

GOAL SPECIFICATION

A successful behavior education program requires not only selection of appropriate goals, but also careful specification of the target behaviors that reflect those goals. In developing behavior intervention programs, a distinction is made between general goals and behavioral objectives. General goals encompass multiple mini-objectives and refer to a progression of specific goals, each of which must be behaviorally defined. For example, the global goal of developing expressive language in a child with speech delays involves a complex series of subobjectives, which includes the learning of various specific sounds, the blending of these sounds into words, the usage of specific words in labeling objects in the environment, and putting words together to form sentences.

Before beginning an intervention, it is important that the target behaviors are defined precisely so that the treatment can be administered in a consistent fashion. When developing these precise definitions, the everyday language system used by a lay person is often not sufficient. A good behavioral definition is expressed through a description of the observable physical characteristics of the behavior rather than in general and more subjective terms, such as those that refer to the cognitive, emotional, intentional, or other inner states of an individual. Typically, good behavior definitions outline the boundary conditions of the response by describing examples of the response. For example, aggression is better defined as a hitting response with hands or kicking with feet, directed at persons other than self or at objects in the environment, rather than as a violent, deliberate, destructive act. Attention might be defined as eyes focused on specific task materials and/or on the face of the teacher who is giving verbal directions.

The formulation of clear and objective response definitions does not occur through a priori logical analysis, but rather requires close observation of a child's behavior. The ideal response definition allows different observers who are simultaneously, but independently, monitoring a specific behavior of an individual to agree upon its occurrence and non-occurrence. Clear specification of goals allows therapists to determine with precision the initial or baseline level of a response, whether intervention is needed, and the extent to which a response changes during an intervention program.

Reinforcement: motivating children to learn

Before discussing reinforcement procedures in detail, it is important to understand exactly what is meant by reinforcement. Within the operant-learning model, a behavior is controlled both by stimulus events that precede it in time and by stimuli that occur after it. *Reinforcement* refers to a process in which a response is increased through the administration of a stimulus event, called a reinforcer, following that response.

It would be difficult to overestimate the importance of reinforcement in the behavioral change process. According to many behavioral psychologists, it is through reinforcement that most new behaviors develop; although it is acknowledged that some behaviors can be acquired without reinforcement through observational learning and also as a result of maturation. It is further asserted that, once behaviors emerge, they will continue to occur only if they serve some functional purpose, that is, if they continue to provide some type of reinforcement to the individual.

TYPES OF REINFORCERS

There are two basic types of reinforcement procedures: positive and negative. *Positive reinforcement* refers to a process in which a stimulus event is delivered after a response occurs and a subsequent increase in the probability of that response occurs. For example, if a mother smiles and says "that is beautiful" after a child colors a picture in a coloring book, and a subsequent increase in the frequency of that child's coloring behavior is observed, it is likely that the mother's smile and praise served as a positive reinforcer for that child.

A second type of reinforcement procedure, which is less frequently employed in clinical-educational situations, but nevertheless very important, is negative reinforcement. *Negative reinforcement*, like positive reinforcement, also refers to a process whereby a stimulus event follows a response and results in a subsequent increase in the rate of that response. However, in contrast to positive reinforcement, it is not the delivery but rather the termination of the stimulus event that produces the effect. An example of negative reinforcement is a teacher who controls her class by showing overtly her dismay by frowning when the students are talking rather than doing their schoolwork, and who then subsequently ceases showing her dissatisfaction immediately after the students behave appropriately. In this example the class's appropriate behavior is negatively reinforced by the immediate termination of the teacher's frowning.

Another example of negative reinforcement is that of a child who controls a mother's attention by crying until the mother pays attention to the child, whereupon the child stops crying. If this sequence of events repeatedly occurs and the mother's attention to the child subsequently increases in frequency, it appears likely that the mother's attention has been negatively reinforced by the child's cessation of crying; that is the child's cessation of crying is a negative reinforcer. Although negative reinforcement techniques are only occasionally employed in programs directed at developing adaptive behavior, the concept of negative reinforcement helps explain how behavior problems, such as tantrums and aggression, emerge and are utilized to manipulate the social environment. Conversely, awareness of this dynamic provides a foundation for reducing maladaptive behavior through the use of extinction. This technique will be discussed in the last section of this chapter.

In addition to these two general types of reinforcers, there are also different types of positive and negative reinforcers. One subtype of these reinforcers is called primary. A *primary reinforcer* is generally viewed as having a biological connection; specifically, it reduces an unpleasant drive state such as hunger or thirst, or some other painful biological state and/or satisfies a basic sensory need, such as a need for physical contact. Primary reinforcers are generally effective, but may temporarily lose potency if the individual gets too much of the reinforcer; for example, if a child is reinforced repeatedly over a short time with a food item, the food item will probably lose its appeal as the child becomes satiated and thus cease to act as a reinforcer.

In contrast to primary reinforcers, there are stimulus events that are not biologically based or "naturally" reinforcing, but become reinforcing through their connection with primary reinforcers. These are called *conditioned reinforcers*. According to conditioning theory, stimulus events such as praise, smiles, prizes, and grades become reinforcing because historically they have been directly associated with primary reinforcers or with other conditioned reinforcers that have had this type of historical association; for example, from this theoretical perspective praise becomes a reinforcer because it has been associated with primary reinforcers such as affectionate hugs or food. As children are socialized their behavior becomes increasingly controlled by conditioned reinforcers. A special kind of reinforcer, called a token reinforcer, is a particularly powerful and useful conditioned reinforcer.

TOKEN ECONOMIES

A reinforcement system which involves the use of token reinforcers or tokens is typically referred to as a *token economy*. Tokens acquire reinforcing power because they can be exchanged for or used to purchase backup reinforcers which the child values. Thus, token reinforcers, such as poker chips, stars, points, check marks, or money, might be used to purchase food, toys, or activities, such as time on a computer or on a trampoline, or other important things the child might desire. Because tokens are associated with a number of backup reinforcers, they are less subject to satiation than primary or other conditioned reinforcers.

In establishing a token economy, the target behaviors to be taught, such as emptying the trash or feeding the dog, must be articulated. Then the tokens that can be earned for performing each behavioral objective must be specified. Next, the backup reinforcers to be exchanged for the tokens must be determined, such as time playing a computer game or interacting with a favorite toy. Finally, the number of tokens required to purchase a backup reinforcer must be specified; for example three tokens might be required to purchase five minutes of time playing a computer game.

Token economies have been employed in a variety of settings, including schools, homes and workplaces, and with a variety of populations, including neurotypical children and children with ASD. There are many reasons to use a token economy. Token economies can be especially useful when goals are more complex and numerous and take time to acquire. Token economies teach a child impulse control because they do not get what they desire right away. It also teaches them the symbolic value of tokens and indirectly the value of money as a medium of exchange. Tokens are easily administered and reduce the reliance on other reinforcers that break up the rhythm of an education session and/or involve the use of unhealthy foods. If the child becomes satiated and no longer enjoys a particular set of backup reinforcers, others can be easily substituted. Tokens can also be easily introduced into naturalistic teaching situations to foster generalization. Finally, they can be phased out gradually as a child learns. In this regard, it is desirable to have children learn because it is fun and not to gain anything, other than the joy of achievement and the occasional approval and affection of those around them.

SELECTING REINFORCERS

Therapists and teachers have a variety of theoretical and practical ways available for selecting reinforcers, including: 1) making a best guess based on information gathered from the child, significant others, or one's intuition, and then experimenting with them to see if they work; 2) using stimuli (primary reinforcers), such as food, that are drive reducing, or stimuli that have become conditioned reinforcers through being associated with primary reinforcers, such as praise; 3) employing stimuli that, because of their novelty and/or complexity, are stimulating to the senses; 4) using high probability responses, for example, giving a child access to a toy that is frequently played with (Premack's principle); and 5) using responses to which the child has been denied recent or long-term access, for example, a child going outside to a playground after having been inside for several days because of rain.

In addition to selecting stimulus events and activities that are likely to be effective when employed with a child, there are a number of other factors that should be taken into account when choosing a reinforcer. These factors include:

ease of application, efficiency, cost, and *naturalness.* Optimally, a reinforcer should be easy to administer. When the reinforcement procedure is both energy and time efficient, teachers and parents can dedicate themselves to other aspects of education and training programs. If a reinforcement procedure takes too long to administer, for example taking a child for a walk, or if it involves too much energy on the part of the person administering it, the procedure may not be employed at all or be administered on an irregular and inconsistent basis. Although teachers and parents can be trained and motivated to apply tedious and/or time-consuming procedures, they are more likely to apply reinforcement procedures that are simple and quick, such as praising or hugging a child.

Reinforcement procedures are considered time efficient not only when they can be quickly applied, but also when they change behavior rapidly. Occasionally a procedure that is time-consuming to apply may be in the long run more time efficient because it changes behavior quickly. When considering cost, the value of the reinforcer itself must be considered. Tangible reinforcers, such as food, are more costly than social reinforcers. From multiple perspectives social reinforcers, such as praise and hugs, are ideal; they are cheap, can be applied easily, and are natural. Ultimately, the best reinforcers are those that work, and work quickly.

REINFORCER ADMINISTRATION

There are a number of other factors that influence whether reinforcement procedures are successful. As indicated in the previous section, selecting an appropriate reinforcer is important. However, even a potent reinforcer may fail, if it is not applied in an appropriate fashion. In order to maximize reinforcer effectiveness, a designated reinforcer should be applied in a *contingent* fashion, that is, only after the desired target behavior occurs. In other words, to reinforce effectively, the behavior to be increased must be reinforced, not some other behavior.

Although this principle makes good intuitive sense, in practice, reinforcers can be easily applied in a noncontigent and inappropriate fashion due to carelessness or inattention, such as when a delay occurs in delivering the reinforcer after the target behavior occurs. When a reinforcer is not provided immediately after the occurrence of a desired target behavior, another behavior may be subsequently emitted and inadvertently reinforced. If, however, the children being reinforced have well-developed language and cognitive skills, contingent and immediate application of the reinforcer is less critical. They can be told why the reinforcer is being given. In contrast, for children whose language repertoire and cognitive skills are not well developed, it is important that the time interval between target behavior and reinforcement be as short as possible in order for the response to be contingently reinforced. When responses are contingently reinforced, it is easier for language-challenged children to see the connection between their behavior and the reinforcer.

The *schedule* and *amount* of reinforcement are two other important factors influencing reinforcer effectiveness. During the early stages of an intervention program when a target skill is being taught, it should be reinforced on a continuous schedule, that is, every time it occurs; specifically because continuous reinforcement leads to more rapid response acquisition. Later, after the response is acquired, it can and should be reinforced intermittently to ensure long-term maintenance of the response.

Regarding the amount of reinforcement, when material reinforcers are employed, generally the greater the amount of a reinforcer given on any occasion, the more likely it is that an increase in behavior will occur. However, there is a parallel consideration relating to frequency of reinforcement. If the target behavior occurs and is reinforced frequently, a larger amount of a reinforcer may result in satiation, which is another way of saying the reinforcer will lose its effectiveness. Thus, the amount of a reinforcer given must be determined by the frequency of occurrence of the target behavior and the schedule of reinforcement. Reinforcer potency is also determined by the length of time the child has been deprived of the reinforcer outside of the training session. When food is employed, it is advisable to have training sessions before meals when the child is more likely to be hungry and to use if possible nourishing foods as reinforcers to ensure that a child's daily nutritional requirements are met.

The general rule of thumb in an educational program is to reinforce frequently in the beginning of a program, to change from a continuous to an intermittent schedule of reinforcement once the target behavior is occurring regularly, and to reduce gradually the amount of material reinforcers given on any particular reinforcement occasion. Optimally, praise should always be associated with material reinforcers and eventually material reinforcers should be faded out entirely and only praise employed. These issues will be discussed further when the topic of maintenance and generalization is covered later in this section.

A final consideration regarding reinforcer administration relates to *consistency of application*. It is important, whether one or more persons is involved in teaching a child, that the reinforcement procedures used be applied in a consistent fashion. This requires personal vigilance and close communication between parents, teachers, and other caretakers. When procedures are inconsistently applied, the likelihood of a child becoming confused and failing to learn is increased.

Response induction and supportive prompts

No matter how judicious the reinforcer selection or how skillful the reinforcer administration, these procedures will be of little consequence if the target behaviors to be taught never or seldom occur; that is, if they do not occur, they cannot be reinforced. Fortunately, a variety of procedures are available for developing behaviors that do not naturally occur. Before discussing these procedures it should be noted that even if a target behavior is occurring at a low rate, reinforcement of these occasional occurrences may be sufficient to bring about behavior increases. However, if this "wait-and-reinforce" strategy proves to be too time-consuming, then alternative procedures for making sure the response occurs should be considered. These procedures include the use of *verbal, visual,* and *manual prompts,* and *shaping.*

Because the use of *verbal prompting* procedures presuppose receptive language skills, these procedures may not be very useful when employed with children who do not have such skills. However, because verbal prompting is clearly an efficient procedure, if it works, this procedure should be tried initially. For example telling a child, "Sit" or "Look at me" may be sufficient to produce a desired response. An alternative method for prompting the occurrence of a behavior involves demonstrating or *modeling* the desired behavior for the child and then reinforcing the child's imitative behavior. Finally, in addition to the verbal and visual prompts, *physical guidance* can be employed, specifically by providing active manual assistance to the child. Depending on the child, when modeling and/or physical guidance procedures are employed, they may be paired with verbal instructions. This pairing helps develop the child's language skills.

All three of the aforementioned procedures introduce a stimulus prompt that precedes or accompanies the target behavior. If these procedures are successfully employed, prompts should then be gradually faded out; specifically, instructions are abbreviated, visual cues are attenuated and eventually removed, and physical guidance is withdrawn. When the goal is to get the child to respond to verbal instructions alone, only visual and physical prompts are faded out. When the goal is to get the child to act spontaneously, that is without any prompts, the verbal cues are also gradually removed.

In contrast to the aforementioned prompting techniques, a fourth procedure for getting a response to occur, shaping, involves the application of reinforcement in a special way. *Shaping* involves differentially reinforcing successively closer approximations to the target behavior. Initially, only very rough approximations to the ultimately desired response are required for reinforcement to occur; then gradually, more exact approximations are reinforced. For example, if a child is being taught to say goodbye, he/she might be initially reinforced for saying "goo," then for "good," and finally for "goodbye." Shaping is particularly applicable when the behavior taught is more complex or difficult to learn. As indicated earlier, although it is possible to use any of the previously cited procedures alone, a combination of the four are often employed.

Discrimination training: teaching children when and where a newly learned behavior is appropriate

The goal of an adaptive behavior training program is not merely to increase the frequency of behavior. In order for a behavior to be considered truly functional and appropriate, it typically must occur in certain places, at certain times, or more generally in the presence of specific stimulus circumstances. That is, as part of learning to respond, a child must learn where and when, as well as how, to respond. Once a child is able to make a response at an appropriate place and/or time, the child is said to have formed a discrimination. A critical tool for helping children form such discriminations is differential reinforcement. *Differential reinforcement* involves reinforcing a response only in the presence of a certain stimulus or set of stimuli and not reinforcing that response in the presence of other stimuli. Instructional and imitation training are two examples of discrimination training programs in which differential reinforcement is employed.

In *instructional training*, a verbal cue is presented to a child, for example "Sit down," and the child is reinforced for producing the correct response, in this case sitting down, to that verbal cue. The child is not reinforced if the child sits down when given another instruction, such as "Come here." In *imitation training* the only difference in the procedure is that the major cue presented is visual; the teacher demonstrates sitting while saying "Do this." Sometimes instructional and imitation training procedures are used together. In order for a child to learn to respond in a discriminative fashion, it is usually necessary to expose the learner repeatedly to the stimulus to which the response should be made as well as to other stimuli to which the response should not be made. This gives the child multiple opportunities to respond in an appropriate fashion and to be reinforced for correct responses. A discrimination training program is terminated when the child reliably makes the appropriate response in the presence of the appropriate stimulus.

Although failures by the child to respond appropriately, accompanied by nonreinforcement, can be conceived of as learning opportunities, it is best to minimize such errors, particularly when teaching children with ASD who are more likely to have a history of failure. The most effective way of reducing errors is to teach easier discriminations first and to use prompts as necessary, gradually fading these special aids until the discrimination can be made independently.

In many behavior training programs, the behaviors that are taught are not simple, but rather involve a set of multiple responses arranged in a particular sequence or *response chain*, such as in a self-help training program focused on teaching a child to feed him/herself. Within a response chain, each response in the chain provides the discriminative stimulus for the next response in the chain. For example, in a self-feeding program a child has to learn to pick up a spoon, then bring the spoon to the food, put food on the spoon, bring the spoon to the mouth, put the food in the mouth, and withdraw the spoon from the mouth. In order to acquire this complex series of responses, the child has to learn not only each of the component responses, but also to make a series of discriminations in order to perform the responses in the proper order.

To develop an effective *chaining* procedure, the component responses of the behavioral sequence must be first identified and then each component taught in a sequential fashion before proceeding to the next component. This type of behavior chain can be taught by either starting with the first response in the chain and then working forward (*forward chaining*), or with the last response in the chain and then working backward (*backward chaining*). Reinforcement is initially administered for a single component response, then for two component responses emitted in the proper sequence, then three component responses in proper sequence, and so on until only the last response in the chain is reinforced. Chapter 6 presents examples of the use of chaining procedures for developing complex sensorimotor behaviors.

Maintenance and generalization

The terminal goal of any educational intervention program is to ensure that behaviors taught are maintained over time and generalized to appropriate situations beyond the teaching environment. In instances where maintenance and generalization do not spontaneously occur, the teaching program must be expanded. Although early behavior therapists and educators typically trained and then hoped that maintenance and generalization would occur, this strategy was often not successful. For this reason, a variety of techniques were developed to promote maintenance and generalization, many of which were originally described by Stokes and Baer (1977).

Although conceptually, there is a distinction between *maintenance* and *generalization*, these two training objectives share much in common. Both refer to a situation in which the original training program is not in effect. When behavior is maintained over time, there occurs a type of situational generalization, that is, a generalization from a situation in which the training stimuli are present to one later in time in which the training program is absent or modified. Thus, the maintenance environment is almost identical physically to the training environment except the original training program is not in effect. If learning is not maintained over time, the original or a modified intervention program must be reintroduced. In contrast to a maintenance environment, a generalization environment is physically different from the environment in which training has taken place. For example, a child might in a school training environment be taught to identify two-dimensional red objects (pictures) and then subsequently in a home generalization environment be asked to identify three-dimensional objects that are red.

Although a multiplicity of training strategies for producing maintenance and generalization have been suggested by past research, many of these strategies can be classified under one of two approaches. The first approach, a common-stimulus strategy, involves approximating within the training situation the conditions that are or will be present in the maintenance or generalization settings. Ideally this approximation in the training situation should be based on a systematic analysis of the physical structure of other settings in which the response is appropriate. This approach assumes that the more key components the training and maintenance/generalization settings have in common, the greater the probability that maintenance/generalization will occur. These common-stimulus components can relate to the reinforcement and prompting procedures employed, the educational agents applying the procedures, and the other nonsocial and physical features of the settings.

The natural or non-training environment is perhaps best characterized as a place where minimal prompts are given, reinforcers are most often social in nature, where material reinforcers, such as food, are used only infrequently, where reinforcers are administered in an intermittent and variable fashion, and where delays may occur between the emission of a behavior and its subsequent reinforcement. Based upon this characterization, the common-stimulus strategy suggests that during training prompts should be gradually removed and that material reinforcers, initially applied in a continuous fashion, should be gradually faded out and replaced by social reinforcers which have been paired with the material reinforcers. Subsequently, these social reinforcers should in turn be thinned out and provided only intermittently and on an unpredictable schedule.

In addition to these changes in prompting and reinforcement practices, the common-stimulus strategy suggests that the social agents in charge of administering educational programs in the training environment should either be the same as those who interact with the child in his or her natural environment or be trained to apply the intervention program in as similar a fashion to them as possible. Group training of all the child's teachers (teacher aides, parents, volunteers, etc.) together is strongly recommended. Finally, the common-stimulus strategy suggests that behavioral therapists should pay close attention to the physical nature of the training environment. In attempting to approximate the generalization setting within the training environment, such features as room size, furniture, presence of other people, visual and auditory distractors, and training materials should also be as similar as possible.

From a theoretical point of view, the common-stimulus approach to programming maintenance and generalization can be conceptualized in terms of a discrimination-learning model. Within this framework, the basic explanation of why maintenance and generalization of responding should occur using a common-stimulus approach is that the child fails to discriminate between the training and non-training environments. In contrast, a cognitive perspective would suggest that those who are taught form a concept concerning how the training and generalization situations are similar despite their differences.

It perhaps has occurred to the reader that the extreme case of the common-stimulus approach would be to make the training environment identical to the generalization setting. The major reasons for not adopting this ultimate variant is that the generalization settings are not typically restricted to one or two situations and that it would be difficult, if not physically impossible, to incorporate the features of all the possible generalization settings into one training setting. Even if it were possible to create this simulation, this approach is likely to be cumbersome and inefficient. In general the major intent of the common-stimulus approach is not to make the training situation identical to non-training settings, but rather to incorporate into the training situation critical elements that control behavior across many settings.

Whereas the first approach just discussed is useful in promoting maintenance and generalization to settings that are similar in many respects to the training setting, the second approach to be described is particularly useful for promoting generalization to situations that are quite different from the training environment. Initially, like the common-stimulus approach, this approach involves conducting the training program and then waiting to see if generalization occurs. If it does not occur, then additional interventions are placed into effect. This approach recognizes that whenever a behavior is learned, it may become connected to a narrow range of cues and that in order for generalization to take place the breadth of the stimuli controlling that behavior needs to be gradually expanded.

One way to broaden the range of strategic stimuli controlling responses is to introduce sequentially these stimuli into the training environment. In this regard Stokes and Baer (1977) point out that if teaching one exemplar of a generalization lesson is not sufficient to produce generalization, then additional exemplars of that generalization lesson should be taught until the lesson is learned. For example, in a socialization program this strategy would dictate that if a child, who is taught to play with another child, does not show generalized play with other children, then additional children should be introduced sequentially into the play-training situation until generalized play occurs with children who have never been in the training situation. Another approach is to teach children to play in a sequential fashion in different social settings that vary in their physical structure, play activities, and the children present.

Although the common-stimulus and sequential training approaches for producing maintenance and generalization are distinctive, they do in fact complement one another. With the common-stimulus strategy, an attempt is made to program generalization during the early phases of training. If this strategy fails or does not produce extensive enough effects, the sequential approach can then be employed as a backup procedure. Ultimately, whichever strategies are employed, it is important to remember that neither maintenance nor generalization is likely to occur if the natural social environment does not support behaviors developed in the training environment.

For example, it is a well-established fact that behavior will be extinguished if it is not at least intermittently reinforced. Thus, if the significant socialization and educational agents in a child's everyday environment, such as in a home or a school setting, are not reinforcing appropriate behavior, maintenance and generalization must be systematically programmed by training these individuals to use appropriate reinforcement techniques. In subsequent chapters, particularly the chapter on self-regulation (Chapter 10), other techniques for producing maintenance and generalization will be described.

Emotion-focused interventions

Over 50 years of research provides support for the efficacy of exposure therapies for treating anxiety, fear, and other intense negative emotional responses. The terms anxiety and fear will be used interchangeably here to refer to responses that are disproportionate to the threat presented by situations offering little or no actual danger. These responses are characterized by moderate to intense physiological responses (e.g. increased heart rate and respiration), verbal expressions of concern, avoidance of specific situations, and other motor expressions. Fear/anxiety responses are particularly maladaptive when they inhibit learning and prevent an individual from entering into everyday living situations.

The goal of emotion-focused interventions is to reduce or extinguish an individual's fears/anxiety in situations that should not evoke these emotions. Chapter 4 provides a more elaborated rationale for using such programs with children with ASD. In this section we discuss a variety of interventions which, although different in their structure, share in common a strategy of reducing anxiety/fear through exposure to a feared stimulus. These interventions include: full exposure, graduated exposure, in-vivo, pictorial, and imagined exposure, reciprocal inhibition, vicarious extinction, and habituation.

Full exposure

Full exposure involves re-exposing an individual to the actual situation that originally evoked the fear. For example, a child is placed back on a pony from which a fall was taken. Full exposure is seldom used with children who have intense and long-standing fear responses. Moreover, discretion regarding its use is recommended for children with fear responses that are milder and of recent origin; specifically because there is a risk that full exposure may intensify rather than lead to the extinction of the fear response.

Graduated exposure

This approach involves presenting a threatening stimulus to an individual in a graduated fashion, for example by increasing the period of time of exposure, by gradually decreasing the distance from the feared object, and/or by gradually increasing the intensity of the stimulus. For example, if a child is afraid of a friendly and affectionate dog, that dog might be brought repeatedly into the same room as the child, initially for just a few seconds, but on subsequent occasions for progressively longer periods of time. After that child's fear response is extinguished or substantially diminished to the dog's presence in the room, the dog might be brought gradually closer to the child. If the child is afraid of the sound of a dog barking, that barking sound might be tape-recorded and presented at gradually increasing intensities. The key when this type of procedure is employed is to not increase the duration, proximity, or intensity of exposure to the feared stimulus until the child is able to tolerate a lower level of exposure, that is at a point when the child's fear response is minimal. Initially, and sometimes well into this procedure, repeated re-exposure at a particular level (duration, distance, or intensity) may be necessary before increasing the level of exposure.

In-vivo, pictorial, and imagined exposure

When graduated exposure techniques were originally developed, the clients were often adults with severe phobic disorders. Rather than exposing them in-vivo to an actual feared stimulus/situation, the individuals were asked to imagine situations that evoked different levels of fear. Using the previous example of a dog phobia, phobic individuals might imagine hearing a dog bark outside when they were safely in the house, then later visualize seeing the dog at a distance in a kennel, and eventually imagine situations where a dog approaches them on the street. The theory behind this imagery exposure procedure, which has received considerable empirical support for its efficacy, is that once individuals become cognitively desensitized to the feared stimulus as imaged, they would then be able to tolerate more easily the feared stimuli in-vivo.

For children with ASD, graduated exposure procedures that involve visual exposure through pictures or videos of a feared stimulus and/or graduated exposure to an actual feared stimulus are recommended rather than imagined exposure. This recommendation is based on clinical and empirical evidence suggesting that children with ASD, as well as younger neurotypical children, are more concrete and visual thinkers who are likely to have difficulty imaging fear-evoking situations in their mind.

Reciprocal inhibition procedures

Reciprocal inhibition procedures are based on the theory and considerable research indicating that certain feelings are incompatible with each other and that it is difficult, if not impossible, to experience feelings of anxiety and fear fully at the same time that one is experiencing feelings of pleasure. From a physiological perspective, pleasurable feelings are associated with parasympathetic activity; such activity is capable of inhibiting anxiety responses which are associated with sympathetic activity.

In order to inhibit anxiety responses, activities or stimuli that produce pleasurable experiences are utilized. Such activities or stimuli might include: food, drink, receiving a massage, other muscle relaxation procedures, wearing a weighted vest, playing with a favorite toy, and being in physical contact with an adult with whom a child feels emotionally secure.

Therapeutically, reciprocal inhibition procedures are typically paired with the aforementioned graduated extinction procedures. For example, if a child with autism enjoys experiencing deep pressure, deep pressure might be applied while the child is being exposed in a graduated fashion to a feared stimulus, either in-vivo or through pictures.

Vicarious extinction

Vicarious extinction involves exposing a child, with a fear response to a particular situation, to an individual or individuals who show pleasure or joy in that same situation. For example, if a child with ASD is afraid to go swimming, he/she might be exposed to children who are having great fun in a swimming situation. This exposure could be in-vivo, to the actual fear-evoking situation, or through a video of that situation. Theory and research with typically developing children suggest that such an exposure can reduce fear responses to a point where a child is able to approach the feared situation. Vicarious extinction can be used in conjunction with the graduated exposure and reciprocal inhibition procedures previously described.

Habituation

Habituation refers to a process which is quite similar, if not identical, to that which takes place during exposure (extinction) therapies. It refers to a process in which there is a decrement in responding to a stimulus that occurs when that stimulus is repeatedly presented. For example, if a child becomes upset when exposed to a high-pitched sound or a bright light (or other sensory stimuli to which a hypersensitive response is shown), that light or sound, or a less intense variant of that light or sound, is repeatedly presented. The theory is that over time the sensory nervous system will be retrained and that eventually the child should be able to tolerate such a stimulus without any or minimal visible upset. Whereas, extinction is directed at reducing the overt fear response, habituation is ostensibly directed at changing the biological substrate underlying this response. It seems likely, however, that the exposure (extinction) procedures described earlier also directly affect these same hypothetical biological processes.

Cognitive-behavioral and self-regulation techniques

In this section, cognitive-behavioral and self-regulation techniques are described in conjunction because most cognitive-behavior techniques have a self-regulatory function and conversely most self-regulatory techniques have a cognitive component. Given the many cognitive deficiencies that are commonly associated with ASD, it is not surprising that children with ASD have difficulty regulating their behavior. From a cognitive perspective, a wide variety of cognitive problems, including problems related to attention, memory, metacognition, executive functioning, and theory of mind (see Chapters 8, 9, and 10), have been proposed to account for the other deficiencies associated with ASD.

Cognitive-behavior therapy first emerged as an important part of the behavior therapy movement in the 1960s. Since that time, applied research has demonstrated the efficacy of this approach for a broad array of clinical and academic problems in children and adults. Cognitive-behavior therapy has also been successfully employed in intervention programs for children with an array of developmental disabilities, including ASD. This approach was developed based on the assumption that cognitions control behavior and that cognitions are subject to the same sort of environmental influences as overt responses. Although it has been acknowledged that not all behavior is cognitively driven, it has also been recognized that behavior development is greatly enhanced as cognitive development occurs. Two of the major vehicles that cognitive-behavior therapists utilize in changing cognitions, that is the way people think, are visual images and verbal behavior. The assumption is that visual images and words can control thinking and thinking in turn controls overt actions and feelings.

In order to change the verbal behavior that controls cognitions and in turn actions in children with ASD, several major problems are confronted. The first is that many children with ASD have little if any expressive language. For these children, many of the cognitive-behavioral techniques described here are not able to be employed as part of their intervention program. However, several visually oriented procedures can be utilized to influence their thinking processes and in turn behavior. For children with ASD who have expressive language, a second problem is confronted: specifically their language does not always control their actions. For these children, verbal control or regulation of their actions must be taught. In this section, both visually oriented and verbally oriented techniques for influencing thinking and behavior are described, including modeling, pictorial instruction, verbal instruction, correspondence training, self-instruction, executive functioning, and metastrategic interventions.

Modeling, imitation, and observational learning

Modeling and imitation are used to refer to the changes in behavior that occur through observing the actions of other people (models). Through observation of others, children can learn adaptive behaviors as well as maladaptive behaviors. They can also acquire fears vicariously by watching individuals who are traumatized in particular situations or conversely they can have their fears extinguished by watching individuals who show no fear in potentially threatening circumstances. Finally, through observation, children can learn not only how to respond, but also the appropriate time and place for a response.

Although early in their development children with ASD often do not spontaneously imitate the behavior of those around them, they can be taught to do so through prompting and reinforcing imitative behavior (see Chapter 3). Because many children with ASD are often adept visual learners, the use of modeling as a teaching tool makes particular sense. Typically, real-life models are employed. However, the use of video models is also recommended because children with autism often spontaneously imitate such models, perhaps because video models are quite consistent and predictable in their behavior. The use of video models may also be more convenient and cost effective than real-life models because videos can be easily and repeatedly introduced. Once children with ASD learn to spontaneously imitate the action of others, their capacity for learning exponentially increases.

Pictorial instruction

During pictorial instruction, children are provided visual cues to guide their behavior. For example, visual schedules have been employed to inform children with autism about the nature and flow of their daily activities and to cue them about what they should do next. Visual recipes can also be employed to teach them how to perform complex activities, such as brushing teeth or setting a table. The pictorial cues serve as visual templates or models that can be imitated.

Verbal instruction

One of the most frequently utilized techniques employed by parents and teachers is verbal instruction. Although the vast majority of cognitive training programs for children with ASD contain a verbal component, verbal prompting procedures are often not sufficient and need to be supplemented through the addition of other types of prompts, including physical assistance and modeling, as well as the reinforcement techniques described earlier in this chapter. Techniques for teaching children to follow verbal instructions are described in Chapter 3.

From a theoretical perspective, there are a variety of explanations for why children with ASD who have well-developed language skills often fail to learn from verbal instruction. Whitman (1987, 2004) has speculated that they have problems focusing on the pertinent cues contained in verbal instructions, associating words with actions, and using speech to control motoric behavior. Given the difficulties children with ASD have in learning through traditional verbal instructional methods, alternative methods of establishing verbal control can be utilized to facilitate performance. Two such alternatives include correspondence training and self-instruction.

Correspondence training

Correspondence training has been utilized to increase a wide variety of academic, social, and personal behaviors, such as listening, appropriate sitting, sharing, appropriate posture, and choosing nutritious snacks (Whitman, 2004). Correspondence training is based on the social convention that there should be a relationship between what children say and what they do. Developing correspondence between verbal and nonverbal behavior in children with ASD is especially appropriate because of their language control deficiencies. Past research indicates that children with ASD often fail to self-regulate and are excessively dependent on others for guidance and direction (Whitman, 2004). Correspondence training establishes the child as the locus of control through teaching them how to verbally self-regulate. Because correspondence training develops a habit of verbal self-control, it can be used to foster maintenance and generalization.

Correspondence training can proceed in one of two basic sequences: 1) teaching children to do what they say they will do (say-do), or 2) teaching children to accurately report (say) what they actually did (do-say). In the say-do approach, children are specifically taught to say what they will do in a particular situation. Subsequently, their behavior is monitored to evaluate whether they did what they said they would do. If they do what they said they were going to do (e.g. perform a household task), they are reinforced. Conversely in do-say correspondence training, children learn how to monitor their behavior (e.g. what they ate at a meal) and report what they did. Correspondence is again developed by reinforcing word–action congruence. This type of correspondence training is particularly important because children with ASD have great difficulty monitoring their behavior and as a consequence do not have a well-developed self-image because they are not self-aware.

Self-instruction

In addition to verbal instructional and correspondence training procedures, a third verbal training technique, self-instruction, has been employed with children with developmental delays. Self-instruction is similar to external instruction, except that it requires the child to instruct themselves during the training process. Self-instruction is also very similar to correspondence training in that the relationship between verbal and nonverbal behavior is reinforced.

Although usually conceptualized as two distinct therapeutic techniques, both say-do correspondence training and self-instructional training utilize an individual's own verbal behavior to guide his or her nonverbal behavior. Thus, as in correspondence training, the emphasis in self-instruction is upon developing self-regulatory speech, that is self-verbalizations are programmed to control nonverbal behavior. However, self-instruction involves a more complex and dynamic teaching algorithm than that which is employed in correspondence training as well as a more complex set of verbal cues to be learned by the child. Self-instruction assists children through supplying words/strategies and then helping them to understand the meaning of those words/strategies by teaching them to use the words to guide and regulate their actions (Whitman, 2004).

The training sequence typically proceeds as follows: 1) a teacher/model performs a task (e.g. an arithmetic problem) while talking out loud, stating specifically how the task should be performed; 2) the child then performs the task, assisted by the teacher who provides verbal guidance/instructions; 3) next the child performs the task while self-instructing out loud, that is telling him/herself what should be done and then doing it; 4) the child then whispers the instructions while completing the task; and finally 5) the child completes the task while guiding his/her performance through covert self-instruction. There are several important problem-solving skills often included in a typical self-instruction routine, such as: 1) problem definition ("What do I have to do?"); 2) attention to the task and response guidance ("I need to _____."); 3) standard setting, self-evaluation, and self-reinforcement ("Good, I did that one correctly."); and 4) skills for coping with errors ("I made a mistake; however, I can fix it and go on.").

Before self-instruction is adopted as a training procedure, it is important to determine whether a child has reasonable expressive skills; specifically a child should be able to string words together into sentences and show some rudimentary capacity to regulate verbally his/her own behavior. There are several reasons to use a self-instructional rather than an external instructional format. The use of self-instructional training paradigm allows the teacher to monitor systematically whether the child understands, as reflected in their verbalizations and actions, how to perform a particular task and whether the child's verbalizations actually control his/her behavior.

Executive functioning and metastrategic interventions

In contrast to the previously discussed self-management procedures, which have been derived for the most part from applied behavioral research and clinical practice, the interventions discussed in this section evolved from cognitive-developmental research and theories (Whitman, 2004). Children with ASD have been found to use fewer and simpler cognitive strategies than typically developing children in memory, learning, and problem-solving situations. Children with ASD do not appear to be particularly strategic; instead they rely on cues from others to direct their behavior and have great difficulty generalizing the use of strategies they do employ to new situations.

Although research indicates that specific cognitive task skills can be readily taught to children with ASD through the use of techniques such as self-instruction, these children lack the requisite higher-order metacognitive and executive functioning capabilities to apply these skills in other situations. In particular, they lack awareness concerning what they have learned and know, and how what they know can be used in other problem-solving situations. Interventions focusing on developing these capabilities are especially appropriate for children with ASD given their extreme passivity in learning situations.

Executive functioning involves active self-control rather than control from the external environment. It involves planning, making strategic decisions, then acting, and finally monitoring the results of one's actions. It is guided knowledge, plans, and goals. Metacognition refers to the process of asking questions about what one knows and how this knowledge can be employed to guide decision-making in specific situations. In contrast to self-instructional training, where children are taught to use strategies in specific problem-solving situations, metacognitive and executive-functioning instructional programs emphasize using what one has learned previously in new problem-solving situations.

Metacognitive and executive-functioning training programs for children with autism should contain the following components:

1. Active involvement should be encouraged through sensitizing children about the relationship between their personal effort, that is the importance of working hard and successful performance.

2. In order to catalyze their active involvement, self-awareness should be promoted through having the children analyze and examine in a problem-solving situation what they know about the requirements of a task being confronted. They are asked to examine their cognitive repertoire for possible task solutions and if they know what to do, to implement those strategies, or if they do not know what to do, to recognize their need for assistance and to ask for help, and finally to assess after implementation whether a problem has been solved. Self-monitoring and checking skills are taught to ensure that the children deploy strategies effectively.

3. In addition to being given instruction about how to make decisions in a specific problem-solving situation, information concerning the usefulness of specific decision-making strategies in other situations is provided.

In contrast to the self-instructional programs described in the last section, the emphasis during executive functioning and metacognitive training is less on the development of specific strategic skills and more on coordinating the use of these skills across problem-solving situations. Children with ASD need to be taught to recognize the general importance of being strategic and to discriminate when a previously learned skill is applicable in a new situation. However, to develop a general strategic orientation, programming must focus first on ensuring that the child is in possession of specific strategies necessary to solve different tasks, and then on teaching him or her to select appropriately and utilize these various strategies as different types of problems are presented.

For example, a child might be taught in a sequential fashion different basic math skills (addition, subtraction, multiplication, and division) and then taught to utilize appropriately these various strategies when problems requiring their use are randomly presented. In order to perform effectively, the child needs just to learn to identify the type of math problem with which he or she is confronted and then to choose the appropriate strategy for solving the problem. Thus, the goal of this type of training is to first teach him or her to be strategic (to use cognitive strategies) and then to be metastrategic (to evaluate the applicability of different strategies in different situations), and finally to implement the appropriate strategy and monitor whether it is successful.

Summary

Because children with ASD vary considerably in their language competency, it is important that their linguistic skills be systematically evaluated prior to the development of a cognitive training program. Children with minimal receptive and expressive language typically have to be taught through procedures which emphasize the use of visual prompts, often in conjunction with manual and verbal prompts. If these procedures are employed, emphasis should be placed on gradually fading the manual prompts and bringing their behavior under visual and then, if possible, verbal control. Training should also stress the development of both basic expressive (e.g. use of words and simple sentences) and receptive (e.g. instruction-following) language skills. As these language skills are developed, more complex cognitive instructional techniques can then be utilized. Chapter 3 describes procedures for developing basic receptive and expressive language skills.

Children with receptive and expressive language skills, who are able to follow adult verbal directives and to monitor and describe their own actions, are in a position to benefit from more advanced cognitive training programs. For children with established, but more rudimentary language skills, correspondence training procedures should be employed; specifically because these procedures make less demand on the language system and are directed at helping the child understand the relationship of words and actions. For children with better developed language skills, self-instructional procedures can be employed.

Based on our present state of knowledge, it appears that self-instructional training will be most beneficial for children who have developed language proficiency but still have difficulty processing more complex verbal directives from socialization agents and using these directives to regulate their own behavior. Self-instruction teaches children to be more strategic in a verbal self-regulatory sense; more specifically, to process information given by others and to use this information subsequently to direct verbally their own behavior. Finally, for children with highly developed language skills, who have learned how to employ various specific cognitive strategies in problem-solving situations, executive and metacognitive training components should be utilized to help them generalize their strategic knowledge to new learning situations.

Reduction of maladaptive behavior

Children with ASD manifest a wide range of behavior deficiencies. For example, they are frequently deficient in their self-help, motor, language, and social skills. Because of their extensive deficiencies, it is somewhat surprising to find that some intervention programs seem more concerned with reducing maladaptive behavior rather than increasing adaptive behavior. From our perspective, the emphasis during intervention should be almost exclusively on developing adaptive behavior skills, including skills that help children with ASD communicate their needs so that they do not need to act inappropriately.

Behavior reduction programs can be most easily justified if the intent is to make a child more receptive to adaptive-behavior development programs. These programs may be particularly warranted for children whose maladaptive behavior prevents their entrance into educational situations or interferes with their ability to function once they are in such situations. When behavior reduction programs are needed, a wide variety of techniques can be employed, including extinction, differential reinforcement, and punishment procedures, such as response cost and time-out. These procedures and reasons for selecting one of them over the others are discussed in this section.

Extinction

To fully appreciate the rationale for and the potential utility of extinction procedures, it is important to know that most behavior, whether adaptive or maladaptive, is developed and maintained through positive reinforcement. During *extinction*, this developmental process is reversed by withholding reinforcement, which typically results in a decrease in behavior. In order to successfully apply an extinction procedure, the reinforcers maintaining a response must be identified. Although conceptually this identification process appears simple, it may be difficult to achieve in reality, particularly if the reinforcers occur only on an intermittent basis. Ultimately it is impossible to know if the reinforcers for a particular response have been identified until they are withdrawn and the effect of this withdrawal on the target behavior is examined.

In order for extinction to occur, it is necessary for reinforcers to be completely withdrawn. For example, if social attention appears to be the reinforcer for a child's inappropriate response, then that attention must be completely withdrawn and the child's behavior consistently ignored. If a therapist, parent and/or teacher occasionally reinforce the behaviors being extinguished, that is they do not all uniformly adhere to the extinction procedure, the target behavior may become even more firmly entrenched and resistant to extinction. The consequences of inconsistent application are vividly seen in a classic case study by Williams (1959) in which a child's bedtime crying behavior was successfully treated through an extinction routine (crying is ignored) administered by the parents and then inadvertently reinstated as a result of an aunt's attention to the child's emotional outbursts.

A number of factors must be considered in deciding whether to use an extinction procedure in a particular situation. One of these factors relates to the length of time it takes for this procedure to reduce an inappropriate response. Typically, the extinction process is a gradual one. The exact rate of extinction depends on the history and schedule of reinforcement that produced the inappropriate behavior. When the target behavior has had a long history of occurrence and been reinforced on an intermittent schedule, extinction typically occurs more slowly and may not be the procedure of choice. In contrast, extinction will occur more rapidly when the behavior is of recent origin and has been continuously reinforced. Another major factor that mitigates against using an extinction procedure has to do with the nature of the inappropriate behavior to be decreased. If the behavior results either in destruction of the physical environment, in serious self-injury, or in injury to others, the use of extinction is not advisable, particularly given the possibility that a decrease in such inappropriate behaviors will only occur gradually.

In the initial stages of most extinction programs, the targeted inappropriate response may actually increase in frequency and intensity as the child tries to reinstate the favorable consequences, that is to regain the reinforcer that has been withdrawn. If at this point, a parent or teacher abandons the extinction protocol, because of their perception that the procedure is not working, and reinforces the child, the inappropriate behavior will become even more firmly entrenched. During the later stages of an extinction program, once extinction has resulted in a decrease in behavior, the response may again temporarily increase in frequency (spontaneously recover), as if the child is testing the waters to see if reinforcement might again be forthcoming. Because such "spontaneous" response increments commonly occur, educational personnel must take care not to interpret these increases as signs of program failure and make sure that the behavior is not reinforced.

Differential reinforcement

Although the aforementioned limitations may dictate against using a simple extinction program, this procedure is often quite effective when combined with positive reinforcement for some desirable alternative behavior. When these procedures are used in combination, extinction often occurs more rapidly, and the temporary increases in the inappropriate behavior, noted previously, may not occur. Most importantly, whereas the use of extinction alone does not guarantee that a child will behave more appropriately, the use of both positive reinforcement and extinction procedures is directed not only at decreasing maladaptive behavior (e.g. crying), but also at increasing alternative more adaptive responses (e.g. talking). This joint procedure is called differential reinforcement.

Differential reinforcement refers to a technique in which one or more behaviors are reinforced while other behaviors undergo extinction. The main objective of a differential reinforcement procedure may be to increase a desirable behavior, decrease an undesirable behavior, or both. Differential reinforcement procedures can also be employed to increase a response, such as talking, in one situation (e.g. during recess) and to decrease the same response in other situations (e.g. in church). This effect is accomplished by reinforcing the target response in the presence of certain stimuli and not reinforcing this response in the presence of other stimuli. From a social perspective, a behavior can be considered inappropriate categorically, that is, wherever it occurs, or only sometimes, depending upon where it occurs. For example, a child's "aggressive" behavior, such as roughhousing with other children, might be deemed always inappropriate or only inappropriate in certain types of situations, such as in a classroom, but not in others, such as in the playground.

When a differential reinforcement procedure is employed with an inappropriate behavior that is considered always inappropriate and placed on extinction, one of two basic procedures for reinforcing alternative behaviors can be used. One procedure involves reinforcing any behavior other than the inappropriate behaviors that are placed on extinction. For example, a hyperactive child who is frequently out of his seat in a classroom might have all out-of-seat behaviors in the classroom placed on extinction and all in-seat behaviors positively reinforced, whether the child is involved in study behaviors or just sitting there, doing nothing in particular. This procedure is commonly referred to as DRO or differential reinforcement of other behavior.

In contrast, a second differential reinforcement procedure involves selectively reinforcing one desirable behavior or a set of desirable behaviors, rather than reinforcing all other behaviors. Sometimes the desirable behaviors are incompatible with the undesirable behavior, because the two sets of behaviors cannot occur at the same time. For example, if the objective of a program is to reduce a repetitive response, such as finger flicking, the differential reinforcement procedures might involve ignoring this response and reinforcing the child only when his/her hands are used to play appropriately with a toy.

Punishment

In addition to extinction and differential reinforcement procedures, a variety of techniques, classified as punishment, have been used to decelerate inappropriate behavior. Punishment can refer to either the withdrawal or presentation of a stimulus event following a response; in both cases these actions must result in a decrease in the frequency of that response in order to be labeled punishment. Both types of punishment procedures are discussed in this section.

TIME-OUT AND RESPONSE COST

Two procedures that bear some similarity to extinction techniques and to each other have been used to decrease the inappropriate behaviors of children with ASD. These procedures are *response cost* and *time-out* from positive reinforcement, commonly referred to as time-out. Response cost is like time-out in that a loss of a positive reinforcer is involved. Technically both are defined as punishment procedures.

Unlike extinction, response cost involves the loss of a specific positive reinforcer that a child currently has access to or is in his or her possession, such as receiving a weekly allowance or playing games on a computer. In contrast, extinction involves the discontinuation of a reinforcer that has been historically given for a response, such as praise. Frequently response-cost procedures are used in conjunction with token economies, in which misbehavior results in the loss of tokens earned for appropriate behaviors. Sometimes the positive reinforcers lost, when response cost procedures are used, are privileges, such as the right to go outside to play or watching television. For example, if a child hits his brother, the response cost for hitting might involve the temporary loss of television privileges.

In contrast to response cost, time-out involves the loss of an opportunity to receive positive reinforcers for a certain period of time. During time-out the individual might be removed from an environment where positive reinforcers are immediately available, such as a playroom where toys are present and social contact is possible, and placed in a room where these stimuli are not present. This procedure is called exclusionary time-out. Another way of implementing time-out from positive reinforcement involves putting a child who misbehaves, for example in a classroom situation, in a chair facing a corner of the room. This procedure is called non-exclusionary time-out.

Whichever procedure is employed, the nature of the environment from which and to which an individual is timed-out must be taken into consideration. Research points out that time-out is effective only when the environment from which the child is excluded, such as a classroom, is really a source of positive reinforcement and conversely when the time-out environment itself is not positively reinforcing. For example, if a child is sent to his room, but has access to his computer, this exclusion might not serve as a punishment. There are several other potential problems with exclusionary time-out procedures. These procedures are sometimes cumbersome, because they are time-consuming to administer and often necessitate a person to monitor the child. For these reasons, non-exclusionary time-out procedures are generally recommended over exclusionary time-out procedures.

APPLICATION OF AVERSIVE STIMULI

In contrast to time-out and response cost, some punishment procedures do not withdraw positive reinforcers, but rather involve the administration of aversive stimuli. Currently, this type of procedure is not widely employed. Moreover, depending on the aversive stimulus employed, this type of procedure may be viewed as inhumane. For example, the use of electric shock, even if effective, to reduce self-injurious behaviors has been thought by many to be inappropriate. A variety of other more innocuous aversive stimuli have been used in punishment programs; for example placement of lemon juice in the mouth has been employed with children who engage in pica behaviors (placing inedible objects in the mouth and sometimes swallowing them) and pepper solution on fingers has been used with children who suck their fingers so frequently that it results in dental problems. In addition to these primary (intrinsically aversive) punishers, conditioned punishers, typically some type of verbal reprimand or warning, have also been used. Similar to the process by which neutral stimuli, such as praise, acquire positive reinforcing properties through association with primary reinforcers, like food, neutral stimuli, such as the word no, can become punishers when associated with primary punishers.

Overcorrection

Several punishment procedures are difficult to categorize because they appear to be a combination of time-out, response cost and/or aversive-stimulus application procedures. *Overcorrection* is the most prominent example of this type of procedure. Overcorrection is actually a general name for an array of procedures that require the misbehaving individual to restore an environment disturbed by his or her deviant behavior, not only to its original state but to an improved state, and/or to practice more appropriate modes of responding within the environment in which the misbehavior occurs. These two general types of procedures have been referred to, respectively, as *restitutional* and *positive-practice* overcorrection.

An example of a restitutional overcorrection procedure that has been employed is requiring an aggressive child to clean up a soft drink that has been spilled during an aggressive throwing episode and then to mop up the entire floor of the room in which the episode occurred. An example of a hybrid procedure is requiring a child who has had a toileting accident to clean himself (restitution) and then to practice repeatedly going to the toilet, specifically performing a sequence of appropriate toileting behaviors, including pulling pants down, sitting down on toilet, getting up, and pulling up pants (positive practice). Overcorrection procedures have been used to decrease a variety of inappropriate behaviors, including stereotypy, social aggression, and temper tantrums.

Selection of a punishment procedure

When the decision to employ some type of a punishment procedure has been made, a number of factors must be considered. These factors relate to the overall efficacy of the techniques considered, undesirable side effects associated with the application of the techniques, convenience of administration, and social acceptability. In general, punishment procedures, when properly employed, are usually effective. Nevertheless, considerable concern has been raised about the use of punishment procedures because of the possible undesirable effects that may occur; specifically that punishment may result in anxiety responses, suppression of socially desirable patterns of behavior, and avoidance by the punished individual of persons administering the punishment and of the situations in which the punishment is administered. However, these types of effects can be ameliorated, if not prevented, when punishment procedures are judiciously used in conjunction with positive reinforcement programs.

Another very practical consideration that has a bearing on the selection of punishment procedures relates to the amount of time and energy that must be expended in their application. Some procedures, for example verbal disapproval, have an obvious advantage over others that are considerably more time-consuming to administer, such as overcorrection. Other punishment techniques also vary on this dimension. For example, time-out can be a very lengthy procedure when it involves removing a child from one room to another and monitoring the child while in that time-out situation. In contrast, time-out can be more efficient, such as when a child is merely removed to the periphery of a classroom.

When punishment techniques are applied, it is imperative to keep several things in mind. First, it is critical that the punished response not be inadvertently reinforced. Second, care should be taken that escape from punishment is not possible. If either or both of these situations occur, it will extend the time punishment programs have to be in effect and may result in the program not working at all. Perhaps the most important point to be kept in mind for punishment programs to be effective in the long term is that they should always be used in conjunction with a positive reinforcement program for acting appropriately. For example, a child in a playroom who is punished for aggressive behavior should also be actively reinforced for appropriate play behavior.

In the long run, society's perception and acceptance of a punishment technology will undoubtedly determine the extent of its employment. It is probably accurate to state that currently society tends to shy away from the use of punishment as a child-rearing technique. The reasons for this position are complex, relating to the association of punishment with cruel and inhumane treatment, the production of unnecessary pain, and child abuse. Society has also tended to connect punishment with a means of dealing with criminal behavior and people guilty of wrong doing, not with children with ASD who clearly do not have a fully developed sense of right and wrong.

The current philosophy of most practicing behavior therapists, guided by regulations put forth by state agencies and professional associations, is to use punishment procedures only after other procedures, such as extinction and differential reinforcement, have failed and then to use the least aversive and most socially acceptable alternative procedures, such as response cost and time-out. This more conservative approach is dictated both by societal attitudes about punishment as well as by the belief that if intervention programs focus on developing adaptive behaviors, including the development of communication and other social skills, behavior problems are less likely to evolve in the first place or if they do evolve will be more easily controlled.

Preview

In the remaining chapters of this book, the applicability of the intervention techniques described in this chapter, along with other related techniques, will be examined in specific program areas. These areas include: foundation or core learning skills (Chapter 3), emotional problems and emotional competence (Chapter 4), sensory problems and sensorimotor development (Chapters 5 and 6), language, cognitive, and social development (Chapters 7, 8, and 9), self-regulation (Chapter 10), and behavioral problems (Chapter 11). After discussing the rationale for intervening in each of these areas, specific behaviors that often need to be targeted for treatment will be described, along with specific intervention techniques for addressing these behaviors. Each chapter concludes with a presentation of specific program examples.

References

Stokes, T. & Baer, D. (1977). An implicit technology of generalization. *Journal of Applied Behavior Analysis, 10,* 349–367.

Whitman, T. L. (2004). *The development of autism: A self-regulatory perspective.* London: Jessica Kingsley Publishers.

Whitman, T. L. (1987). Self-instruction, individual differences and mental retardation. *American Journal of Mental Deficiency, 92,* 213–233.

Williams, C. (1959). The elimination of tantrum behavior by extinction procedures. *Journal of Abnormal and Social Psychology, 59,* 269–271.

Recommended readings on learning theory-based interventions

Alberto, P. & Troutman, A. (2006). *Applied behavior analysis for teachers* (7th ed.). Upper Saddle River, NJ: Pearson Merrill Prentice Hall.

Cooper, J., Heron, T., & Heward, W. (2007). *Applied behavior analysis* (2nd ed.). Upper Saddle River, NJ: Pearson Merrill Prentice Hall.

Malott, R. (2008). *Principles of behavior* (6th ed.). Upper Saddle River, NJ: Pearson Prentice Hall.

Martin, G. & Pear, J. (2007). *Behavior modification: What it is and how to do it* (8th ed.). Upper Saddle River, NJ: Pearson Prentice Hall.

O'Donohue, W. (1998). *Learning and behavior therapy.* Needham Heights, MA: Allyn & Bacon.

Plaud, J. J. & Eifert, G. H. (1998). *From behavior theory to behavior therapy.* Boston, MA: Allyn and Bacon.

Sarafino, E. (2004). *Behavior modification: Principles of change* (2nd ed.). Long Grove, IL: Waveland Press.

Scheuermann, B. & Webber, J. (2002). *Autism: Teaching does make a difference.* Belmont, CA: Wadsworth/Thompson Learning.

Umbreit, J., Ferro, J., Liaupsin, C., & Lane, K. (2007). *Functional behavioral assessment and function-based intervention: an effective practical approach.* Upper Saddle River, NJ: Pearson Merrill Prentice Hall.

Chapter 3

Core Learning Skills

In this chapter, the importance of developing core learning skills during the initial stages of intervention programs for children with ASD is discussed. These core skills are targeted to replace deficiencies shared in common by many children on the spectrum. Core skills are building blocks, critical prerequisite tools, that allow these children to learn more quickly. These skills are considered essential to the success of any early intervention program because of the significant impact they have on later development.

The core skills to be discussed in this chapter include: attention, joint attention, social referencing, imitation, request-making, labeling, instruction-following, matching, and sequencing. Another core response that will be examined is not really a skill, but it has great impact on learning and development, specifically the child's attachment to parents and other important socialization agents (see Table 3.1). In the following sections we describe the importance of each of these core behaviors along with general intervention strategies that can be utilized in teaching them. At the end of this chapter, specific examples of core skills education programs are provided.

Table 3.1 Core learning skills

Attention
Joint attention and social referencing
Imitation
Receptive and expressive language
    Request-making (gesture or verbal)
    Labeling
    Instruction-following
Matching
Sequencing
Attachment/bonding

Attention

Attention is a prerequisite for the development of more complex cognitive processes. It is quite common for children with ASD to have attention difficulties.

A companion problem, hyperactivity, also occurs with great frequency in this population. Therefore, it should not be surprising that children with ASD are sometimes diagnosed as having attention deficit hyperactivity disorder (ADHD). Co-morbid disorders, such as autism and ADHD, are sometimes viewed as being separate entities with different underlying causal structures. In contrast to this viewpoint, Whitman and Ekas (2008) suggest that ADHD and its symptomatology emerge as a result of the sensory, language, social, and other cognitive deficiencies and problems associated with autism spectrum disorders.

Parents and teachers commonly report that children with ASD have particular difficulties attending in learning situations. It is interesting to note, however, that although these children can be easily distracted and their focus may often wander, paradoxically, their attention is sometimes captured by seemingly unimportant and irrelevant cues upon which they fixate for long periods of time. This problem, which is sometimes referred to as stimulus overselectivity because it involves a limited consideration of environmental cues, is also observed in children with learning and motivation problems.

In a typically developing child, attention is directed more to social than nonsocial stimuli, often toward another person's eyes (see review by Klin, Jones, Schultz, Volkmar, & Cohen, 2002). In contrast, Klin et al. (2002) reported reduced fixation time on a person's eyes to be a good predictor of autism. Moreover, greater fixation on objects than people has been associated with more extensive autistic symptomatology. Klin et al. (2002) raise interesting hypotheses about the relationships between mouth and eye-fixation times and the development of language and social competence. They suggest that both mouth and eye fixation are important for language acquisition because the mouth provides information about the formation and structure of sounds and words and the eyes provide nuanced information about the referents and meanings of words. Moreover, it seems likely that attention to facial cues is a critical prerequisite for joint attention.

Speculation regarding the precise nature of attention problems of children with ASD suggests a range of potential deficits rather than a single deficit, including an inability:

- to orient to a stimulus

- to sustain attention to a stimulus for long periods

- to shift attention from one stimulus to another, that is, to disengage attention from one object in order to engage another

- to broaden attention focus.

Research suggests, however, that many of the aforementioned attention characteristics may not be reflective of a basic underlying deficiency or defect. That is, children with autism can and do orient to a stimulus, can sustain attention to a stimulus for long periods of time, can disengage and shift attention from one stimulus to another, and are not always over-selective in their attentional focus (Whitman, 2004). Nevertheless, children with ASD seem to engage in paradoxical behaviors, sometimes appearing to ignore completely their environment and at other times continually changing the focus of their attention.

If the attentional problems of individuals with autism do not represent in and of themselves basic defects, a question is raised as to why they do occur. In this regard, there are many potential answers. They may attend to one stimulus to the exclusion of others because it is intrinsically reinforcing, that is because of its appealing sensory qualities. For example, some children with ASD appear to be drawn to objects that have a certain sound or visual quality. Alternatively, the unique attentional style of individuals with ASD may evolve as a way of regulating unpleasant emotions in social situations. From this perspective, inattention and selective attention represent general coping mechanisms through which children with autism learn to deal with social situations that are over-demanding. Attention characteristics, such as eye-gaze avoidance, a tendency to look at objects using peripheral perception, and an "unwillingness" to share attention with other people, are possible examples of these coping mechanisms at work (Whitman, 2004).

Another explanation for the attentional problems of children with ASD is that they focus on narrow aspects of the environment because they have difficulty perceptually integrating or deriving meaning from "complicated" stimulus patterns. Relatedly, some researchers suggest that children with autism have a problem using cues to direct their actions if the cues contain complex information that is social in nature and must be interpreted. This theory may explain why children have difficulty sharing attention with others and following the gaze of others. That is, children with autism may not share attention or follow the gaze of others because such acts require an understanding of complex social cues. This type of deficiency could also explain why children with autism have difficulties in educational situations which emphasize social communication as a critical part of the instructional process (Whitman, 2004).

Intervention perspectives and strategies

Because attention is a critical prerequisite for learning and socialization, it is important that intervention programs establish as a priority helping children with autism to focus their attention in an appropriate manner. Because attentional deficiencies in children with autism can have many possible causes, the root cause or causes for a particular child's attentional problem need, if possible, to be isolated. For example, it may be that the causes are related to emotional, sensory, cognitive, language, and/or social difficulties. Moreover, in developing a specific intervention program, the role that the physical environment plays in influencing attention must also be considered.

Before designing an intervention strategy for children with attentional problems, the following types of questions should be posed:

- Are there aspects of the physical environment that are serving to distract the child which can be eliminated?

- Does the child show a hypersensitivity to specific stimuli in particular settings?

- Does the child seem anxious?

- If the child is being asked to perform a task, is the task too difficult? Does he/she have the prerequisite skills to perform the task? Relatedly, is the child being provided sufficient supports, such as verbal, visual, and physical prompts or cognitive strategies to perform the task?

- In instructional (or other social) interactions, is the parent or teacher presenting information too rapidly or in an inconsistent fashion?

Depending on the answers to these types of questions, general procedures, such as outlined in Chapter 2, should be considered. For example:

- If specific stimuli in the physical environment distract the child's attention, these stimuli should be removed if possible. As the child's attention improves, these stimuli can be gradually reintroduced. More generally, structured interventions should initially take place in settings that are simple and contain only the requisite materials and furniture necessary for the program.

- If the child shows hypersensitivity to specific stimuli, which in turn make it difficult to attend, these stimuli should be removed. If they cannot be removed, sensory extinction or other programs described in Chapter 5 should be utilized to deal with the hypersensitivity problem.

- If the child's attentional difficulties are related to an anxiety problem, the emotion-focused procedures described in Chapter 4 should be considered. If, however, the child's emotional upset is temporary, attempts to engage the child's attention should be delayed until the child is able to calm him/herself.

- Because a child's attentional problems in educational situations can be related to the specific curriculum that is in place or the way the curriculum is delivered, the structure of this program should be examined to ensure that the task is developmentally appropriate and proper instructional supports are in place.

- Depending upon the child's language and cognitive skills, verbal instruction should be employed to help the child semantically organize tasks being taught in a training/educational program (see Chapter 10).

Whereas the aforementioned procedures address external and underlying causes for a child's attentional problems, others, such as those employed in behaviorally oriented programs, directly focus on the attentional response itself. Behavior interventions are particularly useful for increasing a child's attention to another person or specific instructional materials. Most behavioral training programs use a combination of prompting and reinforcement procedures. For example, a child might be verbally or physically prompted to attend to a specific stimulus, such as a picture in a book, then reinforced when he/she looks at that picture. In the early stages of an intervention, children are often directed to look at their parent/ teacher who reinforces the child for "good looking." Such attention to teacher is particularly critical when the teacher is demonstrating to a child how to perform a particular skill.

Numerous other objectives are often pursued as part of a behaviorally oriented attention training program. For example, once the momentary attention of a child is captured, he/she might be reinforced for gradually sustaining attention to a task, such as a motor task involving putting pegs in a board or an academic task involving arithmetic problems. A child might also be reinforced for selective attention to one stimulus or a specific set of stimuli. For example, in a socialization program a child might be reinforced for looking at the individual who is talking to him/her and not at other individuals in the group. It is also important for children to learn to shift their attention and scan their environment. For example, if a child is asked to point to the largest of a group of objects, such as an array of different-sized animals, the child needs to learn to look at each object before making a selection. In this case the child during training would first be reinforced for looking at each animal and then reinforced for selecting the largest animal. For specific program examples, the reader is referred to the end of the chapter.

Joint attention

What distinguishes children with ASD from typically developing children is not so much the fact that they don't interact with others or form relationships, but rather the ways in which they interact. For example, although they show some attachment behaviors, approach parents to make requests, make occasional eye contact, and even take part in games requiring taking turns, they are not inclined to share actively their interests and achievements with others and/or conversely to share in the interests and activities of others; that is, they do not share attention jointly with others. Early in development most children with autism are unlikely to point to objects in order to engage the attention of others, look where others are pointing, or shift their gaze back and forth from an object, such as a book, to an individual who is reading to them.

Joint attention is critical for: acquiring oral language, deciphering other people's communications and the nonverbal facial expressions that accompany such communications, learning vicariously through observation, developing empathy, and understanding the minds of others. Research indicates that joint attention is related to both later social and cognitive development as well as the development of early basic imitation, play, and language skills in children with autism (Bono, Daley, & Sigman, 2004; Whalen, Schreibman, & Ingersoll, 2006). More generally, some researchers feel that joint attention may be a key to understanding the development of autism. (See reviews by Carpenter & Tomasello, 2000, and Mundy & Stella, 2000.)

Mundy and Burnette (2005) propose that joint attention skills are already impaired in infants with autism, inhibiting proper attention deployment, social information-processing, and social learning. As a consequence they become isolated from a typical pattern of social exchange, resulting in social impairment as well as neurobehavioral disorganization and neurodevelopmental pathology. In a review of research, Mundy and Crowson (1997) point out that joint attention deficiencies reliably discriminate samples of young children with autism from children with other developmental delays and suggest that this deficiency, along with deficiencies in play and imitation, are among the best early predictors of autism. Moreover, these authors indicate that because joint attention is dynamically linked to later social and cognitive development, it is a pivotal skill that needs to be targeted at the onset of an early intervention program.

Intervention perspectives and strategies

Joint attention has been defined as involving "behaviors used to follow or direct the attention of another person to an event or object and to share an interest in that event or object" (Siller & Sigman, 2002, p. 77). Joint attention involves not only responding to bids for attention by others, but also soliciting the attention of others.

Joint attention is developed using behavior-focused procedures similar to those employed in attention training programs, that is a combination of prompting and reinforcement techniques. For example:

- A child might be taught to look where a teacher is pointing. In such programs, the teacher typically gives a verbal directive, e.g. "Look at the spaceship," and then points at the spaceship. If necessary, the child can be physically oriented toward the spaceship. When the child looks at the spaceship, the teacher reinforces the child, specifically by praising the child, e.g. "Good looking," and then allows the child to play with the spaceship.

- Alternatively, a child might be asked to show a teacher a toy which he/she is playing with and reinforce the child for sharing his/her interest.

When joint attention programs are implemented, objects toward which joint attention is to be directed should have high intrinsic appeal to the child (see program examples section at the end of this chapter).

Social referencing

Another characteristic closely related to joint attention is social referencing. As infants grow and become interested in their caretakers and other people, they tend to spend more time looking at them. This interest likely springs from the fact that adults provide infants with stimulation, objects of value (e.g. food), and emotional support. Along with this general social interest comes a specific tendency for infants to focus visually on adults in situations that are unusual, ambiguous or confusing, a phenomenon known as social referencing. Adults become sources of information for infants in such situations, as a consequence influencing the infants' behavior and feelings. During social referencing infants shift attention from a new or strange object (or person) to a parent in a back and forth manner, apparently for the purpose of gaining information about how to interpret the meaning of the strange object/person and whether it constitutes a threat (Whitman, 2004).

Deviating from this normative pattern, children with ASD spend less time looking at their caregivers, even in situations that are unusual or ambiguous. When they do look at their caretaker's face, they do not appear to use the information contained in facial cues to guide their behavior. For example, if children with ASD encounter a strange object, their reaction to the object does not seem to be greatly influenced by whether their caretakers are smiling or showing fear. Perhaps this social referencing deficit occurs because children with autism are overwhelmed by the sensory complexity of their physical and social environment and thus as a consequence obtain little information or assistance from others to resolve their confusion. When children with autism find their environment chaotic and fear-evoking, they are likely to control it through withdrawal, rigid routines and attentional fixations, rather than using their social environment as a source of support.

Intervention perspectives and strategies

Social referencing develops in children once they become aware that a parent, teacher or some other individual is a source of information that is important for their well-being; for example, whether a stranger is a friend, where a particular food object is located, or how to do something. Social referencing evolves directly from a child sharing attention with a parent or teacher and coming to value what that individual has to offer. Children are more likely to engage in social referencing if they are securely attached to their parent/teacher and trust them. They are also more likely to engage in social referencing once they learn to imitate the actions of others, particularly actions which provide them access to pleasurable outcomes.

Although formal intervention programs for developing social referencing in children with ASD do not exist, there are several general strategies that parents can utilize to attract their children's attention when they are distressed and/or needy. Most importantly, parents must learn to interpret their children's nonverbal communication signals and respond in a sensitive way to these signals. As parents become more aware of their children's needs and are able to satisfy those needs, the child is more likely to look, both literally and figuratively, to their parents when they require emotional, physical, and instrumental support. In addition, as children turn to their parents for assistance, parents should help their children communicate what they want either through gestures or words. As children learn that their parents can be very helpful in times of need, they will increasingly seek them out for assistance. As a consequence parents will become a source of aid, comfort, and information.

Imitation

Along with joint attention and play, imitation is an early reliable discriminator of autism (Mundy & Crowson, 1997). Imitation is a key process that shapes learning during infancy and childhood, influencing motor development, play, social interaction, communication skills, and knowledge acquisition, including socioemotional understanding. Imitation is a skill that is manifested early in the human life cycle. During normal development, infants are drawn to the faces of their caretaker and imitate with increasing frequency their facial expressions. These imitations are part of a larger social interactional dance that begins shortly after birth between infants and their parents.

The difficulties children with ASD have in imitating the actions of others is well documented. Imitation defects seem to be universal in this population. Although children with ASD can improve their imitative skills over time, their disability in this area differentiates them from both typically developing children and children with other handicaps, including children with a formal diagnosis of mental retardation. They often show deficiencies in both spontaneous and requested imitation. Although children with autism appear to manifest a general imitative deficit, their ability to imitate simple actions involving objects seems less impaired than their ability to imitate body movements, such as oral-facial movements. Relatedly, imitation of body movements having social significance and/or involving sequential action are more difficult for them (Rogers, Cook, & Meryl, 2005).

Increasingly, research is investigating how imitation is related to motor, social, cognitive, and language development. For example, an increase in reciprocal imitation skills in young children with autism has been associated with increases in social communicative behaviors, including language, pretend play, and joint attention (Ingersoll & Schreibman, 2006). Relatedly, imitation, along with joint attention and toy play, have been found to be early predictors of communication development (Toth, Munson, Meltzoff, & Dawson, 2006).

Several different processes have been suggested to produce the imitation deficit in children with ASD, including executive-functioning deficiencies, motivational problems, sensory integration and motor problems, social interaction deficiencies, low verbal ability, dysphasic and action representation problems, and deficits in self–other mapping (Rogers, Cook, & Meryl, 2005). Because social imitation requires attending to other people, it has also been suggested that imitative deficiencies may also occur because of an attentional and/or social interpretational deficiency (Leekam & Moore, 2001).

In summary, although imitation deficits are not unique to autism, given that they also occur in individuals with a range of other developmental delays, these deficits seem to be pronounced in persons with ASD. In a meta-analysis of action imitation research in children with ASD, Williams, Whiten, and Singh (2004) concluded that children with this disorder show a marked and highly significant delay in normal imitative development, but not an absolute deficit. These imitation deficiencies are thought to be so important that they have been given the status of a core or basic deficit. Intervention research has, however, clearly established that children with ASD can both learn imitative skills and generalize them to new environments (e.g. Ledford, Gast, Luscre, & Ayres, 2008). Once they become imitative, children with autism are able to acquire new skills, including language, motor behaviors, emotional expressions, and social protocols. Some researchers theorize that imitation also helps them to understand the minds of other people and social conventions as well as to self-regulate during social interactions (Smith & Bryson, 1994).

Intervention perspectives and strategies

Early intervention programs for children with autism typically focus on developing imitative behavior as a prelude to teaching specific motor, language, and social behaviors. It is assumed that once children with autism become imitators, they will be better able to learn informally through observing others in social situations like play.

The procedures for teaching a child to imitate are well developed and widely employed. Typically, the following types of program steps are employed:

- A child is invited verbally to imitate the actions of a teacher/parent who serves as a model (e.g. the teacher/parent might say "Do this," or "Do this, point to your nose," while simultaneously demonstrating the action desired).

- If the child performs the modeled action, it is reinforced (e.g. "Good job.").

- If the child does not imitate the demonstrated action after several trials, he/she is physically assisted in completing the action and then provided a reinforcer.

- Gradually, physical and specific verbal prompts are withdrawn, until the child can perform the modeled action without assistance.

- To strengthen and generalize imitative behaviors, different actions are modeled by the teacher/parent, initially in structured situations (e.g. at a table) and subsequently in everyday situations.

- The ultimate objective of imitation programs is to get the child to spontaneously imitate the actions of others without prompting.

- If inappropriate actions are imitated (e.g. aggressive behaviors), such responses should not be reinforced, and if necessary explicitly discouraged.

The reader is referred to the final section of this chapter for specific intervention examples.

Core receptive and expressive language responses

Language deficiencies are a core diagnostic characteristic of autism. Estimates suggest that around 50 percent of children with autism do not acquire speech as a primary mode of communication (Prizant, 1996). Based on parental report, it appears that some children with autism lose their language abilities after a period of normal development. It is common for children with autism who have difficulty with expressive language to echo words spoken to them. Echolalia is also found in neurotypical children who are just beginning to acquire language.

As a group, children with ASD vary considerably in their language development. Some children have minimal receptive and expressive speech while others develop elaborate language skills; however, even this latter group has difficulty engaging in dynamic discourse with others and comprehending the intricacies and nuances of social communications. The fact that children with autism have language deficiencies should not be surprising given their problems in preverbal communication (e.g. limited use of social gestures) and deficiencies in maintaining eye contact, joint attention, and imitation (Whitman, 2004).

Intervention perspectives and strategies

In the next sections, procedures for developing three core language behaviors are described. These behaviors are object-labeling, request-making and instruction-following. These behaviors serve as basic building blocks for later language and social development.

OBJECT-LABELING

A significant change in development occurs when toddlers begin to realize that objects have names and that words are connected to objects in their environment. Knowing the names of objects allows toddlers to make the transition from gestural to verbal communication. Through words they begin to communicate their thoughts to others. Through words they make requests of others for objects they desire and through words they are able to think more easily about objects in their world when those objects are not physically present. As language emerges and cognitive maturation occurs, the world acquires coherence and stability and objects acquire a quality of permanence.

During early childhood, neurotypical children acquire labels for objects as they hear adults repeatedly associate specific words with specific objects. This process is delayed, sometimes for a considerable time, in children with autism. However, through early intervention this delay can be considerably abbreviated. Techniques for teaching labels for objects to children with ASD are well established and easy to implement. The typical sequence of steps in an object-labeling program is as follows:

- The child is asked by a parent/teacher to identify a specific object (e.g. a ball), specifically by asking "What is this?"

- If the child responds correctly by saying "ball," he/she is immediately reinforced.

- If the child is not able to provide the name of the object, it is supplied, after a delay (e.g. "What is this?"—delay—"Ball.").

- To ensure that children have the word for an object (e.g. ball) in their verbal repertoire, verbal imitation training procedures may need to be employed before an object-labeling program commences.

- Imitation training proceeds until the child is able to provide the label (ball). If necessary, the verbal labels can be developed through shaping.

- As the child is learning the name of one object, the above steps are repeated with other objects.

During the early stages of teaching object-labeling, the process may proceed slowly. As the child begins to understand the nature of the request being made, training typically progresses in a more rapid fashion. Once children learn the names of various objects, they can then be taught to identify specific physical features (e.g. color, shape, size, number) of objects, positional descriptions (e.g. in front of, on top of, behind), action descriptions (e.g. the boy is running), and other attributional descriptions (see Chapter 7). It is often desirable for this type of training to occur initially in a more structured fashion (e.g. at a table) and then extended as training proceeds to ensure generalization to objects in the child's everyday living environment.

REQUEST-MAKING

During early infancy, neurotypical children begin to make their needs known, first through their gestures and later through their vocalizations. Their early proto-communication signals are quite diverse, ranging from putting their arms out to be held, pointing to what they want, crying, and other nonverbal utterances. Parents rapidly learn to interpret their infants' early communication signals and begin to carry on a rich dialogue with them. Eventually, as their children begin to acquire language, they quickly learn to use words to make requests.

Many infants with autism do not utilize proto-communication signals or have a quite restricted range of these responses for making their needs known. In such cases their parents may have great difficulty discriminating what their children want. Conversely, because toddlers with autism are slow to develop expressive and receptive language skills, they have difficulty communicating their needs. These deficiencies may result in the child becoming frustrated and developing behavior problems. Often request-making is taught before or in conjunction with labeling because children rapidly learn that language can be used to satisfy their needs, thereby increasing their desire to communicate.

For these reasons, behaviorally oriented programs place considerable emphasis during the early stages of intervention on teaching children with autism to use gestures/signs and words to make requests. As a child begins to acquire expressive speech, the typical steps in a request-making program are as follows:

- The parent/teacher perceives the child wants something (e.g. a cookie) and proceeds to ask the child "What do you want?"

- If the child says "cookie," he/she is reinforced by being given the cookie.

- If the child cannot say what he/she wants, the parent/teacher provides words for the child to use. For example, after asking the child "What do you want?" the word "cookie" is provided. The child is then asked to say "cookie."

- If the child says "cookie," or tries to provide some vocalization, then he/she is given a cookie.

- If the child has difficulty saying "cookie," the response is shaped, with increasingly better approximations of the word "cookie" reinforced until the child is actually able to say "cookie."

- Eventually, the child is taught to elaborate upon the response to "What do you want?" by saying "I want a cookie."

It is critical for children to learn that if they ask, that is make a request, they often get what they want; thus they are reinforced for asking. Conversely, if they do not ask, they should be reminded to use their words. Children who are not ready to verbalize or for some reason cannot, can be taught, using a program quite similar to that just described, to sign or use gestural language or some other alternative procedure, like the Picture Exchange Communication System (PECS), to express their needs (see Chapter 7).

Instruction-following

The initial stages of the development of the self-regulatory system begins with social control. The main technique that parents employ during infancy and early childhood involves bringing the child under verbal control, that is teaching the child to follow verbal directions. During the first year of life, neurotypical infants learn to follow simple instructions, such as "Come here," "Stand up," and "Roll me the ball." The ability to follow more complex instructions rapidly develops as their vocabulary and cognitive skills expand in scope. Once children learn to respond to instructions, verbal directives can be used to teach a wide variety of complex motor, social, language, and cognitive skills.

Instruction-following behaviors often develop slowly in children with autism. Fortunately, the techniques for teaching these children to follow instructions are well developed and have been employed as part of early intervention programs for over 40 years. During instructional training the following steps typically occur:

- The child is presented an instruction, such as "Sit down." If the child sits down, reinforcement is provided, such as praise ("Good sitting!").

- If the child does not comply with the instruction "Sit down," a prompting procedure is introduced; for example, a modeling prompt is employed. (Before this procedure is used, the child should have gone through the imitation training program described previously in this chapter.) The child is told to "do this, sit down" and the response is then demonstrated/modeled for the child. If the child then sits, reinforcement is provided.

- If the child still does not comply with the instruction "Sit down," a second prompting procedure is employed, alone or in conjunction with the modeling prompt. Specifically, the child is told to "Sit down," then shown how to sit, and finally if he/she does not comply, the child is gently physically guided into a sitting response, whereupon reinforcement is given.

- Once the child reliably sits with the prompting procedures in place, these prompts are gradually faded until the child's sitting response is cued only by the verbal instruction ("Sit down."). If both physical guidance and visual/modeling prompts are employed, physical guidance should be gradually faded and then subsequently modeling prompts.

- As the child is learning to respond to one instruction, other simple instructions should be introduced into the training program. Eventually, the child can be taught to comply with increasingly complex instructions, such as "Go to the toy box and bring me the ball."

In summary, during the early stages of training the child is reinforced for following instructions, even when visual and physical prompts are employed. Later once the child learns to sit through the use of prompts, prompts are faded and reinforcement is given only for unprompted behavior. This instructional training protocol can be used to teach complex behaviors, such as self-help skills (e.g. toothbrushing) and leisure skills (e.g. playing a game).

Visual matching

Another core skill, visual matching, is also taught using verbal directives. Visual matching can be employed to teach a wide range of discriminations and concepts, such as color, shape, size and number skills, body parts, letter and word identification. Matching behavior is somewhat similar to imitative behavior. However, whereas imitation involves replicating verbally/motorically the responses of another person, matching involves an examination of various stimuli and making a determination, through word or action, that two (or more) stimuli are the same. Although matching often involves the visual modality, auditory, tactile, olfactory (smell), and gustatory (taste) stimuli can be utilized in a matching program.

Intervention perspectives and strategies

In teaching a child to match stimuli, the training protocol is quite simple and involves the following steps:

- A child is given a set of visual stimuli (pictures or three-dimensional objects); for example, a child might be shown pictures of four animals, a cow, chicken, pig, and horse. With the pictures in front of the child, he/she is given another picture which is identical to one of the four animals (e.g. a chicken) and told to "Put like with like." If the child is able to do this, he/she is reinforced.

- If the child is not able to provide the correct matching response, he/she is visually cued by the instructor who points to the picture that is like the one the child has been given to match. At this point, the instructor can verbally elaborate on why the pictures are similar, although such elaboration is more appropriate once basic matching skills are developed. Physical guidance can also be employed. Initially, the child is reinforced for matching responses even though prompts are provided.

- If prompts are employed, they should be gradually faded until the child can match without assistance.

The tasks involved in a visual matching program can be made progressively more complex by increasing the number of stimuli placed in front of the child (e.g. six animals instead of four) and by providing pictures that are rich in detail and/or are only slightly different from each other. Matching programs not only help develop discrimination skills but also can help develop attentional responses, such as scanning and shifting attention from one object to another and/or from one part of a stimulus to other parts. Matching programs can also be employed to develop labeling skills (e.g. "Put chicken with chicken."). Once visual matching skills are mastered, similar programs can be introduced for teaching children to match auditory, tactual, olfactory (smell), and gustatory (taste) stimuli. Such matching programs, involving different modalities, help the child to generalize the concepts of same and different.

Sequencing

Sequencing is a critical core skill because children need to learn that daily activities and complex behaviors often follow a temporal or a logical sequence. For example, children need to learn that waking up follows sleeping, and that grooming, dressing, eating, and going to school occur in predictable sequences, and that a complex response, such as toothbrushing, is composed of a set of component behaviors that occur in a particular order. In the process of learning to sequence, children learn important concepts, such as first, next, and last. Although sequencing is a valuable skill for all children to learn, it is a particularly valuable skill for children with ASD given their preference for routines; specifically because it helps them understand that the events in their world are often predictable and orderly. Like matching, sequencing is taught through the use of prompts and reinforcement procedures.

Intervention perspectives and strategies

Although there are a variety of ways to teach sequencing skills, the use of pictures is initially recommended because of the visual approach to thinking employed by children with autism. When visual stimuli are used, the typical steps in a sequencing program are as follows:

- A series of pictures of an activity are presented to the child in random order, for example of a mother going grocery shopping. The pictures displayed might consist of a mother making a grocery list, getting into the car, driving to the grocery store, shopping, and paying the check-out person.

- The child is asked to put the cards in the order the mother performs the steps when going to the grocery. Initially, the child may need to be prompted, e.g. "What does the mother do first?", next, etc.

- If the child does not perform a step or steps correctly, feedback is given through visual and verbal prompts. For example, pointing to the card of the mother preparing a grocery list, the child is told that first the mother makes out the grocery list. Similar prompts are given as necessary for each of the steps.

- Prompts are removed once the child is able to put the pictures in sequence. Reinforcement is initially given for prompted responses. However, once the child begins to learn, reinforcement is given only for unprompted correct responses.

If a child has reasonably well-developed language skills, the child should not only place the cards to be sequenced in order, but also be asked to describe verbally what the mother is doing. The aforementioned training protocol can be employed in teaching children response sequences that occur in self-help activities (e.g. toothbrushing), leisure time activities (e.g. board games), academic tasks (e.g. arithmetic problems), and community activities (e.g. grocery shopping). When teaching sequencing skills, the visual stimuli to be sequenced should, if appropriate, be associated with specific stimuli from other modalities, for example each picture might be associated with a specific verbal label or a unique sound. Conway, Pisoni, and Kronenberger (2009) argue that sound provides a supporting framework or scaffold that humans use in interpreting and processing sequential information.

Attachment

Attachment in neurotypical children

From an evolutionary perspective, attachment behaviors serve to keep children close to their parents, thus ensuring their physical safety and the preservation of the human species. Attachment relationships are also considered necessary because they provide emotional security to children, which in turn allows them to actively explore their environment. Finally, attachment relationships are important because they influence the perceptions children have of people, including their parents. As a consequence of a child's early attachment experiences, a "working model" is formed concerning what people are like and how they are likely to treat you, particularly in close relationships.

The formation of attachment in neurotypical children to their parents begins very early; in the case of the attachment of the child to his/her mother, it likely begins prenatally. Already at birth, or shortly thereafter, infants are able to discriminate their mother's voice and smell from other women. Although the attachment relationship between mother and child, as well as between father and child, seems to occur automatically, it is in fact greatly influenced by the child's experiences with their parents. To the extent that those experiences are pleasurable and satisfying, a secure attachment is likely to evolve. Parents who are able to read their infants' signals and respond effectively to their needs are more likely to have securely attached children. For example, during early development, parents, who are able to detect when their infant is hungry, in need of a diaper change, soothing or social interaction, and in turn are able to respond in a way to satisfy these needs, are likely to have children who are emotionally drawn to them.

Sometimes, however, the child's attachment to the parent does not develop smoothly and the child may either not seek out their parents, respond in an ambivalent fashion to them, or actively avoid them. When an attachment relationship does not develop or is insecure in nature, the reasons are complex and are related to parenting characteristics, such as parental stress, inexperience, insensitivity, neglect, inconsistent or harsh disciplinary practices, and/or the characteristics of the child, such as a child with a serious illness or a difficult temperament. The nature of the attachment relationship between infant and parent may change over time, for the better or worse, as parents and their children change and mature. For further general information on child attachment the reader is referred to child development texts by Berk (2009) and Lightfoot, Cole, and Cole (2009).

Attachment in children with autism

Clinical reports of children with ASD treating their parents as objects, for example like pieces of furniture, has led to the suggestion that they have an attachment deficit. Theoretically, a variety of child factors have been hypothesized to inhibit the development of attachment behaviors in children with ASD, including anxiety, problems in interpreting nonverbal expressions of emotion, an inability to make inferences about other people's mental states, and neurotransmitter and hormonal disturbances (see reviews by Huebner & Kraemer, 2001; Gillberg & Coleman, 1992). Although children with autism have been characterized as being unable to develop close emotional bonds with other people, research suggests otherwise, specifically that they can and often do become attached to their parents/caretakers.

Studies that employ the "strange situation" paradigm for assessing attachment indicate that children with ASD miss their parents when they are left alone in a room, that they are relieved when they are reunited with their parents, and that they prefer the company of their parents to a stranger; all signs that a specific attachment has been formed. Other research suggests, however, that although children with ASD often do form attachments, such attachments are not always of a secure type and are sometimes difficult to categorize. It should be noted that these studies have typically been conducted later with children with ASD than with neurotypical children, due to the fact that the diagnosis of autism is not usually made before a child reaches two or three years of age. For this reason, such studies are not able to provide information on how such attachments initially develop or whether attachment formation is typically delayed (Whitman, 2004).

A number of critical questions concerning the attachment relationships of children with ASD are in need of answers. For example, are attachment relationships more impaired in certain subgroups of children with ASD? What is the relationship between child IQ and attachment style? How do the attachment styles of children with ASD differ from those of children without a developmental disability and children with other types of developmental disabilities? It seems likely that a number of the characteristics commonly associated with autism, including hypersensitivity, inattention, hyperactivity, language difficulties, self-regulation deficiencies, social and cognitive problems, and behavioral problems (e.g. irregular sleep habits) could exert considerable influence on the formation, nature, and complexity of the attachment relationship. Moreover, it is quite possible that the attachment relationship itself influences the general development of children with autism.

Research is beginning to provide preliminary answers to some of these and other questions. For example, in adults with high functioning ASD, research suggests that there is little relationship between attachment security and autistic symptomatology as well as IQ (Taylor, Target, & Charman, 2008). However, there is evidence that attachment in toddlers with autism is a better predictor of level of play behavior than the child's disorder (Naber et al., 2008).

In addition to the characteristics of children with ASD, it is quite possible that the social context surrounding these children influences attachment formation, including factors such as parental grief, depression, stress, and difficulty in interpreting their children's signals. In this regard, it is interesting to note that mothers of securely attached children with ASD are more sensitive to their children's cues, more inclined to understand the motives underlying their children's behavior as well as more resolved to their child having a diagnosis of autism (Koren-Karie, Oppenheim, Dolev, & Yirmiya, 2009; Oppenheim, Koren-Karie, Dolev, & Yirmiya, 2009). For further information regarding attachment and autism, the reader is referred to a review by Rutgers, Bakermans-Kranenburg, van IJzendoorn, and van Berckelaer-Onnes, 2004.

Even if children with ASD form secure emotional attachments with their caretakers, as some research suggests, it does not follow that these children form articulated conceptualizations about who their parents are or about human relationships in general. The development of such a conceptual model assumes an ability on the part of the child to understand his/her own mind and those of other people, empathize with others, and to generalize attributions formed in one interpersonal situation to other people; these are cognitive abilities that are often deficient in children as well as adults with autism (see review by Sigman & Capps, 1997).

Intervention perspectives and strategies

Although early conventional wisdom suggested that children with ASD could not develop attachment relationships with their parents, clinical experience and research indicates otherwise. Children with ASD often do develop positive attachment relationships with their parents, particularly with their major caretaker who is typically the mother. They often enjoy parental affection, seek out their parents when they are needy, and are comforted by their parents when they are in distress. Moreover, they usually prefer interacting with their parents than people with whom they have little contact.

Nevertheless, it also appears that a number of child and parental factors can interfere with the development of a positive and secure attachment of children with autism to their parents and other individuals. Many of the same characteristics that lead children to be diagnosed as autistic can also create social relationship problems. Children with ASD are more needy. They often have sensory problems, motor problems, and a multitude of physical problems. They display fear and anxiety, particularly when they confront new situations. They may be severely restricted in their eating habits and have sleep problems. Because of their cognitive, language, and social deficiencies, they have difficulty communicating their needs and responding to the needs of others and as a consequence are more likely to develop behavior problems.

Because of these delays and problems, children with ASD can be a source of considerable stress for their parents. Parents may also, before and especially after the diagnosis of their child, be in a stage of denial and grief, making it difficult for them to respond to their children. Moreover, because of their children's developmental deficiencies, parents may have difficulty reading their children's signals and responding to their needs. Without assistance, these social relationship problems can get worse and may interfere with a child's ability to develop a secure attachment with their parents.

From a clinical and educational perspective, it is important to recognize the importance of the social relationship between children with ASD and their parents. A parent's effectiveness in helping their children cope with their developmental deficiencies is powerfully influenced by the quality of this relationship. In order to ensure that this relationship is a positive and secure one, it is critical for early intervention programs to address the needs and challenges confronting these parents, including their grief, their anxiety, their sources of stress, and their needs for appropriate social and professional supports. These programs must help parents, as well as educators, to understand the behavioral dynamics of children with autism, to interpret the meanings of their children's communications, to respond effectively to their children's needs, and to recognize their children's vast potential for growth. This book is directed at providing parents and professionals with a comprehensive understanding of autism, helping them appreciate how the characteristics of this disorder influence social relationships and development, and assisting them in developing a trusting relationship with their children.

To help children with ASD develop a secure attachment with their parents, the following points should be kept in mind in designing specific intervention programs:

- Parents must become adept at understanding their children's needs and helping their children communicate these needs.

- Parents need to be consistent and positively reinforcing in their interactions with their children.

- Although parents need to set limits for their children, they should avoid the use of aversive punishment procedures (see Chapter 2).

- When their children become upset, parents need to help them emotionally self-regulate and be a source of comfort for them.

In the next section, specific intervention examples for developing core skills and behaviors are presented.

Program examples

Attention

OBJECTIVE

Teach the child to attend to a set of materials on a work surface upon the presentation of such materials and/or when told to, "Look."

MATERIALS

For this procedure, you will need a variety of work materials, or materials you may use for work purposes in the future.

PROCEDURE

There are many different methods available for teaching this skill. One method involves teaching the child a specific response enabling the child to orient to the materials.

1. For pictures:

    a) Place one or two pictures upside down on a work surface and instruct the child to turn the pictures over, thus increasing the likelihood that he/she will attend to the pictures as they are revealed.

    b) As the child turns the picture over, give the instruction, "Look."

    c) If the child attends to the pictures while turning them over, deliver specific praise for "looking," following the turn of each picture.

    d) Deliver a more valuable reinforcer immediately after the child has turned over all of the pictures, as long as the child is attending to the pictures as he/she turns them over.

2. For objects:

    a) Place one object (e.g. a toy car) on a work surface, covered with a folder or piece of paper.

    b) Instruct the child to move the cover, thus revealing the object.

    c) Upon moving the folder/paper, give the instruction, "Look," and deliver a reinforcer if the child attends to the object.

    d) With either of the above procedures, it is necessary to repeat the procedure several (i.e. 10 to 20) times per session.

e) Alternate pictures and objects used, placing them in different areas of the work surface (e.g. in the middle of the table, to the left, to the right, far from the child, close to the child, etc.) after each trial.

f) As the child succeeds, gradually add more pictures/objects to the work surface, one at a time, requiring the child to attend to all objects before delivering the reinforcer.

ERROR CORRECTION

If the child does not look at the stimulus while completing the response, use prompting to help the child look. For example, point to the pictures or objects, bring the item closer to the child's face and gradually move it toward the table as the child attends, or place a small reinforcer near the object. Deliver a smaller reward to the child when he/she attends to the item following such prompting methods than when he/she attends independently of such prompts.

TIPS/SUGGESTIONS

These procedures outline steps to help children attend to stimuli on a table or work surface. However, sometimes children must attend to items in other locations (e.g. flashcards being held up by a teacher). Consider starting with this procedure and then moving the stimuli slowly away from the table, to the desired end position.

Try not to use excessive verbal prompts (e.g. repeating the child's name or the instruction to "Look") or explanations (e.g. "I want you to find the car; don't look at me, look at the car."), as they are additional prompts that don't necessarily assist with skill acquisition and require additional, time-intensive fading. Along the same lines, while implementing the above procedure it is not necessary to always give the instruction to "Look," because it will be essential for the child to learn to attend without always being instructed to do so. Therefore, it will be helpful to sometimes implement the procedure without giving any instructions to the child, only using physical guidance as necessary.

TROUBLESHOOTING

If your child is having difficulty with this skill, try starting with materials that are intrinsically reinforcing (i.e. the child already likes to look at the items, such as toys the child plays with independently). You may be able to obtain stimulus control quicker using such items and then begin to slowly introduce novel items that may be less appealing to the child.

OTHER TEACHING METHODS

Another method involves placing an object/picture on a work surface and instructing the child to "Look" at the stimulus while simultaneously providing a prompt. There are several different prompts that can be used, but physical prompts (e.g. turning a child's head toward you) may be difficult and unsuccessful with attending procedures. Instead, try using a visual prompt. For example, place a small reinforcer (e.g. piece of a chip) next to or on top of the target stimulus (i.e. work materials). Upon attending to the stimulus (and reinforcer) immediately provide the child with access to the reinforcer. Gradually fade the sight of the reinforcer (e.g. use increasingly smaller pieces of the chip), but provide better reinforcement as the child continues to attend to the stimulus despite the diminishing presence of the reinforcer (e.g. provide a quarter-sized chip to the child when he attends to a toy car that has a dime-sized chip on top of it; provide an even larger chip when the child attends to a car that has an even smaller chip on top of it).

If the child has difficulty with this approach, start with the object and reinforcer placed within 2 inches (5 cm) from the child's eyes and gradually lower the materials to the work surface as the child succeeds with attending.

FUTURE OBJECTIVES

Once the child is attending well to the items, add additional teaching targets. For example, once you obtain the child's attention to the materials, ask him/her to give you one of the materials. This may require additional prompts (see the discrimination program examples in Chapter 5).

Joint attention: attending to pointing

OBJECTIVE

Teach the child to follow the pointing of an adult.

MATERIALS

Have a variety of highly preferred reinforcers available.

PROCEDURE

1. Say to the child, "Look at the _____," and point to the reinforcing object.

2. If necessary, use physical guidance to help guide the child's gaze toward the object.

3. Once the child is looking at the object, provide specific praise and access to the object used or to another tangible/edible reinforcer.

4. Repeat, occasionally switching objects and moving the object in different locations so the child must follow your finger, rather than looking in the same general location each time.

GENERALIZATION

Begin with objects that are close in proximity to the child, but as the child learns this skill, begin placing the objects farther away from the child. Once the child has shown improvement in this skill, point at items in their natural surroundings such as airplanes in the sky, trains, animals at the zoo, or the moon and stars.

TIPS/SUGGESTIONS

Try using objects that move or do something spectacular once the child is looking. For example, use a toy popper and wait to set it off until the child looks toward it when you point. Blow bubbles once the child looks at the bubble wand, where you are pointing. Set up a volcano experiment with vinegar and baking soda; wait to add the baking soda until the child looks to where you are pointing, then the volcano can begin. Some of these techniques may require the assistance of another person.

FUTURE OBJECTIVES

Attempt to teach the child to follow your gaze. For this skill, the child must first learn to look at your eyes. Therefore you may need to implement an attending program that teaches the child to attend to your eyes when you say, "Look," or when you say the child's name. Once the child makes consistent eye contact, use the procedure outlined above to teach the child to look at the object that you are looking at by following your gaze.

Imitation

OBJECTIVE

Teach the child to independently imitate the gross motor movement of an adult when the adult is modeling an action.

PROCEDURE

For quicker acquisition of a generalized imitative repertoire (i.e. a set of skills that enable the child to imitate any motor behavior of a model), it is necessary to introduce some generalization techniques right from the very beginning. This will help to prevent memorization and scrolling and requires the child to attend to the model more closely, thus simultaneously increasing the child's attention to the behavior of others. The following procedure outlines one way of teaching generalized gross motor imitation.

1. Obtain the child's attention and be sure the child is attending to the model.

2. Model the target behavior (e.g. clapping).

3. Within 1 to 3 seconds, physically prompt the child as much as necessary to copy the modeled action.

4. Immediately provide specific praise and a tangible/edible reinforcer.

5. Repeat with a different action, rotating between three to four different actions.

6. Fade prompts for each target behavior individually across trials by decreasing the amount of physical assistance provided during each trial, as long as the child continues to successfully imitate the modeled behavior. Increase the amount of the reinforcer or amount of time with the reinforcer as the child begins to imitate with less intrusive prompts.

7. Introduce new actions once the child is imitating some actions independently.

ERROR CORRECTION

Be careful not to reinforce scrolling. For example, if you model clapping and the child touches his nose but then claps afterwards, do not provide a reinforcer; this is considered an error. To offer a reinforcer at this point would be to reinforce the sequence or chain of touching his nose and then clapping, rather than reinforcing imitation of your modeled response. Instead, place the child's hands down and repeat the trial but be quick to offer assistance before the child makes another error this time. If successful, reinforce the imitation.

GENERALIZATION

To increase the likelihood of response generalization, model the target action differently during each trial. For example, clapping your hands can be done in many ways; clap in front of your body, above your head, to the side of your body, loudly, softly, repeatedly, and so on. Requiring the child to attend to the specific form of your behavior and then imitating the exact action modeled will better ensure generalized imitation. Keep in mind that some of the different forms of behavior may require increased prompt levels (i.e. more assistance).

In addition, when modeling the target behavior, say different versions of the instruction "Do this" (e.g. "Copy me," "Do what I do," etc.). Sometimes model the behavior without saying anything, to allow for opportunities to reinforce a closer form of spontaneous imitation.

Tips/suggestions

Start with a list of target behaviors that the child will learn to imitate (see example list below). It is usually easier to begin with gross motor behaviors because some children have more difficulty with fine motor tasks, and gross motor behaviors tend to be easier to prompt than fine motor. Focus on teaching three to five targets at one time, before moving on to other targets from the list.

In addition, when modeling, do not state the action you are modeling (e.g. do not say "Clap your hands" while clapping) because the goal is to teach imitation, not instruction-following.

Troubleshooting

For more difficult learners, or for children who have not quite mastered the skill of attending, it is easier to have two adults to assist with teaching imitation: one adult to model the action, and one adult to prompt the child while standing behind him/her. This way the modeler can continue to model the action while the prompter assists the child with copying the action accurately. If two adults are not available, be sure to begin teaching in a structured environment with as few distractions as possible.

Other teaching methods

Some children may benefit from video modeling, especially if they enjoy watching television. With this procedure the child may still require assistance with attending to the video, as well as physical assistance to imitate the model.

Example targets

- clapping (clap above your head, to the side)
- tapping (different body parts, different surfaces)
- walking (forward, backward, sideways, quickly)
- sitting (on the bed, on the floor, in a chair)
- waving (high, low, fast, slow)
- holding arms out (above head, in front, one arm, two arms)

- dancing

- spinning

- jumping.

FUTURE OBJECTIVES

Once the child is imitating several novel responses, begin teaching fine motor imitation, and imitation with objects. Imitation with objects is a skill that can be very useful for teaching play skills as well as other behaviors. In addition, begin teaching the child to observe peer models and to imitate their behavior, rather than only the behavior of adults.

Making requests

OBJECTIVE

Teach the child to request desired or needed objects or activities.

MATERIALS

For this procedure, you will need to have at least one (but preferably several) objects/activities available to the child. These objects and activities should be things that the child already has a strong interest in but does not yet request independently.

PROCEDURE

1. Determine what the child currently wants. You can do this by offering items to the child, letting him/her sample the various items, observing the child reaching for an item, or giving the child something he/she wants but leaving out a necessary component (e.g. giving the child ice cream but no spoon).

2. With the desired item in the child's view, ask him/her, "What do you want?"

3. Use most-to-least echoic or imitative prompting to help the child accurately state or sign the name of the item (e.g. immediately say or sign, "Cookie.").

4. Once the child says or signs the name of the item (or an approximation) immediately provide access to the item.

5. Repeat, fading your prompts across trials.

6. Continue until the child has shown disinterest in the item/activity. At this point determine a different item/activity the child may be interested in and continue this procedure using that item. If possible (i.e. if the child wants more than one item at the same time) alternate between trials of various items.

ERROR CORRECTION

If the child says or signs the wrong word, simply repeat your question ("What do you want?") and deliver a model prompt (i.e. say or sign the correct word) until the child responds correctly. If using sign language, you can physically guide the child to sign correctly if a model prompt is ineffective. Once the child responds correctly, give a small amount of the item or activity.

GENERALIZATION

This procedure may need to be initially implemented in a controlled setting, however this is a skill that can be practiced throughout the child's natural environment everyday. For example, if the child wants to go outside, hide a shoe and prompt her to request the missing shoe. Once outside, stop the child before she gets to the slide or swings and have her request that activity. The key is to anticipate or observe the child's wants and needs, and to then teach an appropriate form of communication for receiving desired items or activities.

In addition, teach your child to request without prompts, including the prompt, "What do you want?" To do this, occasionally hold the item in the child's view but do not ask, "What do you want?" You can still prompt the child to request by modeling the correct response (e.g. "Cookie.") but this way the child will learn that he/she can make requests whenever the desire or need is present, and not only when asked the question, "What do you want?"

TIPS/SUGGESTIONS

It is important to note that the reinforcer for a request is the object or activity that the child has requested. You do not need to provide an additional reinforcer or even praise the child for making these requests.

In addition, to maximize learning or practice opportunities, thus increasing the rate of skill acquisition, provide small amounts of the reinforcer to the child. For example, if the child requests candy, give him one or two Skittles, but not a whole handful. Then require the child to continue asking for additional Skittles. Along the same lines, do not provide or allow access to the reinforcer without requiring a request. The child will be less likely to ask for candy if he can reach the candy himself when you walk away, or if another adult/sibling will give it to him without requiring a request.

Take advantage of the time of day and the child's current condition. For example, immediately before lunch is a great time to practice requesting food. In addition, if the child has had a lot of salty food, he may not want any more salty food, and thus may stop requesting. However, after a couple of bites of salty foods or a hot day of running around outside, a child will be highly motivated to request a drink.

In the beginning phases of teaching requesting, do not require that your child says, "I want…," or "please," or "thank you." These phrases are not meaningful to the child just yet, and the added effort it takes to say such carrier phrases may decrease the child's motivation to make a request at all, or may result in the child using other means to access the item (e.g. challenging behavior). The number of words per sentence can be expanded upon later, once the child has a stronger history of using language to communicate.

TROUBLESHOOTING

Make sure that the child currently wants the item or activity you are using at the time that you are practicing. Motivation for the item is the most important component of this procedure. Typical signs that the child is no longer motivated include: not accepting the item, walking away, pushing you or the item away, reaching for something else, and many more similar signs. If the child does not want the item/activity you are using, find out what he/she does want and practice with that.

Initially when training a child to make requests, he/she may become very upset when not given a desired item right away (i.e. until he/she requests the item appropriately). The child may be accustomed to simply reaching for the item, crying, tantrums, or any number of inappropriate methods of obtaining wanted or needed items, and therefore may not be expecting this new, perhaps more difficult, requirement of requesting. It is important to help the child by using effective prompting methods so that he/she can quickly make the desired response and thus access the reinforcer more efficiently than with such former methods.

OTHER TEACHING METHODS

Picture exchange communication and other augmentative communication methods are very useful for children who do not speak and for whom sign language is not an option. We recommend seeking specific education in the device you are using with your child.

FUTURE OBJECTIVES

The child must now learn to request items that are not present. This can be done by slowly fading the presence of the item while using the above procedure. For example, put the candy in your fist, or behind your back, or in the cupboard, before asking the child what he/she wants. Or hide an object that the child needs (e.g. crayons for coloring, Mr. Potato Head's shoes, a key to open the door to the game cupboard, etc.). Be creative with the number and type of requests you teach your child. Simply going outside to play can involve several different requests, including shoes, jacket, opening the door, access to particular play equipment, pushing on the swing, singing certain songs, and so on.

Once the child has become fluent in several different requests, and is making several requests per day you may start to require the child to add more words to his/her sentences (e.g. "I want to play," "Let's go outside," "More candy please.").

Labeling objects

OBJECTIVE

Teach the child to independently label an object that he/she sees, either spontaneously or when asked, "What is this?"

MATERIALS

For this procedure, you will need various objects that the child currently does not label. Start with a list of target objects (see example list below). It may be best to target objects with which the child is likely to have a lot of contact (e.g. a spoon vs. a candle). Focus on teaching three to five targets at one time, before moving on to other targets from the list.

PROCEDURE

1. Hold up or place a target object on the table. Be sure the child is attending to the object.

2. Provide a generalized instruction (e.g. "What is this?" "What do you see?" "Tell me what this is," etc.). Sometimes show the object without saying anything, to allow for opportunities to reinforce a closer form of spontaneous labeling.

3. If the child responds correctly, provide specific praise (e.g. "You're right, it is a spoon!") as well as a tangible/edible reinforcer.

4. If the child does not respond within 1 to 3 seconds, provide a verbal prompt (e.g. "Say spoon.") and repeat the prompt every 3 to 5 seconds until the child responds with the correct label or an approximation. Reinforce prompted responses, but without as much enthusiasm and with less preferred items.

5. Repeat with a different object.

6. Fade prompts for each target object individually across trials.

7. Continue until five to ten trials of each target have been presented.

Error correction

If the child makes an error (e.g. says, "Fork," when the object is a spoon), remove the item for 1 to 3 seconds. Re-present the same item and instruction, but prompt immediately with the correct response (i.e. before the child makes the same error). Reinforce the correct response.

Generalization

Be sure to have three to five different examples of each object (e.g. if the target object is a plate, use a plastic plate, paper plate, large and small plates, different colored plates, etc.). This will ensure that the child learns that many different objects can share the same name if they share certain characteristics.

To increase the likelihood of stimulus generalization, mix the targets across trials and use a different example of the target object each trial. For example, for trial 1 (target: plate) use a small paper plate; for trial 2 (target: fork) use a plastic fork; for trial 3 (target: cup) use a Styrofoam cup; and for trial 4 (target: plate) use a large plastic plate, and so on. Requiring the child to respond similarly to multiple exemplars will better ensure generalized labeling.

Tips/suggestions

Keep in mind that some of the different examples of objects may require increased prompt levels (e.g. a wooden spoon looks a lot different from a silver spoon and therefore the child may need additional help labeling the former as a "spoon" even if he/she is already labeling a silver spoon independently).

Troubleshooting

Sometimes it is helpful to use objects that the child enjoys, but does not currently desire. For example, if the child typically likes to eat cookies, but currently does not want one, he/she can learn to label the cookie. Just be sure to give a different reinforcer (i.e. do not give the cookie) for labeling.

If the child does not already request desired objects, consider teaching requesting prior to this procedure. Once the child consistently requests objects, return to this procedure.

EXAMPLE TARGETS

Desirable items:

- ball
- toy animals (e.g. pig, cow, dog, etc.)
- block
- car
- train
- book.

Everyday items:

- cup
- bowl
- spoon
- fork
- plate
- sock.

FUTURE OBJECTIVES

Use the same procedure to teach the child to label the features of objects (e.g. the tiger has a tail, stripes, ears, etc.). Also teach dimensions of objects (e.g. color, shape, size, etc.) so that the child can learn to describe objects.

Following instructions

OBJECTIVE

Teach the child to independently follow basic verbal instructions.

MATERIALS

Have a list of basic, one-step instructions (see example targets on p. 97). The instructions should be easy for the child because the goal of this procedure is to teach the child to complete an action upon hearing an instruction, not to teach the child novel actions.

PROCEDURE

1. Obtain the child's attention and deliver an instruction (e.g. "Clap your hands.").

2. Within 1 to 3 seconds, physically prompt the child as much as necessary to perform the action as instructed.

3. Immediately provide specific praise and a tangible/edible reinforcer.

4. Repeat with a different action.

5. Fade prompts for each target behavior individually across trials. Be careful to also fade model prompts (i.e. clapping your hands while you're instructing the child to clap).

ERROR CORRECTION

If the child performs the wrong action (e.g. touches his head instead of clapping), stop the child (e.g. put his/her hands down), wait 3 seconds, then repeat the same instruction but use a prompt to help the child respond correctly. Deliver a smaller reinforcer for correct responding that follows an error correction.

GENERALIZATION

Give the instructions in a natural, relaxed tone of voice, as opposed to a sing-song or authoritative tone. Do not be too concerned about the exact wording. In fact, it will be more beneficial if the child learns to follow instructions that are presented in several different ways (e.g. "Sit down," "Have a seat," "Sit in your chair," etc.). Once the child has learned several instructions, teach him/her to play games such as Simon Says to generalize learned instructions.

TIPS/SUGGESTIONS

Rotate between three to five different instructions each time you implement this procedure. Repeatedly presenting one instruction before moving on to others may make it difficult for the child to learn new responses. For example, if you repeatedly ask the child to clap his hands until he learns to clap, when you move on to "Touch head" the child may continue to clap his hands, even when presented with the new instruction.

TROUBLESHOOTING

If the child is consistently responding incorrectly, make sure you are not reinforcing a chain of errors. For example, if the instruction is to clap hands, and the child touches his head and then claps his hands, do not deliver a reinforcer, but instead follow the error correction procedure. Also, be sure to use highly effective reinforcers, and to obtain the child's attention before delivering the instruction.

EXAMPLE TARGETS

- clap
- touch (different body parts, different surfaces, etc.)
- walk
- sit
- run
- wave (high, low, fast, slow, etc.)
- arms up
- spin
- jump
- stomp
- raise hand.

FUTURE OBJECTIVES

Once the child can follow basic one-step instructions, you can move on to teaching novel one-step actions, and then basic and novel two-step actions. For two-step actions, mix up combinations of various one-step actions so that the child learns to really listen to your instruction, rather than memorize a pattern of responses. For example, say, "Clap your hands then touch your head," one time, but on the next trial, say "Touch your head then clap your hands," or "Touch your head then stomp your feet." Move on to more functional instructions (e.g. teaching the child how to wash his/her hands) or fun sequences of play behavior (e.g. complete an obstacle course) once the child is able to listen to and follow novel combinations of instructions.

Matching identical objects
OBJECTIVE
Teach the child to independently match an object to an identical object when it is in an array of at least three other objects.

MATERIALS

For this procedure, you will need to have several identical 3D objects. These objects should match in all dimensions (e.g. shape, size, color, etc.). You can also start with matching identical pictures, however keep in mind that children may need to be taught both 2D matching as well as 3D matching (i.e. teaching one skill may not automatically result in the acquisition of the other). Focus on teaching three to five targets at one time, before moving on to other targets from the list.

PROCEDURE

1. Hold up or place a minimum of three different objects on the table.

2. Have the child attend to and scan the objects.

3. Hand the child an object that matches one of the objects on the table.

4. Provide a generalized instruction (e.g. "Match," "Put same with same," etc.) and prompt as necessary.

5. If the child responds correctly, provide specific praise (e.g. "You're right, that's a match!") as well as a tangible/edible reinforcer.

6. Rearrange the materials on the table and occasionally present new materials.

7. Repeat the instruction with a different object.

8. Fade prompts for each target object individually across trials.

9. Continue until five to ten trials of each target object have been presented.

ERROR CORRECTION

Try to avoid errors by increasing your prompt level immediately upon seeing the child making the wrong move (e.g. if you see the child moving toward the wrong item, quickly provide a physical prompt to guide his/her arm to the correct match).

If the child makes an error (e.g. places the cup with the plate instead of the matching cup), remove the items for 1 to 3 seconds. Re-present the same items in the same order, and repeat the same instruction. Prompt immediately to help the child match correctly (i.e. before the child makes the same error). Deliver praise but do not deliver a tangible reinforcer following error correction.

GENERALIZATION

Add more stimuli to the array so that the child must scan to find the match. Use materials that are very similar to each other, but differ along one dimension. For example, use the same-sized paper rectangles that differ in color, so the child must be sure he/she is matching along the correct dimension (i.e. color). Or use similar sized animals, but the child must be sure to attend to the actual features of the animal in order to match correctly.

In addition, puzzles with matching insets are a great, fun way to generalize matching skills, and can help the child learn a new leisure activity. Along the same lines, play matching games (or modifications of) such as Memory, or Pin the Tail on the Donkey.

Tips/suggestions

Using materials that are fun and interesting to the child may help with participation, especially if the child is an early learner. Use Sesame Street characters, trains, or pictures of favorite television show characters as matching stimuli.

Troubleshooting

Be sure you are using a highly effective reinforcer, and that the child is already able to attend to objects. If the child is not attending to the objects, he/she will have a lot of difficulty learning this skill, even with physical prompting.

Future objectives

Matching non-identical objects (e.g. matching a winter hat to a baseball cap when the other objects are a glove and a sock) is often difficult for children to learn. Once the child learns to match identical objects, move on to this more difficult procedure. Keep in mind that the child may need to learn this slowly, and may require additional prompting, despite the fact that he/she can already match identical objects.

Afterwards, focus on teaching the child to match objects to pictures or vice versa. For this skill, the pictures do not need to be actual photographs of the objects, but can be representations of the objects. Just be sure that the picture clearly depicts the object you are trying to teach the child to match.

Sequencing

Objective

Teach the child to sequence the steps of a familiar activity and to describe the activity in sequence.

Materials

You will need to have pictures of the steps of a familiar activity (e.g. washing hands).

Procedure

1. Obtain the child's attention and give him/her the pictures.

2. Instruct the child to put the pictures in order.

3. Prompt as necessary to help the child put the pictures in order. Initially you can use verbal prompts to help the child learn the verbal description that accompanies each picture (e.g. "First you turn on the water.").

4. Upon completion, immediately provide specific praise and a tangible/edible reinforcer.

5. Repeat with a different sequence of pictures.

6. Randomly rotate between two to three different sequences, fading prompts (including verbal prompts) across trials.

Error correction

If the child places the pictures in the wrong order, use a prompt to help him/her correct this error. Do not deliver a reinforcer following an error.

Generalization

Once the child has learned to sequence, have him/her use this skill when completing the sequenced activities. For example, teach the child to wash his/her hands in the appropriate sequence. For this skill, you could use the pictures as prompts, or the verbal description of each step, until the child learns to complete the action in the appropriate sequence. If using verbal prompting be sure to fade such prompting quickly so the child does not wait for the prompt or instruction before moving on to the next step.

Tips/suggestions

Start with short sequences (e.g. three to four steps) and gradually increase to longer sequences of activities. Also, consider starting with sequences of activities that the child enjoys, such as making a preferred snack, or building a train track. Take pictures of the child engaging in these preferred activities from start to finish and then have the child correctly sequence these pictures later.

Troubleshooting

If the child is consistently responding incorrectly, try using pictures of favorite characters performing the activities (e.g. Elmo making the bed). Or use video segments and have the child number the video segments in order (for advanced children). You could also take pictures of you or a preferred friend/family member completing the activities.

EXAMPLE TARGETS

- washing hands

- getting dressed

- eating

- cleaning the room

- making a sandwich

- grocery shopping

- brushing teeth

- math problems.

FUTURE OBJECTIVES

Once the child can independently place the pictures in the correct order, ask him/her to tell you what is happening in each picture. The child may need increased assistance with this step, and depending on the child you may need to initially accept one to two word responses (e.g. "Water on."), gradually requiring full sentences before delivering a reinforcer.

Use the newly learned sequencing skills to prompt the child to complete difficult tasks, such as making a sandwich. You can break the activity down into several steps and teach the child the sequence while he/she is completing the task.

References

Berk, L. E. (2009). *Child Development* (8th ed.). Boston, MA: Allyn Bacon.

Bono, M. A., Daley, T., & Sigman, M. (2004). Relations among joint attention, amount of intervention and language gain in autism. *Journal of Autism and Developmental Disorders, 34,* 495–505.

Carpenter, M. & Tomasello, M. (2000). "Joint attention, cultural learning and language acquisition: Implications for children with autism." In A. Wetherby & B. Prizant (Eds.), *Autism spectrum disorders: A transactional developmental perspective* (pp. 31–54). Baltimore, MD: Brookes Publishing.

Conway, C. M., Pisoni, D. B., & Kronenberger, W. G. (2009). The importance of sound for cognitive sequencing abilities. The auditory scaffolding hypothesis. *Current Directions in Psychological Science, 18,* 275–279.

Gillberg, C. & Coleman, M. (1992). *The biology of autistic syndromes* (2nd ed.). London: McKeith Press.

Huebner, R. A. & Kraemer, G. (2001). "Sensorimotor aspects of attachment and social relatedness in autism." In R. A. Huebner (Ed.), *Autism: A sensorimotor approach in management* (pp. 209–244). Gaithersburg, MD: Aspen.

Ingersoll, B. & Schreibman, L. (2006). Teaching reciprocal imitation skills to young children with autism using a naturalistic behavioral approach: Effects on language, pretend play and joint attention. *Journal of Autism and Developmental Disorders, 36,* 487–505.

Klin, A., Jones, W., Schultz, R., Volkmar, F., & Cohen, D. (2002). Visual fixation patterns during viewing naturalistic social situations as predictors of social competence in individuals with autism. *Archives of General Psychiatry, 59,* 809–816.

Koren-Karie, N., Oppenheim, D., Dolev, S., & Yirmiya, N. (2009). Mothers of securely attached children with autism spectrum disorder are more sensitive than mothers of insecurely attached children. *Journal of Child Psychology and Psychiatry, 50*(5), 643–650.

Ledford, J. R., Gast, D. L., Luscre, D., & Ayres, K. M. (2008). Observational and incidental learning by children with autism during small group instruction. *Journal of Autism and Developmental Disorders, 38,* 86–103.

Leekam, S. & Moore, C. (2001). "The development of attention and joint attention in children with autism." In J. Burack, T. Charman, N. Yirmiya, & P. Zelezo (Eds.), *The development of autism: Perspectives from theory and research* (pp. 105–130). Mahwah, NJ: Erlbaum.

Lightfoot, C., Cole, M., & Cole, S. (2009). *The development of children* (6th ed.). Worth, IL: Worth Publishing.

Mundy, P. & Burnette, C. (2005). "Joint attention and neurodevelopmental models of autism." In F. R. Volkmar, R. Paul, A. Klin, & D. Cohen (Eds.), *Handbook of autism and pervasive developmental disorders: Vol. 1. Diagnosis, development, neurobiology, and behavior* (3rd ed., pp. 650–681). Hoboken, NJ: John Wiley & Sons.

Mundy, P. & Crowson, M. (1997)."Joint attention and early social communication: Implications for research on intervention with autism. *Journal of Autism and Developmental Disorders, 27,* 653–676.

Mundy, P. & Stella, J. (2000). "Joint attention, social orienting and nonverbal communication in autism." In A. Wetherby & B. Prizant (Eds.), *Autism spectrum disorders: A transactional developmental perspective* (pp. 55–77). Baltimore, MD: Brookes Publishing.

Naber, F. B. A., Bakermans-Kranenburg, M. J., van IJzendoorn, M. H., Swinkels, S. H. N., Buitelaar, J. K., Dietz, C., van Daalen, E., & van Engeland, H. (2008). Play behavior and attachment in toddlers with autism. *Journal of Autism and Developmental Disorders, 38,* 857–866.

Oppenheim, D., Koren-Karie, N., Dolev, S., & Yirmiya, N. (2009). Maternal insightfulness and resolution of the diagnosis are associated with secure attachment in preschoolers with autism spectrum disorders. *Child Development, 80,* 519–527.

Prizant, B. (1996). Brief report: Communication, language, social and emotional development. *Journal of Autism and Developmental Disorders, 26,* 173–178.

Rogers, S. J., Cook, I., & Meryl, A. (2005). "Imitation and play in autism." In F. R. Volkmar, R. Paul, A. Klin, & D. Cohen (Eds.), *Handbook of autism and pervasive developmental disorders: Vol. 1. Diagnosis, development, neurobiology, and behavior* (3rd ed., pp. 382–405). Hoboken, NJ: John Wiley & Sons.

Rutgers, A. H., Bakermans-Kranenburg, M. J., van IJzendoorn, M. H., & van Berckelaer-Onnes, I. A. (2004). Autism and attachment: a meta-analytic review. *Journal of Child Psychology and Psychiatry, 45,* 1123–1134.

Sigman, M. & Capps, L. (1997). *Children with autism: A developmental perspective.* Cambridge, MA: Harvard University Press.

Siller, M. & Sigman, M. (2002). The behaviors of parents of children with autism predict the subsequent development of their children's communication. *Journal of Autism and Developmental Disorders, 32,* 77–89.

Smith, L. & Bryson, S. (1994). Imitation and action in autism: A critical review. *Psychological Bulletin, 116,* 259–273.

Taylor, E. L., Target, M., & Charman, T. (2008). Attachment in adults with high-functioning autism. *Attachment & Human Development, 10*(2), 143–163.

Toth, K., Munson, J., Meltzoff, A., & Dawson, G. (2006). Early predictors of communication development in young children with autism spectrum disorder: Joint attention, imitation, and toy play. *Journal of Autism and Developmental Disorders, 36,* 993–1005.

Whalen, C., Schreibman, L., & Ingersoll, B. (2006). The collateral effects of joint attention training on social initiations, positive affect, imitation, and spontaneous speech for young children with autism. *Journal of Autism and Developmental Disorders, 36,* 655–664.

Whitman, T. L. (2004). *The development of autism: A self-regulatory perspective.* London: Jessica Kingsley Publishers.

Whitman, T. L. & Ekas, N. (2008). Theory and research on autism: Do we need a new approach to thinking about and studying this disorder? *International Review of Research in Mental Retardation, 35,* 1–41.

Williams, J. H. G., Whiten, A., & Singh, T. (2004). A systematic review of action imitation in autistic spectrum disorder. *Journal of Autism and Developmental Disorders, 34,* 285–299.

Further reading

Sigman, M. & Mundy, P. (1989). Social attachments in autistic children. *Journal of American Academy of Child and Adolescent Psychiatry, 28,* 74–81.

Chapter 4

Emotion-Related Problems

Relatively little is known about the emotional lives of children with ASD. The reason for this gap in knowledge relates in part to the nature of autism. Because many children on the autism spectrum lack or have only rudimentary expressive language skills, they are not able to share verbally their inner feelings. Moreover, even those children with well-developed language skills have difficulty reflecting on their emotional states, understanding their feelings, and expressing in appropriate ways their emotional needs.

Thus, in order to understand this aspect of the inner life of children with ASD, close attention has to be given to studying the environmental, behavioral, and physiological correlates of their emotions. Fortunately, through investigating the emotional experiences of neurotypical children, researchers and clinicians have become quite skilled in making these types of indirect assessments. Emotions are studied through examining autonomic nervous system responses (e.g. heart rate and respiration), the expressive behavior of the face and body, as well as through verbal report. These various response systems are both reflections of emotions as well as regulating mechanisms, serving to dampen or increase bodily arousal and action. This field of research has provided a valuable window into both typical and atypical emotional development.

Emotional development in neurotypical children

It is important to understand how emotional development proceeds in neurotypical children in order to fully appreciate the differences in how this system emerges in children with autism and influences their overall development. The emotional life of infants is quite rich. For example, infants are able to express a wide variety of basic emotions, including happiness, interest, surprise, fear, anger, sadness, and disgust. Shortly after birth, newborns smile in response to gentle touches and soft voices. They also show distress and even anger in response to painful stimuli, such as a wet diaper or medical inoculations. Sadness may also occur when attractive objects are removed or separation from a caretaker occurs. Fear is often expressed in response to new, unexpected, and intense encounters with the environment. In contrast to later evolving emotions, which are learned and more cognitively controlled, these basic emotions are to a large degree innate and hard-wired.

During the early stages of development, infants are limited in their ability to regulate their emotions. They use mechanisms like sucking, curling their body to the midline, eye-closing, and eye-aversion. Young infants also depend heavily on their caretakers for soothing when their emotions get intense. In addition, they utilize the emotional responses of others as an aid in interpreting and evaluating ambiguous situations, a phenomenon developmental psychologists call social referencing.

In early childhood, a variety of other emotions begin to appear, including shame, embarrassment, guilt, envy, and pride. These emotions emerge as the cognitive system matures, language evolves and socialization occurs. Children begin to reflect on their actions and the actions of those around them, which in turn is associated with a newly evolving sense of self. As these changes occur, they become increasingly adept at expressing their emotional needs, controlling their emotional expressions, and responding to the emotional needs of others.

Infancy and early childhood is also a time when emotional bonds are formed between the caretaker and child. Children develop affectional ties to their parents, with the quality of these ties influenced by a variety of factors, including the child's personality characteristics, caregiver sensitivity and responsiveness, family stress, and the parents' own attachment experiences. These affectional ties subsequently have a profound influence on the children's later social relationships and their ability to relate emotionally to others.

Growth in language and the cognitive system allows for an increase in emotional self-regulation. Children learn to recognize emotional states in others as well as to express verbally their own feelings. Emotional cues from others not only influence their feelings, but also help them respond empathetically to the pain and pleasure of others. As the cognitive system develops, emotions become more textured. Gradually, children learn social rules which help them express their emotions in increasingly refined and appropriate ways. The reader is referred to Berk (2009) and Lightfoot, Cole, and Cole (2009) for further information on emotional development in children.

Emotional competence and adjustment

Goleman (1994) and Sarni (1999) emphasize the importance of emotional competence in the lives of both children and adults. Emotional competence refers to an array of skills that facilitate personal adjustment and the quality of interpersonal relationships. For example, emotionally competent people are able to identify, label, and discuss a wide array of emotions that they experience. They can read the emotional states of other people. They can empathize with others. They understand that there may be an incongruity between what people say about their feelings and their actual feelings. They are aware of the ways emotions can influence a person's actions. They understand how people can maintain simultaneously conflicting feelings, such as sadness and joy, and love and hate. Most importantly, they are able to control and manage effectively intense emotions, such as hostility and fear. As adults and parents they are able to teach others, including their children, how to develop these competencies. Sarni (1999) views emotional competence as developing within the context of social relationships and a person's emotional experiences. She suggests that because of their inability to interpret their emotional experiences and those of others, children with autism are unable to convey emotions in conventional ways.

The development of emotional competence takes on particular importance when examining adjustment in families with children who have autism. Parents who have skills in emotion management are not only better able to manage their own emotions, but also to assist their children with autism and their other children in developing emotional competence. In order to become better emotion managers, parents need to learn how their children with autism operate at an emotional level. In the next sections, emotional development and specific emotional problems and deficiencies are examined in children with autism along with intervention strategies for addressing their emotional needs.

Emotional development and autism

Insights into the emotional lives of individuals with autism come from their personal stories and those of their parents as well as from empirical research. Although any specific characterization about emotional development and autism must be made with caution because of the considerable individual differences in this population, anecdotal and empirical evidence provide a reasonably coherent picture.

Contrary to some popular conceptions, children with autism often display deep emotional responses to their social and physical environment. However, unlike typically developing children, their emotions are often more basic and volatile. Due to their cognitive and social deficiencies, their emotional responses at times seem inappropriate. Their facial expressions, which may appear odd or bland, belie, however, what is a rich and often intense emotional life. Children with autism can and often do react empathetically to the feelings of others, although this response is more reflexive, rather than driven by a deep cognitive understanding of the origins of other people's emotions. They also form attachments to others, particularly their caretakers, however these attachments often do not seem to provide them with the secure base necessary to actively explore their physical and social world nor the foundation to develop deep meaningful social relationships. Because they have a less developed emotional regulation system, they sometimes display fear, anxiety, anger as well as joy in unusual and sometimes socially unsettling ways.

The majority of children with autism display response styles characteristic of children with difficult or slow-to-warm-up (shy) temperaments. Difficult temperament children have a high activity level, are avoidant of new situations and people, display low adaptability, are more negative in mood, and show a high intensity in their affect when sad or upset. Slow-to-warm-up temperament children are low in activity level, avoidant in new situations, low in adaptability, and low in the intensity of their affect when happy or sad (Thomas & Chess, 1977). Both of these temperament types share a common component, an emotion regulation problem; children with a difficult temperament have difficulty controlling their displeasure when upset whereas children in the slow-to-warm-up category control their emotions through avoidance and withdrawal.

Research examining temperament in children with autism has found that they show high levels of negative affect (Schwartz et al., 2005), great variability in affect regulation, ineffective affect-regulation strategies, poor inhibitory control, and difficulties in being soothed (Konstantareas & Stewart, 2006). They have also been reported to be less adaptable and require more intense stimulation from the environment in order to respond (Hepburn & Stone, 2006). Research by Shalom et al. (2006) suggests that children with autism are not impaired in their emotional response at a physiological level, but rather in the manner in which they interpret, express, and react to the emotions that they experience.

In order to function effectively, a calm–alert state is necessary. Paris (2000a) suggests that children with autism demonstrate levels of arousal that tend to the extremes; either lower than desirable or so high that decompensation results. Reviewing evidence from experimental studies with children with autism, Toichi and Kamio (2003) point out that there is support for both a hypoarousal and hyperarousal hypothesis, either of which they speculate could result from an impairment in the reticular activating system in the brain. Hypoarousal is frequently connected with lethargy, indifference and sleep, whereas hyperarousal is associated with intense, often uncomfortable feelings, avoidance, and immobility (Dunn, 1997).

Problems in arousal/activation and affect regulation have been theorized to have a major influence on the development of the sensory, motor, cognitive, language, social, and self-regulatory systems of children with ASD. At a sensory level, children with autism experiencing a high state of arousal often show a pattern of hypersensitivity, particularly in environments that are changing, novel, and/or more intense. In contrast to neurotypical children, they are also likely to show slower habituation responses to sensory input. Conversely, problems of hyposensitivity and the absence of an orienting response toward stimulus inputs, such as pain, hot or cold, seem to be associated with a state of low arousal (Whitman, 2004).

Paris (2000b) suggests that a state of hyperarousal could also explain many of the motor symptoms associated with autism, including muscular tension, gross and fine motor skill, coordination, balance, and motor planning problems. Hyperarousal also appears to be associated with hyperactivity, behavioral disorganization and avoidance. In contrast, low arousal is often associated with a state of low muscle tone, lethargy, and inactivity.

Cognitively, individuals with autism in a state of hyperarousal are likely to be distractable and impulsive, displaying problems in attentional focusing, attention span, attention-shifting, information-processing and short- and long-term memory (Dawson & Levy, 1989). As a consequence, learning is slower and more complex; cognitive and metacognitive processes, such as abstract thinking, problem-solving, executive functioning, social comprehension, self-monitoring and self-understanding, are adversely affected. Although the process is somewhat different, low arousal may lead to a similar pattern of problems which are due to inattention rather than distractibility. In either case, because their level of arousal is less than optimal, learning and performance in individuals with autism are adversely affected.

Gardner and Karmel (1983) suggest that during early infancy, maladaptive arousal patterns alter central nervous system (CNS) organization in permanent ways. In discussing research that indicates highly aroused infants prefer less complex and informative stimuli, they point out that such preferences may be permanently established as functional and structural connections in the brain, thus having a detrimental effect on cognitive development. This preference for noncomplexity displayed by distressed infants bears close similarity to the attentional fixations and stereotyped routines engaged in by children with autism who are under stress.

Arousal/activation and emotion processes may also play a critical role in the development of the language/communication system in children with autism. Bloom (1993) links affective expression with the development of language. She points out that emotional expression competes with language learning for an infant's attention and suggests that a neutral emotional state allows infants to use their limited cognitive resources for early language learning. Her research indicates that one-year-old infants who spent more time in neutral emotional states achieve language milestones, such as first words and multiword speech, earlier than infants who are more emotionally expressive (Bloom & Capatides, 1987). If children with autism are experiencing during their early development more intense and unregulated emotions, this could explain at least in part their language and communication deficiencies.

Finally, social development is likely affected by states of hyperarousal and hypoarousal. This impact on social learning and performance is probably mediated by the attentional problems that result from overarousal and/or underarousal, with inattention or selective attention leading to problems in encoding, processing, and recalling social information. Children who are extremely anxious are less likely to be aware of their social environment, less strategic in their social decision-making, and less able to carry through an orderly plan of social action (White & Roberson-Nay, 2009).

Further insight into how emotional arousal might affect social functioning is provided by research examining facial processing in children with autism. A variety of studies indicate that individuals with autism demonstrate marked abnormalities, compared to non-ASD controls, in the processing of faces, including reduced attention to faces, reduced attention to eyes, increased focus on mouths, poor memory for faces, and impaired recognition of familiar faces (Dalton et al., 2005; Joseph, Ehrman, McNally, Keehn, & Tager-Flusberg, 2005; Kylliäinen & Hietanen, 2006). More generally, individuals with autism tend to use a local or feature-based rather than a holistic or configural approach to processing. In turn, this mode of facial processing has been purported to be associated with a variety of social and communication problems, including joint attention deficiencies, reduced social imitation, poor emotion recognition, and lower social referencing (Sasson, 2006).

In summary, until recently, relatively little attention has been given to studying the emotional states of individuals on the autism spectrum. Existing research, however, points to the profound role that emotions play in the lives of children with autism and the adverse impact on development that results when emotions are not properly regulated. Although intervention programs for helping children regulate and express their emotions in appropriate ways are still evolving, applied research with neurotypical children and children with socioemotional problems provide considerable guidance about how such programs should be structured.

Intervention goals, perspectives, and strategies

In the remainder of this chapter, core skills for developing emotional competence and emotion-based problems that need to be targeted for interventions are examined, along with examples of intervention programs (see Table 4.1). Specifically, we describe intervention strategies for developing emotion awareness, emotion expression, and empathy. Several types of emotional problems commonly associated with autism are discussed, including hyperarousal, anxiety and fear, hypoarousal, and anger.

Table 4.1 Developing emotional competence and emotion-regulation: critical targets for intervention

Emotion labeling (awareness of others' emotions)
Emotion self-awareness
Emotion expression
Empathy
Anxiety and fear
Hypoarousal
Anger

Awareness of others' emotions (emotion labeling)

The processes of becoming aware of other people's emotions and one's own emotions appear to be dynamically interrelated, with the emergence of awareness of others' feelings likely leading to an increase in awareness of one's own feelings and vice versa. In typically developing children, awareness of others' emotions appears in part to be an innate process. For example, we have all observed how one infant's emotional upset, manifested through crying, elicits crying in a nearby infant, or one infant's laughter leads to spontaneous laughter in another infant, a process sometimes referred to as emotional contagion. Imitation likely plays a role in this emotional transfer. As infants imitate the expressions of others, such as smiling, these motoric acts in turn automatically evoke emotions that are wired to these acts (e.g. smiling makes you feel good). This process may explain how empathy evolves. A less reflexive and more mature emotion awareness begins with the emergence of language and the ability of children to verbally label the emotions being expressed by other people.

Research examining emotions in children with ASD suggest that they, like other children, experience the world at an emotional level. However, they are not very aware of the emotions of others or in touch with their own and as a result convey their emotions in unconventional ways: for example, Reddy, Williams and Vaughan (2002) found, after analyzing videotapes and comparing the responses of children with Down Syndrome and children with autism in different play situations, that children with autism displayed lower frequencies of attention and smiles in response to the laughter of others. Their data suggests that children with autism do not learn the same cultural scripts of emotion as other children.

Other research also indicates that children with ASD have difficulties with emotion recognition (Rump, Giovannelli, Minshew, & Strauss, 2009), although older children with ASD seem to have better skills than younger children with ASD (Kuusikko et al., 2009). Because children with autism do not focus their attention as readily on people as they do on physical objects, they are less able as a consequence to access the critical cues that would allow them to encode and interpret human emotions (Kikuchi, Senju, Tojo, Osanai, & Hasegawa, 2009). Research has shown that even when children with autism do look at people's faces, they are less likely to scan the total face, instead often fixating on particular aspects of the face, such as the mouth or the periphery of the face. Because the various facial features in combination provide critical information about a person's emotions, children with autism are denied access to this information. This face-processing style emerges early and likely impacts their social interactions during toddlerhood (Chawarska & Shic, 2009).

From an intervention perspective, awareness of others' emotions is a teachable, albeit a complex response. Although the strategies for teaching emotion awareness to neurotypical children and children with autism are somewhat similar, the general approach utilized with children with ASD is much more systematic in nature. Typically, they are taught to identify various emotions being expressed by a particular individual and then to generalize these emotion identification responses to other individuals. For convenience sake, pictures are often initially employed for this purpose. Subsequent steps in this teaching program, specifically during the generalization phase, utilize videos and in-vivo presentations of people experiencing various emotions. Research by Golan et al. (2010) also points out the usefulness of animated video figures for developing emotion recognition.

When teaching children with ASD to identify emotions in others, their attention must be drawn to relevant facial cues, non-facial body cues, and contextual cues. Contextual stimuli (e.g. receiving a present at a birthday party) can be utilized, not only to provide information to children about what emotion a person is experiencing (e.g. joy), but also to help them gain insight into why that individual is experiencing that emotion. In order to expedite learning during the early stages of intervention, the program is best implemented in a structured setting (e.g. at a table). Eventually, to facilitate generalization, an incidental learning approach is utilized in which children are asked to identify feelings spontaneously expressed by individuals in their everyday living environments.

For example, the following steps are often employed during an intervention:

- The child is shown pictures of an individual displaying different emotions (e.g. joy, anger, sadness, surprise) and asked to identify each of the emotional expressions. If the child makes an incorrect response, corrective feedback is given.

- After completing correctly the previous task on several occasions, pictures of other people expressing the same set of emotions are gradually integrated into the initial set of pictures. Again, the child is asked to identify each of the emotional expressions and given corrective feedback as necessary.

- After completing this task, the child is shown videos of individuals expressing the same set of emotions and asked to identify them. Information provided by contextual cues (e.g. a boy having a toy taken away from him) can be brought to the child's attention, to provide both insight concerning which emotion is being expressed and why it is being expressed.

- The child is asked to identify emotions of people in everyday living circumstances.

The last three steps of this program are designed to facilitate generalization of the emotion recognition response.

Emotion self-awareness

The process of teaching children with autism to become aware of their own emotions is less straightforward and more complex than teaching them to identify the emotions of others. In contrast to the more structured approach used in teaching children to identify the emotions of others, a more naturalistic and introspective approach, incidental learning, is often used to help children identify their feelings as they are being experienced. This incidental learning approach uses naturally occurring events in a child's life as teachable moments. For example, the following steps might be followed in an incidental learning program directed at teaching emotion self-awareness:

- A child becomes upset and starts crying when a strange dog runs toward him/her.

- After the dog goes away, the child is provided assistance in identifying his/ her feelings, as well as what produced them, by asking the child what he/ she was feeling and why.

- If the child is not able to identify his/her feelings and what produced them, the child is prompted, until he/she can say "I was afraid because I thought the dog might hurt me," or some approximation thereof.

In addition, the following procedures can be employed:

- Mirrors can be used to show children the emotional expressions they make (e.g. when they are happy), in order to help them associate their inner feelings with their outer expressions.

- Children can be shown pictures of themselves expressing specific emotions and asked to identify those emotions. They can also be shown videos of emotions that they express in their everyday life.

- Alternatively, when children are expressing an emotion in an everyday living situation, they can be given pictures of themselves (or others) expressing various emotions and asked which picture best expresses what they are feeling.

Once children identify their emotions and reasons for their feelings, they have taken an initial step toward learning how to regulate those emotions. Emotion regulation will be discussed in this chapter and Chapter 10.

Emotion expression

Emotions can be expressed through nonverbal and/or verbal behaviors. The aforementioned procedures can be employed to provide children with autism a way of expressing verbally what they are feeling, as well as to increase their self-awareness. For example children who are enjoying swimming in a pool may be taught to indicate their joy through saying "This is really fun."

Because children with autism often express their emotions in ambiguous and unusual ways, they may need to be taught how to express them in more conventional ways. One approach to teaching children conventional expressions of emotions is through imitation training. For example:

- Children can be shown a video of a child who is happy (smiling and laughing) and then be asked to imitate that happy child's behavior.

- Feedback is then given, either verbally or through modeling, by the teacher/ parent to help the children refine their expression of that emotion.

This type of imitation procedure can be used to help children acquire the postures, gestures, mannerisms, facial expressions, as well as words, including accents and speech rates, associated with various emotions. Actors who learn to express emotions in a more articulated fashion are taught through similar procedures.

Empathy

Empathy involves a process in which one individual is able to respond appropriately to an emotion expressed by another person. Although this process is in part *reflexive*, a result of an automatic mirroring and mimicking process, empathy also involves more *reflective* processes that are directed at understanding the circumstances that produce specific feelings. Children with autism have difficulties with both components of this process.

They have problems with the automatic aspect of empathy because they fail to attend to the emotional cues put forth by individuals and thus are unable to react to these expressions. The imitation training procedure described in the last section can be employed to facilitate the development of this component of empathy. Imitation training can be utilized, not only to help children express more clearly their emotions, but also to facilitate their emotional understanding of what other people are experiencing. Researchers suggest that the mimicking of emotional behaviors and movements produces automatically specific feelings, through feedback from the muscle movements to the brain, autonomic nervous system, and the physiological substrate underlying the emotions. Specifically, mimicking the emotional expressions of others leads the person doing the mimicking to experience the emotions of the person being mimicked. For example, if you mimic the sad or fearful responses of other people, you actually feel some of the sadness or fear those people are experiencing. In other words, imitation of others' emotional behaviors produces an empathetic response (Stel, van Dijk, & Olivier, 2009).

The second aspect of empathy, the reflective component, emerges as children develop a theory of mind. Theory of mind refers to the ability to understand not only what emotions people are experiencing, but also why they are experiencing those emotions, that is, what is going on in the minds of other people as they express emotions. High functioning children with autism appear to be more sensitive to the distress of others than low-functioning children; however they have difficulty responding to this distress in an appropriate fashion (Bacon, Fein, Morris, Waterhouse, & Allen, 1998). Theory of mind deficiencies in children with autism and interventions for addressing these deficiencies are discussed in Chapter 9.

Hyperarousal, anxiety, and fear

Descriptions of persons with autism by those around them, as well as by themselves, suggest that they are easily stressed, anxious, and fearful. Not only do they often show strong reactions to the environment, but they often have difficulty regulating their emotions when they become upset. Temple Grandin described herself as living in a constant state of fear, with seemingly minor events causing an intense reaction. She stated that as she got older her anxiety attacks got worse, escalating into a constant state of physiological alertness, panic attacks, and ultimately depression. She suggested that about half of high functioning individuals with autism have similar problems (Grandin, 1995).

Observation of children with autism suggests that they also display high autonomic reactivity, particularly in new situations, as well as a difficulty in self-regulating this reactivity. Waterhouse (2000), drawing from clinical descriptions of persons with autism, research, and theory, points out the primacy of anxiety in the lives of both children and adults with autism. She speculates that the roots of such anxiety may be biologically and perhaps even genetically based as part of the individual's temperament.

A number of clinical studies have indicated that children and adults on the autism spectrum are at great risk for mood and anxiety disorders (Bradley, Summers, Wood, & Bryson, 2004; Ghaziuddin, Ghaziuddin, & Greden, 2002; Kanne, Christ, & Reiersen, 2009; Kim, Szatmari, Bryson, Streiner, & Wilson, 2000; Muris, Steerneman, Merckelbach, Holdrinet, & Meesters, 1998). For example, Muris et al. (1998) found that 84 percent of individuals with a pervasive developmental disorder in their study met the full criteria for an anxiety disorder. Anxiety and fear in turn can produce attentional problems, hyperactivity, learning difficulties, and social problems, including loneliness, and more generally can have a dramatic inhibiting impact on development (White & Roberson-Nay, 2009).

Anxiety and fear develop as a result of trauma and stimulus overload and persevere because of sensory, cognitive, language, and social deficiencies which prevent effective coping and emotion regulation. Although the terms anxiety and fear are used interchangeably here, anxiety has been described as a state of uneasiness and apprehension about future uncertainties, and fear has been used to describe a feeling of agitation caused by the perception of an assumed danger, such as fear of the unknown, fear of unexpected changes in routine or in the environment, fear of the presentation of an unwanted stimulus, and fear of the removal of a wanted stimulus.

Anxiety and fear often have devastating effects on the behavior of children with autism. These emotions can lead them to avoid situations that evoke these emotions and even result in withdrawal into their own private world. Additionally, children may react by crying, hitting, kicking, or screaming. These types of behaviors may at first seem unprovoked or random in occurrence, but typically they are elicited by a specific set of circumstances. Therefore, it is extremely important to monitor and track the occurrence of such behaviors. While tracking their occurrence, the stimulus events/situations that occur before and after the response need to be carefully examined. These antecedent and consequent events often provide critical information about what is eliciting and controlling the fear/anxiety responses and how interventions should be structured.

Based on over 50 years of research, a variety of techniques have been employed to manage anxiety and fears in nonclinical as well as clinical populations, including with individuals with ASD. Three approaches, described in Chapter 2, are particularly useful: environmental alteration, emotion-focused, and behavior-oriented.

Environmental alteration strategies are more palliative in their focus; that is they are focused on isolating the environmental causes of a particular anxiety/fear response and removing the "offending" stimuli, rather than on directly reducing the anxiety/fear responses to those stimuli. For example:

- If it is determined that sounds of a high frequency and amplitude, or tactile stimuli, which are rough or sticky, cause great emotional upset, these stimuli can be simply eliminated as much as possible from the child's environment. Although this approach can be useful, at least in the short term, it is of limited value if it greatly restricts the activities and environments into which the child can enter.

In contrast to the environmental alteration approach, an emotion-focused approach is directed at reducing anxiety/fear responses in specific stimulus situations. Although there are a wide variety of *emotion-focused* strategies that might be employed, three are mentioned here: extinction, graduated extinction or desensitization, and reciprocal inhibition. Each of these approaches are briefly described, using the example of a child who becomes emotionally distressed when hearing a high-pitched sound:

- If an *extinction* strategy is used, the high-pitched sound is periodically presented at random intervals, until the child gradually shows a reduction in the intensity of the anxiety/fear responses. This approach is most useful for anxiety/fear responses which are of more recent origin and lower in intensity. In contrast, if the child's anxiety/fear response is long-standing and pronounced, the use of extinction is not recommended.

- In contrast to extinction, the *graduated extinction* or *desensitization* approach introduces the fear-evoking stimulus in a more attenuated form. For example, a high-pitched sound might be initially introduced for a very brief period, for example 1 second. Over later presentations this interval is gradually increased as the fear response diminishes to the sound when presented at a shorter duration. A variety of other graduated extinction procedures can also be employed. For example, the pitch and amplitude of the stimulus presented could be gradually increased from low to high or alternatively the high-pitched stimulus could be initially masked by other sounds and gradually unmasked.

- A third approach, *reciprocal inhibition*, can be used in conjunction with either extinction or graduated extinction. This procedure involves presenting to the child a stimulus that competes with the fear-evoking stimulus. This competing stimulus, rather than evoking fear, is a source of pleasure and/or relaxation. For example, the child might be given a favorite food or be engaged in a favorite activity during the presentation of the high-pitched stimulus. The theory underlying this procedure is that, if arranged correctly, the pleasurable stimulus will inhibit the fear response evoked by the high-pitched stimulus, thus changing the valence of the feared high-pitched stimulus from negative to neutral and eventually to positive.

The last general strategy, *behavior-focused*, bears some similarity to emotion-focused approaches. However, whereas emotion-focused strategies are directed toward the emotional symptom, fear, behavior-focused strategies are directed toward the behavioral symptom (e.g. avoidance of fear-evoking situations).

- This strategy positively reinforces the child for approaching fear situations. For example, if a child is afraid of the high-pitched sound of a lawn mower, he/she might be positively reinforced with a highly desired food for gradually approaching closer and closer to the lawn mower. From a theoretical perspective, extinction of the fear response occurs because exposure to the feared stimulus takes place in the presence of the reward, with food evoking a pleasurable response that inhibits the fear response.

The reader is invited to review Chapter 2 for a further discussion of these and other anxiety-reduction techniques and to examine research by Gulsrud, Jahromi, and Kasari (2010) who describe how these techniques and others, such as redirection, ignoring, reassurance and provision of comfort, can be helpful to parents in co-regulating the emotions of their children who have ASD.

Hypoarousal

Just as hyperarousal can have adverse effects on the behavior of children with autism, so too can hypoarousal (Geurts, Begeer, & Stockmann, 2009). Hypoarousal is defined here as a state of physiological and behavioral lethargy. Although the causes of hypoarousal are not well understood, it is clear that this state is not conducive to learning.

Under certain conditions, hypoarousal may simply be an avoidance mechanism, involving behavioral and cognitive withdrawal, that results when children are not able to cope with the demands of their environment. From this perspective, it is a state not unlike depression that is accompanied by helplessness.

- In such instances, the environmental demands may need to be altered to reduce the degree of demand, for example by having a child in an academic situation engage in an easier task rather than a more difficult task.

In contrast, other approaches might be employed to increase arousal to an appropriate level. These approaches include environmental alteration, behavior-focused, and sleep and/or diet modifications.

- Environmental alteration strategies begin with assessing the types of situations/stimuli that are associated with a higher level of arousal for a particular child and then placing the child into those stimulus situations. For example stimuli, such as a brighter lighting level, yellow or red wall colors, window lighting, rock music, and cooler temperatures may serve to energize some children. A related strategy involves evaluating the child's activity level during the day and implementing intervention programs during those parts of the day when the child is most alert and active.

- A variety of behavior-focused strategies can also be useful for children who are lethargic including: reinforcer-based, prompt-based, and setting event strategies. For example, the use of activity-based reinforcers, such as jumping on a trampoline or rough and tumble play, can serve to stimulate the child during an educational program.

- Relatedly, because hunger is sometimes associated with a higher activity level, introducing intervention programs when the child has not eaten for several hours may be advantageous, not only because the child's activity level is higher, but also because food becomes a more potent reinforcer when deprivation has occurred.

- Teachers/parents should also be aware that lethargy and sleepy behaviors can be negatively reinforced, if the child realizes that he/she can escape work by engaging in "tired" responses, such as closing their eyes or falling asleep.

- Another behavioral strategy that can be effective in increasing arousal level involves the use of stimulating prompts and social reinforcers. Teachers, who are more animated and dynamic as they instruct, model, physically prompt, and reinforce during an educational program, are more likely to engage and activate the child.

- Setting events, that is events which transpire before an intervention program is initiated, also need to be evaluated. Just as activity-based reinforcers can serve to activate behavior, so too can having a child engage in more vigorous activities before educational programs are initiated, particularly given that educational interventions are often more sedentary in nature.

- Finally, to the extent that the child with hypoarousal problems has a history of sleeping and eating problems, careful consideration should be given to addressing these problems and ensuring that the child is getting adequate and high-quality sleep and proper nutrition. Procedures for dealing with sleep and eating problems are discussed in Chapter 10.

Anger

Anger, whether expressed verbally through shouting or nonverbally through tantrum behavior and aggression, occurs most frequently when a child is frustrated. Anger problems often result in children with autism becoming socially isolated and excluded from educational and other community settings. Because of the adverse impact that anger-related behaviors have on the angry child and others, interventions directed at helping children with autism control and express their anger in appropriate ways are extremely important.

A multitude of approaches and specific strategies can be employed for helping children with anger and anger-related problems including: emotion-focused, environment-focused, behavior-focused, and cognitive-oriented interventions. Because interventions for dealing with anger-related behaviors will be discussed at greater length in Chapter 11, we only briefly examine here each of these approaches:

- Because anxiety and fear responses can escalate into anger, many of the emotion-focused strategies previously outlined in this chapter for decreasing anxiety and hyperarousal can be useful in preventing this escalation process.

- Environment-focused interventions for controlling anger carefully evaluate the situations in which anger and anger-related behaviors occur. To the extent that the incidence of anger is greater during specific activities, in certain places, and with certain people, this incidence can be reduced through restricting the person with anger problems from entering into those settings. Such a prevention strategy is, however, not always feasible or desirable if entrance into these settings is educationally or socially important. Information derived from environmental assessments can also allow teachers and parents to implement strategies that will enable the child to cope with frustration in a more acceptable manner.

- Coping skills programs are particularly useful when a child's inability to communicate or a lack of social, academic, or job skills create a circumstance in which the probability of failure and frustration is high. In such cases, helping children to communicate their frustrations in more acceptable ways and to develop more adequate skills can assist them in coping with challenging situations.

- Finally, cognitively based and self-regulation interventions which focus on developing emotion-awareness, self-calming behaviors, and problem-solving skills can be quite useful.

The reader is referred to Chapter 2, Chapter 11, and to the program examples in the next section for further discussion of these and other techniques and their application with children with autism who have emotion-related problems and deficiencies.

Program examples

Labeling emotions in pictures

Objective

Teach the child to label the emotions of various people in pictures.

Materials

This program will require several examples of pictures of people expressing various emotions. It is necessary to have multiple examples of each emotion (i.e. four to five pictures of each emotion) so that the child learns to attend to the salient features of the faces in the pictures rather than memorizing a particular label for a particular picture. At this stage, the pictures should be simple and show primarily faces and not the surrounding environment.

Procedure

1. Begin by selecting two to three emotions to target.
2. Obtain the child's attention.
3. Hold up a picture and ask the child how the person in the picture is feeling.
4. Immediately reinforce correct responses.
5. If the child does not answer within 3 to 5 seconds, deliver a verbal prompt to help the child identify and label the correct emotion. Fade these prompts across trials by delivering less of the prompt and/or waiting slightly longer before offering the prompt.
6. Reinforce prompted responses. Gradually fade prompts by delivering more or better reinforcers for unprompted, independent responses.
7. Repeat with a different picture until you have gone through each picture 2 to 3 times.
8. Once the child can independently label four or five examples of an emotion, test the child with a novel example of the emotion. If the child can label novel examples of the emotion, consider it mastered. Add a new target, but continue to practice mastered targets.

Error correction

If the child incorrectly labels the emotion, put the picture down for 2 to 3 seconds, then hold it up again and repeat the instruction, delivering a quicker prompt to help the child answer correctly and avoid the same error. If the child answers correctly this time, deliver praise but do not deliver a tangible reinforcer following error correction. Move on to one or two different pictures, then re-present the erred picture again for additional practice.

TIPS/SUGGESTIONS

Be sure that the child is in an alert state prior to starting an emotion-identifying task because this task requires so much of the child's attention. Play quiet music to relax the overaroused child, or engage an underaroused child in physical activity to energize him/her prior to starting the task.

Help the child attend to the various features of the faces. For example, tell the child to "Look at her mouth," or "Look at his forehead." This will help to ensure that the child is not attending to only one part of the face when analyzing the pictures. In addition, depending on the child's age and language abilities, consider teaching multiple words to describe similar emotions (e.g. tired, sleepy, exhausted).

TROUBLESHOOTING

If the child is having sufficient difficulty with this task, find or create cartoon images that highlight or emphasize one important feature (e.g. a smile or a furrowed forehead and eyebrows). Then add more features to the cartoons so that the child must scan several features to identify the salient ones. For example, start with an image that shows only a smile, and no other features. Then as the child learns that this emotion is "happy," add eyes, a nose, eyebrows, and so on.

GENERALIZATION

Once the child has mastered a few emotions, help the child identify these emotions in other pictures. For example, when looking at pictures in books, see if the child can identify and label the emotions of the people in the pictures. The child may have more difficulty with this task, due to the increased amount of detail. Help the child by prompting him/her to attend to the faces of the people in the pictures.

OTHER TEACHING METHODS

Verbally label the salient features of the various pictures (e.g. smile, slanted eyebrows, frown, etc.) if children have a lot of difficulty learning to attend to the entire face or to environmental events.

EXAMPLE TARGETS

- happy/joy
- sad

- angry/mad
- surprised
- scared/frightened
- tired/sleepy/exhausted
- disgusted
- hurt/in pain
- frustrated
- irritated/annoyed
- confused
- curious/interested
- embarrassed/humiliated
- excited
- jealous
- love struck/in love
- mischievous
- proud
- shocked
- sorry
- shy.

FUTURE OBJECTIVES

Move on to teaching the child to identify emotions based not only on facial expressions, but also on environmental features. These pictures can be a bit more ambiguous, thus requiring an analysis of the surrounding environment to assist with identifying the appropriate emotion. For example, the emotion "scared" can be depicted by a picture of a person who looks shocked and is standing in front of a giant spider. Keep in mind that some emotions are primarily identified by environmental and situational factors, rather than by facial expressions (e.g. jealousy).

Following such training, teach the child to identify emotions based on live demonstrations. To do this, you can role play, or use video examples of emotional situations. For example, show a video of a person being surprised at a birthday party. Ask the child how the person in the video is feeling. If the child has difficulty, pause the video on the person's face so that the child can study the face and take some time to answer. Fade this pause-prompt, so that the child can identify emotions more quickly as they are occurring.

Emotion expression

OBJECTIVE

Teach the child to display facial expressions and body language that coordinate with his/her current state of emotion.

PREREQUISITES

The child should have the ability to describe briefly others' emotions and his/her current emotions and/or thoughts.

MATERIALS

Video clips of people expressing exaggerated emotions (e.g. clips from children and adolescent television shows such as Saved by the Bell and Barney).

PROCEDURE

1. Prepare to prompt and reinforce the following behaviors:

    a) accurately identifying the emotion expressed in the video clip

    b) attending to and labeling the detailed facial and body movements of the individual in the clip

    c) imitating the facial expressions and body language.

2. Show the child a video clip and ask him/her to identify the emotion(s) the character in the video is expressing. For example, show a clip of Saved by the Bell (whose characters tend to express exaggerated emotions) and ask the child how that character is feeling.

3. Tell the child to attend to and label the detailed facial and body movements (e.g. Zach's eyebrows are up and his eyes are wide, his mouth is in the shape of an "o," and his arms are lifted slightly, palms facing up).

4. Have the child imitate the facial expressions and body language.

5. Repeat with a different clip.

ERROR CORRECTION

If the child inaccurately guesses the emotion, point out the surrounding events in the clip. For example, if the child says that the character is scared when he is actually shocked or surprised, explain that he just walked into a room and everyone jumped out of hiding places yelling, "Happy Birthday!" Use this prompting strategy to help the child come to the appropriate conclusions of the emotion the character is experiencing.

GENERALIZATION

Take advantage of natural learning opportunities to teach the child to coordinate affect with emotions in the moment. For example, if you see the child receive a gift he/she has been wanting for a long time, but the child does not express happiness, use this moment to help the child practice such skills. Pull him/her aside and use a mirror to help the child learn to show his/her happiness.

TIPS/SUGGESTIONS

It may help to make the child a list of the particular aspects he/she should attend to. For example, attend to the character's eyebrows, eyes, mouth, forehead, arms, hands, body stance, and so on.

In addition, a mirror may help with imitating. Or videotape the child so he/she can compare his/her response with the original video.

Use these same procedures to teach the child to identify and label his/her own emotions in order to teach more self-awareness.

OTHER TEACHING METHODS

Tape the child in various situations. Later, ask the child how he/she felt during those situations (e.g. "How did you feel when you were playing and the other child stole your toy?"). Then show the child the video to see how his/her actual feelings compare to his/her expressions. Go through the same steps listed above so that the child can identify what emotion he/she appeared to be expressing. Then have the child practice expressing the emotion with appropriate facial and body movements.

FUTURE OBJECTIVES

If your child does not do so already, teach him/her to respond to the nonverbal cues of others by acting appropriately when they see someone else express a certain emotion. For example, if your child sees someone look upset, teach him/her to ask if there is something wrong. Along the same lines, teach him/her to express concern through nonverbal methods (e.g. eyebrows up toward center of forehead, but descending, head tilted to the side slightly, lightly touching other's arm, etc.).

Empathy

OBJECTIVE

Teach the child to identify, reflect, and respond appropriately to the feelings of others.

MATERIALS

You will need a mirror, videos or photographs, or actual people simulating emotions. Video clips of people expressing exaggerated emotions (e.g. Saved by the Bell clips) can also be helpful for this procedure.

PROCEDURE

1. Prepare to prompt and reinforce the following behaviors:

    a) accurately identifying the emotion expressed by someone else

    b) imitating the facial expressions and body language

    c) responding appropriately to the person's emotion.

2. Use a procedure similar to that of teaching affect coordination (see above example). Show the child a video clip or have someone act out an emotion. Ask the child to identify the emotion(s) the person is expressing. For example, show a clip of Saved by the Bell (whose characters tend to express exaggerated emotions) and ask the child how the character was feeling.

3. Have the child imitate the facial expressions and body language.

4. Prompt the child to respond appropriately to the emotion using model prompts and/or verbal prompts to help the child know what to do. For example, if another person is crying, the child should show a concerned face, or a frown, and perhaps ask the person if he/she is okay.

5. Repeat with a different clip/emotion.

ERROR CORRECTION

If the child inaccurately guesses the emotion, point out the surrounding events in the clip. For example, if the child says that the character is tired when he is actually sad (e.g. the character's pet has passed away). Point out signs of sadness, such as frowning, tears, and so on. Use this prompting strategy to help the child come to the appropriate conclusions of the emotion the character is experiencing.

If the child does not express appropriate empathy toward the person, use mirrors or videotapes to help the child to respond more appropriately.

Generalization

Whenever a natural learning opportunity presents itself, take advantage of it. If a child in the classroom starts crying, ask your child to complete the three steps outlined in the above procedure (i.e. steps a, b, and c). Reinforce the use of these skills in a natural context. If you see your child using these skills independently, deliver a highly preferred reinforcer and a lot of praise.

Moreover, be sure to teach the child a few different ways to respond to others' emotions. Some people may not want to talk when they are upset, and it may not be appropriate to hug strangers who are crying.

Tips/suggestions

Role play may be the best option for teaching empathy because you can contrive several scenarios, thus increasing the number of learning opportunities. Just be sure to generalize and take advantage of natural learning opportunities as well.

Remember to teach the child that he/she does not always have to approach others to express empathy. The child can simply remain somber when others are sad, or smile if others are happy. Some children may have difficulty learning to approach others in such delicate social situations (e.g. at a funeral) and thus you may be more successful teaching the child simply to show similar emotions as those around him/her.

Troubleshooting

If the child is having difficulty with empathy, try to determine which of the three steps he/she is having difficulty with. If he/she is inaccurately labeling the emotions of others, teach this skill first. If imitation is the problem, focus primarily on imitating facial expressions before focusing on empathy itself. If the child is not learning how to respond appropriately, try videotaping sessions. Watch the videotape with the child and provide feedback as you go.

Other teaching methods

Teaching the child theory of mind may have an impact on empathy (see Chapter 9).

Future objectives

For more advanced learners, teach more complex emotions and behaviors. Sometimes people express emotions simply by changing their typical behavior, and this change may not be an obvious indicator of the person's emotions. For example, if a happy, bubbly person is behaving differently from normal (e.g. quieter and less energetic) but is not frowning or crying, that person may be upset about something. Teach the child to inquire if the person is okay. Also, be sure to teach social boundaries. For example, some people may prefer to be left alone if upset and the child must learn to recognize such subtle cues and then to respond to those cues.

Reducing anxiety and fear

Objective

Teach the child to approach or remain nearby anxiety or fear-provoking stimuli.

Materials

Prepare both anxiety or fear-provoking stimuli and highly preferred items/ activities. If you use neutral items or even mildly preferred items (i.e. as opposed to highly preferred items), such items may become aversive themselves, rather than decrease the anxiety or fear response.

Procedure

1. Present a negative stimulus briefly, using a hierarchy of least feared to most feared. For example, if the child is afraid of insects, show a picture of their least feared insect (e.g. butterfly) for 1 second.

2. Immediately upon showing the feared stimulus, deliver the highly preferred item and then remove the negative stimulus. This must occur quickly and in that order so the child is receiving the preferred item while the negative stimulus is still present. For example, show the butterfly picture and play music at the same time.

3. Repeat.

4. Once the child is able to demonstrate a calm state or noticeably less anxiety/ fear for two consecutive sessions, gradually expose the child to the negative stimulus for longer periods of time (i.e. extend time by 1 to 5 seconds).

5. As you extend the time, deliver the preferred item for longer periods of time as well. In the beginning, present the preferred item for the same amount of time or longer than the negative stimulus.

6. Once the child is able to inhibit anxiety or fear responses for more than 1 minute in the presence of the negative stimulus, move on to a more feared/anxiety-provoking stimulus (e.g. a picture of an ant).

7. Continue in this fashion, moving up the fear/anxiety hierarchy as long as the child is not exhibiting a fear response. For example, move on to pictures of spiders, and then bumblebees (i.e. if bumblebees are the most feared). Then move on to videos of the insects in the same order. Next, use actual insects in a shoe box or at the zoo.

Tips/suggestions

If your child exhibits very strong anxiety or fear reactions, do not implement this procedure yourself. Contact a professional who has expertise in anxiety or fear behavior.

Some children are calmed by certain reinforcers, such as music, certain television shows, particular toys, sippy cups, and so on. It would be beneficial to use such items that naturally help the child calm down or maintain a calm demeanor.

Other teaching methods

Some children benefit from learning coping skills or calming techniques, which help them to remain calm in the sight or presence of fear or anxiety-provoking stimuli. Some examples of calming techniques include deep breathing, progressive muscle relaxation, self-talk, as well as individualized techniques that may depend on the child (e.g. counting, or reciting the alphabet quietly).

Coping skills to reduce anger-related behavior

Objective

Teach the child various coping skills to calm down when angry.

Materials

It may be helpful to use visual cues to help the child learn to use the various coping skills. Such cues can include a scale to rate anger, picture icons to cue particular coping skills, and/or picture cues or textual prompts to cue appropriate responses after calming down.

Procedure

1. Determine what seems to precede most angry behavior. It is highly likely that several events "set off" the child, however these events can usually be categorized into some general type of antecedent. Examples include not getting his/her way, removal of a particular item, change of schedule/routine, sight of a particular person, sight of work materials, presentation of a demand, and so on.

2. Once you have determined at least one category of antecedents, teach the child coping skills in a calm situation. For example, if you know that the sight of homework materials usually results in angry behavior from the child, work on teaching coping skills when such materials are not present.

3. Each child differs when it comes to effective coping skills. Therefore, try one or two for a while to see if they work and, if not, try something else. Some examples include: identifying and/or rating one's anger, self-monitoring anger bursts, deep breathing, progressive muscle relaxation, tensing and relaxing one muscle, distraction methods, and so on. These can occur in isolation or in combination with other coping skills.

4. When teaching your child to engage in the coping skills, remember that you must reinforce correct practice of these skills, even when the child is already calm.

5. Once the child has learned to engage in the coping skill(s) when calm, introduce slightly upsetting events. For example, if the sight of homework materials typically precede challenging behavior, place a pencil on the table near the child. Cue the child to use the coping skills to remain calm. Once the child has done so, cue the child to respond appropriately (e.g. teach him/her to ask you to remove the pencil or for help when you start presenting the homework itself). Reinforce the child's appropriate response by honoring his/her request.

6. Continue gradually introducing more upsetting events and cuing the child to engage in the coping skills to remain calm and then to respond appropriately.

7. Once the child has mastered the use of these skills in simulated tasks such as these, teach him/her to use these skills in the natural environment when opportunities present themselves. Continue to reinforce the proper application of these skills until the child has demonstrated mastery for quite some time.

ERROR CORRECTION

If the child responds with negative behavior, do not punish the child or threaten the removal of the reinforcer. Instead, prompt him/her to engage in the effective coping skills and, upon doing so, deliver the reinforcer. Practice later with more simulated exercises to give the child more practice using these skills quickly upon feeling the anger.

GENERALIZATION

Fade your prompts and cues. The picture icons can be an effective way of decreasing your verbal prompts. Point to the picture cues instead of telling the child what to do.

TIPS/SUGGESTIONS

Keep in mind that learning coping skills can be a long process. Children may have learned that expressing anger can typically get them what they want quickly or delay a necessary task. It will take a while for them to learn new, difficult skills that will help them to obtain the same results. It will be very helpful for you to also respond less to such anger bursts. Try to avoid attending too much to such inappropriate behavior.

OTHER TEACHING METHODS

Teaching children more advanced communication skills can help avoid such anger problems. In addition, if the stimulus that is evoking such anger can easily be removed, consider doing so. If the problem is a person, such as a sibling, talk to the person about ways they can change their own behavior to stop evoking such responses from the child.

References

Bacon, A. L., Fein, D., Morris, R., Waterhouse, L., & Allen, D. (1998). The responses of autistic children to the distress of others. *Journal of Autism and Developmental Disorders, 28,* 129–140.

Berk, L. E. (2009). *Child Development* (8th ed.). Boston, MA: Allyn and Bacon.

Bloom, L. (1993). *The transition from infancy to language: Acquiring the power of expression* New York, NY: Cambridge University Press.

Bloom, L. & Capatides, J. B. (1987). Expression of affect and the emergence of language. *Child Development, 58,* 1513–1522.

Bradley, E. A., Summers, J. A., Wood, H. L., & Bryson, S. E. (2004). Comparing rates of psychiatric and behavior disorders in adolescents and young adults with severe intellectual disability with and without autism. *Journal of Autism and Developmental Disorders, 34,* 151–161.

Chawarska, K. & Shic, F. (2009). Looking but not seeing: Atypical visual scanning and recognition of faces in 2 and 4-year-old children with autism spectrum disorder. *Journal of Autism and Developmental Disorders, 39,* 1663–1672.

Dalton, K., Nacewicz, B., Johnstone, T., Schaefer, H., Gersbacher, M., Goldsmith, H., et al. (2005). Gaze fixation and the neural circuitry of face processing in autism. *Nature Neuroscience, 8,* 519–526.

Dawson, G. & Levy, A. (1989). "Arousal, attention and the socioemotional adjustment of individuals with autism." In G. Dawson (Ed.), *Autism: Nature, diagnosis and treatment* (pp.144–173). New York, NY: Guilford.

Dunn, W. (1997). The impact of sensory processing on the daily lives of young children and their families: A conceptual model. *Infants and Young Children, 9*(4), 23–35.

Gardner, J. M. & Karmel, B. Z. (1983). "Attention and arousal in preterm and full-term neonates." In T. Field & A. Sostek (Eds.), *Infants born at risk* (pp. 69–98). New York: NY: Grune & Stratton.

Geurts, H. M., Begeer, S., & Stockmann, L. (2009). Brief report: Inhibitory control of socially relevant stimuli in children with high functioning autism. *Journal of Autism and Developmental Disorders, 39,* 1603–1607.

Ghaziuddin, M., Ghaziuddin, N., & Greden, J. (2002). Depression in persons with autism: Implications for research and clinical care. *Journal of Autism and Developmental Disorders, 32,* 299–306.

Golan, O., Ashwin, E., Granader, Y., McClintock, S., Day, K., Leggett, V., & Baron-Cohen, S. (2010). Enhancing emotion recognition in children with autism spectrum conditions: An intervention using animated vehicles with real emotional faces. *Journal of Autism and Developmental Disorders, 40,* 269–279.

Goleman, D. (1994). *Emotional intelligence: Why does it matter more than IQ?* New York, NY: Bantam Books.

Grandin, T. (1995). *Thinking in pictures.* New York, NY: Vintage Books.

Gulsrud, A. C., Jahromi, L. B., & Kasari, C. (2010). The co-regulation of emotions between mothers and their children with autism. *Journal of Autism and Developmental Disorders, 40,* 227–237.

Hepburn, S. & Stone. W. (2006). Using Carey temperament scales to assess behavioral style in children with autism spectrum disorders. *Journal of Autism and Developmental Disorders, 36,* 637–642.

Joseph, R. M., Ehrman, K., McNally, R., Keehn, B., & Tager-Flusberg, H. (2005). "Affective responses to eye contact in children with autism." Poster session presented at the biennial meeting of the Society for Research in Child Development, Atlanta, GA.

Kanne, S. M., Christ, S. E., & Reiersen, A. M. (2009). Psychiatric symptoms and psychosocial difficulties in young adults with autistic traits. *Journal of Autism and Developmental Disorders, 39,* 827–833.

Kikuchi, Y., Senju, A., Tojo, Y., Osanai, H., & Hasegawa, T., (2009). Faces do not capture special attention in children with autism spectrum disorder: A change blindness study. *Child Development, 80*(5), 1421–1433.

Kim, J. A., Szatmari, P., Bryson, S. E., Streiner, D. L., & Wilson, F. J. (2000). The prevalence of anxiety and mood problems among children with autism and Asperger syndrome. *Autism, 4,* 117–132.

Konstantareas, M. & Stewart, K. (2006). Affect regulation and temperament in children with autism. *Journal of Autism and Developmental Disorders, 36,* 143–154.

Kuusikko, S., Haapsamo, H., Jansson-Verkasalo, E., Hurtig, T., Marja-Leena, M., Ebeling, H., Jussila, K., Bölte, S., & Moilanen, I. (2009). Emotion recognition in children and adolescents with autism spectrum disorders. *Journal of Autism and Developmental Disorders, 39,* 938–945.

Kylliäinen, A. & Hietanen, J. (2006). Skin conductance responses to another person's gaze in children with autism. *Journal of Autism and Developmental Disorders, 36,* 517–524.

Lightfoot, C., Cole, M., & Cole, S. (2009). *The development of children.* Worth, IL: Worth Publishing.

Muris, P., Steerneman, P., Merckelbach, H., Holdrinet, I., & Meesters, C. (1998). Comorbid anxiety symptoms in children with pervasive developmental disorders. *Journal of Anxiety Disorders, 12,* 387–393.

Paris, B. (2000a). "Characteristics of autism." In C. Murray-Slutsky & B. Paris (Eds.), *Exploring the spectrum of autism and pervasive developmental disorders* (pp. 7–23). San Antonio, TX: Therapy Skill Builders (Harcourt Health Sciences).

Paris, B. (2000b). "Motor control and coordination difficulties." In C. Murray-Slutsky & B. Paris (Eds.), *Exploring the spectrum of autism and pervasive developmental disorders* (pp. 278–332). San Antonio, TX: Therapy Skill Builders (Harcourt Health Sciences).

Reddy, V., Williams, E., & Vaughan, A. (2002). Sharing humor and laughter in autism and Down's syndrome. *British Journal of Psychology, 93,* 219–242.

Rump, K. M., Giovannelli, J. L., Minshew, N. J., & Strauss, M. S. (2009). The development of emotion recognition in individuals with autism. *Child Development, 80*(5), 1434–1447.

Sarni, C. (1999). *The development of emotional competence.* New York, NY: Guilford Press.

Sasson, N. (2006). The development of face processing in autism. *Journal of Autism and Developmental Disorders, 36,* 381–393.

Schwartz, C., Henderson, H., Burnette, C., Sutton, S., Weisman, A., Zahka, N., et al. (2005). "Variations in error-monitoring and anxiety in higher-functioning children with autism." Poster session presented at the biennial meeting of the Society for Research in Child Development, Atlanta, GA.

Shalom, D., Mostotsky, S., Hazlett, M., Goldberg, R., Landa, Y., McLeoud, D., et al. (2006). Normal physiological emotions but differences in expression of conscious feelings in children with high-functioning autism. *Journal of Autism and Developmental Disabilities, 36,* 395–400.

Stel, M., van Dijk, E., & Olivier, E. (2009). You want to know the truth? Then don't mimic. *Psychological Science, 20,* 693–699.

Thomas, A. & Chess, S. (1977). *Temperament and development.* New York, NY: Brunner/Mazel.

Toichi, M. & Kamio, Y. (2003). Paradoxical autonomic response to mental tasks in autism. *Journal of Autism and Developmental Disorders, 33,* 417–426.

Waterhouse, S. (2000). *A positive approach to autism.* London: Jessica Kingsley Publishers.

White, S. W. & Roberson-Nay, R. (2009). Anxiety, social deficits, and loneliness in youth with autism spectrum disorders. *Journal of Autism and Developmental Disorders, 39,* 1006–1013.

Whitman, T. L. (2004). *The development of autism.* London: Jessica Kingsley Publishers.

Further readings

Bloom, L. & Trinker, E. (2001). The intentionality model and language acquisition: Engagement, effort and the essential tension in development. *Monographs of the Society for Research in Child Development, 66*(4), 1–104.

Schwartz, C. B., Henderson, H. A., Inge, A. P., Zahka, N. E., Coman, D. C., Kojkowski, N. M., Hileman, C. M., & Mundy, P. C. (2009). Temperament as a predictor of symptomatology and adaptive functioning in adolescents with high functioning autism. *Journal of Autism and Developmental Disorders, 39,* 842–855.

White, S. W., Ollendick, T., Scahill, L., Oswald, D., & Albano, A. M. (2009). Preliminary efficacy of a cognitive-behavioral treatment program for anxious youth with autism spectrum disorders. *Journal of Autism and Developmental Disorders, 39,* 1652–1662.

Chapter 5

Sensory Problems

Almost all daily activities require the reception, organization, and management of sensory input from the environment (Baker, 2008). The sensory system sends signals to the brain where they are processed and integrated to form a picture of the environment, which in turn allows for an appropriate response to that environment (Harrison & Hare, 2004). Sensory problems occur when environmental signals do not get organized into appropriate responses. Although formal definitions of autism do not include sensory processing problems as a key defining characteristic of this disorder, the presence of sensory disturbances in children with autism spectrum disorders has been widely acknowledged (Baranek, Parham, & Bodfish, 2005). Harrison and Hare (2004) suggest sensory problems are present in 70 to 80 percent of children with autism. Other studies claim that as many as 95 percent of people with autism display sensory difficulties (Baker, 2008).

In this chapter, we begin by examining sensory processing from a developmental perspective and then discuss sensory problems commonly associated with autism (see Table 5.1). Finally, interventions for addressing sensory problems are described.

Table 5.1 Sensory-related problems that might be targeted for intervention

Hypersensitivity
Sensory overload
Hyposensitivity
Sensory integration difficulties
Sensory fixations
Unusual sensory attractions
Sensory tune-outs

Early sensory processing in neurotypical children

Prior to birth, infants are insulated by the protective cocoon of the womb. Their sensory environment is rich, but fairly orderly in its structure. It is noisy due to the mother's heart beating as well as her breathing, digestive sounds, movements, and voice. As the fetus explores the intrauterine environment, he/she receives diverse types of tactile, proprioceptive (a system based in the muscle joints and ligaments that provides information about where the body is in space), and taste experiences (Maurer & Maurer, 1988). Compared to the world experienced after birth, this pre-birth environment, although rich in sensory stimulation, is relatively muted, homogeneous, and predictable. After birth, the infant's world changes dramatically. Although this post-birth world can be chaotic, intense, and stressful, infants have protective mechanisms, including sucking reflexes, eye closure, and other primitive state-regulation behaviors that help them accommodate to their environment until their neurosensory and neuromotor systems mature. A sensitive caretaking environment also protects the infant from excessive stimulation and assists the infant in this adaptation process.

Despite the fact that infants are confronted with challenges in processing information from the environment at birth, they enter the world with an array of sensory competencies. For example, they are able to respond to touch around the mouth, the palms of their hands, and the soles of their feet. They have taste preferences for sweet liquids. They respond both negatively and positively to an array of smells. They can hear a variety of sounds, particularly within the frequency range of the human voice. Although their vision is the least mature of their senses, they do visually explore their environment. With development and experience, their sensory acuity in these areas, as well as in others, including proprioceptive and kinesthetic senses, rapidly develops. As the sensory receptors mature and the nervous system receives information, infants become increasingly competent in encoding information from the environment. Eventually, this information is organized and objects and events become recognizable.

Children differ considerably in their sensitivity to sensory stimuli, a process affected by genetic factors, experience, an evolving cognitive system, motivational level, fatigue, pain, and sickness. To function effectively, children need to detect differences between stimuli as well as to adapt to stimuli, displaying diminished sensitivity as a consequence of repetitive stimulation. Although sensory adaption reduces sensitivity to some incoming stimuli, it allows attention to be focused on other important aspects of the environment without distraction. For more information on sensory processing and development, the reader is referred to Berk (2009) and Lightfoot, Cole, and Cole (2009).

Sensory processing in children with autism

What is it like to be a child with autism? How is his or her sensory development different from that of other children? For reasons only partially understood, children with autism often appear to differ from typically developing children in their sensory thresholds, specifically in their capacity to detect various stimuli, as well as in their ability to integrate stimuli coming from the various sensory modalities.

What happens, as appears to be case with autism, if the environment is experienced as chaotic? Based on the observations of parents and professionals who interact with children with autism, as well as the self-report of high functioning individuals with autism, like Temple Grandin and Donna Williams (1992), the sensory world of persons with autism not only begins in chaos, but continues to be confusing, as well as occasionally frightening. It is sometimes too bright, too noisy, too abrasive, too pungent, and too bitter. The symptomatology associated with autism presents a picture of individuals with sensory anomalies, who are severely challenged as they attempt to adapt to their environments and who compensate for their limitations by developing unusual ways of relating to their physical and social surroundings (Whitman, 2004).

Individuals with autism, as a group, present a myriad of sensory symptoms. For example, they often appear to experience the sensory world at the extremes, either showing hypersensitivity or hyposensitivity. Interestingly, hypersensitivity and hyposensitivity can co-occur in the same individual (Baker, 2008). For example, a person with autism could have hypersensitive hearing, and at the same time could be hyposensitive to tactile stimuli. Moreover, within a particular sensory modality an individual might have a mixed pattern of sensory experiences. A child could be hypersensitive to certain sounds and hyposensitive to others (Grandin, 2006). Although sensory problems are often reported in terms of a specific modality, problems in one sensory modality often influence functioning in other sensory modalities, thus creating sensory integration problems (Anzalone & Williamson, 2000). Dodd (2004) discusses a particularly intriguing phenomenon referred to as synesthesia or sensory crossover. The individual perceives a particular sensation as completely different from that characteristically experienced by most individuals. For example, a person might experience sound as color, for example seeing red when a particular sound occurs. Other related sensory problems associated with autism include sensory distortions and sensory overload (Baranek, Parham, & Bodfish, 2005; Harrison & Hare, 2004).

Gillberg and Coleman (1992) suggested that abnormal sensory responses to stimuli may constitute the most characteristic symptom of autism not currently contained in the diagnostic criteria for this disorder. O'Neill and Jones (1997), reviewing evidence from clinical and empirical studies, indicated that unusual sensory responses are present in the majority of children with autism during early development and are linked to other aspects of autistic behavior. Research has also revealed that sensory symptoms are not unique features of autism, but are also associated with other clinical diagnoses (Baranek, Parham, & Bodfish, 2005; Ermer & Dunn, 1998; Rogers, Hepburn, & Wehner, 2003).

Baranek, Parham, and Bodfish (2005) summarize evidence suggesting that although unusual sensory features exist at a young age in children with autism, including during infancy, they often decrease over time. Little is known, however, about either the etiology of sensory problems in children with autism or their possible relationships to the other sequelae and symptoms associated with autism. Because sensory symptoms appear to occur early, an argument can be made that they influence the development of autism. Support for this position is provided by Rogers, Hepburn, and Wehner (2003) who found that sensory symptoms are significantly related to overall adaptive behavior. Preliminary research by Lane, Young, Baker, and Angley (2010) suggests that there are different sensory processing subtypes in children with autism and that such subtypes may help promote understanding about how sensory processing influences development. Although relatively little research has investigated the role that sensory problems play in the development of autism, there has been considerable theoretical speculation (Whitman, 2004).

For example, Ornitz (1983) indicates that the behavior of children with autism becomes disorganized because of their inability to modulate sensory input. Disorganization appears to occur for a variety of reasons, including an inability to focus on incoming stimuli, a failure to filter out irrelevant aspects of such stimuli, and/or a failure to process completely information contained in the stimuli. These problems may in turn produce disruptions at an emotional level that further inhibit effective sensory processing, thus preventing coordinated and strategic action. Dunn (1997) has pointed out that although hypersensitivity results in a high level of arousal and activity for some children, for other children hypersensitivity precipitates sensory overload and an ensuing behavioral lethargy and flatness of affect.

The influence of sensory problems on the motor system may be far-reaching and profound (Whitman, 2004). Paris (2000) suggests that problems in processing tactile information may result in impairments in gross motor control (e.g. impaired balance reactions and motor clumsiness), hand control (e.g. impairments in grasp and manipulation skills), oral motor control (e.g. articulation problems), physical problems (e.g. shortening of the hand), and general disruptions in motor development (e.g. feeding, walking, and speech delays). Research by Gepner and Mestre (2002) suggests that children with autism are also less reactive posturally to visually perceived environmental motion than typically developing children. They speculate that hyporeactivity to such visual input may be associated with motor impairments, perhaps accounting for the delays some children with autism experience in achieving major motor milestones, as well as other motor problems, such as rigid gait and writing problems.

Sensory problems may also influence cognitive development in children with autism. Moreover, Huebner (2001) suggests that sensory problems adversely affect social and language development through their impact on cognitive learning. Cognitively, hypersensitive children often appear distractible or narrowly focused on one aspect of their environment; whereas hyposensitivity can be viewed as an attempt on the part of children to deal with the problem of overstimulation by cognitively shutting out a physical and social world that is too intense and chaotic.

Kylliäinen and Hietanen (2006) propose that hypersensitivity to visual stimuli also influences social development. Their research suggests that avoidance of eye contact in children with autism occurs because they become anxious when viewing the rapid eye movements of other people. This avoidance of eye contact in turn leads to problems in communication and as well as interferes with the perception of important social stimuli. Relatedly, reciprocal eye contact appears important in the development of children's attachment to their parents during infancy (Kylliäinen & Hietanen, 2006). Relatedly, research by Hilton et al. (2010) indicates that sensory responsiveness predicts social behavior in children with high functioning ASD.

Finally, Baker (2008) hypothesizes that the unusual and sometimes seemingly bizarre behaviors that characterize autism may be caused by a dysfunction in sensory processing. One of these unusual characteristics is stereotypy, which includes behaviors such as object-spinning, hand-flapping, finger flicking, object tapping, rocking, and hand biting. These behaviors may provide the child with autism positive sensory feedback or alternatively allow the child to execute some control and regulation over their sensory environment.

In summary, a wide variety of theories and research suggest that the sensory problems of children with autism may have a profound effect on their development. However, it is less clear what produces these sensory problems in the first place.

Intervention strategies and perspectives

At present, there is no compelling evidence that the sensory problems of children with autism are related to problems in their peripheral sensory structures; however, there are reports in the literature of children with autism having different types of visual and hearing difficulties (Baranek, Parham, & Bodfish, 2005; Carmody, Kaplan, & Gaydos, 2001; Klin, 1993; Milne, Griffiths, Buckley, & Scope, 2009; Rosenhall, Nordin, Sandstrom, Ahlsen, & Gilberg, 1999; Wiggins, Robins, Bakeman, & Adamson, 2009). Available information indicates that the sensory problems of children with autism may be secondary to their problems in other areas, such as in the arousal/activation or self-regulatory systems, the latter of which includes cognitive and language processes, rather than due to basic defects in the sensory system.

If one adopts the perspective that sensory problems are secondary to their problems in other areas, a diverse set of intervention strategies are available for addressing these problems. For example, if sensory problems are conceptualized as being produced by fear/anxiety responses or a state of hyperarousal, the emotion-focused strategies discussed in Chapter 4 for dealing with these responses can be employed to reduce anxiety/hyperarousal and in turn sensory problems. Alternatively, if sensory problems are viewed as resulting from an immature stimulus processing system, habituation procedures and cognitive and language-based interventions that help the individual process and organize incoming stimuli become treatments of choice. A utilitarian approach would suggest that these various types of procedures be sequentially introduced until one that works is found. However, which intervention strategy is chosen often depends on the specific nature of the sensory challenge and information regarding its origin. In the following sections, interventions for dealing with the following sensory problems will be discussed: hypersensitivity, sensory overload, hyposensitivity, and sensory integration deficiencies.

Hypersensitivity

One of the most common sensory characteristics associated with autism is hypersensitivity. A hypersensitive person has a heightened response to certain sensory stimuli (Cascio et al., 2008). For such an individual, even brief exposures to these stimuli may be overstimulating because of the way the sensations are registered (Dodd, 2004). The surge of sensory input triggers heightened physiological arousal and feelings of pain, stress, and fear, although some children may outwardly appear underaroused and possibly hyposensitive (Wetherby & Prizant, 2000). Hypersensitivities in children with autism are displayed to a wide variety of stimuli, including visual, auditory, tactile, olfactory (smell), gustatory (taste), and vestibular inputs.

Although children with hypersensitivities often avoid certain stimuli, they may also search out specific stimuli if they present an enjoyable experience, such as a child who loves to watch spinning objects. Hypersensitivity to visual stimuli is sometimes referred to as seeing the invisible. For example, a child might notice the tiniest flecks of dust floating through the air or the smallest piece of lint on the floor. Stimuli like bright lights may be painful, leading a child to avoid such stimuli and situations associated with this visual stimulation. A common visual hypersensitivity is an overreaction to fluorescent lights (Dodd, 2004). Children with hypersensitivities to visual stimuli appear to have difficulty knowing which visual information is important and which to disregard (Ayres, 2005). As a consequence, they may have difficulties organizing input received from the visual system, including problems tracking, discriminating, and perceiving objects (Dodd, 2004).

Children with autism sometimes display a hypersensitivity to auditory stimuli. For example, they may be easily bothered by noises, even sounds which most individuals would not find alarming. There are two common ways of reacting to oversensitivity to sound. Individuals either learn to adapt to such sounds or they attempt to shut such stimulation off through avoidance or tuning out (O'Neill & Jones, 1997). Individuals with auditory hypersensitivities often appear easily distracted and inattentive (Grandin, 2006).

Children with a hypersensitivity to touch may not be able to tolerate being touched or coming into contact with certain sensory textures; for example they may be oversensitive to rough clothing fabrics. They may also have an increased ability to detect vibrations (Grandin, 2006). Some individuals with autism seek out certain tactile stimuli, such as deep pressure, whereas others avoid tactile experiences such as light touch, which evoke anxiety (Grandin, 2006; Wetherby & Prizant, 2000).

Research also indicates that some children with autism become agitated when they encounter certain tastes and odors (Bennetto, 2007). The combination of these two systems contributes to an overall perception of flavor. It has been suggested that this type of sensory problem may account for why many children with autism eat only certain foods and are unwilling to try new foods.

Individuals with autism may also avoid certain kinds of motor-related activities and vestibular stimulation. Ayres (2005) suggests that children with autism may not be avoiding the movement itself, but the absence of feeling grounded. For example, children may become distressed when they are swinging by themselves, but less anxious when accompanied by another person (Ayres, 2005). For some individuals, an overactive vestibular sensitivity produces motion sickness (Dodd, 2004). These type of sensory problems may account for the impairments in gross and fine motor movements, difficulties in hand–eye coordination, and posture and balance problems of children with autism (Dawson & Watling, 2000).

Several approaches can be employed to reduce hypersensitivity in children with autism.

- One approach focuses on the emotional response associated with the stimulus to which the child is hypersensitive. This approach makes the assumption that hypersensitivity and hyperarousal are opposite sides of the same coin. To state this assumption another way, hypersensitivity is a problem because it is associated with and influenced by hyperarousal. From this perspective emotional arousal, particularly if it is intense, heightens a person's sensitivity to the environment, in effect lowering the threshold of the sensory response. Furthermore, it is assumed that if the child's emotional response to a stimulus to which he/she is hypersensitive can be reduced or eliminated, the child's hypersensitivity will substantially diminish, if not disappear.

If this perspective is adopted, a wide variety of intervention procedures can be employed to reduce hypersensivity. These procedures include three emotion-focused techniques (extinction, desensitization and reciprocal inhibition) and a behavior-focused technique which is directed at decreasing avoidance of stimuli to which the individual is hypersensitive. The reader is referred to Chapter 4, more specifically the section on hyperarousal, for a discussion of these techniques as well as an environmental approach that is directed at removing the offending stimulus without dealing directly with the hypersensitivity problem.

• Another approach for reducing hypersensitivity that is prominently mentioned in the autism literature is habituation. Habituation, which is discussed in Chapter 2, is technically quite similar to extinction and desensitization procedures. Each of these techniques involves exposing the individual to the stimulus to which he/she is hypersensitive. Extinction and desensitization, which are based on learning theory, have been extensively evaluated and validated through both basic and applied research. In contrast, the empirical evidence for habituation, which theoretically is focused on changing the underlying neurological substrate of the individual who is hypersensitive, is not as well developed.

Sensory overload

Sensory overload is a condition that may be connected with hypersensitivity. Sensory overload occurs when an individual is not able to focus on relevant and important aspects of the environment because of an inability to filter out irrelevant aspects of that environment (Dodd, 2004). Whereas hypersensitivity is a term typically employed to describe a response to a specific stimulus within a particular modality, sensory overload occurs as a response to more complex stimulus arrays, such as those that occur in social interactions which involve a multitude of stimuli in dynamic flux. Existing research suggests that sensory overload is caused by too much stimulation (Dodd, 2004). This problem may in turn explain why children with autism often have difficulty attending to more than one stimulus at a time and why they might focus their attention on unimportant details in the environment and tune out other more important aspects of that same environment.

The sensory fixations that some children with autism spectrum disorders display, such as a fascination with spinning objects, may be their way of coping with sensory overload. Relatedly, self-stimulatory behaviors, like rocking, may serve to block out undesirable environmental stimulation, while simultaneously providing soothing stimulation that reduces the hyperarousal that accompanies sensory overload. Similarly, routines, compulsions, and stereotypic behaviors may help the child exert some control over an overwhelming environment (Wetherby

& Prizant, 2000). If such coping responses, however inappropriate, are ineffective, the overload of sensory input may become so overwhelming that a child will physiologically shut down and tune out the environment.

Interventions directed at reducing sensory overload focus on simplifying stimulus input, by reducing the number of stimuli presented and decreasing the rate of presentation of stimuli.

- In teaching situations, simplifying instructional stimuli allows the child more time to process those stimuli. Similarly, slowing down the rate of presentation of stimuli allows the child to focus on important information. Behaviorally oriented educators prefer structured programs because they provide a more controlled educational environment. A highly structured environment typically provides stimulation that is not only simpler, but also less variable and more predictable. This is the major reason why behavioral approaches are introduced into tightly structured situations during the initial stages of an educational program for young children with autism. As the child acquires basic core skills, intervention programs can then be transferred into more naturalistic and complex living and classroom environments.

- More generally, in designing sensory environments, it is important to evaluate the sensory diet of children with autism; specifically to examine the types of stimulation and activities that are sought out as well as the types of stimulation and activities that are avoided. This assessment should focus not only on behavior, but also on the emotional responses of the child to specific sensory inputs. Well-designed interventions emphasize initially the use of preferred types of stimulation and activities. As intervention proceeds less preferred stimuli, including those that are avoided by the child, can be gradually embedded into a context of desirable stimuli. From a classical learning theory perspective, stimuli that are initially less desirable become more positive through their association with preferred stimuli. Evaluation of a child's sensory diet can also provide useful information for identifying reinforcers that will be pleasing to the child and serve to motivate learning.

Sensory diet, as it is described here, is not so much a treatment but rather a strategy for developing a specific treatment. As originally discussed by Wilbarger and Wilbarger (1991), it refers to the type and amount of sensory input received by an individual. An ideal sensory diet is one that helps the child maintain a level of alertness, emotional calmness, and effective performance. In order to expand a child's sensory diet, while maintaining effective functioning, challenging tasks are interwoven with activities that are satisfying; that is challenging activities are gradually introduced in a way that allows the child to maintain an optimal level of arousal. Sequencing of activities is important. Activities that precede challenging events, as well as activities that occur during and after such events, are critical to the design of an effective sensory intervention program.

In addition, to prevent sensory overload, children can be taught to monitor and self-regulate their arousal level (Williams & Shellenberger, 1996). A prime example of this self-regulation technique is the use of the squeeze machine by Temple Grandin for reducing her anxiety level (Grandin, 1995). The use of deep pressure, as well as the Wilbarger brushing protocol (Wilbarger & Wilbarger, 1991), can be introduced by others or self-introduced by the child, before, during, and/or after challenging activities. Some behavioral programs also use a child's stereotypies as an allowed activity after engaging in challenging tasks. This type of access to stereotypies can serve not only as a reward for good performance, but also as a response to maintain optimal arousal.

Hyposensitivity

Hyposensitivity is another sensory problem associated with autism. For example, some children display reduced sensitivity to pain, cold, and/or loud sounds. Hyposensitive children seem to require a more intense sensory input to experience stimulation. These children often display a low state of arousal and do not notice or at least do not pay attention to their immediate environment. It has been hypothesized that children with hyposensitivities may engage in behaviors, such as repetitively spinning in circles, in order to activate sensations of which they have been deprived (O'Neill & Jones, 1997). When the sensory input is lowered, these individuals may become oblivious to their environment, and their state of arousal may continue to decrease (Wetherby & Prizant, 2000). They may devote their attention to a specific detail in the environment or their attention may become completely unfocused. An alternative hypothesis regarding the origins of hyposensitivity is that, rather than being produced by understimulation, it is, at least sometimes, a response to being overstimulated by the environment.

The approach taken to reducing hyposensitivity varies depending on the child's unique history and the theory adopted to explain the origins of this symptom. Three such theories and intervention strategies based on them include the following:

- For example, if hyposensitivity is conceptualized as a response to a state of sensory overload and hyperarousal, in which the child shuts down and tunes out the environment that is too chaotic and painful, several intervention strategies might be employed. These strategies include: reducing the amount and rate of sensory input, removing the child from a challenging situation to a less demanding environment, reducing the child's level of arousal through use of desensitization and reciprocal inhibition procedures (see Chapter 4), and/or instituting cognitive training procedures directed at helping the child organize their sensory input. Depending upon the child's stage of development, one or more of these procedures might be profitably employed.

- In contrast, if hyposensitivity is viewed as resulting from a state of hypoarousal and limited sensory input, then procedures that focus on increasing the child's arousal level through stimulating activities would be appropriate. Such intervention strategies might include engaging the child in vigorous motor activities that the child finds enjoyable, such as jumping on a trampoline or rough and tumble play, or increasing the intensity of the stimulation which the child ignores, for example speaking louder and with greater animation. Theoretically, it is predicted that such activities will produce a more optimal level of arousal that in turn will help the child orient and attend to the environment to which he/she has been previously oblivious.

- Another theoretical perspective suggests that hyposensitivity may be a function of a child's restricted cognitive orientation to the environment. From this perspective, a sensory fixation on one particular stimulus or set of stimuli inhibits attention to other important stimuli. For example, a child's attention to people may be inhibited if he/she is preoccupied with watching visual images in a computer game. If this theoretical perspective is adopted, intervention strategies might be directed at removing the source of a child's fixation (the computer game), for example by turning the computer off, and/or by redirecting the child's attention, for example to a person speaking to him. This attentional redirection might be accompanied by moving the child's head gently toward the speaker or the speaker could step in front of the computer in order to break the child's fixation.

A related perspective on hyposensitivity as well as hypersensitivity views these disorders as part of a larger sensory integration problem.

Sensory integration problems

The senses provide children with information about the world that surrounds them. During sensory integration, stimuli are received, organized, interpreted, and used to guide behavior. Sensory integration is viewed both as a response that is neurologically based and also as a process that influences the developing neurological structures of the brain. The senses help children to become aware of their environment and prepare them for action. In order for information to be received, the brain must be aroused into an alert state and the body prepared for action. As specific stimuli are repeatedly encountered, the brain habituates or accommodates to these stimuli, thus freeing up its attentional processes for new stimuli (Berk, 2009; Whitman, 2004). Although the senses are often discussed in isolation, information from the various senses needs to be integrated in order for an adaptive response to occur.

Problems occur if the sensory system is not able to register input from the environment and mobilize action. Children who do not register incoming stimulation may either not react at all and/or engage in actions in order to increase the intensity of stimulation. Children who are overly sensitive to certain types of stimulation may become disorganized, show disruptions in their behavior and sometimes initiate responses designed directly to reduce stimulation or to avoid the context in which the stimulation occurs.

Sensory integration therapies have been developed to assist children who have problems of either poor registration and/or oversensitivity; problems which in turn can lead to deficiencies in the processing, organization, analysis, and retention of sensory information. For children who have poor registration of stimuli, therapeutic procedures introduce stimuli that vary in level of intensity, rate of presentation, duration, contrast, points of contact, and/or predictability to enhance functioning. The ultimate goal is to develop in the child an optimal level of alertness and activation as he/she confronts specific stimulus inputs. For children who are overly sensitive to specific stimulus inputs, therapy generally focuses on gradually introducing these stimuli in a way to facilitate habituation and/or prevent stimulus overload (Whitman, 2004). Sensory integration therapies, while sometimes focusing on one specific modality (auditory, visual, touch, taste, smell, vestibular, or proprioception), typically involve other modalities. These therapies are holistic and involve the entire body, including all the senses and the motor system.

Although sensory integration therapy is typically viewed as being a subspecialty of occupational therapy that focuses on helping individuals perform purposeful activities, it often involves procedures derived from other disciplines and specialties. In practice, sensory integration therapy is not one therapeutic procedure but many different procedures with different theoretical underpinnings. For further information on the sensory integration approach, the reader is referred to Cook and Dunn (1998) and Schneck (2001).

Unfortunately, many of the sensory integration therapies that have been developed and heavily utilized have not been subject to rigorous empirical scrutiny. Such treatment intervention research is important, not only to validate the efficacy of these therapies, but also to refine them. Research that has been conducted on these therapies has often yielded mixed or no support regarding their efficacy; this is particularly the case for auditory integration therapies (Whitman, 2004). Techniques for promoting sensory integration that have been validated are, however, available.

In the remainder of this section, we outline a behavioral approach, based on both basic and applied research in the areas of learning and cognition, for promoting sensory integration. To exemplify, we refer to tasks that require children to utilize multiple attributes within a single sensory modality as well as across different sensory modalities for task completion. Initially, the strategy employed in this approach requires the child to learn very simple discrimination tasks, involving a single cue from a single sensory modality. Once the child learns to perform such tasks, the complexity of the discrimination task presented is gradually increased, with the child being required to utilize two and then three cues from a single sensory modality and then to utilize cues from several sensory modalities for task completion.

- For example, a child might initially be required to select a card with a blue circle on it when presented with two cards, one of which has a blue circle on it and the other a red circle. After learning this discrimination task, the child is then presented other similar discrimination tasks requiring the child to select a green or a red circle. This discrimination task is then increased slightly in complexity by requiring the child to select a particular colored circle from three rather than two cards with three different colored circles, then four, and so on. A similar progression of simple discrimination tasks can then be introduced using other modalities, for example employing auditory (soft, loud), tactile (smooth, rough), or taste (sour, sweet) cues.

- After learning such relatively simple discrimination tasks, the complexity of the discrimination task is increased further, with the child now being required to utilize more than one attribute from a modality. For example, the child might be asked to find a small red circle from a set of cards that have circles of various sizes and colors. Task complexity can be further increased by adding other visual attributes; for example the child is asked to find the card with two small red circles.

- In addition to the discrimination tasks involving attributes from a single modality (e.g. visual), cross-modality discrimination tasks can be introduced that require the child to utilize cues from different modalities, for example a task involving tactile and visual cues, such as finding a soft ball from a group of other hard and soft objects.

- Eventually, common objects from everyday living environments can be employed. For example, the child might be asked to find foods that are of a particular size, color, and/or hardness or have a particular taste and/or smell.

In the next section, we present other examples of interventions for helping children with autism with their sensory problems and in Chapter 6 discuss techniques for helping children integrate sensory and motor cues.

Program examples

Reducing sensory overload

OBJECTIVE

Teach the child to attend to relevant stimuli in an overstimulating environment.

PROCEDURE

1. Start by removing as many different stimuli from the environment as possible.

2. If you are in a work-type environment (e.g. school), present work tasks in this less stimulating environment. For example, remove the lights, sounds, and visual stimuli by placing the child in a separate room with the lights off.

3. Work with the child in this less stimulating environment until the child shows improvement in the work tasks.

4. Gradually add in the removed stimuli one at a time, adding an additional stimulus when the child shows improvement in the presence of each new stimulus. For example, turn on some low music while working. Once the child has shown continued progress in work tasks with the music on, add posters on the walls. Then perhaps turn on one of the lights, or bring another child into the room to work in the same environment.

5. Eventually graduate the child to the original location.

TIPS/SUGGESTIONS

It may be helpful to first assess which types of stimuli the child seems to prefer and which types he/she tends to avoid. This way you can use preferred stimuli as reinforcers for tolerating non-preferred stimuli in short amounts.

In addition, teach the child an appropriate method of communication to allow him/her to request a break or removal of aversive stimulation.

OTHER TEACHING METHODS

Some children may benefit from learning how to rate their level of anxiety or stimulus overload on a scale. Depending on their rating, they can implement learned calming techniques to reduce the level of anxiety or arousal. Example calming techniques may include deep breathing, muscle relaxation, squeezing a stress ball, asking for headphones, asking to leave the situation, or listening to music.

In addition, the child may express some subtle signs that he/she is beginning to struggle with sensory overload. For example, the child may start rocking or repeating a specific sound. Become aware of these individual, subtle signs and use them as an opportunity to teach the child to request a break before he/she is completely overwhelmed.

Sensory integration: simple visual discrimination tasks

OBJECTIVE

Teach the child to independently identify an item based on a visual description, when that item is in an array of several similar items.

MATERIALS

For this procedure, you will need materials that are similar in all visual characteristics (e.g. size, shape, color) other than one (e.g. same-sized circles of different colors). Also, it will be helpful to have multiple sets of such objects (e.g. same-sized bears of different colors, same-sized circles of different colors, same-sized blocks of different colors). Focus on teaching at least two targets at a time (e.g. the colors blue and red) before moving on to other targets from the list.

PROCEDURE

1. Place three objects from a set on the table in front of the student (e.g. a blue bear, a red bear, and a yellow bear).

2. Be sure the child is attending to the objects.

3. Provide an instruction (e.g. "Show me blue."). Prompt the child as necessary to help him/her respond correctly.

4. If the child responds correctly, provide specific praise (e.g. "You're right, that's blue!") as well as a tangible/edible reinforcer.

5. Repeat with a different set of objects and/or a different description (e.g. red).

6. Rotate the order of the objects and the materials being used, as well as the instruction (e.g. first ask for blue, then red, then mix up the objects and ask for red again, then use different objects and ask for blue, etc.).

7. Fade prompts across trials.

8. Continue until five to ten trials of each target description have been presented.

9. Once the child has demonstrated mastery of the two targets (e.g. red and blue), introduce a third target (e.g. green). Have at least three objects present at all times. Continue to ask for the mastered targets occasionally.

10. Continue in this pattern, introducing one more target each time he/she demonstrates mastery.

Error correction

If the child makes an error (e.g. picks up the yellow when asked to find the blue item), remove the items for 1 to 3 seconds. Re-present the same items, in the same order, and give the same instruction, but immediately prompt the child to respond correctly (i.e. before the child makes the same error). Provide praise, but do not provide a tangible reinforcer following error correction.

Generalization

Once the child has demonstrated mastery of two to three target descriptors (e.g. blue, red, and green), test them with other objects (i.e. objects not used during training). For example, when coloring a picture, place a blue, red, and green crayon in front of the child and ask him/her to color the picture green.

Tips/suggestions

This same procedure can be used to teach visual discrimination along other dimensions, such as size (e.g. big, tall, small, little, wide, long, short) as well as shape (e.g. circle, square, rectangle) and any other visual descriptions. It can also be used to teach discrimination of other senses, such as tactile (e.g. smooth, rough, hard, soft), taste (e.g. sweet, sour, salty), or auditory (e.g. loud or quiet).

Troubleshooting

If the child continues to make errors, be sure he/she is attending to the objects. You may need to teach the child to attend to objects prior to attempting this procedure. Also, using most-to-least prompting may help avoid errors, and thus increase skill acquisition, especially in the beginning phases of this procedure.

Other teaching methods

Sensory integration therapy is another method used to help children integrate input from several different stimuli or from several of the senses.

FUTURE OBJECTIVES

Teach the child more complex discriminations that require attention to more than one dimension. For example, ask the child to find the big yellow circle, or the short red crayon. Move on to common, everyday stimuli (e.g. foods, dishes, clothing) and perform this procedure in the appropriate environment (e.g. if using foods as the stimuli, do this in the kitchen).

Sensory integration: complex discrimination (single-modality)

OBJECTIVE

Teach the child to independently identify an item based on a complex description that requires attention to more than one characteristic, when that item is in an array of several similar items.

PREREQUISITES

The child must already be able to discriminate various objects using a single modality (e.g. sight, touch, taste, sound, or smell) and when given a simple description of that object when it is in an array of several similar objects (e.g. discriminating the red circle when it is among several same-sized circles of various colors).

MATERIALS

For this procedure, you will need several materials that are similar in all visual characteristics (e.g. size, shape, color) other than two (e.g. circles that are different colors and different sizes, or a variety of same-sized shapes of different colors). Also, it will be helpful to have multiple sets of such objects (e.g. animals, shapes, blocks, etc.).

Focus on teaching at least four different descriptions at one time (e.g. blue, red, small, big), and mix up the order and pairing of the descriptions (e.g. small blue, big blue, small red, big red) before moving on to other targets from the list. The targets you choose should be targets the child has already mastered in the basic discrimination procedure (e.g. if you are choosing size and color, the child should already be able to discriminate big vs. little, and red vs. blue, etc.).

PROCEDURE

1. Place four objects from a set on the table in front of the child. Be sure to include an opposite for each object you place in the array so the child must attend to both characteristics of your description. For example, place a big blue square, small blue square, big red square, and small red square on the table.

2. Have the child attend to the objects.

3. Provide an instruction describing two characteristics (e.g. "Show me the small blue square."). Prompt the child as necessary to help him/her respond correctly.

4. If the child responds correctly, provide specific praise (e.g. "You're right, that's the small blue one!") as well as a tangible/edible reinforcer.

5. Repeat with a different set of objects and/or a different description (e.g. big red).

6. Rotate the order of the objects and the materials being used, as well as the instruction (e.g. first ask for "small blue," then "big red," then mix up the objects and ask for "small red," then use different objects and ask for "big blue").

7. Fade prompts across trials.

8. Continue until five to ten trials of each target description have been presented.

9. Once the child has demonstrated mastery of the four descriptors, introduce a different description (e.g. "long blue" or "short red") as well as additional colors and shapes. Continue to ask for the mastered targets occasionally.

10. Continue in this pattern, introducing one new target each time the child demonstrates mastery.

ERROR CORRECTION

If the child makes an error (e.g. picks up the big yellow when asked to find the small yellow item), remove the items for 1 to 3 seconds. Re-present the same items, in the same order, and give the same instruction, but prompt immediately with the correct response (i.e. before the child makes the same error). You can provide praise, but do not provide a tangible reinforcer following error correction.

GENERALIZATION

Once the child has demonstrated mastery of two to three target descriptors (e.g. color and size, size and shape, shape and color) test other objects (i.e. objects not used during training). For example, when coloring a picture, place a blue, red, and green crayon as well as a blue, red, and green marker in front of the child and ask him/her to color the picture with a green crayon, or a blue marker.

TIPS/SUGGESTIONS

This same procedure can also be used to teach discrimination of combinations of other senses, such as tactile (e.g. smooth, rough, hard, soft), taste (e.g. sweet, sour, salty), or auditory (e.g. loud, quiet).

TROUBLESHOOTING

If the child continues to make errors, be sure he/she is attending to the objects. You may need to teach the child to attend to objects prior to attempting this procedure. Also, using most-to-least prompting may help avoid errors, and thus increase skill acquisition, especially in the beginning phases of this procedure.

FUTURE OBJECTIVES

Teach the child more complex discriminations that require the use of more than one sensory modality (e.g. visual and tactile). For example, ask the child to find the hard red square or the big soft square (use felt and wood or tile and help the child to feel the items). Create scavenger hunts that require the child to search the toy box for a long thin Lego, raid the cupboards looking for the long yellow fruit, or search the backyard for the tall yellow flower.

Sensory fixations

OBJECTIVE

Redirect the child's attention away from objects/stimuli of fixation.

MATERIALS

For this procedure, gather highly preferred reinforcers. Ideally, choose items that share common characteristics to the stimuli with which the child is fixated. For example, if the child is fixated by falling objects (e.g. he/she picks up grass and watches it fall), consider bubbles as an appropriate alternative. You may also want to use a timer for this procedure.

PROCEDURE

1. Determine if the object of fixation is inappropriate due to the object itself (or the child's behavior when he/she is engaged with the object) or because of the amount of time the child spends with the object.

2. If the object or behavior itself is disrupting daily functioning, consider removing the object completely and replacing it with something similar but more appropriate. This may need to be a gradual process. For example, if a teenage child loves to watch preschool-age television shows, slowly start exposing the child to more age-appropriate television shows (e.g. Funniest Home Videos). Allow the child to access the former shows contingent on watching the new shows for x amount of minutes. Or, if the child watches the same scene in a movie repeatedly, require him/her to watch the entire movie, or disable the rewind/fast forward buttons.

3. If the fixation is problematic due to the amount of time the child spends engaged with the object/activity, consider setting time limits. Use a visual timer to help the child recognize how much time he/she has left to spend with the object. In the beginning, you will need to provide an alternate reinforcer to the child when he/she steps away from the object/activity. Start with a lot of time allotted to the child; base the time on how much he/she already spends with the object and choose a time very close to that. For example, if the child plays a computer game for 3 hours a night, start the timer at 2 hours and 55 minutes. Slowly decrease the amount of time he/she can spend on the computer (e.g. by 3 to 5 minutes each time).

ERROR CORRECTION

If the child does not end the activity when instructed to do so, use prompting to help the child. Be sure to deliver reinforcers once the child has stopped engaging with the activity.

TIPS/SUGGESTIONS

It is important to note that simply removing the object/activity without a decent replacement will not solve this problem. The child will likely find another object to fixate on, or he/she may exhibit challenging behavior in search of the original object.

OTHER TEACHING METHODS

Teach your child how to play appropriately with the object of fascination. For example, if the child is fixated on the visual images in a computer game, teach him/her to actually play the game, rather than to simply watch the images. Remember that additional reinforcers will be necessary to help the child learn such a skill.

References

Anzalone, M. E. & Williamson, G. G. (2000). "Sensory processing and motor performance in autism spectrum disorders." In A. M. Wetherby & B. M. Prizant (Eds.), *Autism spectrum disorders* (pp. 143–166). Baltimore, MD: Brooks Publishing Co.

Ayres, A. J. (2005). *Sensory integration and the child: Understanding hidden sensory challenges.* Los Angeles, CA: Western Psychological Services.

Baker, A. E. (2008). The relationship between sensory processing patterns and behavioral responsiveness in autistic disorder: A pilot study. *Journal of Autism & Developmental Disorders, 38,* 867–875.

Baranek, G. T., Parham, L. D., & Bodfish, J. W. (2005). "Sensory and motor features in autism: Assessment and intervention." In F. R. Volkmar, R. Paul, A. Klin, & D. Cohen (Eds.), *Handbook of autism and pervasive developmental disorders: Vol 2, Assessment, interventions, and policy* (3rd ed., pp. 831–857). Hoboken, NJ: Wiley & Sons.

Bennetto, L. (2007). Olfaction and taste processing in autism. *Biological Psychiatry, 62,* 1015–1021.

Berk, L. E. (2009). *Child development* (8th ed.). Boston, MA: Allyn Bacon.

Carmody, D., Kaplan, M., & Gaydos, A. (2001). Spatial orientation adjustments in child with autism in Hong Kong. *Child Psychiatry and Human Development, 31,* 233–247.

Cascio, C., McGlone, F., Folger, S., Tannan, V., Baranek, G., Pelphrey, K. A., & Essick, G. (2008). Tactile perception in adults with autism: A multidimensional psychophysical study. *Journal of Autism and Developmental Disorders, 38,* 127–137.

Cook, D. & Dunn. W. (1998). "Sensory integration for students with autism." In R. Simpson & B. Myles (Eds.), *Educating children and youth with autism* (pp. 191–240). Austin, TX: Pro-Ed.

Dawson, G. & Watling, R. (2000). Interventions to facilitate auditory, visual, and motor integration in autism: A review of evidence. *Journal of Autism and Developmental Disorders, 30,* 415–421.

Dodd, S. (2004). *Understanding autism.* Sydney, Australia: Elsevier.

Dunn, W. (1997). The impact of sensory processing on the daily lives of young children and their families: A conceptual model. *Infants and Young Children, 9*(4), 23–35.

Ermer, J. & Dunn, W. (1998). The sensory profile: A discriminate analysis of children with and without disabilities. *American Journal of Occupational Therapy, 52*(4), 283–290.

Gepner, B. & Mestre, D. (2002). Brief report: Postural reactivity to fast visual motion differentiates autistic children from children with Asperger Syndrome. *Journal of Autism and Developmental Disorders, 12,* 231–238.

Gillberg, C. & Coleman, M. (1992). *The biology of autistic syndromes* (2nd ed.). London: McKeith Press.

Grandin, T. (1995). *Thinking in pictures.* New York, NY: Vintage Books.

Grandin, T. (2006). *Thinking in pictures: My life with autism.* New York, NY: Vintage Books.

Harrison, J. & Hare, D. J. (2004). Brief report: Assessment of sensory abnormalities in people with autistic spectrum disorders. *Journal of Autism and Developmental Disorders, 34,* 727–730.

Hilton, C. L., Harper, J. D., Kueker, R. H., Lang, A. R., Abbacchi, A. M., Todorov, A., & LaVesser, P. D. (2010). Sensory responsiveness as a predictor of social severity in children with high functioning autism spectrum disorders. *Journal of Autism and Developmental Disorders, 40,* 937–945.

Huebner, R. A. (2001). *Autism: A sensorimotor approach in management.* Gaithersburg, MD: Aspen.

Klin, A. (1993). Auditory brainstem responses in autism: Brainstem dysfunction or peripheral hearing loss. *Journal of Autism and Developmental Disorders, 23,* 15–35.

Kylliäinen, A., & Hietanen, K. (2006). Skin conductance responses to another person's gaze in children with autism. *Journal of Autism and Developmental Disorders, 26,* 517–525.

Lane, A. E., Young, R. L., Baker, A. E., & Angley, M. T. (2010). Sensory processing subtypes in autism: Association with adaptive behavior. *Journal of Autism and Developmental Disorders, 40,* 112–122.

Lightfoot, C., Cole, M., & Cole, S. (2009). *The development of children* (6th ed.). Worth, IL: Worth Publishing.

Maurer, D. & Maurer, C. (1988). *The world of the newborn.* New York: Basic Books.

Milne, E., Griffiths, H., Buckley, D., & Scope, A. (2009). Vision in children and adolescents with autistic spectrum disorder: Evidence for reduced convergence. *Journal of Autism and Developmental Disorders, 39,* 965–975.

O'Neill, M. & Jones, R. S. P. (1997). Sensory-perceptual abnormalities in autism: A case for more research? *Journal of Autism and Developmental Disorders, 27*(3), 283–293.

Ornitz, E. (1983). The functional neuroanatomy of infantile autism. *International Journal of Neuroscience, 19,* 85-124.

Paris, B. (2000). "Characteristics of autism." In C. Murray-Slutsky & B. Paris (Eds.), *Exploring the spectrum of autism and pervasive developmental disorders* (pp. 7–23). San Antonio, TX: Therapy Skill Builders (Harcourt Health Sciences).

Rogers, S. J., Hepburn, S., & Wehner, E. (2003). Parent reports of sensory symptoms in toddlers with autism and those with other developmental disorders. *Journal of Autism and Developmental Disorders, 33,* 631–642.

Rosenhall, U., Nordin, V., Sandstrom, M., Ahlsen, G., & Gilberg, C. (1999). Autism and hearing loss. *Journal of Autism and Developmental Disorders, 29,* 349–357.

Schneck, C. (2001). "The efficacy of a sensorimotor treatment approach by occupational therapists." In R. Huebner (Ed.), *Autism: A sensorimotor approach to management* (pp. 139–178). Gaithersburg, MD: Aspen.

Wetherby, A. M. & Prizant, B. M. (2000). *Autism spectrum disorders.* Baltimore, MD: Paul H. Brookes Publishing.

Whitman, T. L. (2004). *The development of autism: A self-regulatory perspective.* London: Jessica Kingsley Publishers.

Wiggins, L. D., Robins, D. L., Bakeman, R., & Adamson, L. B. (2009). Brief report: Sensory abnormalities as distinguishing symptoms of autism spectrum disorders in young children. *Journal of Autism and Developmental Disorders, 39,* 1087–1091.

Wilbarger, P. & Wilbarger, J. L. (1991). *Sensory defensiveness in children aged 2–12.* Denver, CO: Avanti Educational Programs.

Williams, D. (1992). *Nobody nowhere.* New York, NY: Doubleday. (Republished 1999, London: Jessica Kingsley Publishers.)

Williams, M. & Shellenberger, S. (1996). *How does your engine run? A teacher's guide to the Alert Program for self-regulation.* Albuquerque, NM: Therapy Works.

Chapter 6

Sensorimotor Deficiencies

Motor impairments have been widely observed in children with autism spectrum disorders. Because of the critical impact that the sensory system has on motor development, motor behaviors are often referred to as sensorimotor behaviors. Although these impairments are not a part of the formal diagnosis of autism, their impact on overall development is generally acknowledged. The range of sensorimotor impairments that have been associated with autism spectrum disorders is quite broad and include both delays and deficiencies in gross motor behaviors, such as crawling, walking, and running, and fine motor behaviors, such as shoe-tying and writing.

The organization and structure of motor development

As infants' muscles develop and their nervous system matures, they acquire progressively more complex motor skills. Motor control of the body proceeds in a cephalocaudal fashion, that is head control emerges first, followed by control of the arms, trunk and finally the legs. Motor development also proceeds in a proxomodistal fashion from the center of body outward; control of the head and trunk occurs before control of the extremities, such as the hands and fingers. Although environmental restrictions can produce developmental delays, early motor development appears to be mostly a function of genetically influenced maturational patterns. As development proceeds and motor actions become increasingly complex, the impact of the social environment on motor development becomes progressively more important.

Major milestones of development are marked as infants master new motor skills. During early development, gross motor skills emerge, including lifting self by arms, grasping, rolling from back to side and eventually sitting, crawling, and walking. With each new achievement in this realm, infants are able to interact in new ways with their surrounding physical and social environment. Gradually, motor skills become more refined as children learn to walk up stairs, run, jump, and build with blocks. Complex motor skills are acquired as children learn to put a sequence of actions together, enabling them to perform activities, such as eating, bathing, toothbrushing, and dressing, and sports activities, such as soccer, baseball, basketball, and gymnastics. Delays in motor development, like those observed in children with autism, can have adverse effects on the overall development of the child and result in deficiencies in areas such as language and social interaction. For more information regarding motor development in neurotypical children, the reader is referred to Berk (2009) and Lightfoot, Cole, and Cole (2009).

Motor characteristics of individuals with autism spectrum disorders

From a developmental perspective, parents, clinicians, and researchers have noted that children, later diagnosed with autism, display problems in self-feeding, dressing, and general manual dexterity. Delays in meeting the major motor milestones and developing fundamental movement skills also sometimes occur (Pan, Tsai, & Chu, 2009; Teitelbaum, Teitelbaum, Nye, Fryman, & Mauer, 1998). Results of a study by Baranek (1999) are intriguing in that they suggest that motor as well as sensory problems are present in children with autism when they are 9–12 months old and that these problems might be used in conjunction with social and language deficiencies to distinguish young children with autism from typically developing children.

Motor problems have also been mentioned as one of the key characteristics of individuals with Asperger Syndrome (AS). For example, Gillberg (1989) found that 83 percent of the individuals with this disorder have relatively poor motor skills; in particular he noted that they were generally clumsy and had an awkward way of walking that has been described as rapid and arrhythmic. Other motor problems that have been noted include difficulties in throwing and catching a ball, problems with balance, and difficulties in tying shoelaces and with handwriting (Attwood, 1998).

Whereas motor problems are viewed as an important feature of AS, children with autism have sometimes been portrayed as displaying normal motor development and even possessing special competencies in this domain. However, as already indicated, a variety of research challenges this perspective and suggests that children with autism have at least as high an incidence of motor problems as children with AS (Jansiewicz et al., 2006; Manjiviona & Prior, 1995; Rinehardt, Bradshaw, Brereton, & Tonge, 2001).

In a review of research, Smith (2004) evaluated the claim that motor problems are characteristics of specific subgroups within the autism spectrum. After examining motor skills in individuals with high functioning autism (HFA) and

AS, she concluded that an AS–HFA distinction does not hold up in the motor domain. It is still possible that motor abilities may vary across other portions of the autism spectrum, e.g. between individuals with HFA and those with lower functioning autism (LFA). Support for such a relationship is provided by Baranek, Parham, and Bodfish (2005), who summarized evidence suggesting that cognitively advantaged individuals are more motorically competent than less cognitively advantaged individuals.

Although motor problems have frequently been observed in populations with autism spectrum disorders, they are certainly not unique to these disorders. Children with a variety of other developmental problems, such as mental retardation and attention deficit disorder, also exhibit an array of motor symptoms. There is, however, evidence that specific motor difficulties may be distinctively associated with autism, such as imitation deficits (Baranek et al., 2005; Williams, Whiten, & Singh, 2004).

Motor symptoms can be conceptualized as falling into two categories, involuntary and voluntary. Involuntary motor behaviors are reflexive and non-intentional, but nevertheless serve an adaptive function. Although little is known about the developmental course of involuntary movement problems in children with ASD, there is evidence that this type of motor response is negatively related to IQ and co-morbid with mental retardation (Baranek et al., 2005). In contrast, voluntary motor behaviors include a cognitive and intentional component. After reviewing research on voluntary movements, Baranek et al. (2005) suggested that children with autism have particular problems performing non-repetitive gross and fine motor tasks that include complex and novel features. More recently research has indicated that individuals with autism have problems reprogramming already planned movements (Nazarali, Glazebrook, & Elliott, 2009) and coordinating movements involving both sides of their body (Staples & Reid, 2010).

Little is known about the specific processes that influence motor behavior. It is not clear whether the early occurring motor problems associated with autism are a function of defects in the motor system, the arousal/activation system, the sensory system, or a combination of these and other defects. For example, it is possible that during infancy early stress and associated sensory problems lead to disorganized motor behavior. In turn, motor problems may restrict the availability of motor coping resources available for dealing with stress, which then further exacerbates the child's emotional and sensory problems (Als, 1982).

As mentioned in the last chapter, children with autism spectrum disorders have difficulties registering sensory inputs and utilizing sensory data as they interact with their environment. They commonly display problems in orienting responses, filtering incoming stimulation, habituating to stimulation, and processing and interpreting sensory information—particularly information that is complex and requires integration from multiple modalities. Thus, it should not be surprising that children with ASD have problems using sensory information to guide motor action.

Some research has suggested that motor dysfunction in autism is related to motor planning problems, including dyspraxia (Rinehardt et al., 2001). Motor planning is a complex process which requires conscious attention and effort (Paris, 2000). Dyspraxia, a common problem in children with autism, refers to difficulties in formulating a goal, figuring out how to accomplish a goal, and executing an action; steps that obviously have a strong cognitive as well as a motor component. Children with dyspraxia find it particularly difficult to learn new tasks (Huebner, 2001).

Another theory regarding motor problems in children with autism is that these problems are simply a function of a developmental immaturity. This immaturity may not only be biological in nature, but also related to the restricted interactions that children with autism have with their environment. For example, children with autism, like younger developing typical children, have been found to display a high frequency of ambiguous or inconsistent handedness. Children with this characteristic often switch hands when engaging in a task. Eventually, however, as these children mature, one of their hands usually becomes dominant (Hauck & Dewey, 2001).

Although the relationships between motor functioning and development in other areas, including cognitive functioning, speech acquisition, socioemotional behavior, and self-regulatory behavior, have been of interest to autism researchers, the importance of these relationships is only beginning to be studied (Baranek et al., 2005). Motor development has long been proposed as playing a critical early role in the development of the cognitive system (Piaget, 1970). Children's perception of the world changes dramatically as locomotion increases (Smith & Thelen, 1993). From a sensory and cognitive perspective, a motorically advanced child not only comes into more contact with the environment, but is also able to explore more fully that environment through active manipulation. Evidence of the close interrelationship between motor and cognitive development also comes from neurological research examining the co-activations of the neocerebellum and the dorsolateral prefrontal cortex (Diamond, 2000).

The motor system also likely plays a critical role in social development through its influence on the acquisition of motorically based language skills and social behaviors. Delays in the motor arena not only hamper the development of skills necessary for social interaction, such as those involved in early play and leisure activities, but also mark children as different, as a consequence stigmatizing them. Most of the proposed relationships between motor development and functioning in other domains need to be systematically examined in children with autism spectrum disorders.

In summary, research indicates that children with autism spectrum disorders have a variety of motor delays and problems. Less is known about the impact of these motor delays and problems on their overall development. It is evident, however, that both gross and fine motor skill deficiencies and motor planning problems can, and often do, greatly restrict the ways these children learn and interact with their environment.

Intervention approaches

In this section, two contrasting approaches for remediating sensorimotor deficiencies are described: sensorimotor therapies and behavior intervention. Whereas the first approach is more biological in orientation, and directed at developing broader sensory and motor competencies, the second approach is focused on developing specific sensorimotor skills.

Sensorimotor therapies

Sensorimotor therapies are commonly employed by occupational and physical therapists in their work with children with autism. Occupational therapy focuses on the development of fine and gross motor skills and the reduction of sensory processing problems. Occupational therapists are found in a variety of settings including hospitals, schools, and private clinics. Occupational therapy bears many similarities to physical therapy, but differs in its emphasis on helping an individual to function in their everyday environment. In contrast, physical therapy is directed at developing or retraining general mobility and is likely to focus on gross motor problems, low muscle tone, gait problems, and strength deficits.

Different general sensorimotor approaches have been identified by Schneck (2001). One approach involves the use of sensory stimulation to elicit appropriate motor responses. Treatment can include more passive procedures, which involve the therapist guiding an individual's movement, or more active procedures, which integrate the child into activities that provide specific sensory inputs and require certain movements. In contrast, a second approach gradually introduces challenging sensory input for the purpose of helping individuals to adapt to that input. Unlike the first approach, it is not typically applied in the context of a goal-directed activity. Finally, a third approach is directed at organizing sensory input for the individual when sensory processing deficits lead to problems in adaptive responding; the goal being to improve the way the sensory system integrates and uses sensory input. It contrasts with the other approaches in that it is more individualized, often involves the active participation of the child, and typically uses a variety of equipment. In addition to the therapies mentioned, there are a variety of sensorimotor programs developed for children with autism spectrum disorders that emphasize physical activity, physical exercise, movement, and sports activities, such as Daily Life Therapy (Kitahara, 1983/1984).

Although disturbances can occur in any of the senses, sensorimotor integration programs emphasize exercises that promote motor development through affecting three systems: the tactile (a system based on the skin surface and the nerves that serve it), the proprioceptive (a system based in the muscle joints and ligaments that provides information about where the body is in space), and the vestibular (a system, based mostly in the inner ear, that influences body movement and balance). Ayres (1979), in what has become a classic work, *Sensory Integration and the Child*, outlines a variety of therapeutic activities that are designed to promote overall sensory integration; many of these activities involve the use of equipment-based exercises.

One such activity employs a scooter board, a board mounted on four wheels that allows movement in any direction. Typically, the child lies on the scooter in a prone position and engages in a variety of activities, such as spinning and riding down a ramp, which are designed to provide a complex array of sensory inputs. A second piece of equipment frequently utilized in sensorimotor integration therapy is a bolster swing. The swing consists of a core with padding and a cover that is around 6 feet (180 cm) in length and 3 feet (90 cm) in circumference. Ropes attach the swing to an overhead hook. The child sits or lies on the core and swings back and forth. Various activities, such as picking up objects from the floor while the bolster is moving, provide the child with a variety of vestibular, proprioceptive, and tactual inputs, as well as other types of stimulation. Ayres (1979) points out that one of the prime purposes of these activities is to develop an inner sense of direction and locus of control during interactions with the environment in order to generate a sense of self-confidence and mastery.

A variety of other sensorimotor techniques have also been used by therapists. For example, to address problems of tactile oversensitivity, techniques that involve the handling of different textured materials, deep pressure (e.g. hugs and massage) and habituation (gradual introduction of materials that produce unpleasant sensations) have been employed. For proprioceptive problems, jumping on a trampoline and joint-compression have been used. For vestibular problems, techniques, such as walking on a balance beam, balancing on a large moving ball, and engaging in exercises that involve crossing the midline of the body (e.g. right hand on left part of torso and stair climbing) have been employed. For more specific information on sensorimotor programs and occupational therapy, the reader is referred to Schneck (2001) and Rydeen (2001).

Behavior intervention

In this section we describe basic behavior intervention strategies for developing sensorimotor behaviors. Sensorimotor behaviors vary considerably in their complexity, ranging from walking, jumping, dressing, and writing to playing soccer. Table 6.1 presents a list of the types of behaviors that might be targeted for intervention. Because these skills are influenced by a variety of processes in addition to motor, including arousal/emotion, sensory, cognitive, and language processes, the intervention strategies employed also vary considerably.

Table 6.1 Examples of sensorimotor behaviors that might be targeted for intervention

Early developmental skills
> Sitting
> Reaching
> Walking

Self-help skills
> Bathing and personal hygiene
> Self-feeding
> Toothbrushing
> Self-dressing

Household tasks
> Washing and drying dishes
> Setting a table
> Cooking
> Vacuuming

Pre-academic and academic tasks
> Drawing and copying
> Printing and writing

Community survival skills
> Street-crossing
> Using public transportation
> Making emergency calls

Leisure skills
> Toy play
> Playing board games
> Playing baseball, soccer, football

Anzalone and Williamson (2000) emphasize several factors that influence how children interact with their environment, including their ability to maintain alertness, to focus selectively on relevant aspects of the environment, and to control their emotional reactivity. In children with autism, deficiencies in motor functioning are often related to impairments in an individual's ability to execute movements even though they have the physical capacity to perform such actions.

In order to execute both simple and complex motor behaviors, children must be able to visualize the goal to be enacted, formulate a plan for achieving that goal, and then place that plan into action. Implementation of this process involves making a decision to act as well as how to act, and then acting, using sensory cues to guide the movement as it unfolds. Imitative and sequencing behaviors, previously discussed in Chapter 2, are two fundamental building blocks that are strategically important for teaching sensorimotor skills. Other core learning skills mentioned in Chapter 2 are also critical components of sensorimotor training programs, including attention and joint attention, receptive language and expressive language.

Because of the numerous processes involved in executing a motor behavior, it is recommended that intervention programs should, depending on a child's specific pattern of strengths and limitations, incorporate one or more of the following components:

- Ensure that the child is in a quiet alert state—neither sleepy nor overexcited. If the child reacts to the teaching situation with fear and/or hypersensitivity, procedures described in the chapters on emotion (Chapter 4) and sensory processes (Chapter 5) should be introduced into the intervention program.

- Help the child understand the nature of the action to be performed in a particular situation. For children who have adequate expressive verbal skills, help them verbalize the plan of action, that is have them describe what they should do. For children with limited verbal skills, visual templates of the action should be provided.

- Teach the child to focus on the cues that serve to guide the motor behavior, such as visual cues provided by a teacher/parent modeling that behavior, verbal cues describing the action to be performed, and visual and proprioceptive cues provided by the motor action itself.

- Provide physical guidance when the child is not able to perform a particular motor behavior.

The following intervention procedures are particularly helpful in teaching children sensorimotor skills: verbal instruction, modeling and imitation training, chaining, shaping and reinforcement, self-instruction, correspondence training, and discrimination training. In order to illustrate how each of these procedures can be employed in teaching a complex sensorimotor skill, a program for developing toothbrushing behavior will be used as an example. Before describing these procedures, it should be emphasized that the first step in any behavior education program is to describe in detail the specific response components of the skill to be taught. The component skills for toothbrushing, which could be enumerated even further, are listed in Table 6.2.

Table 6.2 Sequence of steps in a toothbrushing program

1. Pick up toothbrush
2. Put water on toothbrush
3. Remove cap from toothpaste
4. Place toothpaste on toothbrush
5. Replace cap on toothpaste
6. Brush outer surfaces of teeth
7. Brush top surfaces of teeth
8. Brush inner surfaces of teeth
9. Fill cup with water
10. Rinse mouth
11. Rinse toothbrush
12. Put toothbrush and toothpaste away

VERBAL INSTRUCTION

In any motor skill program, the general rule of thumb is to provide only the minimal amount of assistance necessary to teach a skill. Initially, children should simply be asked to brush their teeth. If they can perform this act when given a general verbal directive ("Brush your teeth."), it can be concluded that they do not have a performance deficiency. If, despite knowing how, the child does not brush his/her teeth at appropriate times of the day, he/she must be taught to do so. Discrimination training procedures, described later in this section and in Chapter 2, can be employed for this purpose.

If it is established that the child is not able to brush his/her teeth when given a general verbal request, specific verbal cues should be provided, directing the child to perform each of the steps described in Table 6.2 (e.g. "Pick up your toothbrush," "Put water on your toothbrush," etc.). If the child is then able to perform the designated actions when given specific verbal directives, these verbal directives should be provided as necessary and subsequently faded out.

Modeling and imitation training

If verbal instruction is not effective, this procedure should be combined with a modeling procedure, where a child is told and shown what to do. If a child is able to perform the various steps when given verbal and visual (modeling) cues, the next step in the program is to gradually fade out the visual cues and then the verbal cues.

An alternative procedure, also involving visual cues, is to provide the child a picture book depicting each of the steps in the toothbrushing sequence and to show him/her how to use it. This visual recipe should also be faded. Care should be taken to ensure that a child does not become dependent on this visual aid. The ultimate goal of all behavior education programs is to promote, whenever possible, self-regulation and full autonomous action.

Physical guidance

If verbal and visual cues are not sufficient to prompt appropriate toothbrushing, verbal cues should be used in conjunction with physical guidance. More specifically, the child should be told what to do and then physically assisted in the actual doing. Once the child is able to perform the toothbrushing steps with physical assistance, this assistance should be gradually faded and then subsequently the verbal cues.

Chaining

Because toothbrushing involves a sequence of steps or a chain (see Table 6.2), training typically focuses on the first step in the chain, then the second step, third step, and so on, until the child gains proficiency. When chaining is employed, prompts (verbal, visual, and/or physical guidance) should be given as necessary for each step. As the child gains proficiency in performing each specific step, prompts are removed until the total toothbrushing sequence is performed without assistance. In the next section, program examples are provided describing in greater detail different kinds of chaining procedures.

Shaping and reinforcement

As children learn, their ability to perform specific acts may be only rough approximations of how these acts should be ideally performed; for example the act of brushing the outside of the teeth may be only cursory at best. Initially, rough approximations of the desired response are reinforced. As performance improves over time, only more proficient approximations are reinforced, while less proficient approximations are put on extinction; this process is called shaping.

SELF-INSTRUCTION AND CORRESPONDENCE TRAINING

As mentioned, the ultimate goal of training is to get children to brush their teeth without having to be told; that is, to be able to self-regulate and operate autonomously, independent of adult instruction or supervision. Two particularly helpful procedures for teaching children with verbal skills to self-regulate are correspondence training and self-instruction. Both of these procedures involve teaching children to say what they should do and then to do it, that is perform the action. Children who can self-regulate in this manner are gradually assuming cognitive control of their behavior. The reader is referred to Chapter 2 for a further description of these procedures and to Chapter 10 for a fuller discussion of self-regulation and its development.

DISCRIMINATION TRAINING

In a training program, the child must not only learn specific skills, but also learn when and where to perform them. For example, children need to be taught not only to brush their teeth, but also when and where they should brush them, for instance after all meals and at the bathroom sink. In a discrimination training program, after the child learns how to brush his/her teeth, the child is then reinforced for doing so only at specific times and in specific places (see Chapter 2 for further information on discrimination training).

SUMMARY

The procedures outlined here for teaching toothbrushing can be employed in developing both simple and complex sensorimotor skills (see Table 6.1). From a process perspective these procedures are designed to: promote the child's understanding of what a sensorimotor skill entails, help the child focus on relevant instructional and task-related cues, acquire requisite motor skills, and finally put a motor plan into action. In the next section, examples of other behavior-oriented, sensorimotor training programs are provided.

Program examples

One-step toy play

OBJECTIVE

Teach the child to imitate one-step actions with toys.

MATERIALS

Gather toys that the child is already interested in so that he/she will be more inclined to participate in the activity. Do not use materials that the child uses to engage in repetitive, stereotypic behaviors, or materials that the child has difficulty giving up. Instead, choose items that the child shows interest in, but will share with others when asked to do so.

PROCEDURE

1. Say, "Do this," and model a single-step action that is common to the object. For example, roll a car forward, put a toy phone up to your ear, or stack a block on top of another block.

   a) If the child imitates the action, immediately deliver praise and a reinforcer.

   b) If the child does not imitate the action within 1 to 3 seconds, use prompts to assist him/her with imitating. Deliver praise and a smaller reinforcer than what you would use if he/she imitated without your help.

2. Repeat with a different action and object.

3. Model different one-step actions with the objects so that the child learns more than one way of playing with a toy. For example, put a phone up to your ear, or press the buttons on the phone, or hang up the phone. For additional examples, see the example list below.

ERROR CORRECTION

If the child does not imitate your action (e.g. spins the wheels of the car instead of rolling it back and forth), remove the toy or stop his/her action. Model the original action again and immediately prompt the child to imitate correctly. Deliver praise but do not deliver a tangible reinforcer following error correction. Repeat the trial, quickly delivering a prompt in order to avoid the same error, this time reinforcing the prompted response.

GENERALIZATION

Use many different examples so that the child can perform the task with multiple toys. For example, use several different types and colors of cars, purses, phones, and so on. In addition, teach several actions with each toy so that the child does not learn to respond only to the presence of the toy (e.g. the car can go up a ramp, in the garage, or into a carwash). In addition, by varying your actions you are ensuring that the child is actually imitating your behavior, and not simply learning a rote response.

TIPS/SUGGESTIONS

Verbal imitation or speech skills are not necessary for this procedure. However, consider adding verbal responses to the procedure for children who have such skills, in order to build on speech as well as social skills.

TROUBLESHOOTING

If the child consistently makes errors, start prompting more quickly, before the error occurs. Consider using two people to teach this skill: one person to model the behavior, and one person to physically prompt the child. Reinforce correct, prompted responses, using differential reinforcement to fade your assistance. In addition, be sure that you are using highly preferred reinforcers, and delivering the reinforcers very quickly following correct responses (i.e. within 1 to 5 seconds).

EXAMPLE TARGETS

Doll:

- put the doll in bed
- comb the doll's hair
- seat the doll at the table.

Car:

- drive down the ramp
- crash into another car
- park into a parking space on a car mat.

Crayons:

- draw on paper
- put in crayon box.

Barn animals:

- place animal in barn
- open or shut door of barn
- make horse jump the fence
- put rooster on the roof.

Trains:

- drive train down the track
- attach another car to the train
- put doll/animal in train.

FUTURE OBJECTIVES

Next, use this same procedure to teach two-step toy manipulations. Initially, teach commonsense, two-step play chains (e.g. put a horse in the train wagon then move the train down the track). But once the child is responding independently to such logical actions, begin to teach random, unrelated two-step actions (e.g. put a doll in a sand bucket, then put the train in the barn). The rationale for teaching such illogical steps is to avoid teaching children rote responses with objects, and to increase actual imitation. It is essential that the child have a strong repertoire of imitation skills to further develop other play and social behaviors.

Tracing lines

OBJECTIVE

Teach the child to trace lines of various lengths and curvatures.

MATERIALS

For this procedure, you will need paper and a writing utensil. It may be best to prepare the lines that the child will trace ahead of time (see example targets on p. 69).

PROCEDURE

1. Use the example targets as a guide to teach tracing. Start with teaching vertical lines until the child has mastered this skill, and then move on to horizontal and curved lines.

2. Provide the child with the materials and the instruction to trace the line.

3. Prompt the child, as needed, to help him/her trace the line.

4. Give the child a reinforcer. Initially reinforce even if the child needed assistance.

5. Repeat, practicing as much as possible, for at least ten consecutive trials.

6. Fade prompts until the child can independently trace the line. When fading prompts, differentially reinforce responses that require less assistance (i.e. more independent responses equal better reinforcement).

7. Move on to the next target, but continue to have the child practice tracing lines that he/she has already learned to trace independently.

ERROR CORRECTION

If the child makes an error, erase and redo the line, or move on to the next line, increasing your assistance to avoid the same error. Try fading your assistance more gradually or use one of the tips in the troubleshooting or tips/suggestions sections.

GENERALIZATION

Once the child can accurately trace lines, connect the lines to form shapes, such as a triangle or square. Have the child trace simple drawings that use these same lines, such as a house, clock, flower, or bicycle.

TIPS/SUGGESTIONS

It may be easier for the child to start tracing lines that are thicker than the desired target width. Alternatively provide the child with a writing utensil that is easier to hold, or draws a thicker line (e.g. a marker) to help reduce the amount of error. Fade the thickness of the lines or writing utensil so that the child is eventually able to trace thin lines (i.e. as drawn with a sharpened pencil) with a pencil or thin-tipped marker.

When preparing materials, make the lines as transparent as possible so that the child can easily see the line he/she is tracing. Avoid using dark black ink because it will be difficult for the child to see that he/she is tracing accurately.

Help the child to trace in the same way each time. For example, if he/she is tracing a circle, teach the child to start at the same spot each time, and to curve around in the same direction. Such consistency will help the child learn a motor movement, making it easier to make the transition to drawing instead of tracing.

TROUBLESHOOTING

If the child is having difficulty tracing without assistance, be sure that he/she is holding the writing utensil correctly (i.e. using a pincer grip with the thumb and first two fingers). If he/she is not holding the utensil correctly, take some time to practice this skill before continuing with tracing, drawing, or writing tasks. Also consider the child's hand dominance. Perhaps the child is using the wrong hand to trace.

If the child is having difficulty tracing the entire length of the line (i.e. he/she traces half of the line but then veers off course), try placing a sticker or small piece of candy at the end of the line so he/she is more motivated to track the line to its end point. If the child is having difficulty with curved lines, move on to slanted lines first then come back to curved lines and circles.

Remember that a lot of practice is necessary to master any skill, especially difficult motor tasks such as handwriting. If the child does not enjoy this task, break up the practice across the session or day, rather than doing several trials in a row. Also consider reserving a highly preferred reinforcer to use only during this task.

OTHER TEACHING METHODS

Handwriting without tears is another great resource for teaching tracing and beginning handwriting skills.

EXAMPLE TARGETS

- 2", 4", 6", and 8" vertical lines
- 2", 4", 6", and 8" horizontal lines
- 2", 4", 6", and 8" curved lines (vertical or horizontal)
- 2", 4", 6", and 8" circles
- 2", 4", 6", and 8" slanted lines
- 2", 4", 6", and 8" vertical and horizontal connected lines (forwards, backwards, or upside down L).

FUTURE OBJECTIVES

Once the child has mastered some of the lines in the example targets list, begin teaching the child to trace upper case letters that use the same line directions he/she has learned to trace independently. Then move on to lower case letters.

Fade the sight of the lines in order to assist the child with learning to copy lines in addition to tracing. Begin to fade the lines by using lighter and lighter colors of ink, or make thinner and thinner lines until the line is no longer visible and the child is copying rather than tracing the line. Another approach to fading involves gradually changing the lines into dashed lines. Slowly increase the space between the dashes, eventually making only dots at the beginning and ends of the lines. Then fade the dots until there is nothing left for the child to trace.

Self-feeding

OBJECTIVE

To teach the child to independently feed him/herself using hands and/or utensils.

MATERIALS

Gather all materials you would normally have for mealtime, including utensils, plates or bowls, and food.

PROCEDURE

The following procedure outlines one way of teaching a child to self-feed using total-task presentation and shaping. Total-task presentation involves teaching all of the steps involved in the task during each session.

1. Start by doing a task analysis of the steps involved in self-feeding. To do this, break down the task into small steps. These steps may be different for each child and some children may require more steps than others (see example task analyses on the following page).

2. Start with step 1, providing the child with only as much physical assistance as is necessary. For example, if the child is eating pancakes, cut the pancakes into bite-sized pieces ahead of time unless the child is ready to work on knife skills. Assist the child with picking up the fork and holding it correctly. Try to use as light a touch as possible, fading this assistance after each bite.

3. Move on to the next step (e.g. help the child pierce a piece of pancake with the fork).

4. Move through each step, always attempting to decrease your physical guidance, allowing the child the opportunity to perform the step independently. For example, instead of holding the child's hand over the fork, hold the wrist. On the next step hold the child by the elbow. Continue fading your guidance until eventually you are not touching the child at all.

5. Deliver praise whenever the child completes a step with less assistance.

6. Immediately deliver a reinforcer upon completion of the entire chain (e.g. after the child has eaten a piece of food). This reinforcer will need to be in addition to the food the child is eating. This is necessary because the child may be accustomed to eating food more quickly and easily when someone else feeds him/her. Therefore additional reinforcement is necessary for completing the difficult task of feeding him or herself.

7. Continue until the child has finished eating, fading assistance with each bite.

TIPS/SUGGESTIONS

While it may be difficult, try to avoid using verbal prompts or reminders throughout this or any self-help task (e.g. "Keep eating."). Verbal prompts are very difficult to fade, and the child may become dependent on hearing the verbal reminder before he/she attempts the task. Instead, only deliver a verbal instruction at the beginning of the task (e.g. "Time to eat.").

In addition, this skill may be easier for the child to learn if he/she is eating something desirable. It also may be helpful to use reinforcers that the child does not need to hold (e.g. turn on music for a few seconds) because you will not need to retrieve the reinforcer from the child when it is time for him/her to take the next bite.

OTHER TEACHING METHODS

This skill can be taught using other methods, including forward or backward chaining (see the following Dressing program example). Regardless of the methods used, it is essential to fade prompts as quickly as possible to ensure complete independence.

EXAMPLE TASK ANALYSES

Example 1:

1. pick up fork

2. hold fork correctly

3. pierce a piece of food

4. bring food to mouth

5. close mouth around fork

6. slide fork out of mouth

7. repeat.

Example 2:

1. pick up fork

2. pierce piece of food

3. eat food.

Dressing

OBJECTIVE

To teach the child to independently put on all of his/her clothes.

PROCEDURE

The following procedure outlines one way of teaching a child to get dressed using backward chaining. Backward chaining involves teaching the last step of a chain first. This has several benefits, one of which is quicker access to a reinforcer in the beginning phases of teaching independent dressing, because as soon as the child finishes the last step, the task is complete and the child should receive a reinforcer.

1. Start by doing a task analysis of the steps involved in getting dressed. These steps may be different for each child and some children may require more steps than others (see example task anaylses on the following page).

2. Starting with step 1, physically assist the child through each step of the chain except the last step, providing only as much assistance as is necessary. Do not require the child to attempt these steps independently yet. For example, if the child is learning to put on his shirt, physically assist him with picking up the shirt, putting his head through the big hole, and putting each arm through the sleeves (one at a time).

3. For the last step of the chain, fade your assistance as much as possible, allowing the child the opportunity to perform this step independently. For example, allow the child to pull down his shirt (i.e. last step of the chain) independently.

4. Immediately deliver praise and a reinforcer upon completion of the chain.

5. Once the child can successfully complete the last step without any assistance from you, start teaching the second to last step (e.g. putting his second arm through the sleeve) by fading your assistance during that step. Allow the child to continue completing the last step (i.e. pulling shirt down over belly) independently. Provide praise for completing the steps independently, but only provide a tangible reinforcer after the entire chain is complete (e.g. the child's shirt is on).

6. Continue until the child can complete all of the steps independently.

Tips/suggestions

While it may be difficult, try to avoid using verbal prompts or reminders throughout this or any self-help task (e.g. "Put your arm in, pull your shirt down."). Verbal prompts are very difficult to fade, and the child may become dependent on hearing the verbal reminder before he/she attempts the task. If the end goal is for the child to get dressed without being asked to do so (e.g. when he/she wakes up in the morning) it may be helpful to use a visual schedule to guide the child through a routine (e.g. a morning routine).

If taking data on backward chaining procedures, it is only necessary to take data on the current teaching target. For example, if you are working on teaching the last step of putting on a shirt, take data on the prompt level needed for the child to complete that last step. Once you have moved on to teaching the child to put his/her arm through the second sleeve, take data only on that step, unless you observe the child regressing in a previously learned step.

Other teaching methods

This skill can also be taught using other methods, including forward chaining, total-task presentation (i.e. teaching all steps at once), or using visual schedules or visual prompts. Regardless of the methods used, it is essential to fade prompts as quickly as possible (including visual prompts) to ensure complete independence.

Example task analyses

Example 1:

1. pick up shirt

2. make sure tag is in back (closest to child)

3. put head through hole

4. pull down over head

5. put left arm in sleeve

6. pull sleeve

7. put right arm in sleeve

8. pull sleeve

9. pull shirt down.

Example 2:

1. put head in big hole

2. put first arm in

3. put second arm in

4. pull down.

Example 3:

1. put on shirt

2. put on underwear

3. put on pants

4. put on socks.

Completing household tasks

OBJECTIVE

Teach the child to complete various daily household tasks independently.

MATERIALS

Various materials needed to complete the target tasks should be placed in a location that is easily accessible to the child. In addition, it may be helpful to use a visual prompt of some sort (e.g. a written list of tasks, or a picture or object schedule). Using such a method may help the child to obtain independence because the child must refer to the list/schedule rather than asking an adult what is to be done.

PROCEDURE

1. Choose two to three tasks to teach the child. Write these tasks on a list or set up a picture/object schedule.

2. Present the list/schedule to the child and instruct the child to do his/her chores.

3. Assist the child by standing behind him/her and physically guiding the child to point to the first task.

4. Initially, state the name of the task out loud (e.g. "Set the table.").

5. Physically assist the child with each step of the task until it is complete.

6. Guide the child back to the list/schedule to point to and start the next task.

7. Initially, provide reinforcers to the child for completing components of the task even if he/she requires assistance. For example, when learning to set the table, give the child a high five when he/she puts all the plates on top of the place mats, and then again after the child puts all the forks in their place. Consider using tokens throughout the task and allowing the child to exchange the tokens for a larger reinforcer after the child has completed the entire list/schedule of tasks.

8. Provide excited praise and a larger reinforcer (or opportunity to exchange tokens for a reinforcer) after the entire list/schedule is complete.

9. Repeat daily with the same tasks. Discontinue stating the name of the task when the child points to it on the list and gradually fade your physical prompts and distance from the child until he/she is able to complete the task list independently.

10. Use differential reinforcement to reward the child for responding more accurately and independently as you fade your assistance.

ERROR CORRECTION

As you begin fading assistance the child is more likely to make a mistake. If this happens, quickly increase physical assistance to help the child complete the step correctly. This may require restarting the task. For example, when learning to wash dishes, if the child puts a dish in the drying rack before it is completely clean, place the dish back in the sink and help the child re-wash the dish. Provide praise once the dish is clean, but do not offer a reward following error correction.

GENERALIZATION

Attempt to fade the chore list or schedule. This can be done gradually (e.g. fading the size of the pictures so they become increasingly smaller and eventually disappear) or attempt to remove the list completely. Regardless of whether or not the child continues to use a visual prompt, it is necessary to fade the use of any verbal prompts (e.g. telling the child to set the table) so that the child completes these tasks when they need to be completed, rather than only when told to do so.

Tips/suggestions

If the chores will change day to day (e.g. only take the trash out on Thursday) it may help to use a calendar to remind the child which tasks must be completed each day. In addition, to promote success start with tasks that the child is likely to enjoy doing.

Troubleshooting

If the child engages in challenging behaviors during a particular task, consider removing that task from the list, temporarily or permanently. Determine a way to reduce the aversive properties of the task. For example, if the child cries when you attempt to teach him or her how to vacuum, consider having the child wear headphones while vacuuming to reduce the noise. Be sure to reward the child for completing the tasks, even if assistance is required. However, be careful not to show the reward while he/she is exhibiting such challenging behaviors (e.g. if the child is crying, do not hold up a Skittle and say, "Stop crying and you can have your Skittle." Instead, physically guide the child through the task and then provide reinforcers upon task completion).

If the child is consistently making errors on one particular task, consider removing that task and replacing it with something that is less difficult. Meanwhile, practice skills that will enable the child to eventually learn to complete the former task independently. For example, if the child has trouble making her lunch independently because she cannot spread the peanut butter, work on spreading with a knife more often and in more structured settings until the child masters this skill. Then reintroduce the task into the chore list.

Other teaching methods

For daily tasks, it may be best to teach the child to complete the task at the same time each day (e.g. make the bed every morning after getting dressed) rather than using a list/schedule.

Future objectives

Once the child is able to complete two to three tasks independently, gradually add more tasks to the list. Keep in mind that you may need to temporarily increase your assistance with these new tasks.

EXAMPLES OF HOUSEHOLD TASKS

- washing/drying dishes
- loading/unloading the dishwasher
- setting the table
- cooking
- cleaning the table/counters
- making lunch for next day
- taking out the trash
- vacuuming
- dusting
- sorting dirty laundry
- folding towels, socks, or other laundry
- putting away clean laundry
- making the bed
- changing the sheets
- picking up toys/items on the floor.

Throwing a ball

OBJECTIVE

Teach the child to throw a ball to another person from multiple distances.

MATERIALS

For this procedure you will initially need two people to assist the child. When choosing a ball, keep in mind that some children may need to start with a larger ball (e.g. a beach ball) and gradually fade to a smaller ball (e.g. a baseball).

PROCEDURE

1. Start with one assistant (prompter) standing behind the child, and the other assistant (catcher) standing across from the child, about 2 feet (60 cm) away.

2. The catcher should instruct the child to throw the ball.

3. The prompter should immediately use physical prompts to help the child throw the ball to the catcher. Using the child's dominant hand, help the child raise the ball near his/her ear (or above the head if it is too heavy to hold in one hand), bend the elbow(s), extend the arm(s), and then release the ball toward the catcher.

4. Deliver praise and a reinforcer to the child after each successful throw, even if assistance is required.

5. The prompter should gradually fade his/her physical assistance until the child can throw the ball to the catcher independently.

6. Once the child can throw independently from two feet (60 cm) away gradually increase the distance between the child and the catcher (e.g. by one foot (30 cm)).

7. Each time the catcher increases his/her distance from the child, the prompter should provide additional physical assistance to help the child successfully throw longer distances. The prompter should fade such assistance as quickly as possible.

8. Use differential reinforcement to reward more independent responses.

Error correction

If the child drops the ball or does not throw it far enough, do not offer praise or a reinforcer. Try again at the same distance, increasing physical assistance if necessary. If the child makes two errors in a row, slightly decrease the distance between him/her and the catcher. Practice at the decreased distance, rewarding successes with praise and reinforcers.

Generalization

Once the child has learned this skill, play catch outside on the playground, in the pool, in a field, or on a baseball diamond. Substitute same-age peers as the catcher. Play catch in a circle with other peers; require the children to say the name of the peer they throw the ball to prior to throwing.

Troubleshooting

If the child's muscle development is preventing him/her from throwing a heavier ball, try teaching the child to throw a balloon first, then a foam ball, a beach ball, and then a tennis ball, gradually increasing the weight of the ball. Practice other tasks that require the child to do some light weightlifting (e.g. putting away soup cans when you get home from the grocery store).

If the child does not enjoy this activity, perhaps put the task on hold and teach the child something more enjoyable, such as hitting the ball with a bat. Be sure that you are using highly preferred reinforcers while teaching this task. Remember that the child should not have access to the reinforcers unless he/she is responding correctly (i.e. initially with assistance, but eventually independently).

FUTURE OBJECTIVES

Attempt to decrease the size of the ball that the child is throwing. If the child is having difficulty catching the ball, use the same procedure to teach the child to catch the ball. Perhaps teach the child to throw a ball into a basket.

References

Als, H. (1982). Toward a syntactic theory of development: Promise for the assessment and support of infant individuality. *Infant Mental Health, 3,* 229–243.

Anzalone, M. E. & Williamson, G. G. (2000). "Sensory processing and motor performance in autism spectrum disorders." In A. M. Wetherby & B. M. Prizant (Eds.), *Autism spectrum disorders* (pp. 143–166). Baltimore: Brooks Publishing Co.

Attwood, T. (1998). *Asperger's Syndrome: A guide for parents and professionals.* London: Jessica Kingsley Publishers.

Ayres, A. J. (1979). *Sensory integration and the child.* Los Angeles, CA: Western Psychological Services.

Baranek, G. (1999). Autism during infancy: A retrospective analysis of sensory-motor and social behaviors at 9–12 months of age. *Journal of Autism and Developmental Disorders, 29,* 213–224.

Baranek, G. T., Parham, L. D., & Bodfish, J. W. (2005). "Sensory and motor features in autism: Assessment and intervention." In F. R. Volkmar, R. Paul, A. Klin, & D. Cohen (Eds.), *Handbook of autism and pervasive developmental disorders: Vol. 2. Assessment, interventions, and policy* (3rd ed., pp. 831–857). Hoboken, NJ: John Wiley & Sons.

Berk, L. E. (2009). *Child Development* (8th ed.). Boston, MA: Allyn Bacon.

Diamond, A. (2000). Close interrelationship of motor development and cognitive development and of the cerebellum and prefrontal cortex. *Child Development, 71,* 44–56.

Gillberg, C. (1989). Asperger syndrome in 23 Swedish children. *Developmental Medicine and Child Neurology, 31,* 520–531.

Hauck, J. A. & Dewey, D. (2001). Hand preference and motor functioning in children with autism. *Journal of Autism and Developmental Disorders, 31,* 265–277.

Huebner, R. A. (2001). *Autism: A sensorimotor approach to management.* Gaithersburg, MD: Aspen.

Jansiewicz, E. M., Goldberg, M. C., Newschaffer, C. J., Denckla, M. B., Landa, R., & Mostofsky, S. H. (2006). Motor signs distinguish children with high functioning autism and Asperger's syndrome from controls. *Journal of Autism and Developmental Disorders, 36,* 613–621.

Kitahara, K. (1983/1984). *Daily life therapy* (Vols 1, 2 & 3). Tokyo: Musashino, Higashi, Gakuen School.

Lightfoot, C., Cole, M., & Cole, S. (2009). *The development of children.* Worth, IL: Worth Publishing.

Manjiviona, J. & Prior, M. (1995). Comparison of Asperger Syndrome and high functioning autistic children on a test of motor impairment. *Journal of Autism and Developmental Disorders, 25,* 23–39.

Nazarali, N., Glazebrook, C. M., & Elliott, D. (2009). Movement planning and reprogramming in individuals with autism. *Journal of Autism and Developmental Disorders, 39,* 1401–1411.

Pan, C., Tsai, C., & Chu, C. (2009). Fundamental movement skills in children diagnosed with autism spectrum disorders and attention deficit hyperactivity disorder. *Journal of Autism and Developmental Disorders, 39,* 1694–1705.

Paris, B. (2000). "Characteristics of autism." In C. Murray-Slutsky & B. Paris (Eds.), *Exploring the spectrum of autism and pervasive developmental disorders* (pp. 7–23). San Antonio, TX: Therapy Skill Builders (Harcourt Health Sciences).

Piaget, J. (1970). "Piaget's theory." In P. H. Mussen (Ed.), *Carmichael's manual of child psychology* (Vol. 1, 3rd ed., pp. 703–732). New York, NY: Wiley.

Rinehardt, N., Bradshaw, J., Brereton, A., & Tonge, B. (2001). Movement preparation in high-functioning autism and Asperger Disorder: A serial choice reaction time task involving motor reprogramming. *Journal of Autism and Developmental Disorders, 31,* 79–88.

Rydeen, K. (2001). "Integration of sensorimotor and neurodevelopmental approaches." In R. Huebner (Ed.), *Autism: A sensorimotor approach to management* (pp. 209–244). Gaithersburg, MD: Aspen.

Schneck, C. (2001). "The efficacy of a sensorimotor treatment approach by occupational therapists." In R. Huebner (Ed.), *Autism: A sensorimotor approach to management* (pp. 139–178). Gaithersburg, MD: Aspen.

Smith, I. M. (2004). "Motor problems in children with autistic spectrum disorders." In D. Dewey & D. E. Tupper (Eds.), *Developmental motor disorders: A neuropsychological perspective* (pp. 152–168). New York, NY: Guilford Press.

Smith, l. B. & Thelen, E. (1993). *A dynamic systems approach to development: Applications.* Cambridge, MA: MIT Press.

Staples, K. L. & Reid, G. (2010). Fundamental movement skills and autism spectrum disorders. *Journal of Autism and Developmental Disorders, 40,* 209–217.

Teitelbaum, P., Teitelbaum, O., Nye, J., Fryman, J., & Mauer, P. (1998). Movement analysis in infancy may be useful for early diagnosis of autism. *Proceedings of the National Academy of Sciences, 95,* 13982–13987.

Williams, J. H. G., Whiten, A., & Singh, T. (2004). A systematic review of action imitation in autistic spectrum disorder. *Journal of Autism and Developmental Disorders, 34,* 285–299.

Chapter 7

Language and Communication Problems

Language and communication deficiencies are a core diagnostic characteristic of autism. Estimates suggest that around 50 percent of children with autism do not acquire speech as a primary mode of communication. For those who do acquire speech, there is considerable variation in the timing and patterns of language acquisition (Whitman, 2004). Early speech characteristics include echolalia, pronoun reversal and peculiar word use (Hobson, Lee, & Hobson, 2010). If children with autism acquire more advanced speech, they typically display a variety of problems relating to articulation, syntax, morphology, prosody, and pragmatics (Diehl & Berkovits, 2010). They also frequently display peculiar paralinguistic features relating to vocal quality, intonation, and stress patterns (Paul & Sutherland, 2005). As a consequence they have difficulty engaging in dynamic discourse with others and comprehending the intricacies of social communications, even though their expressive language skills are otherwise well developed. Many of these aforementioned characteristics are also displayed by children with Asperger Syndrome (Attwood, 2006).

Most intervention programs for children with autism spectrum disorders place a major emphasis on teaching receptive and expressive language behaviors. Because both home-based and school-based education programs use verbal instruction as a major tool for teaching, it is imperative that these children become proficient in the use of language as early as possible and to the fullest extent possible. Language provides a foundation and is a prerequisite for the development of many motor, cognitive, and social skills. As indicated in Chapter 3, basic language skills, such as labeling, making verbal requests, and responding appropriately to verbal instructions, are core behaviors that are essential for learning and development. Moreover, language is an important vehicle for regulating the behavior of children with autism spectrum disorders as well as for teaching them how to regulate their own behavior. In this chapter, we briefly examine language development in neurotypical children and children with autism spectrum disorders and then describe language/communication behaviors that need to be targeted to help children with ASD achieve proficiency in this domain. We then discuss traditional and behavioral interventions directed at developing language, and communication skills, and in the final section provide examples of specific behavior-focused programs.

Communication and language development in typical children

Primitive communication behaviors occur early in development, as babies begin to share attention with caretakers regarding objects of mutual interest and look to their caretakers to help them interpret their environment. During typical development, preverbal gestures and joint attention acts help pave the way for oral language. Intentional preverbal communication develops early, followed by first words, word combinations, sentences, and discourse grammar. Although language development emerges in earnest around two years of age, infants are born into the world showing a preference for certain sounds, particularly those expressed by their mothers. Their expressive abilities gradually evolve, proceeding from a limited set of sounds to cooing and babbling and eventually to sounds approximating words. Children learn early that words refer to objects in their environment and that words are a way of making requests for specific objects they desire.

During the second year of life, as children acquire an increasing number of words, they begin to express themselves and to understand others in increasingly complex ways. Vocabulary growth leads to increases in the child's ability to put words together and use them in different contexts. Eventually, as vocabulary increases in complexity and variety, children begin to form sentences. As children learn to communicate in sentences, they also begin to master grammatical rules and select words and word orders appropriate to particular contexts. Most importantly, children learn to use language to communicate their desires as well as to respond to the needs of others around them. As speakers and listeners, children begin to communicate in earnest when their interpretations of a communication are shared in common with others. Children gradually acquire knowledge that helps them regulate both what is said and how to express it in a way that is understandable to others.

There is a dynamic relationship between children's language and their social and cognitive functioning. Through language children express their needs, make demands, regulate their own and other people's behavior, communicate their feelings, explore and respond to their social environment, come to better understand themselves and imagine worlds different from the one in which they live. Language helps children escape reality and become whoever or whatever they wish to be. It also allows them to more readily understand the minds of other people. In short, language plays a critical role in shaping children's perceptions of the world as well as how they interact with it. For further information on language development the reader is referred to texts on child development by Berk (2009) and Lightfoot, Cole, and Cole (2009).

Communication and language in children with autism

Although children with autism vary considerably in their language development, all have difficulty communicating. Some children have minimal receptive and expressive speech while others develop complex language skills; however, even this latter group has difficulty engaging in dynamic discourse with others. For children who acquire speech, their language deficiencies can be summarized as including problems in: words and grammar, pragmatics, which includes the rhythmic features of language, conversational conventions, taking the listener's perspective into consideration, and the use of narrative. Phonological (sound) development in children with autism, while slower, appears to resemble that of other children; however, the meanings they attach to words are often idiosyncratic, tied to specific concrete objects and contexts. Among children with autism who develop more complex language, their grammar and syntax, while similar to neurotypical children, show a variety of anomalies, such as unusual word strings, less sophisticated grammar rules, past tense difficulties, pronoun reversals (e.g. I for you), misuse of passive sentences, and problems in the production and comprehension of questions (Sigman & Capps, 1997; Whitman, 2004).

Thus, despite the fact that some children with autism develop fairly normal grammar, their use of language nevertheless remains problematic; perhaps because they have less experience with the dynamic reciprocal social interactions that would help them understand the nuances of words and more generally the pragmatics of language. Their conversations, which are often characterized by perseveration on specific topics, irrelevant detail, and tangential shifts in topic, appear to satisfy more their own needs than to share attention with others or to understand another person's point of view.

Children with autism also frequently show idiosyncratic interpretations of other people's speech, as well as problems in speech modulation, loudness, pitch, stress, and rhythm. They are less likely to use intonation stress to convey meaning or interpret utterances. Conversations with children with autism typically break down when they are questioned. They also have a tendency to interrupt others, as well as difficulties in elaborating on other people's comments and maintaining a logical dialogue flow. These latter problems may relate to a broader difficulty that children with autism have with being able to understand the perspective of others (Sigman & Capps, 1997; Whitman, 2004).

In contrast to expressive language, less is known about language comprehension in children with autism. Research suggests that children with autism do not attend to speech in the same way as other children and are better at visual than auditory/ verbal processing. Because of their attentional problems and visual processing preferences, it is not surprising that they also have problems understanding the meanings of speech, particularly those aspects of speech which are more symbolic in nature (see review by Watson, 2001).

Many of the aforementioned expressive and receptive language characteristics, as well as others, are displayed by children with Asperger Syndrome. Gillberg (1989) includes among the diagnostic criteria for this disorder the following speech and language characteristics: superficially perfect expressive language, formal pedantic speech, odd prosody, peculiar voice characteristics, and impairments in comprehension, including a tendency to misinterpret both the literal and implied meanings of words (see also Attwood, 2006 for a further discussion of these characteristics).

Given that speech is acquired in a social context, children with ASD, due to their early preferences for social isolation and solitary activities, seem to be at a unique disadvantage; specifically because they have been deprived of the type of early language stimulation enjoyed by typically developing children. Tager-Flusberg (1996) points out that children with autism seldom use language to share or seek information. They are often unresponsive to the verbalization of others and do not frequently initiate, expand, or elaborate as they converse. Tager-Flusberg (1996) suggests that these problems evolve because children with autism fail to understand that other people's viewpoints are often not the same as theirs; that is, they do not have a theory of mind.

Travis and Sigman (2001) suggest that two developmental reorganizations, hypothesized to be critical for language development, do not occur in the same way in children with autism as in neurotypical children. These two reorganizations relate to the emergence of communicative intentions and symbolic ability. Communicative intentions typically occur around nine months when infants begin to show awareness that their behaviors/signals have an effect on others. As a result, they reproduce behaviors that elicit desirable consequences. Symbolic ability begins around 11 to 13 months when infants become aware that signs can be substituted for the objects to which they refer. This recognition leads to the use of "symbolic" gestures and words to communicate their needs and interests. Thus, from this perspective, the roots of the language deficiencies in children with autism emerge early in development.

The fact that children with autism have communication deficiencies is also not surprising given their problems in preverbal communication (e.g. limited use of social gestures), maintaining eye contact, social-referencing, and imitation. Several core problems have been proposed as being responsible for the communicative deficits of children with autism, including failures to attend to speech, joint attention deficiencies, symbol use limitations, and emotion-regulation problems (Marans, Rubin, & Laurent, 2005; Paul & Sutherland, 2005; Tager-Flusberg, Paul, & Lord, 2005; Wetherby & Prizant, 2005). A somewhat similar, but broader, perspective on language acquisition is suggested by Bloom and Trinker (2001). Although their theory of language acquisition was not put forth to explain language development in children with autism, it suggests that in order to understand the language acquisition process of these children, their unusual cognitive, emotional, motor, and social characteristics all need to be considered.

Research examining the connections between language and communication problems and other autistic characteristics has been until recently quite limited. Increasingly, however, studies have indicated a dynamic relationship between the language and communication deficiencies and other symptomatology associated with autism (Hale & Tager-Flusberg, 2005; Paul & Sutherland, 2005). For example, in a population-based twin study, Dworzynski, Happé, Bolton, and Ronald (2009) found a correlation between communication and social difficulties. Further, language impairments in children with autism have been associated with both theory of mind and visual-perspective taking problems (Farrant, Fletcher, & Maybery, 2006).

Traditional interventions focusing on language development: an overview

Approaches for developing language and communication skills in children with autism spectrum disorders vary considerably. For the most part, these approaches were developed by speech and behavior therapists. Although they are not formally trained as speech therapists, behaviorally oriented therapists have made major contributions to the development of speech programs for young children with autism, including approaches such as discrete trial training and natural language learning. Many of the behavioral techniques used in these programs have been standardized, employed widely, and empirically evaluated. These techniques, and the principles upon which they are based, have become incorporated into the broader discipline of speech therapy.

In the next sections, a general overview is provided of speech therapy programs, alternative communication programs, and a more controversial approach, auditory integration training, for fostering language development. In the final sections, behavioral approaches for teaching expressive and receptive language are described along with specific program examples.

Speech therapy

Speech therapy is probably the most frequent intervention employed with young children with autism spectrum disorders. The goals of speech therapy vary considerably depending on the developmental level and capabilities of the recipient. Some programs are directed at developing basic receptive and expressive language skills. Other programs emphasize speech morphology, syntax, and content, as well as the pragmatic components of speech, that is how speech is used in maintaining a conversation through turn-taking, responding in a relevant fashion, staying on topic, being clear, and recognizing the speaker's intent. Still other programs focus on speech articulation and the paralinguistic and prosodic features of speech, including pitch, timing, volume, and stress. Not all programs focus on oral speech and language usage; some emphasize preverbal and nonverbal aspects of communication, that is communications that convey messages without words. For example, such programs might concentrate on developing appropriate eye contact, use of gestures, appropriate facial expressions, joint attention, and alternative communication systems, such as signing.

Specific programs for achieving these goals vary in where they take place, the clinic, school and/or home, and in the degree to which they are developmentally oriented, that is whether they systematically build on existing language skills rather than just providing practical language skills necessary for everyday living. Home and clinic-based speech programs are more likely to be used with younger children, whereas school-based programs are employed more often with older children. Ideally, home-based programs should always be developed in conjunction with clinic and/or school-based programs to ensure that training is extensive and intensive and that speech achievements are generalized across different environments and people.

Historically, behaviorally oriented speech and communication training programs were more directed at meeting the immediate needs of the child and family. Currently, these types of programs are typically utilized as part of a broader and more comprehensive developmentally oriented language plan. Developmental programs are directed at systematically building language from its simple to more complex forms. This type of program is particularly appropriate for children whose language skills are developing more rapidly. However, in instances where language development is significantly delayed and children are not responsive to a more ambitious developmentally oriented program, interventions can be directed at meeting the immediate functional needs of the child, that is a program which is more pragmatic and limited in its goals, focused on teaching basic receptive and expressive verbal skills and/or nonverbal communication skills.

Although Wetherby and Prizant (1992, 2005) stress the importance of developmental speech programs, they also point out that a priority should be placed on helping participants communicate verbally and/or nonverbally so that they can be effective in their daily social interactions. For example, they suggest that program goals should initially include helping children make requests and eliciting joint attention. Further they emphasize that attention should be given to understanding the communicative functions of problem behaviors so that children can be taught alternative and more appropriate ways of expressing frustration and controlling their emotions.

Wetherby and Prizant (1992, 2005) also recommend that the natural environment be used to teach important language responses and that emphasis be placed on helping family, peers, and significant others interact more effectively with children with ASD. This guideline was developed in recognition of the fact that communication is a transactional event in which two or more people are involved, each of whom must be able to understand and respond to the words/ gestures as well as the intent of the other's communication.

Traditionally, speech therapists have focused on the person with an autism spectrum disorder and have provided only general support to parents and significant others. However, as parents and teachers have become more actively involved in the children's total intervention program, speech therapists have expanded their role to include consultation. The consultation approach is typically employed in conjunction with a program administered in a clinical setting by the speech therapist. It involves establishing a partnership between the speech therapist and individuals who are in close contact with children with ASD, including parents, teachers, and peers. This partnership is directed toward establishing speech and communication goals and best treatment practices. How this partnership proceeds varies considerably depending on the speech therapist and those who seek consultation. Although consultation is used to formulate and transmit general goals and approaches, ideally it also involves the speech therapist training significant individuals in the child's life to implement the speech/communication program (Ogletree, 1998).

Alternative communication training

Typically alternative communication programs are employed when children with autism are unable or have difficulty acquiring speech. Many of these programs utilize behavioral procedures to teach children how to utilize communication devices and tools. A wide range of materials and technologies exist for facilitating communication, such as cards with pictures and words on them and language devices with prerecorded messages that can be activated through a variety of responses. The technology for assisting communication has become increasingly sophisticated as computer software evolves and is interfaced with sound/speech synthesizers. For example, computers can be used to convert pictures, printed words, and other symbols into a speech format (Whitman, 2004).

Less technology-driven, alternative, communication approaches include the Picture Exchange Communication System (PECS) and sign language, both of which are widely employed (Whitman, 2004). These systems have been popular choices for historical, pragmatic, and economic reasons, as well as because of their established utility. Specific considerations that influence the choice of a communication system include: the sensory and motor capabilities of the child, the system's potential for expansion into more complex language forms, the child's motivation to use the system, the system's exportability into natural settings, and the ability of recipients to understand the communication. The PECS and sign language approaches are briefly described here.

PICTURE EXCHANGE COMMUNICATION SYSTEM (PECS)

Visual communication systems are frequently utilized with children with autism who have limited language skills (Whitman, 2004). These visual systems provide both a means of responding to the verbal communications of others as well as a method for expressing one's needs and desires. The visual communication abilities of children with autism are often better than their verbal abilities. Visual systems utilize pictures with words or objects on them, or combinations of the two, for communication purposes. They also involve the use of some type of physical aid, such as a communication board, a notebook, or other devices to carry pictures. Portability and convenience of use are especially important considerations in selecting a particular system. The PECS program, developed by Bondy and Frost (1993, 1994), is the most widely known of these visual systems.

During PECS training, objects or activities are chosen that serve as reinforcers for the child. During the initial stages of training, a child is prompted to put a picture of a desired object/activity (e.g. a cookie) in the hand of the parent/teacher, who in turn verbalizes what the child wants ("You want a cookie!"), and then gives the child the object (the actual cookie). As training proceeds, prompts are gradually withdrawn to encourage the child to initiate spontaneously a request for the desired object/activity through the use of the proper picture card. Subsequent training focuses on teaching the child to request other objects and desired activities, thus allowing the child to choose from a range of objects/activities the one most preferred at a particular time and to express that choice by giving the appropriate picture of the preferred object/activity to the parent/teacher. This step requires that the child learn to discriminate between objects/activities. Later stages of training focus on teaching the child to respond to questions by using single and multi-picture responses. Pictures should be associated with words as part of a total communication package in order to facilitate speech. For more complete information on PECS, the reader is referred to Bondy and Frost (1994).

Another approach that is somewhat similar to the PECS training system is facilitated communication. The facilitated communication approach is employed with individuals who have limited or no verbal abilities. The facilitator provides the child support in using an augmentative communication device, such as a computer or a communication board. Critics of this approach contend that the facilitator, not the child, is dictating the communication response, that is the child does not actually learn to communicate independently. This approach has also been criticized because it has not been subjected to rigorous empirical scrutiny. Reviews of existing research examining this therapy offer little evidence for its efficacy (Mostert, 2001). Because facilitated communication is similar in its intent to other more accepted approaches, such as PECS, that are directed at either augmenting or providing a child with an alternative means of communication, parents, therapists, and teachers are strongly encouraged to consider these other approaches.

SIGN LANGUAGE

When children with autism have difficulty acquiring speech, sign language may become a treatment of choice, depending on the child's sensory, motor, and cognitive capabilities. For some children, signs are easier to teach than oral speech responses. Because no physical aids are required, signing is easily exportable to any communication situation. Moreover, sign language systems can be employed to express or receive messages of a highly complex nature. Sign language can be taught using an array of prompting and reinforcement procedures, such as formats like those of discrete trial and natural language training which are discussed in the last section.

The major drawback of a signing approach is that signing may not be understood by those with whom the child interacts. Therefore, in order to be useful, training programs need to teach not only the child, but also significant others in the child's life to sign. Signing programs, although typically employed when traditional oral communication training programs fail, may aid in the acquisition of speech. Unless extensive auditory and other physical impairments exist, signing procedures for children with autism are typically paired with speech as part of a total communication package. One signing program commonly employed with speech-delayed children is American Sign Language. For a concise review of signing and other alternative communication systems, the reader is referred to Scheuermann and Webber (2002).

Auditory integration training

In addition to the aforementioned approaches for developing communication, auditory integration training (AIT) is sometimes employed to assist in the development of listening skills and speech (Ogletree 1998). AIT is typically utilized with individuals who display hypersensitivity to sound. Hearing is obviously essential for perception, speech, and learning. Because auditory input influences arousal levels and attentional responses, disruptions in auditory processing can lead to a variety of cognitive, linguistic, and socioemotional problems. Children with autism often have difficulty in sound and speech processing. They also sometimes engage in socially unusual behaviors in order to avoid or to produce certain sound stimuli, behaviors that some clinicians theorize originate from an auditory integration deficiency. In order to assist children with this deficiency, various approaches have evolved to facilitate auditory integration.

One popular approach is the Berard Method, which was developed by Guy Berard, a French otolaryngologist (Berard, 1993). This method assumes that people vary in their level of sensitivity to sounds and that for some individuals hypersensitive hearing can result in pain and consequently attentional and learning problems. As part of the Berard method, an audiogram is obtained to evaluate auditory abnormalities, to determine the thresholds at which a person hears sounds at different frequency levels, and to establish a baseline against which to evaluate treatment effectiveness. Treatment is directed at reducing hypersensitivity problems.

Berard believes, just as muscles can be retrained through physical exercises, that the hearing system can be retrained as well. In order to retrain the auditory system, a broad range of low and high frequency sound stimuli are presented randomly through headphones to the listener. Frequencies at which hearing is painful are attenuated through the use of a filtering system. Treatment typically consists of half-hour sessions over a 10- to 20-day period. Although Berard does not maintain that the auditory problems of children with autism cause their disorder, he believes that treatments directed at improving auditory functioning can reduce problems that are associated with hearing difficulties, such as attentional and learning problems.

Support for the efficacy of this method is mixed. Anecdotal reports suggest improvements in language, tactile, and social functioning, as well as a reduction in sound hypersensitivities. Although such reports of successes abound, including those described by Stehli (1990, 1995), empirical research yields at best an incomplete picture regarding the method's efficacy (Goldstein, 2000; Mudford et al., 2000). At present, more research is needed to evaluate the general utility of this approach, specifically to assess what types of individuals, if any, benefit from this procedure and to provide insights into why this procedure is effective, if indeed it is. The reader is referred to Chapter 5 for other approaches that are employed to reduce auditory hypersensitivity problems.

Behavior intervention perspectives and strategies

Since its inception in the middle of the last century, behavior intervention programs for children with autism have emphasized the development of language skills (Lovaas, 2003). The techniques implemented in these programs have been employed not only by behavior therapists, but also have become major tools used by speech therapists. In this section, we examine two salient behavior training approaches: discrete trial training and natural language learning.

Discrete trial training was developed by Ivar Lovaas to teach children with severe language delays, including children with autism. Because this training approach is standardized and designed to be easily exportable, it can be and typically is transferred to nonprofessional, paraprofessional, and professional individuals, including parents, teachers, teacher aides, volunteers and more generally any individual who interacts on a regular basis with children. Although the structure of the speech program is developed by qualified speech and behavior therapists, the parents, teacher aides, volunteers, and others are extensively involved in the implementation of the training program. Both the parent/paraprofessional training and child therapy components of the intervention are intensive and extensive in nature.

Discrete trial training, a variant of applied behavior analysis, is a highly structured approach that employs a variety of behavioral techniques, including the extensive use of prompts (verbal, imitation and physical) and reinforcement. Each trial begins with the therapist/teacher giving the child a distinct cue, for example asking "What is this?" or saying "Point to the ___" while showing the child a picture of an object or the actual object. The trial ends when the child makes a correct response, either prompted or unprompted, and is reinforced, or when the child is unable to make the correct response within a prescribed period of time. Typically, the child is taught in blocks of five or more trials, either consecutive, or nonconsecutive and intermixed with trials directed at teaching other responses, until the child is able to reliably make each targeted response to a fixed criteria, (e.g. gets four out of five responses correct). After learning occurs, maintenance and generalization programs are put in place to ensure that the child retains what has been learned and to extend the use of language into everyday living environments (see Chapter 2). If maintenance of what has been taught does not occur, the original training program is partially or totally reinstated.

Because it is highly structured, discrete trial training often takes place at a table or on the floor where training materials are organized and readily available. Once the child begins to learn in this structured training environment, the intervention program is gradually transferred to a less structured and normalized setting in which a natural language training approach is introduced.

In contrast to discrete trial training, the natural language training approach is implemented in everyday living environments. In one variation of natural language training, the structure of the program is more spontaneous, dictated basically by the child's behavior and interests. For example, if a child is bouncing a ball, he/she might be asked what it is, or "What are you doing with the ball?" If the child is able to provide a correct response, (e.g. "ball"), he/she is reinforced (e.g. "Yes, that is a ball."). If the child is not able to respond, he/she is prompted (e.g. "That is a ball. Say ball."). In other variations of natural language training, parents/teachers arrange the environment in order to increase the probability of specific child language responses. For example, stimuli, such as a ball, which are employed during discrete trial training, are strategically introduced into the natural environment. In this approach, as in discrete trial training, very similar teaching procedures are employed.

Discrete trial training, natural language training, and other forms of behavior education programs all have certain critical features in common. These features include:

- selecting and carefully defining the target behaviors to be developed

- deciding on the training techniques, which typically include some type of prompting and reinforcement procedures

- programming the target behavior to occur with sufficient frequency so that it can be reinforced

- implementing the intervention in a way so as to ensure that target behaviors occur in appropriate situations, are maintained over time, and are generalized to appropriate social settings.

These procedures are described at some length in Chapter 2 and in the next section which presents examples of behavior therapy programs directed at developing language skills.

Table 7.1 Language/communication behaviors that are targeted in comprehensive intervention programs

---

Proto-communication (use of gestures, e.g. nodding)
Sound production
Word production
Labeling (tacting) (see Chapter 3)
Request-making (manding) (see Chapter 3)
Vocabulary building
Instruction-following (simple and complex) (see Chapter 3)
Phrase/sentence development
Pronoun use
Syntax and grammar skills
Preposition use
Use of action verbs
Use of different verb tenses
Passive versus active verb usage
Question production and comprehension
Conversational speech
Prosody (e.g. pitch, intonation, rhythm, and loudness)

The process of selecting target behaviors to be taught in a behavior intervention program is guided by whether they make developmental sense, that is whether they build on previous learning, and are useful. Table 7.1 presents a partial list of such behaviors, ordered in a sequence that makes developmental sense. Because language training programs are complex, it is important that they are developed with the professional assistance of speech therapists and/or certified applied behavior analysts. For a more complete description of such programs, the reader is referred to books like *Teaching Language to Children with Autism or Other Developmental Disabilities* by Mark Sundberg and James Partington (1998) and *Teaching Individuals with Developmental Delays* by Ivar Lovaas (2003).

Program examples

Labeling actions

OBJECTIVE

Teach the child to label (i.e. tact) pictures of actions using a noun-verb combination.

MATERIALS

Gather several different pictures of people/animals completing various actions. To promote generalization, you should have at least four different examples of each action.

PROCEDURE

1. Hold up a picture and ask the child to tell you what is happening in the picture (e.g. "What is he doing?" or "Can you tell me what's happening in this picture?").

    a) If the child responds correctly with a noun-verb combination (e.g. "He's swimming," or "Girl is running.") immediately deliver specific praise ("That's right, the girl is running.") and a tangible reinforcer.

    b) If the child responds with the correct verb, but does not provide a noun, prompt the child to rephrase the sentence to include the noun. For example, if the child responds, "Swimming," to a picture of a boy that's swimming, say, "That's right, he's swimming. Say, 'the boy is swimming.'" Once the child repeats the correct noun-verb combination, provide a small or short reinforcer.

    c) If the child does not respond at all, deliver a prompt so that the child responds correctly. Provide a small or short reinforcer.

2. Repeat with a different picture, randomly rotating between three to five different actions, using four to five different pictures for each action. Continue until each action has been presented 5 to 10 times.

3. Fade prompts until the child has demonstrated mastery of the target by reliably responding correctly and independently (i.e. accurately labeling four different examples of an action using a noun-verb combination without prompts).

4. Once an action target has been mastered, introduce a new action. Continue to practice and generalize mastered targets occasionally to maintain the skill.

ERROR CORRECTION

If the child responds incorrectly (i.e. states the wrong action), repeat your instruction and immediately provide a prompt to help the child respond correctly. When the child responds correctly, provide praise, but do not deliver a tangible reinforcer following an error correction. Following one to two other trials, re-present the erred trial. Be prepared to prompt more quickly to avoid the same error; reinforce the prompted trial.

GENERALIZATION

Once the child has mastered an action, begin using the skill in more natural locations. For example, when looking at a picture book, ask the child to tell you what is happening in the pictures. It may help to create a book that has specific pictures of the actions that the child has already mastered. This is something the child can do with you as an art project.

TIPS/SUGGESTIONS

Choose actions that are common and relevant to the child and easy to identify in pictures. For example, choose actions such as cutting, crying, reading, writing, swimming, or painting. For some children, it may be relevant to teach actions such as typing, texting, calling, or exercising. For additional examples, see the example list below. Do not use actions such as sitting, standing, or watching, which are too vague and difficult to identify in pictures (e.g. a picture of a boy who is smiling and sitting in a chair could be labeled as smiling or sitting). Also, use pictures that are clear and universal. If you are unsure about the pictures you have chosen, show them to several people to see if they all identify the same action.

TROUBLESHOOTING

If the child does not attend to the pictures, try using pictures of his/her favorite cartoon characters. Or begin by teaching the child to label live actions that are enjoyable to him/her. For example, tickle the child and ask, "What am I doing?" Or, when the child is riding his/her bike, stop the bike and ask, "What are you doing?" Once he/she answers correctly allow him/her to resume riding.

EXAMPLE TARGETS

- skating
- yelling
- swinging
- washing (clothes, dishes, a car, the dog)

- flying

- waving

- fishing

- riding a bike

- eating

- drinking.

FUTURE OBJECTIVES

Next teach the child to label live actions of adults and/or children (e.g. "What am I doing?" "What are you doing?" "What's happening on the playground?"). Also, determine if the child can receptively identify pictures when given the action (e.g. "Find the picture of the girl that is yawning."). Receptive identification and expressive identification are two very different skills that often require individual focus and training. Do not assume that mastery of one of these skills (e.g. tacting/ labeling the action) will result in the automatic acquisition of the other (e.g. identifying an action). In addition, begin expanding the length of the sentences the child provides (e.g. add words such as "the," "and," "is," as well as additional nouns such as, "washing the dishes," "doing the laundry," etc.).

Also, begin fading your questions about the pictures to assist with spontaneity. Perhaps instead of asking the child what is happening, simply present the picture to the child. When the child labels an action without you asking him/her to do so, provide enthusiastic praise and highly preferred reinforcers.

Song and phrase completion

OBJECTIVE

Teach the child to finish a common song or phrase that is started by someone else.

MATERIALS

For this procedure, you will need a list of common songs (e.g. "Twinkle, Twinkle, Little Star") or phrases (e.g. "See you later, alligator."). Adjust the songs and phrases to be age-appropriate and relevant to the child.

PROCEDURE

1. State the beginning of a common song/phrase (e.g. "Old McDonald…").

a)   If the child finishes the song/phrase, immediately deliver a reinforcer and praise.

b)   If the child does not finish the song/phrase, provide a prompt to help him/her respond correctly. Once the child responds, provide praise but do not deliver a tangible reinforcer.

2.   Repeat, mixing trials of three to five songs/phrases, until you have done five to ten trials of each target song/phrase.

3.   Fade prompts until the child has demonstrated mastery of the target by reliably responding correctly and independently (i.e. finishing the song/ phrase within 3 seconds without prompts).

4.   Once a song/phrase has been mastered, introduce a new song/phrase. Continue to practice and generalize mastered targets occasionally to maintain the skill.

ERROR CORRECTION

If the child responds incorrectly (e.g. repeats (echoes) your part of the song/phrase or finishes with an incorrect response), simply repeat the beginning of the song/ phrase and quickly prompt the child to respond correctly (e.g. "Old McDonald had a farm…, say, '…E I E I O.'") until the child responds correctly. Once the child responds correctly, give light praise (e.g. "That's right!") but do not deliver a tangible reinforcer following error correction. Present a different trial, and then return to the erred trial, being prepared to prompt more quickly to prevent the same error from happening again; reinforce the prompted trial.

GENERALIZATION

Initially you may need to begin this procedure in a more controlled setting, such as at a table or in a location where typical academic tasks are learned. However, once the child masters the target song/phrase, begin using this skill in a more natural context. For example, sing "Old McDonald" while playing with a farm set, on a car ride, or when visiting a petting zoo. Present phrases at times when they would typically be used (e.g. when leaving, say, "See you later…" waiting for him/her to say "Alligator."). Be prepared to temporarily increase assistance when presenting mastered targets in new locations/situations.

TIPS/SUGGESTIONS

If the child can read, use a textual prompt rather than a verbal prompt to help the child finish the phrase. Write the words you want the child to say on a piece of paper or a note card, and hold up the card after you begin the phrase. Fade the use of the card by waiting an additional second to present the card, or by writing fewer words on the card.

For some children, the reinforcer may be completing the song in a fun way (e.g. use a hand puppet for the farmer and present different animal toys when you sing about them).

TROUBLESHOOTING

If the child is having difficulty learning this skill, you might be starting this goal too early in the child's development. Prior to beginning such a complex language procedure the child should already be requesting (manding) and labeling (tacting) spontaneously (i.e. without prompts, other than, "What do you want?").

If the child is having difficulty maintaining interest in this activity, consider ways to increase motivation by altering the activity itself. For example, start with phrases such as, "I want…," having the child finish the phrase by stating what he/she wants and then giving that item to the child as a reinforcer. Or sing a song about an object that the child wants (e.g. if he/she wants a cookie, teach the song, "Who Stole the Cookie from the Cookie Jar."). If the child can already request a cookie, have him/her fill in the blanks, rather than finish the phrase. Point to the cookie when it's time for him/her to say, "cookie," and then reward the child with a piece of the cookie as you finish the song.

OTHER TEACHING METHODS

If the child is echoing your every word, a different prompting method may be required involving two people. For this method, one person must present the beginning of the song/phrase to the child, while the other person stands behind the child and states the part of the phrase that the child should echo. For example, the person standing in front of the child will say, "Twinkle, twinkle…" The person who is standing behind the child will quickly (i.e. before the child begins to echo the first person) deliver the lines that the child will echo, "little star." The child should echo the person behind him/her, at which point the first person should immediately deliver a highly preferred reinforcer.

This may take a few trials for the child to understand who to echo. If the child repeats the words of the first person, stop and start the trial over again. The second person should be quick to deliver the appropriate lines for the child to repeat. The second person should fade the prompts by decreasing the volume of his/her voice, delivering less of the phrase, and/or using a time delay of one additional second.

If two people are not available, try using a tape recorder to present the prompts. Keep in mind that a tape recorder must be faded as well, which can be done in the same manner as if a person were prompting.

FUTURE OBJECTIVES

Teach the child to respond to phrases that are more specific (e.g. "My name is…" or, "I like to eat…"). In addition, teach some non-familiar phrases, opposites, and associations (e.g. "Socks and…" or "Peanut butter and…" or "Hot and…").

Also once the child has learned some beginner intraverbal behavior (i.e. responding to your verbal statements with a related but different statement), teach the child to answer basic questions. Begin with simple questions that have clear answers (e.g. "What is your name?") as opposed to questions whose answers may vary depending on the situation (e.g. "How are you?"). Keep in mind that the child will need specific training on different types of questions, such as what, where, who, why, and when. Some of these questions will be more difficult to answer than others.

Answering "wh" questions about topics

OBJECTIVE

Teach the child to answer various "wh" questions about different topics.

MATERIALS

No materials are needed for this procedure unless you are using a visual or textual prompt.

PROCEDURE

1. Ask a question about a topic (see example targets on the following page). Don't ask a question if you don't know the answer. For example, if you ask what the child had for breakfast, be sure you are already aware of the answer. Vary questions/topics across trials.

2. Prompt the child to answer the question by modeling the correct response.

3. Reinforce the correct response.

ERROR CORRECTION

If the child responds incorrectly (i.e. provides the wrong answer), repeat your question and immediately provide a prompt to help the child respond correctly. When the child responds correctly, provide praise, but do not deliver a tangible reinforcer following an error correction. Following one to two other trials, re-present the erred question. Be prepared to prompt more quickly to avoid the same error; reinforce the prompted trial.

GENERALIZATION

Begin asking the child "wh" questions that he/she has not been trained to answer. For example, when going to the dentist, ask the child questions about the trip, such as why people go to the dentist, or what the dentist did while the child was there.

TIPS/SUGGESTIONS

Initially, choose topics that are of interest to the child. If the child can read, a textual prompt will be easier to fade than a verbal prompt (i.e. write the answer down for the child to read as opposed to telling him/her what to say).

TROUBLESHOOTING

If the child repeats your question, it may help to have another instructor available to prompt the child. One helper can stand facing the child and deliver the question. The second helper can stand behind the child and immediately provide the child with an echoic prompt (i.e. verbally model the answer for the child to echo) or deliver a textual prompt (i.e. present a written answer for the child to read aloud). Reinforce the response only if the child provides the answer without repeating the question. See the previous program example (Song and phrase completion) for more information on this prompting method.

EXAMPLE TARGETS

Example topics and questions	Example answers
Breakfast	
What do you eat for breakfast?	Pancakes
When do you eat breakfast?	In the morning
Taking a shower	
Why do you have to take a shower?	To get clean
Where do you take a shower?	In the bathroom
School	
Who do you see at school?	Tommy and Mary
What do you do at school?	Play and write letters
Where do you go to school?	Alphabet Elementary

FUTURE OBJECTIVES

Teach the child to provide answers that may change from day to day. For example, ask the child what he/she ate for breakfast that morning. Or ask the child where his/her mom/dad/sibling/pet is currently. You will need to be sure of the answers prior to asking such questions. If the child is not able to recall past events, teach that procedure first or simultaneously (see Chapter 8). Also teach your child to ask other people questions, and to wait for the answers.

Asking conversational questions

OBJECTIVE

Teach the child to ask questions in order to expand and sustain conversations.

MATERIALS

No materials are needed for this procedure unless you are using some sort of visual or textual prompt.

PROCEDURE

1. Present a statement to a child. If the child has already learned how to reciprocate social information, start by using similar statements (e.g. "I really like Princess Jasmine.").

2. Prompt the child to then ask you a question related to your statement, or reciprocate and then ask a question. For example, the child can say, "I like Cinderella. Do you like Cinderella?"

   a) If the child asks the question, answer the question and simultaneously provide an additional reinforcer.

   b) If the child does not ask a question within 3 to 5 seconds, use a more intrusive prompt. Once the child asks a question, answer the question and deliver praise and a smaller, or less preferred reinforcer than what you would deliver if he/she had asked with a less intrusive prompt.

3. Repeat with a different set of statements/questions.

4. Fade your prompts across trials, using differential reinforcement to better reward more independent responding (i.e. when the child asks you a question without requiring a prompt to do so).

ERROR CORRECTION

If the child does not ask a question but instead talks about the topic, provide a cue (e.g. a hand gesture or a question mark) to prompt the child to ask you a question. If he/she does not respond to the cue use a more intrusive prompt (e.g. echoic or textual). Be sure to fade the use of such prompts across trials.

GENERALIZATION

Once the child is able to ask questions in such structured situations, begin to generalize to more naturally occurring situations. For example, when a conversation strikes up, use your effective prompting methods to help the child remember to ask questions during this conversation. Provide reinforcers to the child (e.g. specific praise) following successful conversations in which he/she asked at least one question.

TIPS/SUGGESTIONS

Visual and textual prompts can be very helpful prompts for this procedure. Write down the question you want the child to ask on a note card and hold it up briefly as a prompt. Or show a picture of a question mark when you want the child to ask a question. This can be useful when generalizing too, because you will not have to interrupt the conversation to remind the child to ask a question.

When using textual prompts write down only part of the question for the child to read aloud. The child will then have to complete the question independently. Keep the text general, so the child can learn to ask similar questions in a variety of conversational situations (e.g. "Do you…?" "How about…?"). Initially the child will need help finishing these questions, but such assistance should be faded quickly.

OTHER TEACHING METHODS

Initially, you can role play scenarios. Create scripts and act them out with the child. It may help to make comic strip scripts that combine visual and textual information, which can be very appealing to a lot of children. Consider videotaping the scripts so that the child can watch them with you later. Along the same lines, video modeling can be another method that is helpful for teaching social and conversation skills such as these.

FUTURE OBJECTIVES

Once the child regularly asks questions during such reciprocal conversations, expand to other types of conversations. For example, present the child with vague information (e.g. "I got a book from the library yesterday.") and prompt him/her to ask for more information (e.g. "What book did you get?"). Also move on to teaching more advanced conversation skills, including increasing the number of back and forth conversation "volleys," interpreting and using slang and idioms, or other figures of speech, and answering more advanced "wh" questions (e.g. about past events).

Pronouns

OBJECTIVE

Teach the child the appropriate use of some basic possessive pronouns.

MATERIALS

You will need something for people to hold in order to show ownership or possession. Consider using something that the child desires so that he/she will be motivated to look for the object.

PROCEDURE

1. Give an object to someone:

   a) yourself

   b) the child

   c) another person (female)

   d) another person (male)

   e) two other people (male or female or both)

   f) the child and one other person.

2. Ask the child who has the object.

3. Prompt as necessary for the child to respond with the appropriate pronoun:

   a) You have it.

   b) I have it.

   c) She has it.

   d) He has it.

   e) They have it.

   f) We have it.

4. Reinforce correct pronoun usage.

ERROR CORRECTION

If the child states the wrong pronoun, interrupt him/her, restate the question and then help him/her state the correct pronoun. Point out who is holding the item (e.g. a girl is holding the item so you say, "She is holding it."). If the child names the person holding the item (e.g. "Billy is holding it."), acknowledge the correct response, but then prompt him/her to use the pronoun before delivering a reinforcer.

GENERALIZATION

Do this in less structured environments and throughout the day when natural opportunities present themselves. If the child wants something, ask him who has it. If he needs to order at a restaurant ask him which person is your waiter/waitress (i.e. correct response is, "She is our waitress," while pointing). When appropriate, if you catch the child using names instead of pronouns have the child restate the sentence using a pronoun. However, be careful not to encourage only the use of pronouns, as opposed to people's names.

TIPS/SUGGESTIONS

It may help if the child is already able to discriminate between males and females when it comes to the pronouns, "he" and "she," although understanding gender is not a prerequisite to this skill. Moreover, teaching the child a rule statement (e.g. "When it is you and one or more people, you say 'we.'") may assist with the acquisition of this skill, if the child is able to understand and follow rule statements.

OTHER TEACHING METHODS

If you do not have enough people available, use dolls (e.g. Barbie and Ken) or pictures to demonstrate the different pronouns.

FUTURE OBJECTIVES

Move on to other pronouns (e.g. him, her, me, you) and use them for sentences other than possession (e.g. "Who is swinging?").

Voice modulation

OBJECTIVE

Teach the child to modulate the volume and/or pitch of his/her voice.

PROCEDURE

1. Ask the child to repeat a word or phrase in a particular volume or tone voice (e.g. loud, soft, high, low).

2. Model the desired volume or tone.

3. Only reinforce correct vocal imitations.

ERROR CORRECTION

If the child does not imitate correctly, interrupt his/her response and give the instruction again, prompting by exaggerating your volume or tone. If the child continues to have difficulty, a shaping procedure may be helpful. This requires reinforcing approximations to the desired response. A certified behavior analyst or a speech pathologist will be able to assist you with shaping desired vocal responses.

GENERALIZATION

Once the child is able to imitate accurately, use a model to help the child respond in a more appropriate tone of voice throughout the day. For example, if asking a child a question and the child responds very loudly, tell the child to repeat the answer quietly. Model the child's appropriate response and have him/her imitate. Reinforce correct imitations. Deliver reinforcers any time the child is responding in a more appropriate tone of voice throughout the day (i.e. when he/she otherwise would have been too loud or soft).

TIPS/SUGGESTIONS

The child may respond well to a visual cue, such as a scale of loudness or pitch. You must first teach the child how to rate his/her voice on the scale, by teaching the child to say a word or phrase at each level on the scale. For example, teach the child to say a word at a level 5 (loud voice) by yelling the word or phrase. Do this for each level. Use a color coded or numbered scale that helps the child discriminate between the different levels.

TROUBLESHOOTING

Do not reinforce anything the child says in the inappropriate tone or volume of voice. For example, if the child asks for cookies in a high pitched, sing-song voice, do not give him/her the cookies until the child asks in a more moderately pitched, even-toned voice.

OTHER TEACHING METHODS

You can video or audiotape the child talking to help the child learn what he/she sounds like to others.

Answering yes or no

OBJECTIVE

Teach the child to respond to the question, "Do you want this?" by saying, "Yes," or nodding his/her head when the item is desired, or saying, "No," or shaking his/her head when the item is not desired.

MATERIALS

For this procedure, you will need a few preferred items (e.g. favorite foods, toys, etc.) as well as non-preferred items (i.e. items the child will not accept when offered). It is typically easier to teach yes/no when using highly preferred items and highly non-preferred items.

PROCEDURE

1. Hold up a preferred or non-preferred item.

2. Say, "Do you want this?"

    a) If the child is indicating he/she wants the item (e.g. the child is reaching for the item), immediately prompt by saying, "Yes," or nodding your head. Once the child repeats the word or action, deliver the item immediately.

    b) If the child is indicating that he/she does not want the item (e.g. the child is pushing it away or refusing to look at the item, immediately prompt by saying, "No," or shaking your head. Once the child repeats the word or action, remove the item from his/her sight.

3. Repeat, mixing trials of yes and no, until the child is no longer motivated for the preferred items or you have done at least ten trials of each, yes and no.

4. Fade prompts by using a time delay, waiting one additional second before prompting. If the child responds correctly before you prompt, give him/her more of the reinforcer or give the reinforcer for longer periods of time.

ERROR CORRECTION

If the child responds incorrectly to a preferred item (e.g. says, "No," when he/she actually wants the item), remove the item for 3 seconds. Re-present the item, delivering the prompt more quickly. If the child responds correctly this time, deliver a preferred item, but give less of it or for less time than usual in order to prevent reinforcing a pattern of incorrect responding.

If the child responds incorrectly to a non-preferred item (e.g. says, "Yes," when he/she actually does not want the item), give the item to the child for 3 seconds. Remove and then re-present the item, delivering the prompt more quickly.

GENERALIZATION

Initially, you may need to teach this skill in a structured setting. However, you should quickly begin teaching this skill in many different locations and with many different items and people. For example, if you start teaching this skill in the basement at a table, quickly transition to the play area on the floor (e.g. "Do you want to play with the doll?"), then up in the kitchen when it's snack time (e.g. "Do you want some Cheetos?").

Begin using less preferred items that the child wants (e.g. if the child drinks water when she is thirsty but does not otherwise want water, teach her to respond yes to water when she is thirsty). Also use more neutral items to teach the child to say, "No" (e.g. toys she doesn't want to play with currently, although the toy may be preferred at other times).

Teach the child to respond with yes/no when the question is phrased differently (e.g. "Do you want a piece of broccoli?" or "Would you like one?" or "How about a piece of chocolate?").

TROUBLESHOOTING

If you notice that the child is learning to say, "Yes" quicker than, "No" be sure you are allowing adequate and equal practice of both responses. In addition, mix trials, so that the child must respond to one to two trials with, "Yes," and then one to two trials with "No," rather than teaching all of one or the other (i.e. massed trials). Try using items that are highly non-preferred (e.g. vegetables) to teach the child to respond with, "No." Reinforce correct responses to non-preferred items by giving the child a highly preferred item.

If the child does not respond at all, try using items that are even more highly preferred. Increase the value of the reinforcers by depriving the child of the preferred item(s) for a couple of days before teaching. If, on the other hand, the child is responding with inappropriate behavior, try using items that are not as valuable until the child has better developed this skill. In addition, use more neutral items to teach "No," if the presence of a highly non-preferred item is too upsetting.

TIPS/SUGGESTIONS

If using food during this procedure, break it up into small pieces so that the child will maintain motivation for longer periods of time which will allow for more trials. Initially, avoid giving the child something that you must take away. For example, try using a puzzle, and giving the child one piece at a time, rather than using a toy that you must retrieve from the child in order to conduct another trial. However, if the child's most highly preferred items are such toys, then it is important to use such items. If possible, try to wait until the child has stopped touching or playing with the toy before taking it back.

Another prompting method for nodding/shaking the head (i.e. rather than imitation or full physical prompting) involves tapping the child's chin. Lightly tap under the child's chin to help the child nod, or tap the side of his/her chin to help the child shake his/her head. Fade this prompt by tapping more lightly, then just gesturing toward the child's chin, or wait an additional second before prompting. In addition, prompts for vocal responses can be faded by providing less of the word (e.g. say, "Yeh" instead of "Yes") or by decreasing volume (e.g. whisper "Yes").

OTHER TEACHING METHODS

If the child is having difficulty saying yes or no, or nodding/shaking his/her head, then try using another response form, such as a picture exchange. Have the child show or give you a "yes" icon when he/she wants the item, or a "no" icon when he/she does not want the item. The child does not need to be familiar with picture exchange to learn this method however you should refer to the requesting (manding) protocol in Chapter 3. Another option is to have the child use some sort of hand signal to indicate yes/no, or a voice output communication device.

Keep in mind that saying yes/no vocally or with a universal head nod/shake will allow the child to communicate more quickly and with more people than some alternative approaches, and should therefore be considered before trying something else.

FUTURE OBJECTIVES

Start to teach the child to respond with yes/no to questions about activity preference (e.g. "Do you want to color?" or "How about we go get a haircut?"). Keep in mind that when initially teaching this skill you must honor the child's responses by providing him/her with the activity when he/she says yes, and allowing escape from an activity when he/she says no.

Move on to teaching the child to respond to different yes/no questions about preferred and non-preferred items/activities. (e.g. "Can I have your toy?"), as well as fact-based questions (e.g. "Do cats have whiskers?" or "Do cows say meow?"). Different types of yes/no questions will require additional training, despite the fact that the response is the same (i.e. yes or no) because of the different controlling conditions of the response (i.e. the different questions or statements preceding the response as well as the typical consequences following the response).

References

Attwood, T. (2006). *Complete guide to Asperger's syndrome.* London: Jessica Kingsley Publishers.

Berard, G. (1993). *Hearing equals behavior.* New Caanan, CT: Keats.

Berk, L. E. (2009). *Child development* (8th ed.). Boston, MA: Allyn Bacon.

Bloom, L. & Trinker, E. (2001). The intentionality model and language acquisition: Engagement, effort and the essential tension in development. *Monographs of the Society for Research in Child Development, 66*(4), 1–104.

Bondy, A. & Frost. L. (1993). Mands across the water: A report on the application of the picture-exchange communication system in Peru. *The Behavior Analyst, 16,* 123–128.

Bondy, A. & Frost. L. (1994). The picture exchange communication system. *Focus on Autistic Behavior, 9,* 1–17.

Diehl, J. J. & Berkovits, L. (2010). "Is prosody a diagnostic and cognitive bellwether of autism spectrum disorders?" In A. Harrison (Ed.), *Speech disorders: Causes, treatments, and social effects* (pp. 159–176). New York, NY: Nova Science Publishing.

Dworzynski, K., Happé, F., Bolton, P., & Ronald A. (2009). Relationship between symptom domains in autism spectrum disorders: A population based twin study. *Journal of Autism and Developmental Disorders, 39,* 1197–1210.

Farrant, B., Fletcher, J., & Mayhery, M. (2006). Specific language impairment, theory of mind, and visual perspective taking: Evidence for simulation theory and the development role of language. *Child Development, 77,* 1842–1853.

Gillberg, C. (1989). Asperger syndrome in 23 Swedish children. *Developmental Medicine and Child Neurology, 31,* 520–531.

Goldstein, H. (2000). Commentary: Interventions to facilitate auditory, visual and motor integration: Show me the data. *Journal of Autism and Developmental Disorders, 30,* 423–425.

Hale, C. M. & Tager-Flusberg, H. (2005). Brief report: The relationship between discourse deficits and autism symptomatology. *Journal of Autism and Developmental Disorders, 35,* 519–524.

Hobson, R. P., Lee, A., & Hobson, J. A. (2010). Personal pronouns and communicative engagement in autism. *Journal of Autism and Developmental Disorders, 40,* 653–664.

Lightfoot, C., Cole, M., & Cole, S. (2009). *The development of children* (6th ed.). Worth, IL: Worth Publishing.

Lovaas, O. I. (2003). *Teaching individuals with developmental delays: Basic intervention techniques.* Austin, TX: Pro-Ed.

Marans, W. D., Rubin, E., & Laurent, A. (2005). "Addressing social communication skills in individuals with high-functioning autism and Asperger syndrome: Critical priorities in educational programming." In F. R. Volkmar, R. Paul, A. Klin, & D. Cohen (Eds.), *Handbook of autism and pervasive developmental disorders: Vol. 2. Assessment, interventions, and policy* (3rd ed., pp. 977–1002). Hoboken, NJ: John Wiley & Sons.

Mostert, M. (2001). Facilitated communication since 1995: A review of published studies. *Journal of Autism and Developmental Disorders, 31,* 287–313.

Mudford, O., Cross, B., Breen, S., Cullen, C., Reeves, D., Gould, J., & Douglas, J. (2000). Auditory integration training for children with autism: No behavioral benefits detected. *American Journal on Mental Retardation, 105,* 118–129.

Ogletree, B. (1998). "The communicative context of autism." In R. Simpson & B. Myles (Eds.), *Educating children and youth with autism: Strategies for effective practice* (pp. 141–172). Austin, TX: Pro-Ed.

Paul, R. & Sutherland, D. (2005). "Enhancing early language in children with autism spectrum disorders." In F. R. Volkmar, R., Paul, A., Klin, & D. Cohen (Eds.), *Handbook of autism and pervasive developmental disorders: Vol. 2. Assessment, interventions, and policy* (3rd ed., pp. 946–976). Hoboken, NJ: John Wiley & Sons.

Scheuermann, B. & Webber, J. (2002). *Autism: Teaching does make a difference.* Belmont, CA: Wadsworth.

Sigman, M. & Capps, L. (1997). *Children with autism: A developmental perspective.* Cambridge, MA: Harvard University Press.

Stehli, A. (1990). *The sound of a muscle.* New York, NY: Doubleday.

Stehli, A. (Ed.) (1995). *Dancing in the rain.* Westport, CT: The Georgiana Organization.

Sundberg, M. & Partington, J. (1998). *Teaching language to children with autism or other developmental disabilities.* Pleasant Hill, CA: Behavior Analysts.

Tager-Flusberg, H. (1996). Brief report: Current theory and research on language and communication in autism. *Journal of Autism and Developmental Disorders, 26,* 169–172.

Tager-Flusberg, H., Paul, R., & Lord, C. (2005). "Language and communication in autism." In F. R. Volkmar, R. Paul, A. Klin, & D. Cohen (Eds.), *Handbook of autism and pervasive developmental disorders: Vol. 1 Diagnosis, development, neurobiology, and behavior* (3rd ed., pp. 335–364). Hoboken, NJ: John Wiley & Sons.

Travis, L. & Sigman, M. (2001). "Communicative intentions and symbols in autism. Examining a case of altered development." In J. Burack, T. Charman, N., Yirmiya, & P. Zelazo (Eds.), *The development of autism: Perspectives from theory and research* (pp. 279–308). Mahwah, NJ: Erlbaum.

Watson, L. (2001). "Issues in early comprehension development of children with autism." In E. Schopler, N. Yirmiya, C., Schulman, & L. Marcus (Eds.), *The research basis for autism intervention* (pp. 135–150). New York, NY: Kluwer Academic Plenum Publishers.

Wetherby, A. & Prizant, B. (1992). "Facilitating language and communication development in autism: Assessment and intervention guidelines." In D. Berkell (Ed.), *Autism: Identification, education and treatment* (pp. 107–134). Hillsdale, NJ: Lawrence Erlbaum.

Wetherby, A. M. & Prizant, B. M. (2005). "Enhancing language and communication development in autism spectrum disorders: Assessment and intervention guidelines." In D. Zager (Ed.), *Autism spectrum disorders: Identification, education, and treatment* (3rd ed., pp. 327–365). Mahwah, NJ: Lawrence Erlbaum Associates.

Whitman, T. L. (2004). *The development of autism: A self-regulatory perspective.* London: Jessica Kingsley Publishers.

Chapter 8

Cognitive Deficiencies

Examination of the cognitive characteristics of children with autism reveals a different picture from that observed in neurotypical children. Whereas for neurotypical children the world becomes increasingly organized, understandable, and predictable, for children with autism it often remains chaotic, confusing, and frightening. Cognitive development is uneven in children with autism, with delays and deficiencies occurring in both simple and complex cognitive processes. We begin this chapter by examining cognitive development in neurotypical children and children with autism. Then we describe intervention strategies and specific programs for addressing cognitive deficiencies commonly associated with autism.

Cognitive development in neurotypical children

Although newborns appear to experience their world as an incoherent mixture of sensations, they rapidly acquire a rudimentary understanding of their environment. Their interactions with this environment reflect a growing ability to process, store, and use information. During the first year, they learn that objects have permanence and continue to exist even when they are out sight, and that objects, differing in various ways, can still be categorized together based on their similar perceptual characteristics. They also begin to coordinate their motor actions with their perceptions.

During early childhood, children begin to internalize external objects through the use of images, gestures, and words. Pretend play emerges. They begin to understand the mental states and intentions of others and to engage in primitive forms of causal reasoning. As they transition into middle childhood, their thinking becomes more organized and flexible. Their world also becomes more predictable as they discover that objects remain the same even when they undergo peripheral changes. They can think about alternatives as they engage in problem-solving. Their memory capacity and knowledge base expands as they begin to understand their memory and how cognitive strategies can enhance their ability to remember.

During adolescence, children begin to think logically as they seek to understand their reality. They also think more abstractly and are less bound by what they are observing. Adolescents begin to envision possibilities and futures that differ from their present realities. They begin to understand their own thought processes and what they know and do not know. With the transition to adulthood, knowledge acquisition continues; thinking becomes flexible; and a recognition develops, that answers to questions may vary depending on the social and physical context. Problem-solving skills become more pragmatic as life responsibilities are confronted. For further information on cognitive development in neurotypical children, the reader is referred to texts on child development by Berk (2009) and Lightfoot, Cole, and Cole (2009).

Cognitive functioning in children with autism spectrum disorders

Early in the history of autism claims of a general intellectual deficit underlying this disorder were common. This view seemed to be based on the fact that persons with autism were frequently assessed as having mental retardation. Mental retardation is characterized by significantly sub-average intellectual functioning that exists in conjunction with adaptive behavior deficiencies in at least two or more of the following skill areas: communication, self-care, home living, social skills, community use, self-direction, health and safety, functional academics, leisure, and work. To receive a diagnosis of mental retardation, an individual must display both intellectual and adaptive behavior deficiencies before age 18, deficiencies that research indicates are positively correlated (Kenworthy, Case, Harms, Martin, & Wallace, 2010).

Using these criteria, it should not be surprising that children with autism are often diagnosed as having mental retardation. They typically display a variety of skill or behavior deficiencies, most frequently in the communication, social interaction, leisure, academic, and vocational areas. Children with autism, who are considered functioning at a lower developmental level, often display deficiencies in other areas as well, such as in self-care. In addition, many children with autism score in the significantly sub-average range of intellectual functioning on intelligence tests, that is an IQ score of approximately 70 to 75 or below. Estimates of the incidence of mental retardation in persons with autism vary considerably; most commonly, they are in the 50 percent to 80 percent range (Whitman, 2004).

It is important, however, to note that when evaluating their cognitive status, the IQ scores of persons with autism are less informative than their pattern of performance on specific subtests of an IQ assessment. Persons with autism often display an uneven pattern of strengths and weaknesses. Typically, they score higher on subtests that measure nonverbal abilities than on those that assess verbal abilities. They do better on subtests that assess short-term memory than on subtests that assess social knowledge and comprehension. They also do better on subtests evaluating visual organization abilities. However, they are more likely to have problems with subtests that require sequencing skills. If one subscribes to the notion that intelligence is composed of not one general ability, but rather multiple abilities, persons with autism would be characterized, relative to their overall IQ, as having a profile of contrasting cognitive abilities and disabilities (Whitman, 2004).

Some people question whether the IQ tests that are given to children with autism are fair, because these children frequently have language deficiencies and IQ tests have a strong verbal component. Even when their language skills are well developed, children with autism appear to have difficulty tracking the directions of the test administrator, perhaps because of the unconventional ways they use and understand language. They also have difficulty attending in the social situations in which the test is given. Thus, estimates of the IQs of children with autism may be low because of the social nature of testing situations and the verbal format of the IQ test. Such estimates may particularly disguise their competencies in nonverbal areas.

Nevertheless, it should be noted that IQ tests that assess verbal skills and verbal learning are good predictors of academic achievement in schools; however it is also important to note that most schools have a conventional language-based curriculum. Such an IQ test may, however, not be a good predictor of the performance of children with autism who are placed in a curriculum which is more visually oriented and highly structured and takes into consideration their social limitations; that is, a curriculum which is more individualized and utilizes the special competencies of the student.

In describing intelligence, a distinction needs to be made between the basic process or processes underlying intelligence and the developmental achievements in various domains assessed by intelligence tests. At its most basic process level, researchers often view intelligence as an index of the speed with which information is processed. One provocative hypothesis suggests that even though persons with autism are impaired in certain areas like social comprehension, most are unimpaired in their speed of processing, that is in the basic underlying foundation of intelligence.

In a study by Scheuffgen, Happé, Anderson, and Frith (2000), this hypothesis was supported. The speed of processing of children with autism on an inspection time task was compared with that of age-matched, normally developing children, who had IQs one standard deviation above average. The results suggested that children with autism were not deficient in their speed of processing, despite the fact that they had lower IQ scores than the comparison group. More generally, the results imply, at least for some children with autism, that their low scores on intelligence tests may not be a function of a deficit in speed of processing, but rather are due to defects in other areas.

Currently, there is more discussion, research, and theorization about the cognitive characteristics of persons with autism than any other feature of this disorder. There is fairly uniform agreement that this population displays a variety of cognitive deficits, including deficiencies in semantic memory, emotion recognition, knowledge of other people, self-knowledge, problem-solving skills, and abstract thinking. These deficits in turn have often been used to explain their social interaction and communication difficulties. It should also be noted that many of the social and language deficiencies associated with autism have cognitive components, including those related to pragmatic communication, question-asking, joint attention, imitation, pretend play, executive functioning, and theory of mind (Whitman, 2004).

In contrast, there is also increasing recognition that islands of cognitive abilities exist in this population and that cognitive processes, such as attention, discrimination, rote memory, visual-spatial perception, and certain types of object knowledge, are unimpaired or less impaired. Moreover, there are sometimes even areas of special cognitive abilities, such as those displayed by autistic savants (Whitman, 2004).

In summary, as a result of recent research and as data from intelligence testing has been more closely analyzed, a new perspective has emerged, that the cognitive deficits associated with autism are not due to a general intellectual deficit, but rather are of a more specialized nature. It is now acknowledged that intelligence tests provide only limited information about the cognitive abilities and disabilities associated with autism and that more attention needs to be given to examining specific cognitive processes, and possible deficits in areas such as information-processing, executive functioning, and metacognition, as well as deficiencies in academic areas such as reading comprehension.

Interventions focusing on cognitive delays and deficiencies

Historically there has been considerably less focus on cognitive goals in intervention programs for children with autism than on sensorimotor, language, and social skill development. This de-emphasis on cognitive goals is somewhat paradoxical given the prominent role cognitive theories have played in explaining this complex disorder. A variety of theories suggest that disturbances in the cognitive system not only play a major role in understanding the etiology of autism, but also should serve as major targets for intervention programs for young children with autism (Whitman, 2004).

Table 8.1 presents a list of key cognitive processes and skill areas in which research suggests that children with autism have delays and deficiencies. Several of the processes, attention, attention shifting, and joint attention have been previously discussed in Chapter 3 as core processes that drive early development. Several others, social cognition and executive functioning, will be covered in Chapters 9 and 10 when social interaction and self-regulation processes are discussed. In the remainder of this chapter, we discuss the importance of developing holistic processing, short-term and long-term memory, abstract thinking, pretend play, and academic skills, as well as describe specific intervention strategies for addressing deficiencies in these areas. We also examine how special strengths in areas such as visual processing can be employed as key learning tools. Finally, specific examples of intervention programs are provided.

Table 8.1 Cognitive processes and skills that often need to be targeted for intervention

Attention (discussed in Chapter 2)
Attention shifting (see Chapter 2)
Joint attention (see Chapter 2)
Imitation (see Chapter 2)
Holistic processing
Short-term memory
Long-term memory
Categorization and concept formation (abstract thinking)
Pretend play
Cognitive flexibility (see Chapter 10)
Visualization and visual memory

Executive functioning (see Chapter 10)
    Planning (problem definition)
    Searching (examining alternatives)
    Metacognition
    Strategy selection
    Monitoring and evaluation
    Impulse control (response inhibition)
    Working memory

Social cognition (social understanding, theory of mind, empathy) (see Chapter 9)

Academic skills
    Mathematics
    Reading
    Spelling
    History

Holistic processing deficiencies

Visual object recognition is a fundamental cognitive skill. It is an important prerequisite for abstract learning, problem-solving, and goal-directed action. Prior to 18 months of age, neurotypical children perceive objects more as multiple fragments rather than as an integration of these fragments into a whole. During the period of 18 to 24 months, these children begin to develop object-oriented perception. In contrast, the perceptions of children with autism appear to remain bound to fragments that do not coalesce into a whole object (Smith, 2009).

Frith and Happé (1994) theorized that persons with autism display an abnormality in information-processing, more specifically a failure of holistic processing or what they referred to as "weak central coherence." Individuals with weak central coherence tend to concentrate on one or a few aspects of a perceptual task or an environment; that is, they process at a local level and fail to integrate the local details of a complex stimulus into a global percept. Although research support for this theoretical position has been somewhat mixed (Jordan, 1999), recent research suggests that individuals with more extensive autistic symptomatology have more global visual processing problems (Grinter et al., 2009).

Moreover, research has emphasized the difficulties individuals with autism have in processing social information. Gross (2005) found a significant relationship between style of information-processing and recognition of human emotions. Children with autism made fewer global responses and more errors in recognizing human emotions than children without autism. A study by Hill, Berthoz, and Frith (2004) also suggests that individuals on the autism spectrum have more difficulty processing their own emotions and perhaps as a result are less able to regulate them. Information-processing style seems to relate not only to an individual's ability to identify emotional states, but also to understand what is going on in the minds of other people. Burnette et al. (2005) found a relationship between weak central coherence and theory of mind measures. The local information-processing style of individuals with autism could also explain some of their executive-functioning deficiencies and performance problems on complex cognitive tasks.

In addition, information-processing style appears to be related to the emotional state of the individual who is processing sensory input. Basso, Schefft, Ris, and Dember (1996) found that positive mood was directly associated with global processing and inversely related to a local bias. It may be that complex stimuli either elicit a high state of emotional arousal in children with autism because of an information-processing deficiency and/or that these children are more prone to process information at a local level when emotionally agitated.

Intervention perspectives and strategies

Based on existing research and theory, several intervention strategies will be discussed for helping children with ASD cope with tasks that are composed of a complex configuration of stimuli. The intervention strategies to be described focus respectively on environmental, emotion, behavior, and cognitive processes. To exemplify these strategies, an emotion-identification task is employed, one that past research suggests is associated with use of a local (i.e. non-holistic) information-processing style by children with autism.

ENVIRONMENTALLY FOCUSED STRATEGIES

These intervention strategies are often utilized to ensure that the learning environment is devoid of distractions that divert a child's attention. These strategies are also sometimes directed at modifying the complexity of a task given to a child, specifically by presenting a simplified version of the task and gradually increasing its complexity. For example, in an emotion identification task, rather than having a child identify an emotion expressed by a person, a cartoon face could be employed that both simplifies the face while accentuating its key features, such as a turned-up mouth or a wrinkled forehead. Research by Rosset et al. (2008) found that children with ASD were able to use a configural strategy in processing emotional expressions when cartoon faces were employed. Over time, the features of the cartoon face can be increased in complexity as other features are added to the face, including features nonessential for emotion identification. The task might be modified further by substituting pictures of a real person expressing an emotion and finally by presenting a video of a person or an actual person in a real-life situation reacting emotionally to a specific stimulus, such as a child experiencing joy when given a birthday cake. Thus, this intervention procedure is directed at helping the child identify facial features necessary for emotion identification, through task simplification and by focusing attention on key features of that task.

EMOTION-FOCUSED STRATEGIES

Emotion-focused strategies are particularly appropriate when a child is upset, overexcited or conversely is lethargic. In order to perform well on complex visual tasks or sensorimotor tasks, a child must be properly alert, not overaroused or underaroused. An alert state is more likely to promote attention and a holistic orientation, as well as to allow a child to shift attention in order to scan and evaluate more strategically various aspects of an emotion identification task, such as facial features indicative of joy or surprise. In order to reduce overarousal, techniques that serve to soothe and relax the child, such as quiet music, massage, or a weighted vest, can be employed (see Chapters 2 and 4 for other techniques).

In order to increase arousal in an underaroused child, activities that energize the child, such as jumping on a trampoline, can be introduced before complex tasks are presented.

BEHAVIOR-FOCUSED STRATEGIES

A behavioral strategy that employs prompts can be used to teach a child to scan strategically the entire face of the person expressing an emotion, including physical prompts, such as pointing at relevant features of the face. Reinforcement should be applied when the child engages in appropriate scanning behavior and is able to focus on important facial features. This strategy is often employed in conjunction with cognitive strategies.

COGNITIVE-BEHAVIOR FOCUSED STRATEGIES

Because children with autism are delayed in their language development, they have difficulty taking advantage of semantic cues in organizing and processing information from the environment (Sahyoun, Soulières, Belliveau, Mottron, & Mody, 2009). Their approach to processing information from the environment is more visuospatial than linguistic. Nevertheless, even though children with autism manifest language delays, like typically developing children they can benefit from training that uses verbal cues and labels to help them semantically organize their perceptions. Verbal labels when systematically associated with visual stimuli, such as a picture of a child with a big smile, can assist a child in identifying the emotion being expressed. For example, words can be used to identify the specific emotion being expressed (e.g. joy), to label relevant features of an emotion (e.g. the smile), thereby making those features more salient, to characterize how each feature (e.g. mouth, eye, forehead, etc.) is employed in emotion expression, and even to point out to the child how what is happening in the person's environment might produce a particular emotional state. These verbal descriptors help children not only to organize their perceptions, but also to make accurate discriminative responses.

Memory

Although research on memory in children with autism is increasing, less work has been done in this area relative to other cognitive processes, such as attention and social perception. Early perspectives on memory functioning indicate that children with autism have good rote memories. Case studies have indicated that some individuals with autism, including some autistic savants, display better than average and even exceptional memories for certain kinds of material. Research has provided a more refined view of memory processes in this population. For example, research has established that, like typical children, memory improves with age in children with autism. Individuals with autism often do as well as non-autistic persons when material to be remembered is visual in nature, but have more problems recalling material when it is presented auditorially, particularly if the material is verbally presented. Moreover, they appear to have more difficulty in remembering information that is complex and semantically meaningful. There is also evidence that individuals with autism who are mentally retarded have more severe memory impairments (see reviews by Renner, Klinger, & Klinger, 2000, and Whitman, 2004).

In a particularly fascinating study, Millward, Powell, Messer, and Jordan (2000) found that children with autism were less likely to recall events performed by themselves than those performed by a peer. In contrast, non-autistic children were more likely to remember events performed by themselves. The authors point out that these results are consistent with theories that suggest children with autism are less aware of themselves, less self-conscious, and less likely to self-monitor, and as a consequence do not develop a well-defined sense of self. Moreover, the results are consistent with theory of mind and metacognitive perspectives which contend that children with autism do not understand their own minds (Whitman, 2004).

Intervention perspectives and strategies

Not surprisingly, because memory is a cognitive process, most strategies for improving memory in children with autism are also cognitive in nature. Before discussing these strategies, other strategies should be noted. Emotion-focused strategies can be very useful under certain circumstances, specifically if there is evidence that a child is anxious (see Chapters 2 and 4). Anxiety inhibits information-processing as well as retention of material. Moreover, environmentally focused strategies should be utilized if the learning environment is filled with distractions (see Chapter 2). In addition, behavior-focused procedures, such as shaping and chaining, can be useful in increasing memory in an incremental manner (see Chapter 2).

Finally, there are a myriad of cognitive strategies for improving memory. Six of these will be discussed here because they are directed at either capitalizing on existing strengths or remediating deficiencies that are associated with autism. These strategies are: visual, attentional, rehearsal, chunking, semantic, and metamemorial.

VISUAL STRATEGIES

Because children with autism often find visual materials easier to remember than verbal materials, attempts should be made to translate verbal memory tasks into visual tasks or to create a task where words and visual cues are conjoined. For example, if the task involves remembering the names of classmates, pictures of the classmates, along with their names and other verbal descriptors, should be employed as a memory aid. Children with autism also often have difficulty remembering, or at least articulating, what they did at school. Again, pictures of what they did at school might be employed as memory retrieval cues. Over time, the pictures should be faded as children learn to convert visual memory cues into words.

Attentional strategies

Because attentional problems are common in children with autism, a second cognitive approach can be very useful in promoting retention of information. Often memory problems are not memory problems per se, but a reflection of the fact that the child is not listening to what is said and/or is not looking at instructional stimuli. To promote memory of material presented verbally, the material should be presented only when the child is making eye contact with the parent/teacher. When material is presented visually, a teacher or parent should prompt the child's attention by asking the child to look at the material to be remembered, pointing if necessary, to direct the child's attention to the relevant material and then reinforcing the child for "good looking."

Rehearsal strategies

In addition, having children verbalize what they are seeing or what they have just heard a teacher/parent say helps them both to focus attention and to boost recall. Relatedly, having children rehearse what they should remember by making them draw what is to be remembered, along with repeating what is to be remembered, can be very helpful in ensuring that they have placed the information into memory. Moreover, repetition by the teacher/parent of what children must remember can also be helpful, if not overutilized, and serve as a type of passive rehearsal for the child (teacher repeats directions rather than child).

Chunking strategies

Chunking can also be an effective strategy when there is a list of non-related items to be remembered, such as a phone number. Chunking involves reducing a child's memory load by having the child group the items to be remembered. For example, if the memory task involves teaching children to remember their phone number, rather than learning all of the digits together, the child should be taught to group the numbers into one set of three and one set of four, which makes for an easier memory task; for example, it is easier to remember 5–8–9 and 6–1–3–4 than 5–8–9–6–1–3–4.

Semantic strategies

Semantic strategies are helpful if the items to be remembered can be grouped conceptually. Although children with autism have difficulty with abstract concepts, they can learn such concepts, particularly if the concept has explicit visual exemplars. For example, it is easier for children to recall what they did at school if they are asked to tell what they did at recess, in reading and at lunch rather than just being asked a general question about what they did at school. Strategic questioning by parents/teachers helps children organize their memory.

Metamemory strategies

A higher order cognitive strategy for improving memory involves developing awareness in children with autism that certain types of information need to be remembered and/or are more difficult to remember, and that if they use some of the aforementioned strategies as memory aids they can improve their memory. In other words, children learn that remembering is important, that they will need to remember, and that they have at their disposal tools to help them remember. Metamemorial training helps to address a basic deficiency in children with autism, that is, that they do not reflect on the contents of their own mind. For further information on how metacognitive training interventions can be used for instructional purposes, the reader is referred to a recent book by Waters and Schneider (2009).

Abstract thinking

Children with autism tend to understand the world in concrete terms (Waterhouse, 2000). They have difficulty comprehending abstract ideas; instead they react in a literal fashion to the words of others, thus making it difficult for them to understand humor, deceitful behavior, metaphorical expressions, and idiomatic speech. This autistic style of thinking is likely to be a function of the way language is learned. More specifically, their concrete approach to thinking is probably related to the fact that they acquire language later in childhood, relying instead for an extended period of time on visual thinking as a vehicle for understanding and representing the world.

By its nature, visual thinking is iconic, with visual images closely tied to the concrete aspects of environmental stimuli. Temple Grandin discusses how she had to convert abstract ideas into pictures in order to understand them. For example, she points out that words, like church, conjure up for her specific images of all the churches she has ever seen, rather than a general image of a church (Grandin, 1995). One consequence or correlate of concrete visually oriented thinking is that it leads to an interesting pattern of strengths within a context of many limitations.

For example, on IQ tests, like the Wechsler Intelligence Scales for Children, individuals with autism often do better on subtests requiring visualization skills, like the block design, but have difficulty with others that require interpretation of word meanings, concepts, and social situations, like the similarities and information subtests (Whitman, 2004).

Intervention perspectives and strategies

Given that abstract thinking is required in a wide variety of academic, vocational, and other everyday tasks, it should not be surprising that interventions directed at helping children to think abstractly also vary. However, most programs utilize diverse examples to illustrate a concept in action. For example, if the concept of same/alike is being taught to a child, the child is presented with a range of stimuli that are alike in various ways; some of which are exactly alike. Prompting and reinforcement procedures are employed in teaching the child to identify stimuli that are exactly alike.

More specifically, a child might be asked to match a picture of two large red circles with an identical picture from a group of pictures with objects varying in number, size, color, and shape. On subsequent trials, the child is then asked to match other pictures, for example, one small blue square with one small blue square, and so on. In teaching children to match objects, they are asked to "Put like with like." If they are able to do this, they are verbally reinforced (e.g. "Good matching."). Verbal feedback is also given, explaining why it was a good match (e.g. "Yes, this one also has one large blue circle."). If a child makes an incorrect selection, feedback is given concerning why it was incorrect and the child is asked to select again.

Other abstract thinking programs include teaching children to group objects conceptually according to function, for example things you eat, ride in, or wear. Children can also be taught locational concepts (e.g. in front of, on top of, inside of), distance concepts (e.g. near, far), speed concepts (e.g. things that go fast or slow), different forms of precipitation (e.g. rain, snow, hail), animate versus inanimate objects, and so on.

Because children with autism often have great memories, it is important to use a wide variety of stimuli (pictures, objects) to illustrate a concept in order to prevent rote learning. Concept acquisition occurs when a child can reliably identify instances of a concept operating (e.g. objects which are cars) when stimuli (cars) not previously employed in earlier concept teaching lessons are presented. Concept acquisition is an example of stimulus generalization, in which the same response is made in different situations that share certain specific properties in common. Table 8.2 presents a list of concepts commonly taught as part of early intervention programs for children with autism.

Table 8.2 Concepts commonly taught as part of early intervention programs for children with autism

Women	Food
Men	Vegetables
Animals	Fruits
Birds	Trees
Color	Plants
Shape	Flowers
Number	Insects
Size	Reptiles
Location	Churches
Clothes	Houses
Matching	Furniture
Age	Chairs
Real vs. make believe	

Cognitive and behavioral flexibility

Children with autism frequently think and act in stereotyped and repetitive ways. This type of behavior is particularly maladaptive if it interferes with strategic action and learning. Attempts to disrupt such behavior sometimes create emotional turmoil. In order to develop flexible ways of thinking and acting, children need to be taught how thinking and acting in different ways can be interesting, productive, and sometimes essential.

Intervention perspectives and strategies

Some children with autism, for example, become upset if a parent drives them home from school by a new route. If the parents consistently take different routes home, the child will learn that there is not only one way of getting home. The children might also be shown a detailed map that indicates different routes from their school to home and be asked to show their parents one route for going home, and then asked to show a second and third way, and so on. Reinforcement is given for finding new ways.

Another example of a program to develop flexibility is to give a child a set of blocks and ask him/her to build something, then subsequently ask the child to use the same blocks to build something different. Reinforcement is provided only for building novel structures. In the next section, the use of pretend play as a forum for teaching flexibility is examined.

Pretend play

Because of their tendency to view the world in a literal and fixed fashion, rather than flexibly, children with autism have difficulty pretending; that is they tend to view the world as it has been and is, not how it could or might be. Pretend play, or as it is sometimes referred to, symbolic play, creates imaginary worlds and uses objects to represent other objects. In typically developing children, pretend play emerges during the second year of life. In contrast, with children on the autism spectrum, such play is usually initiated at an older age and when it does emerge it is typically less frequent, less spontaneous, less varied in its form, and less complex. Impairment in pretend play has been associated with language, social skill, and emotion regulation deficiencies (Marcu, Oppenheim, Koren-Karie, Dolev, & Yirmiya, 2009).

Jarrold (1997) hypothesizes that children with autism have problems with pretend play because of an executive dysfunction, specifically a difficulty inhibiting a dominant response. During pretend object play, children have to inhibit actions normally elicited by an object; for example, in pretending a pencil is a telescope, a make-believe response, looking through it, has to be substituted in place of an established response, drawing.

Intervention perspectives and strategies

From a behavioral perspective, in order to teach children to pretend, pretend must be defined specifically and examples of pretend play developed for teaching purposes. Pretend play becomes truly dynamic when children learn to go beyond the specific responses taught to invent new ways of acting, reacting, and thinking about their world. Children with autism appear to have problems holding multiple representations of the world simultaneously, one which reflects the real world and the other a pretend world (Bigham, 2010). Although there are many definitions of pretend play and examples of such definitions, it will be defined for the present purposes as a response where children imagine that one object is another or that they are someone that they are not. For example, children could pretend that a bowl is a hat, a stick is a sword, pebbles are money, or that they are an astronaut or a superhero.

In teaching children how to pretend, modeling and role playing are useful techniques (see Chapter 2). These techniques can be used in conjunction with videos, which depict individuals, such as doctors, lawyers, teachers, carpenters, plumbers, and superheros, as they engage in their trade. Parents and teachers might develop plays with scripts, with different children assigned to different roles and then have the children change roles. Drama clubs might be specifically developed that serve both children with autism and neurotypical children.

Building cognitive flexibility should be a key goal of pretend play, in order to counter the tendency of children with autism to engage the world in a fixed, stereotyped, and repetitive way. Because they tend to learn scripts in a rote fashion, it is important to vary the scripts to encourage flexible rather than repetitive and stereotyped behavior. The bowl, which was a hat, becomes a treasure chest. The doctor who gave a patient medicine, now cleans and bandages a wound. When children go for a pretend ride in their car, they should be taught to pretend that they sometimes go one way home and sometimes another. They learn that blocks used to build pretend houses can be employed to construct many different types of houses as well as other edifices, and that superheros perform all kinds of feats as they save the world and help people in distress. Creativity should be reinforced when the child responds in novel ways.

Academic skills

The proceeding sections and Table 8.1 list and describe various basic cognitive processes, such as attention, memory and abstract thinking, in which children with autism are often deficient. Because of these deficiencies, it should not be surprising that children on the autism spectrum also have difficulties with academic subjects that require the use of these processes. Typically, children with autism require adult assistance at school and home to complete their schoolwork. Although children with autism have difficulty with most areas of the academic curriculum, they have particular problems in areas like mathematics and reading comprehension, especially with material that cannot be simply learned by rote and requires understanding of abstract concepts and/or semantic encoding of information. In areas like reading, which sometimes involve material requiring social understanding, comprehension may also be compromised because of theory of mind deficiencies, which are discussed in the next chapter.

Upon reading this chapter and other chapters in this book that include descriptions of intervention approaches for developing basic cognitive processes like attention, memory, and problem-solving, it should be evident to the reader that such programs do not focus on improving these processes in the abstract, but rather on utilizing these processes in specific task situations, including academic tasks. Thus, many of the aforementioned interventions described for developing basic cognitive, language, and self-regulatory processes can also be employed to help children with autism with their academic studies and to work more independently when doing their schoolwork.

Utilizing cognitive strengths

Although cognitive deficiencies and delays are a key characteristic of autism, there is also evidence that many individuals with autism spectrum disorders display specific islands of enhanced abilities relative to other areas of functioning. Sometimes these abilities are developed to such an extent that they are described as having a savant quality.

Savant characteristics or the savant syndrome is often used to describe the presence of remarkable and sometimes amazing abilities that exist within a context of mental and behavior deficits. These savant characteristics are most common in individuals with autism, but are also found in individuals with mental retardation and various types of brain damage. Rimland (1978) reports that savant abilities may occur in about 10 percent of people with autism. Estimates of the frequency of savantism are related, however, to how this syndrome is specifically defined. Examples of savantism, which are more common than clear definitions of this syndrome, include people whose gifts involve special sensory (particularly visual and auditory), motor, memory, or other cognitive abilities, and extraordinary accomplishments in areas like art and music (Treffert & Wallace, 2002). For example, savants may have a prodigious memory, a capacity to produce a musical piece after hearing it only once, special drawing abilities, or the ability to display amazing feats of calculation. The special abilities that autistic savants demonstrate are, however, not typically useful from a vocational standpoint.

There is considerable speculation about why children with autism develop certain abilities and not others. Perhaps the most prominent theory is that a defect or injury in the left hemisphere results in a reorganization of the brain and the enhancement of functions associated with the right hemisphere. Mottron and Burack (2001) emphasize that autistic savants, as well as many non-savant individuals with autism, display patterns of relative strengths in the context of limitations. They suggest that a vertical imbalance exists in autism; specifically that the relationship between lower and higher psychological (and brain) processes is disrupted and that overdeveloped lower processes, such as sensory recognition and reproduction, interfere with the development of higher processes, such as abstract thinking and social reflection. Conversely, it could be argued that the lack of development of higher processes catalyzes the emergence of special abilities to compensate for abilities that do not develop or are lost. Because of the striking and often similar patterns of abilities and disabilities in autistic savants, some researchers suggest that this unusual syndrome may provide unique windows into the functioning of the brain.

Perhaps the most commonly noted "special" or better developed ability associated with autism is the ability to perform well on visual tasks. Temple Grandin describes in great detail how she thinks in pictures and how her visual abilities provide her special insights into the world around her. Grandin has also expressed her frustration with a society that evaluates thinking and intelligence mostly in terms of verbal skills and points out that many successful thinkers are visual, not verbal, in their thinking style (Grandin, 1995).

Intervention perspectives and strategies

The intervention implications that can be derived from recognizing special cognitive abilities, such as visual, are myriad. For example, a book by Miller (2008) depicts how artistic skills can be used for visual communication. Moreover, visual prompts, including pictures, videos, and human models, can be invaluable tools for facilitating learning in children with autism; for example, in teaching them how to perform a motor task such as toothbrushing, a cognitive task, such as arithmetic, a complex domestic task such as cooking, or a language task such as reading with expression. Visual cues can be employed not only in teaching children how to make responses, but also to help them understand how to sequence those responses and where to employ them. Visual stimuli can help children understand the flow of daily activities and help them anticipate when changes are going to occur. Pictures can also be employed to teach abstract concepts and how the same word (e.g. car) can be used to describe objects that vary considerably in their visual appearance. Recent research also indicates how visual materials can be employed to help individuals with Asperger Syndrome develop humor appreciation, in other words a sense of humor (Samson & Hegenloh, 2010). With creative teachers, most daily living skills and academic subjects can be taught through a visual curriculum accompanied by verbal instruction.

In the next section, examples of specific programs to enhance cognitive functioning are presented. For further information on important cognitive processes and strategies for developing them, the reader is also referred to books on learning and memory by Scott (2009) and Baddeley, Eysenck, and Anderson (2009) as well as a recent literature review on teaching children with autism to read for meaning (Randi, Newman, & Grigorenko, 2010).

Program examples
Recalling recent events using a visual cue

OBJECTIVE

Teach the child to recall recent personal events.

MATERIALS

For this program, you will need a digital camera.

PROCEDURE

1. Take a picture of the child when he/she is engaged in an activity (e.g. swinging, painting, playing a game on the computer).

2. Immediately show the picture to the child and say, "What are you doing?" (You don't have to print the pictures, just show the digital image on the camera.)

3. Immediately following the cessation of the activity, show the picture to the child and ask what the child did (e.g. "What did you do at recess?" or "What game did you play on the computer?").

   a) If the child answers correctly, deliver a reinforcer.

   b) If the child does not answer, prompt him/her to answer correctly. Deliver a reinforcer if the child answers correctly following the prompt. Use differential reinforcement to fade such verbal prompts.

4. After about 5 to 10 minutes, show the picture to the child and ask about the activity again.

   a) If the child answers correctly (i.e. same answer as in step 2) immediately deliver a reinforcer.

   b) If the child does not answer, use verbal prompts to help him/her answer the question.

5. Repeat every 10 to 15 minutes.

6. Implement this program several times throughout the day, every day and with several different activities/pictures per day.

ERROR CORRECTION

If the child gives the wrong answer (e.g. says an incorrect activity), turn away for 5 seconds. Then turn back and ask the question again, providing the picture prompt and/or a verbal prompt to help the child answer correctly. Deliver praise but do not deliver a reinforcer following error correction. Repeat a few minutes later, but be ready to prompt quickly to avoid the same error.

GENERALIZATION

Fade the use of the pictures by using a time delay procedure. Ask the child about the activity and wait 5 seconds before showing the picture. Next time wait 8 seconds, then 10 seconds, 15, 20, and so on. If the child answers the question before you show the picture, deliver excited praise and a highly preferred reinforcer.

Once you have faded the use of the pictures, wait for longer periods of time before asking the child about the activity. Instead of asking the child immediately following the activity, wait 1 minute before asking. Next time wait 2 minutes, 3, 5, and so on.

TIPS/SUGGESTIONS

If you do not have access to a digital camera, anticipate what activities the child will do that day and print generic pictures or picture icons of the activities. Use these pictures or icons as cues instead of actual pictures of the child engaging in the activity. Also consider using verbal prompts other than echoic. For example, if the child was swinging at recess, you could say, "It was such a nice day outside. I thought I saw you near the swings…" The child may be able to use such a prompt to then say, "Yeah I was swinging at recess." If not, then an echoic prompt may be necessary (e.g. "Say, 'I was swinging.'").

TROUBLESHOOTING

If the child is not responding to any cues, spend some time teaching the child to describe actions in pictures and actions of him/herself and others in a structured setting before moving on to teaching this task. Also, be sure that you are reinforcing correct responses immediately, using effective, highly preferred reinforcers.

OTHER TEACHING METHODS

If the child cannot already describe actions in pictures, this visual cue may not be effective. Instead, stop the child in the middle of the activity and ask the child what he/she is doing. Use verbal or textual prompts (if the child can read) to help him/her deliver a correct answer. Continue the procedure, leaving out the visual prompt.

In addition, sometimes asking about specific events (e.g. "What did you do at recess?" or "What did you eat for lunch?") rather than broader occasions (e.g. "What did you do at school today?") may assist with recall.

EXAMPLE TARGETS

Ask the child about events such as:

- recess ("What did you do?" "Who did you play with?" "What was the weather like?")

- lunch ("What did you eat?" "Who did you sit with?")

- art, music, or gym class ("What happened in gym class today?")

- play-dates

- movies.

FUTURE OBJECTIVES

Continue this procedure to help the child discuss events that happened yesterday, over the weekend, over the summer or holidays, and so on.

Concept formation: same

OBJECTIVE

The child will group items that are similar along some dimension (e.g. features, functions, classes, etc.) and thus fall into the same category.

PREREQUISITES

Typically this program is more successful if the child can already match identical objects and pictures prior to moving on to this program.

MATERIALS

The materials needed for this program depend upon which concepts you are teaching. When using objects/pictures, be sure to have several examples of each object/picture. For example, if teaching the child to group items into similar categories of animals, prepare three to five different dogs, three to five different cats, three to five different cows, etc. so that the child learns that certain animals (e.g. dogs) share similar features that make them fall into the same category (i.e. dog). Other categories can be school supplies (e.g. different types of pencils, rulers, calculators, etc.), kitchen utensils, foods, farm animals, and so on.

PROCEDURE

1. Place four to six different objects in an array in front of the child. For example, place a dog, cat, pig, horse, and cow in front of the child.

2. Give the child a non-identical object/picture that is similar to one of the objects in the array (e.g. a Collie to match to the German Shepherd). Ask the child to, "Match the same," or "Find the similar item."

   a) If the child correctly matches the two similar items, immediately deliver praise and a reinforcer.

   b) If the child does not respond within 3 to 5 seconds, use a prompt to assist the child. Deliver a reinforcer once the child responds correctly. Use differential reinforcement to fade the use of prompts across trials.

3. Rearrange the items, removing some and adding new ones too.

4. Repeat steps 1 to 3 until you have asked the child to match approximately 10 to 20 times, with at least three different items.

ERROR CORRECTION

If the child matches to the wrong item, remove the items for 5 seconds. Then re-present them in the same order and deliver the same instruction, quickly prompting the child in order to avoid the same error. Deliver praise but do not deliver a tangible reinforcer following error correction. Ask one or two different questions, and then re-present the erred target. For example, if the child places the brown cow with the cat instead of with the black and white cow, remove or cover all the items for 5 seconds. Re-present the materials and ask the child again to match the items, this time pointing to the black and white cow. When the child matches correctly say, "Yes, they are both cows, so they are similar." Rearrange and ask one or two different questions. Then re-present the brown cow, gesturing toward the black and white cow. If the child matches correctly this time immediately deliver a reinforcer. Fade the gestural prompt across successive trials.

TIPS/SUGGESTIONS

It may help to use items that the child enjoys looking at, such as animals or vehicles. This will help maintain the child's interest and attention to the activity. However do not allow the child to play with the materials, because it may be difficult for the child to listen to instructions while playing.

In addition, you may want to teach the child to respond to the word "different" at the same time as teaching "same" to minimize confusion and thus maximize efficiency with these concepts. To teach "different," place two items in front of the child. Hold up an item that is similar to one of the two items in front of the child. Ask him/her to find the "different" one. The child should identify the item that is not similar to the item you are holding.

TROUBLESHOOTING

If the child is having difficulty, start with objects that differ only on one dimension. For example, use the same toothbrushes, only different colors. Or use the exact same number two pencils, but different sizes. Slowly add more differences, one dimension at a time. This will help the child learn to recognize similar features of the items.

GENERALIZATION

Once the child has mastered this skill, ask the child to sort similar items. For example, he/she can sort laundry into similar piles, such as shirts, pants, socks. Or he/she can help clean up the play room by sorting certain objects with other, similar objects. Emptying the dishwasher is another convenient time to teach generalization of this skill because the child can sort the dishes based on their type (e.g. wooden spoons go in this drawer, spatulas go in this drawer, etc.).

OTHER TEACHING METHODS

Matching does not need to be the only method for teaching concepts. You can ask the child to label certain concepts (e.g. "What are these animals?"). Or to teach gender, show the child various pictures of males and females, asking him/her to state whether it's a boy, girl, man, or woman. For prepositions, the child can place objects in specific locations (e.g. on top of the table, behind the chair, etc.). To teach quantities, have the child match a written numeral (e.g. 4) to the correct quantity of counting bears when there are three to four different piles of bears to choose from. The key is to have multiple examples of the concepts available to the child as well as multiple responses (i.e. expressive and receptive).

EXAMPLE CONCEPTS

- same/different
- gender
- animals
- color
- shape
- number

- size

- location

- clothing

- food

- age

- real vs. make believe.

FUTURE OBJECTIVES

Next, focus on teaching the child to identify items by the various features, functions, and classes of those items. Also, move on to more difficult concepts, such as more than, less than, equal, none, emotional states, and so on.

Identifying pictures by features, functions, and classes

OBJECTIVE

The child will identify pictures of items based on their features, functions, or classes.

PREREQUISITES

Typically this program is more successful if the child can already identify the pictures by their names and/or label the pictures. In addition, matching identical objects and pictures, as well as non-identical matching should already be learned prior to moving on to this program.

MATERIALS

For this program you will need pictures of objects in various classes (see the Example list below). You should have several examples of each picture and of each class. For example, there should be three to five pictures of dogs in the animal group, and eight to ten different types of animals.

PROCEDURE

1. Place four to six pictures in an array in front of the child.

2. Ask the child to identify a picture by its feature (e.g. "Give me the one that has a tail."), function (e.g. "Show me something you eat."), or class (e.g. "Find the tool.").

    a) If the child correctly identifies the picture, immediately deliver praise and a reinforcer.

    b) If the child does not respond within 3 to 5 seconds, use a prompt to assist the child. Deliver a reinforcer once the child responds correctly. Use differential reinforcement to fade the use of prompts across trials.

3. Rearrange the pictures, removing some and adding new ones too.

4. Repeat steps 1 to 3 until you have asked the child to identify approximately ten features, ten functions, and/or ten classes.

ERROR CORRECTION

If the child chooses the wrong item, remove the pictures for 5 seconds. Then re-present the pictures in the same order and deliver the same instruction, quickly prompting the child in order to avoid the same error. Deliver praise but do not deliver a tangible reinforcer following error correction. Ask one or two different questions, and then re-present the erred target. For example, if the child chooses "pencil" when asked to find a picture of an animal, remove all pictures for 5 seconds. Re-present the materials and ask the child again to find an animal, this time pointing to the picture of the tiger. When the child chooses the tiger say, "Yes, the tiger is an animal." Rearrange and ask one or two different questions. Then ask again, "Where is an animal?" while gesturing toward the tiger. If the child chooses the tiger, this time immediately deliver a reinforcer. Fade the gestural prompt across successive trials.

GENERALIZATION

Once the child has mastered this skill with the pictures used during training, generalize to other pictures, including pictures in books. Create activities that combine this skill with other skills, such as art projects that require finding animals in a magazine, cutting them out and pasting them to a poster board. If the child can use this skill with objects, contrive situations where the child will have to find objects in the environment in order to complete an action. For example, while baking cookies, ask the child to find something you can mix with so that you can mix the batter.

Tips/suggestions

It may help to use pictures that the child enjoys looking at, such as Sesame Street characters. This will help maintain the child's interest and attention to the activity.

Troubleshooting

If the child is having significant difficulty, consider teaching one type of description at a time (i.e. feature, function, or class). Also, consider using objects instead of pictures, as some children prefer one or the other.

Other teaching methods

Some children learn features better with objects or manipulative pictures. For example, cut and laminate two pictures of tigers. Cut out the individual features from one of the pictures (e.g. tail, legs, paws, stripes, whiskers, eyes, ears) and Velcro them to the first picture. Then have the child match the features as you say, "Which one has a tail?"

Example targets

- animals
- furniture
- tools
- food
- drinks
- school supplies
- vehicles (or modes of transportation)
- electronics
- appliances
- toys
- clothing
- make-up
- jewelry
- playground equipment.

FUTURE OBJECTIVES

Next, focus on teaching the child to label the various features, functions, and classes of objects. Use the pictures/objects as prompts, but eventually fade the prompts so the child can, "Name some animals," without visual or verbal prompts. Also move on to more detailed descriptions, such as naming/identifying writing utensils, kitchen tools, things you take to the beach, vehicles that go in the water, underwater animals, and so on.

Pretend play activities: imitation

OBJECTIVE

Teach the child to imitate various pretend play activities, both with and without objects. This is a prerequisite to other, more advanced pretend play behavior.

PREREQUISITE SKILLS

For this procedure, it is necessary for the child to already reliably imitate the actions of an adult, specifically two-step actions with objects (e.g. toys) and multi-step gross motor actions (e.g. random sequences of gross motor behaviors such as clap, stomp, then touch your head).

MATERIALS

Gather toys and other objects that the child is already interested in so that he/she will be more inclined to participate in the activity with you. Do not use materials that the child uses to engage in repetitive, stereotypic behaviors, or materials that the child has difficulty giving up. Instead, choose items that the child shows interest in, but will share with others when asked to do so. You can use anything from a pillow to a toy school bus.

PROCEDURE

1. Obtain the child's attention and say, "Do this," and model a one-step pretend play action. For example, put a doll inside a car, or put money inside a toy cash register. Model actions both with and without objects. For example, pretend to yawn, or lay your head down on a pillow and close your eyes.

   a) If the child imitates the action, immediately deliver praise and a reinforcer.

b) If the child does not imitate the action, use prompts to assist him/her with imitating. Deliver praise and a smaller reinforcer than you would use if he/she imitated without your help.

2. Repeat with a different action or object.

3. Once the child is responding without your help, add more steps to the actions. For example, put on a toy stethoscope and then hold it up to a doll's chest. Or take a brush out of a purse, brush your hair, then put the brush back in the purse and close it.

ERROR CORRECTION

If the child does not imitate your action (e.g. he/she plays with the doll instead of putting it in the car) remove the toy or stop his/her action. Model the correct action again and immediately prompt the child to imitate correctly. Deliver praise but do not deliver a tangible reinforcer following error correction. Repeat the trial, quickly delivering a prompt in order to avoid the same error, this time reinforcing the prompted response.

GENERALIZATION

Use objects creatively. For example, instead of putting a doll in a car, put the doll on a wide block and pretend the block is a car. Use the block for additional actions so that the child learns to use objects for different purposes.

Use many different examples so that the child can perform the task with multiple toys. For example, use several different types and colors of cars, purses, phones, pillows, and so on. Vary the action(s) so the child learns to perform many actions. In addition, by varying your actions you are ensuring that the child is actually imitating your behavior, and not simply learning a rote response.

TIPS/SUGGESTIONS

Verbal imitation or speech skills are not necessary for this procedure. However, consider adding verbal responses to the procedure for children who have such skills, in order to build on speech as well as play and social skills.

TROUBLESHOOTING

If the child consistently makes the same error, consider teaching multi-step imitation with objects again. Also, be sure that you are using a preferred reinforcer, and delivering the reinforcer quickly after the imitation has occurred, even if you needed to prompt the child. Just remember to deliver more and better reinforcers for more and better independent responding, and do not deliver a reinforcer following an error.

Future objectives

The next step should involve the child following basic commands to pretend an action. For example, you might instruct the child to pretend to be a dog, or to pretend he/she is asleep. For this skill, the child must already be able to follow basic commands (e.g. sit down, jump, touch your head, clap hands) as well as discriminate amongst various objects (e.g. finding a ball when you ask him/her to and it is in an array of four to six other objects). If the child can read, use scripts to add speech to the play activities. Vary the scripts often, so that the child does not learn a rote response but, instead, learns many ways to pretend play.

Written single-digit addition

Objective

Teach the child to solve written single-digit addition problems.

Materials

For this procedure, you will need to gather small counting objects, such as bears or blocks. In addition, gather writing tools, such as paper and a pencil, or chalk and a chalkboard.

Procedure

1. Write a single digit addition problem on the paper or chalkboard (e.g. $1 + 3 = $ _____).

2. Assist the child with reading the problem out loud.

3. As the child reads, help him/her count the correct number of objects for each digit and place those objects under the correct digit. For example, place one bear under the number 1. Then, count three bears and place them under the number 3.

4. Help the child move all of the objects to the other side of the equal sign and count the combined objects.

5. Assist the child with writing the number corresponding to the total number of objects counted.

6. Praise the child and provide him/her with a reinforcer.

7. Repeat with different single-digit addition problems, fading your assistance across each trial.

8. Fade the use of the objects across trials by placing them farther away from the numbers and eventually not using them at all. Provide better reinforcers when the child is able to complete the math problems without your assistance and/or the use of the objects.

ERROR CORRECTION

If the child counts incorrectly, interrupt the child and have him/her start counting again, offering your assistance. Once he/she counts correctly, provide praise and allow the child the opportunity to complete the math problem by writing the correct numeral.

If the child does not write the correct numeral, erase and assist the child with writing the correct response. Praise the correction, but do not provide a tangible reinforcer following error correction. Try a different equation that results in the same answer to give the child another chance to write the number correctly.

GENERALIZATION

Once the child has begun to master the concept of addition, begin to practice the skill in other locations, such as outside with sidewalk chalk. If the child is earning an allowance or tokens, have him/her add newly earned pennies or tokens to current ones to see if he/she has enough money to earn a prize or to purchase a gumball from the gumball machine. Give the child a worksheet with several math problems, instead of individual problems. Present the problems to the child verbally, instead of in written form. Also practice using flashcards to develop fluency. You can make it a game by timing the child. If there are several children present, play a competitive game such as Around the World. In this game, children sit in a circle. Two children stand up next to each other as the teacher presents a math problem. The first child to answer moves on to stand next to the third child in the circle, while the other sits back down. The first child to go around the entire circle without sitting wins. An alternative is to play in teams and track points for each correct answer.

TIPS/SUGGESTIONS

Have the child point to each number in the equation, including the addition and equals signs, as he/she reads the equation out loud. Also, present the equations in multiple formats (e.g. $1 + 3 =$ ____, or $3 + 1 =$ _____, as well as both horizontally and vertically). Start with teaching only a few digits at a time (e.g. numbers 1 to 5 and then numbers 6 to 9). Do not focus on only one particular digit (e.g. all + 1s) unless you teach two or three digits simultaneously. This will help prevent the child from always responding the same (e.g. always adding 1 to the other number, even if the equation requires adding more than 1).

TROUBLESHOOTING

If the child is consistently counting incorrectly, put the addition program on hold and focus on teaching counting objects with a 1:1 correspondence. For example, teach the child to count pennies or other small objects one at a time (as opposed to rote counting where the child simply lists numbers in order). If, on the other hand, the child does not need the objects, simply fade the use of the objects more quickly.

If the child is having difficulty during counting, cover up all but one of the numbers. Have the child gather the correct number of objects for that number, then uncover the next number and repeat.

OTHER TEACHING METHODS

Use an abacus instead of small objects. Or have the child draw little objects or dots under each number. Be sure that you fade such prompts so that the child can solve the problem without needing such assistance.

There are several helpful resources available for teaching math to students with learning disabilities. TouchMath is a technique that has been helpful for several children, with and without disabilities. Consider combining techniques of reinforcement with some other learning approaches, such as TouchMath. Fading the use of prompting methods involved in these other approaches is absolutely necessary for the child to do math independently.

FUTURE OBJECTIVES

Next, focus on teaching the child to solve single-digit subtraction problems. Make sure the child focuses on the math sign (e.g. + or − for addition or subtraction). Then move on to double-digit addition and subtraction.

References

Baddeley, A. D., Eysenck, M., & Anderson, M. C. (2009). *Memory*. Hove: Psychology Press.

Basso, M. R., Schefft, B. K., Ris, M. D., & Dember, W. N. (1996). Mood and global-local visual processing. *Journal of the International Neuropsychological Society, 2,* 249–255.

Berk, L. E. (2009). *Child development*. Boston, MA: Allyn Bacon.

Bigham, S. (2010). Impaired competence for pretense in children with autism: Exploring potential cognitive predictors. *Journal of Autism and Developmental Disorders, 40,* 30–38.

Burnette, C. P., Mundy, P. C., Meyer, J. A., Sutton, S. K., Vaughn, A. E., & Charak, D. (2005). Weak central coherence and its relations to theory of mind and anxiety in autism. *Journal of Autism and Developmental Disorders, 35,* 63–73.

Frith, U. & Happé, F. (1994). Autism: Beyond theory of mind. *Cognition, 50,* 115–132.

Grandin, T. (1995). *Thinking in pictures*. New York, NY: Vintage Books.

Grinter, E. J., Maybery, M. T., Van Beek, P. L., Pellicano, E., Badcock, J. C., & Badcock, D. R. (2009). Global visual processing and self-rated autistic-like traits. *Journal of Autism and Developmental Disorders, 39,* 1278–1290.

Gross, T. F. (2005). Global-local precedence in the perception of facial age and emotional expression by children with autism and other developmental disabilities. *Journal of Autism and Developmental Disorders, 35,* 773–785.

Hill, E., Berthoz, S., & Frith, U. (2004). Brief report: Cognitive processing of own emotions in individuals with autistic spectrum disorder and in their relatives. *Journal of Autism and Developmental Disorders, 34,* 229–235.

Jarrold, C. (1997). "Pretend play in autism: Executive explanations." In J. Russell (Ed.), *Autism as an executive disorder* (pp. 101–140). Oxford: Oxford University Press.

Jordan, R. (1999). *Autism spectrum disorders: An introductory handbook for practitioners.* London: David Fulton.

Kenworthy, L., Case, L., Harms, M. B., Martin, A., & Wallace, G. L. (2010). Adaptive behavior ratings correlate with symptomatology and IQ among individuals with high-functioning autism spectrum disorders. *Journal of Autism and Developmental Disorders, 40,* 416–423.

Lightfoot, C., Cole, M., & Cole, S. (2009). *The development of children.* Worth, IL: Worth Publishing.

Marcu, I., Oppenheim, D., Koren-Karie, N., Dolev, S., & Yirmiya, N. (2009). Attachment and symbolic play in preschoolers with autism spectrum disorders. *Journal of Autism and Developmental Disorders, 39,* 1321–1328.

Miller, E. (2008). *The girl who spoke with pictures.* London: Jessica Kingsley Publishers.

Millward, C., Powell, S., Messer, D., & Jordan, R. (2000). Recall for self and other in autism: Children's memory for events experienced by themselves and their peers. *Journal of Autism and Developmental Disorders, 30,* 15–28.

Mottron, L. & Burack, J. (2001). "Enhanced perceptual functioning in the development of autism." In J. Burack, T. Charman, N. Yirmiya & P. Aelazo (Eds.), *The development of autism: Perspectives from theory and research* (pp. 131–148). Mahwah, NJ: Erlbaum.

Randi, J., Newman, T., & Grigorenko, E. L. (2010). Teaching children with autism to read for meaning: Challenges and possibilities. *Journal of Autism and Developmental Disorders, 400,* 890–902.

Renner, P., Klinger, L., & Klinger, M. (2000). Implicit and explicit memory in autism: Is autism an amnesic disorder? *Journal of Autism and Developmental Disorders, 30,* 3–14.

Rimland, B. (1978). "Savant capabilities of autistic children and their cognitive implications." In G. Serban (Ed.), *Cognitive defects in the development of mental illness* (pp. 43–65). New York, NY: Brunner/Mazel.

Rosset, D. B., Rondan, C., Da Fonseca, D., Santos, A., Assouline, B., & Deruelle, C. (2008). Typical emotion processing for cartoon but not for real faces in children with autistic spectrum disorders. *Journal of Autism and Developmental Disorders, 38,* 919–925.

Sahyoun, C. P., Soulières, I., Belliveau, J. W., Mottron, L., & Mody, M. (2009). Cognitive differences in pictorial reasoning between high-functioning autism and Asperger's syndrome. *Journal of Autism and Developmental Disorders, 39,* 1014–1023.

Samson., A. C. & Hegenloh, M. (2010). Stimulus characteristics affect humor processing in individuals with Asperger syndrome. *Journal of Autism and Developmental Disorders, 40,* 438–447.

Scheuffgen, K., Happé, F., Anderson, M., & Frith, U. (2000). High intelligence, low IQ? Speed of processing and measured IQ in children with autism. *Development and Psychopathology, 12,* 83–90.

Scott, T. (2009). *Learning and memory.* Boston, MA: Allyn & Bacon.

Smith, L. (2009). From fragments to geometric shape. *Current Directions in Psychological Science, 18,* 290–294.

Treffert, D. & Wallace, G. (2002). Islands of genius. *Scientific American,* June, 76–85.

Waterhouse, S. (2000). *A positive approach to autism.* London: Jessica Kingsley Publishers.

Waters, H. S. & Schneider, W. (2009). *Metacognition, strategy use, and instruction.* New York, NY: Guilford.

Whitman, T. L. (2004). *The development of self-regulation: A self-regulatory perspective.* London: Jessica Kingsley Publishers.

Chapter 9

Social Interaction Problems

Children with autism spectrum disorders (ASD) display a broad pattern of deficiencies in social interaction. From a diagnostic perspective, these social deficits are considered a core characteristic of autism. During the early stages of development, these deficiencies are not always apparent, either because social development is on track or, as is probably more often the case, because differences in this area are more subtle and less easy to detect. As children with autism enter into the second year of life, however, their social difficulties become increasingly apparent. By the time they are three years of age, their overall development in the social realm is often markedly delayed. In contrast to children who are diagnosed with autistic disorder, the social deficiencies of children with Asperger Syndrome are less obvious during early development, but become increasingly evident once they enter into school and attempt to develop close social relationships.

In this chapter, we begin by contrasting the social development of neurotypical children with that of children with ASD. We then focus on several areas in which children with autism spectrum disorders manifest social deficiencies, specifically in play, close relationships, theory of mind, understanding social rules, community engagement, safety behaviors, and leisure skills. In each of these areas intervention strategies are discussed. Finally, examples of specific social skill programs are provided.

Social development in typical children

When children are born, they are not particularly social individuals. They are driven by their biological needs for food and sleep in order to develop physically. However, during the early months of life, their social abilities rapidly emerge as they begin to make eye contact with their parents. As mothers and fathers interact with them, through speech, gaze, and changes in facial expressions, infants begin to vocalize (e.g. coo), change expressions (e.g. smile), seek social attention, and imitate.

Eventually, infants develop a special bond with their parents, forming close emotional ties with them. With the emergence of this attachment relationship, babies begin to look to their parents for information about how to interpret and react to their environment, a process called social-referencing. They turn to their parents in times of stress to seek comfort. Using parents as a secure base, they also start to actively explore their physical and social environment.

During early childhood, children begin to develop relationships with individuals outside the family, including their peers. This social interest is reflected in a change in their play activities. Initially, play is more solitary, involving minimal interaction with other children. As young children become more aware of their social environment, they begin to play next to their age-mates (parallel play) and gradually become more interactive and cooperative in their play with them. During the preschool years, peer interaction expands. Children learn from other children, with imitative behavior becoming common. Friendships gradually develop, initially based on mutual patterns of interests. Eventually, friendships deepen as children adjust to the likes and dislikes of their peers, and intimacy develops. The pattern of relationships children have with other children is greatly influenced by their relationships with their parents and their evolving cognitive and communication skills. For further information on social development in children, the reader is referred to books on child development by Berk (2009) and Lightfoot, Cole, and Cole (2009), as well as an article by Beauchamp and Anderson (2010) who present a conceptual framework for examining the development of social skills.

Social interaction deficiencies in children with autism

Despite the fact that young children with autism often become attached to their parents, sometimes use nonverbal skills, such as gestures, to make requests, and may show turn-taking skills during play, they usually show marked limitations in these and other areas of social interaction, particularly in situations requiring joint attention, social initiation, and dynamic social reciprocity. They often manifest difficulties in: maintaining eye contact, using adults as a social reference to interpret ambiguous social situations, expressing empathy, engaging in social play with peers, following social protocols, and developing friendships. Their facial expressions, which are sometimes bland or inappropriate, seem to reflect a lack of understanding of social cues. Most importantly, children with autism are less able than their neurotypical peers to benefit from experiences in social environments which are less structured and require that they learn vicariously through observation (Whitman, 2004).

Although the social deficiencies of children with autism become more apparent as they grow older, there are considerable individual differences in their general pattern of development. Some children are almost totally nonresponsive to the social environment. Others react to social overtures and even initiate social interaction, but do so in immature and unusual ways. Wing and Gould (1979) suggest that the social interaction styles of children with autism spectrum disorders can be grouped into three types: aloof, passive, and active, but odd. Children who are aloof are cut off from social contact, often become upset when they are close to others and typically reject social overtures. In contrast, children in the passive group, while not making social overtures, accept such overtures from others without becoming upset and may even enjoy social contact. The last group consists of children who spontaneously approach people, but do so in unusual, one-sided and inappropriate ways. This group has a higher level of overall competency than the other two groups.

Like children with autistic disorder, children with Asperger Syndrome also show impaired social behavior, despite their more normal language and cognitive development. Gillberg and Gillberg (1989) suggest that to be labeled as having Asperger Syndrome a child should have at least two of the following social impairments: an inability to interact with peers, a lack of desire to interact with peers, a lack of appreciation of social cues, and/or socially and emotionally inappropriate behavior. They also indicate that nonverbal communication impairments should be present for a diagnosis to be made. Specifically, the child should have at least one of the following characteristics: a limited use of gestures, clumsy/gauche body language, limited facial expressions, inappropriate expressions, and/or a peculiar stiff gaze.

Hobson (1993, 2005) views the difficulties that children with autism display in peer and adult interactions—including those relating to social gesturing, sharing experiences, joint attention, affect coordination, emotion perception and expression, imitation, attachment behavior, and self-development—as evidence of their broader difficulty in intersubjective engagement. As a consequence of this intersubjective difficulty, children with autism are constrained in their ability to acquire knowledge about other people's and their own mental and emotional states and to develop language and communication skills.

Several factors are associated with the social development of children with autism, including age, IQ, and social supports. Growth in social competencies typically occurs with increasing age. Moreover, IQ correlates positively with the degree of social development, with higher IQ children typically acquiring more extensive social skills than lower IQ individuals. Most importantly, home, school, and other intervention programs can have a profound and positive effect on the social development of children with autism (Whitman, 2004).

Interventions focusing on social deficiencies

The topic of interventions focusing on social deficiencies and social skills training is a complex and important one. The need for such interventions for children with autism is self-evident, given their marked social deficiencies. Moreover, a strong argument can be made for making social skills training a part of the regular school curriculum, given the many problems that children without a developmental disability have in this area and the fact that personal, academic, and vocational success are strongly correlated with social adaptation.

The development of a comprehensive social skills training program is still emerging. The overall effectiveness of some interventions that have been popular, such as those using social stories, are now being questioned (Kokina & Kern, 2010). Although we know a lot as parents and teachers about developing math, reading, and other academic skills, we know considerably less about helping our children become socially competent human beings. What is clear, however, is that with appropriate support structures and interventions, social behaviors can be taught. In fact, since the inception of early intervention programs, the historical stereotype of children with autism being withdrawn, nonaffectionate, and noninteractive has dramatically changed.

In developing a comprehensive social skills training program, interventions must focus on a diverse set of behaviors. These behaviors can be grouped into several categories: core skills, social play, social engagement and friendship, theory of mind and empathy, social protocols and rules, and community engagement. Some of the key behaviors that fall into these various categories are presented in Tables 9.1, 9.2, 9.3, and 9.4.

During the initial stages of a social skills program, emphasis needs to be placed on developing core skills, which are prerequisites for developing complex social skills. These core skills (e.g. imitation, joint attention, social referencing, attachment, and instruction-following), along with interventions for developing them, are discussed in Chapter 3. A variety of research points out the importance of these core responses, and particularly joint attention, for the development of later social responsiveness (Clifford & Dissanayake, 2009; Yoder, Stone, Walden, & Malesa, 2009). Most early social skills training programs are implemented in play settings, where basic skills, such as sharing and turn-taking, are taught (see Table 9.1). As the child develops, more complex skills necessary for social and community engagement are emphasized. These interventions focus not only on teaching behavior skills, but also on developing an understanding about how the minds of others work and about the social protocols and rules that facilitate harmonious and safe interaction with others and the social community at large. In the remainder of this chapter we discuss the importance of these various social skill areas along with strategies for teaching them.

Table 9.1 Social and community behaviors that might be targeted for intervention

Core skills
    Imitation (see Chapter 2)
    Joint attention and social referencing (see Chapter 2)
    Attachment (see Chapter 2)
    Instruction-following (see Chapter 2)

Social play
    Isolate play
    Parallel play
    Interactive play
        Sharing
        Turn-taking
        Playing by the rules of the game
        Winning and losing gracefully

Social engagement and friendship

Theory of mind and empathy

Social protocols (following rules)

Community engagement
    Safety behaviors
    Shopping
    Eating in a restaurant

Social play

Play is a process that evolves from infancy into adulthood. Play is generally viewed as an activity vital to a young child's development. It is a vehicle through which children explore their environment and learn how to interact with it, thereby influencing their sensorimotor, cognitive, and socioemotional development. Through play children learn about how their physical and social environment operates, including what it looks, sounds, feels, smells, and tastes like, as well as how it responds. Through play children learn about permanence and change in the structure of the environment, cause and effect relationships, and how objects can be used. From these experiences children form internal representations of objects in the environment and thinking processes evolve that allow the child to organize, and even to transform reality through symbolic and imaginary play actions. Play helps children try out new roles, solve problems, work cooperatively with others, and formulate and execute plans.

Play can be distinguished in a variety of ways: including by its diversity, complexity, functionality, its social versus asocial orientation, and its symbolic versus concrete nature. Typically, children show a progression: 1) from object exploration to using toys in specific and conventional ways; 2) from solitary play to parallel play, and eventually to cooperative play with other children; and 3) from concrete to symbolic and imaginary (pretend) play. For more general information on play, the reader is referred to Berk (2009), Lightfoot, Cole, and Cole (2009) and Chapter 8 in this book.

An inability to engage in appropriate play in nonsocial and particularly social contexts is considered to be one of the early distinguishing characteristics of children with autism. Although they do play, research indicates that the play of children with autism is characterized by its: 1) stereotyped nature, with objects often serving as sources of repetitive self-stimulation; 2) preoccupation with specific toys, as well as specific aspects of a toy; 3) absence of functional and normative interactions with toys; 4) lack of imagination and a pretend orientation; 5) concrete and nonsymbolic nature; 6) solitariness and nonsocial quality; and 7) simplistic and scripted structure.

Parents notice early on that their children with autism: do not play with toys in usual ways, are interested in developmentally simpler toys, are quite restricted in what toys they interact with, and may develop an obsessive attachment to toys, often keeping them close, but not playing with them. Children with autism who are operating at a higher intellectual level may show more functional play, more diverse and complex interactions with toys, more social play and a greater tendency to engage in imaginary or pretend play. Nevertheless, their approach to play still has a certain fixed and nonspontaneous quality (Siegel, 1996; Sigman & Capps, 1997).

Research evaluating children with autism has often used social play as an assessment forum, specifically because play with others provides a vehicle for examining the development of social, language/communicative, and cognitive skills. Several studies indicate that children with autism engage in less social play than both typically developing children and children with other developmental delays (Rogers, Cook, & Meryl, 2005; Sigman & Ruskin, 1999). Functional play skills, along with responsiveness to bids for attention and initiation of requesting behaviors, have been found to be childhood predictors of gains in language skills in adolescents with autism (Sigman & McGovern, 2005). Conversely, it appears that a child's language skills affect their play skills. In addition, results of a study by Blanc, Adrien, Roux, and Barthelemy (2005) indicate that both level of play and communication skills in children with autism are associated with their ability to self-regulate.

Lewis (2003) has suggested that although there is general support for a play–language correlation in typically developing children, the nature of this relationship in children with autism is likely to be more complex, specifically because children with autism show play deficits even when compared to non-autistic children who have a similar language ability. Russell (1997) suggests play deficits may occur because children with autism do not use the language they have to regulate verbally their play behaviors, in contrast to neurotypical children who have better developed verbal regulation skills.

Researchers have also suggested that children with autism have play difficulties because of the problems they display in sensory processing, arousal modulation, selective attention, and shifting attentional focus. Others have suggested that their play deficiencies may be related to their dyspraxia and executive control problems (see review of theory and research in this area by Baranek, Reinhartsen, & Wannamaker, 2001). Because play provides a major context for the development of complex social interactions, it is not surprising, given their play deficiencies, that children with autism have difficulty forming meaningful social relationships with others.

In summary, play provides an opportunity for interacting with, exploring and learning from the environment. Historically, play therapy, influenced by psychoanalytic theory, was seen as a vehicle for helping children to express fears and re-enact social conflicts. Through observing play, therapists attempted to gain insights into children's problems. More recently, through the contributions of fields like developmental and behavioral psychology, play has become a major vehicle not only for understanding socioemotional functioning, but also for fostering sensorimotor, cognitive, linguistic, social, and emotional development in children with autism (e.g. Manning & Wainwright, 2010).

Intervention perspectives and strategies

Although play can be particularly challenging and frustrating for children with autism, it is also an invaluable tool for helping them develop. Through an assessment of children in play situations, a profile of their strengths and limitations can be developed that in turn guides the structure of the play therapy. Through play programs, children with autism can be taught object play, imaginary play and social play skills. From a basic process perspective, they can be taught attentional, imitation, motor-planning, and language responses. Moreover, play can be employed to help them tolerate and process sensory stimuli as well as to regulate their emotions. It can also be used as a vehicle for generalizing skills taught in more structured situations.

In establishing a play program, a variety of therapeutic/educational strategies and structures have been employed. At one end of a continuum the structure is quite flexible and child-based, in the sense that the child's own actions become the critical foundation upon which therapy is built. In contrast, other programs are more explicitly structured; after an assessment of their strengths and limitations, children are taught specific skills. Often less structured approaches to play therapy tend to be more an art form and for that reason are more difficult to replicate and transfer to parents and volunteers. In contrast, structured approaches, because of their explicit nature, can be readily taught to others. Both types of programs focus on creating a positive motivational environment for children. Less structured programs typically try to keep children motivated by letting them take the lead in activities which they choose. Structured behaviorally oriented programs also provide choices to children, but utilize their interests and behaviors to build specific skills. In both types of programs children can be further motivated through the explicit use of reinforcers and incentives.

Most play programs also use prompts to promote development. Structured behavioral programs, however, are more specific in the designation of the prompts (e.g. visual, verbal, and manual) to be employed, how these prompts should be sequenced, and how they should be faded out. For example, research by Charlop-Christy, Le, and Freeman (2000) indicates how video modeling can be an effective approach for teaching and promoting generalization of a wide variety of play and communication skills. Most structured programs try to provide enough support to maintain the children's motivation and performance. Whereas both unstructured and structured play programs typically occur in naturalistic settings, structured programs are implemented in more tightly controlled environments. They pay special attention to the play space and play materials, arranging these spaces and materials in order to achieve specific program objectives. Many structured programs, at least initially, create play spaces that are smaller, less distracting, and orderly.

Interventions designed to foster play behaviors should take into consideration the child's current level of motor, language, and cognitive development and their general behavioral capabilities and build upon them. Certain core skills, including joint attention, imitation, and instruction-following, are essential prerequisites for developing social play skills and meaningful social relationships.

Choice of partners is also critical in programs designed to promote social play. Often adults are initially employed as partners, specifically because of their ability to be more sensitive initiators, responders, and supporters of play. Neurotypical peers can be introduced later in a gradual fashion, after they are given training on how to interact with the child with autism. Peer-mediated techniques are particularly useful in teaching general play skills, such as turn-taking and helping. Optimally, all play programs should be designed to allow growth in the complexity of the skills taught and to promote generalization of play skills into a variety of everyday environments.

Programs directed at developing social play skills need to assess whether the child has the prerequisite basic play skills. Play, which involves interactions with specific objects in the environment, e.g. toys or a game, requires one type of skill set. Play which involves interactions with other children requires another type of skill set. For example, a board game might require a child to throw dice, count the dots on the dice, and move a marker on a board the number of spaces indicated by the count. If the child cannot perform these steps, he/she must be taught the steps, either before or while playing that game with another child. If the goal of a play program is to establish interactive pretend play with another child involving a set of toys, the intervention should focus initially on teaching pretend toy play to the child with autism without another child being present, and then progress to teaching two children to pretend play interactively with the same set of toys. In addition, social play programs require that other behaviors be taught such as: sharing, turn-taking, playing by the rules of game, and winning and losing gracefully. Without these types of skills, meaningful social play is not likely to develop.

Most structured social play programs employ the behavior-focused intervention strategies described in Chapter 2. Modeling and role playing, verbal instruction, physical assistance, shaping, feedback, and reinforcement procedures are used to teach proper play and social responses. Wherever possible, social play interventions should utilize materials, activities, and games in which the child shows intrinsic interest. For example, if a child loves to swim, then water-based games might be used to develop social play. Research indicates that embedding natural reinforcers into an intervention program can be a very effective teaching tool (Koegel, Vernon, & Koegel, 2009). For further information on play, the reader is referred to Chapter 8 for a discussion of pretend play, to various other chapters where incidental learning programs are described (see Subject Index), and to the program examples section at the end of the chapter.

Social engagement and friendship

Friendships and more formal peer relationships provide a context in which children utilize social skills as well as develop an understanding of social rules, a sense of personal identity, and an appreciation of individual differences. Social relationships are also a source of emotional satisfaction. Although children with ASD have peer acquaintances, their contacts with them are often casual in nature. While children with autism can be taught a range of social skills, such as making eye contact, initiating and responding to social contacts, and giving compliments, they find it difficult to use these skills in a spontaneous and flexible fashion in social situations. Higher functioning children with autism who possess more complex linguistic and social skills have a better chance of developing and sustaining a social relationship than children with less advanced skills. Typically, however, their social relationships are relatively superficial in nature. It is frequently assumed that children with autism spectrum disorders cannot develop deeper friendships because of an inability to understand the minds and emotions of others. (See the next section for a discussion of theory of mind and interventions for developing it.)

In a review of theory and research on friendship, Bauminger and Kasari (2001) point out that even though children with autism can explain what a friend is, they appear to view friendships in more instrumental terms; for example, it allows them to say that they have a friend. Their descriptions of pictures of friends and friendships tend to emphasize superficial details, like color of hair or frequency of contact, rather than the dynamic social, cognitive, and affective aspects of the friend and social relationship. Although children with autism seem to understand what loneliness means, they don't necessarily associate loneliness or lack of friends with feelings of sadness. Bauminger and Kasari (2001) suggest that interventions directed at friendship development should be individualized, according to the developmental level of the person, and optimally contain components that not only target the acquisition of specific behavioral skills, but also focus on developing the social and emotional meaning of friendship. They further recommend that peers, parents, and teachers be recruited to develop, support, and sustain friendships.

Intervention perspectives and strategies

Although play provides a forum for the initial development of friendships, deeper friendships involve a close emotional tie that is reciprocal, stable and typically manifested across situations, including in and out of school. The skill sets required for developing deeper friendships are quite complex and emerge over time as cognitive and language development occurs. Table 9.2 presents a list of component behaviors that facilitate the development of social relationships and friendships. Because of the deficiencies that children with autism display in these areas, they are frequently the targets of social skills training programs.

Table 9.2 Behaviors that might be targeted as part of a social skills training program

Person recognition and name utilization
Social gesturing
Sharing interests
Emotion recognition (see Chapter 4)
Emotion expression (facial and body) (see Chapter 4)
Making social overtures
Responding to social overtures
Listening

Eye contact
Greeting and saying goodbye to people
Showing appropriate affect (e.g. smiling at appropriate times)
Introducing oneself
Expressing concern about others' welfare
Helping others
Complimenting (giving and receiving compliments)
Expressing interest in others
Anger control
Negotiating and compromising
Conflict resolution
Apologizing
Support and information seeking
Reciprocal interaction/reciprocity
Respecting physical boundaries
Appropriate physical contact
Expressing affection
Voice modulation
Polite speech
Appropriate assertive behavior
Expressing appreciation

The specific social behaviors listed in Table 9.2 vary considerably in their level of complexity. Some of the behaviors are relatively simple and can be taught through behavior-focused interventions, such as person recognition, name utilization, making and responding to social overtures, greeting and saying goodbye to people, introducing oneself, giving and receiving compliments, and the use of polite speech. Other behaviors require an understanding and interpretation of social situations, such as how and when to: express concern about others' welfare, show affection, listen, ask questions, negotiate, and compromise.

Video aids can be quite useful for providing information regarding: social situations that require interpretation, examples of social skills in action, and feedback about social behaviors that are inappropriate (Nikopoulos & Keenan, 2007). In addition, behavior rehearsal and role playing can be effective strategies for teaching many social skills. More naturalistic group-oriented interventions, which focus on teaching skills in everyday settings, have face validity and show promise, but need to be more carefully evaluated (Frankel et al., 2010; Koenig, De Los Reyes, Cicchetti, Scahill, & Klin, 2009). In general, behavior-focused approaches, including ABA, are the most commonly employed interventions used in social skills training programs (Reichow & Volkmar, 2010). Cotugno (2009) points out that in designing group-oriented programs, specific skill instruction needs to be based both on individual needs as well the needs of the group as a whole.

For more extensive information on social skills programs for children with autism, the reader is referred to books by Bellini (2008) and Ingersoll and Dvortcsak (2009), and a review of social skills interventions by Reichow and Volkmar (2010). Moreover, several program examples are presented at the end of the chapter. In addition, other social skills necessary for developing friendships are discussed in the next three sections. More generally, the reader should be advised that comprehensive evidence-based programs for teaching complex social skills are still evolving (Rao, Beidel, & Murray, 2008). In the next section, we discuss theory of mind, which has been found to be a predictor of friendship quality (Bauminger, Solomon, & Rogers, 2010).

Theory of mind and empathy

The area of social cognition involves the study of how people's thought processes are related to their social context. Research in this area focuses on how people think about their thought processes as well as those of other people. Hypotheses concerning the latter topic are part of a prominent literature that has been referred to as theory of mind. Theory of mind researchers study how the mental states of others (e.g. their desires, beliefs, intentions, and knowledge) come to be understood by those around them (see review by Tager-Flusberg, Joseph, & Folstein, 2001).

Within the experimental literature, children's "theory of mind" has been studied in structured situations, including one which utilizes a false belief paradigm. In this type of research, a child is asked a question concerning a situation about which he/she holds knowledge in common with another child, but also possesses unique knowledge. For example, two children are shown Crayolas placed in a blue box. Subsequently, one (informed) child becomes privy to additional information (the Crayolas have been taken out of the blue box and put in a red box) that the other (uniformed) child does not have. Informed children, who have developed an understanding of the minds of others, will report that the uninformed children (who have not seen the Crayolas taken out of the blue box and put in the red box) will think the Crayolas are still in the original blue box. Children, less advanced in their understanding of the minds of others, will indicate that uninformed children will think as they do—that the Crayolas are in the red box.

Theories about how children in general and children with autism understand the world around them are embedded in a broader developmental and cognitive psychology literature. These theories raise questions about the ability of children with autism to think abstractly, to distinguish between mental and physical reality, to differentiate between imaginary, fictional, and real events, and to understand their own selves. Some researchers suggest that children with autism have a primary deficit in understanding the minds of other people and how other people's mental states (desires, beliefs, and knowledge) influence their behavior in social interactions (Baron-Cohen, Tager-Flusberg, & Cohen, 2000).

Other researchers disagree and suggest that children with autism do not understand others' minds because they do not develop a sense that they themselves have a mind, or if they do possess this general knowledge, do not understand or appreciate the contents of their own mind. Although children in general vary in their ability to know their own minds and to understand what they know and do not know, children with autism have particular difficulty thinking about their own thought patterns; that is they have a metacognitive deficit. Metacognition refers to the self-knowledge that individuals have about their cognitive states and mental processes (Flavell, 1979).

In order to explain the problems children with autism have in understanding both their own minds and the minds of other people, one theorist, R. Peter Hobson, has emphasized the critical role that social experience plays in this process (Hobson, 1993). He emphasizes that cognitive development occurs in an interpersonal context and that to understand the mind as a social entity, the social context in which it arises must be considered. Hobson points out that what children typically learn in social transactions is not a theory of other people's minds, but a knowledge about people. Children learn about people's subjective states through having experiences with people. Through social encounters with others, children gain a sense of self and a sense of other's attitudes and feelings.

Hobson (1993) views autism as a condition in which individuals have a limited understanding regarding the subjective and psychological experiences of other people; that is they do not really know what is going on in other people's minds. He suggests that the difficulties that children with autism have in peer and adult interactions—including those relating to social gesturing, sharing experiences, joint attention, affect coordination, emotion perception and expression, imitation, attachment behavior, and self-development—are evidence of their broader difficulty in social engagement. As a consequence of these social difficulties and limited social experiences, children with autism are constrained in their ability to acquire knowledge about other people's mental and emotional states, their own selves, and language and communication, thereby also restricting their ability to form mental representations about others and themselves.

Hobson (1993) emphasizes that emotional understanding also involves cognitive processes, including the ability to make inferences about other's emotional states based on knowledge of one's own internal emotional states, a process typically referred to as empathy. Empathy involves identifying another person's emotions and responding to those emotions in an appropriate fashion. A variety of research indicates that children with autism show impairments in empathetic responding (Auyeung et al., 2009) as well as in understanding other people's mental states (David et al., 2010).

Consistent with Hobson's conceptualizations, research in cognitive and developmental psychology points to the critical role that the social environment plays in the cognitive development of both neurotypical children and children with autism (Berk, 2009; Lightfoot, Cole, & Cole, 2009; Whitman 2004). From this perspective autism can be conceptualized as a condition in which children are disconnected from their social environment and as a consequence do not have an opportunity to develop an understanding of either themselves or other people. Accordingly, interventions directed at helping children with autism develop such understandings must focus on helping them reconnect with their social environment.

Intervention perspectives and strategies

It is important to note that under certain circumstances children with autism spectrum disorders do learn to understand their own minds as well as the minds of other people. In order to assist in the development of this understanding, cognitively focused interventions can be very useful. Although a cognitive therapeutic approach has received little careful clinical or research attention in the autism intervention literature, it has been successfully employed with children with other developmental disabilities. When this approach is used with children with autism, its goal should be to develop awareness of their and other people's thoughts, emotions, and behavior; specifically, it should focus on helping them:

- to monitor and articulate what they know and are feeling about what is happening in their social world

- to understand the role that their experiences and those of other people play in shaping a person's knowledge, emotional responses, and behavior

- to appreciate that their view of the world is sometimes the same and sometimes different from that of other people because of these experiences

- to make inferences, based on their knowledge of other people's social experiences, about what other people are thinking and feeling in specific circumstances.

Therapeutically, to assist children with autism in developing self-knowledge and knowledge about other people, they need to be taught to examine what is happening in the world around them, as well as their own personal actions and feelings. Although all young children, whether autistic or not, have difficulties articulating what is happening around them and monitoring their own actions and reactions, children with autism have a marked deficiency in this regard (see Lind & Bowler, 2009 for a discussion of self-awareness).

Once children with autism spectrum disorders become more proficient in describing the events that are occurring in their world, they can be taught to reflect on how these events influence their feelings and thoughts and vice versa. This personal monitoring and inferential phase is designed to enhance their self-knowledge, a metacognitive process that further develops their self-awareness. Once they develop this self-knowledge, the next step is to help them utilize this knowledge to make sense of their social world.

After being taught to monitor and make inferences about how the world around them influences their feeling and actions, children with autism spectrum disorders can then be more easily taught to monitor what is happening to other people and to make inferences about how these other individuals' experiences and actions influence their thoughts and feelings. Finally, children with ASD should be taught to compare their experiences of the world with those of others and to make inferences about why other people might sometimes be experiencing similar thoughts and emotions as their own and at other times experiencing different thoughts and emotions.

This therapeutic process is at a conceptual level a rather complex one. At a more practical level, it is somewhat simpler and involves getting children to reflect, by articulating out loud their observations, thoughts, and feelings about their world, and to understand how this world influences their actions and reactions as well as those of other people. This process can be promoted by asking the child questions such as: What just happened? How did it make you react/feel? What just happened to "Joe"? Why did he react the way he did? How would you react/feel if what happened to "Joe" happened to you? As necessary, parents/teachers can help the child by providing insights and answers to the child. In addition to reviewing the events of the day as they occur or in retrospect, the use of videos of actual events and also fictional stories can be very useful. Because videos and stories can be stopped, repeated and analyzed, the child's observations and inferences can be sharpened through the questioning, reflection, and review process.

Teaching others is also a learning opportunity for parents and teachers. Although adults, including parents and professionals, have greater self-awareness and understanding of the minds and hearts of other people than children with ASD, the process of having to help children with ASD develop these skills should sharpen both their own self and social awareness. As adults become more aware of their own and others' personal dynamics, they will be better able to help the children they are teaching.

Social protocols and rules

An important component of social competence involves understanding and following social protocols and rules. Social rules are more formalized (e.g. do not run in school) while social protocols are less so (e.g. do not stand too close to others, while talking to them). In some instances, children and adults only become aware of social rules and protocols after they violate them and experience the critical reactions of others. Children with autism spectrum disorders often lack awareness of both formal and informal social rules, as well as the negative reactions of others when they do not follow them; and thus, not surprisingly, they frequently violate such rules. Research by Loveland et al. (2001) suggests that children with autism have problems identifying examples of inappropriate social behavior. Table 9.3 presents a list of some common social protocols/rules.

Table 9.3 Examples of social protocols and rules

Don't chew with your mouth open.
Wash your hands before eating.
Don't interrupt others while they are talking.
Don't run in the halls at school.
Excuse yourself when you burp.
Cross the street when the traffic light is green.
Don't cut into the lunch line, wait your turn.
Talk softly when you are in the library.
Share your toys with your friends.
Don't hit or kick other children.
Ask to be excused when you wish to leave the dinner table.
Raise your hand and wait to be called upon before talking in class.

Intervention perspectives and strategies

Following social rules/protocols is an example of what behavior therapists call rule-governed behavior. Children learn about rules by finding out first what they are. They learn to obey rules when they are positively reinforced for following them and/or after receiving negative feedback for not following them. Many, if not most rules, can be stated in a positive way (e.g. talk quietly), or in a negative fashion (e.g. don't yell). In general, learning occurs more rapidly through reinforcing appropriate behavior than punishing inappropriate behavior. The basic reason for this disparity in outcomes is because punishment only tells children what not to do, but does not teach them what to do. It should also be noted that children are much happier when they are praised than when they are punished.

In teaching a child to follow rules, a cognitively focused procedure, correspondence training, which is discussed in Chapter 2, is often employed. Utilizing this procedure involves teaching children a particular rule, for example, "Raise your hand and then wait to be called upon before talking in class." They are asked to verbalize the rule and then to follow it. If they subsequently follow this rule in class, they are positively reinforced ("Good, you said you would raise your hand and you did."). If they do not follow the rule, they are asked what the rule is and then asked to follow it. If they then follow the rule, they are positively reinforced. Conversely, they should not be allowed to speak without raising their hand.

Through correspondence training programs, children come to understand the meaning of specific social protocols/rules and to follow them. Indirectly, they learn that it is not proper (i.e. hypocritical) to say you are going to do something and then not to do it, or to do something else. As their words (stating a rule) come to control their behavior, children can be taught to state these words (rules) to themselves before acting. When they learn to do this, not only their words, but their thoughts (i.e. subvocalizations) control their behavior. In summary, because children with autism have problems in following social rules as well using language in a way that directs their behavior, correspondence training programs, such as that just described, helps them not only to be more appropriate in their behavior, but also to self-regulate their actions. More will be said about this topic in Chapter 10 when self-regulation is discussed.

Community engagement, safety, and leisure skills

The last category of skills, which includes community engagement, safety, and leisure behaviors, are often not included when social skills training programs for children with autism are discussed. Yet these behaviors should be incorporated as part of a social skills intervention because many, if not most, of these skills include a social aspect. Table 9.4 lists examples of behaviors that fall into this general category.

Table 9.4 Examples of community engagement, safety, and leisure skills

Community skills
    Ordering at a restaurant
    Shopping at a grocery store
    Using public transportation
    Performing tasks appropriately and independently in a work setting

Safety behaviors
    Providing personal information (name, address, and telephone number)
    Calling for help when there is an emergency
    Crossing streets appropriately
    Following evacuation plans when there is a fire

Social leisure skills
    Playing cards
    Playing board games
    Engaging in a group sports activity

One reason autism spectrum disorders are often classified as a developmental disorder is that individuals with this type of disability are often not able to act in an independent fashion in a community setting. For example, older children and adults with autism spectrum disorders should ideally be able to perform without assistance tasks, such as shopping, eating at a restaurant, and taking public transportation. In addition, to be independent, they must be able to take care of themselves in emergency situations. Finally, becoming independent also means that individuals must learn how to occupy themselves in recreational/leisure activities when they are not involved in other daily life activities. Parents of children with autism spectrum disorders often discuss the supervision burden they must bear in monitoring their children when they are not involved in structured programs.

Intervention perspectives and strategies

In teaching children the types of skills listed in Table 9.4, many of the behavior and cognitively focused intervention strategies discussed in Chapter 2 are appropriate, depending on the skill taught. One procedure not specifically discussed, *coaching*, can also be particularly useful. It involves a combination of behavior-focused and cognitive strategies. For example, in teaching an adult with an autism spectrum disorder to use public transportation, the coach would accompany the "student" while he/she engages in this activity.

Coaching initially involves both telling and showing students what they need to do and then gradually fading these verbal and visual supports, requiring the students to tell and show the coach what they must do. Feedback is provided to the students who have difficulty articulating and performing the requisite steps, which in this example might include: walking to a bus stop at an appropriate time, getting on the bus and paying a fare, getting off and later getting on the bus at an appropriate location, and then walking to a final destination. Defining the specific steps is a critical part of the coach's responsibility. Coaching procedures are particularly useful in teaching more complex tasks, such as performing in a job situation, crossing streets, and engaging in board games or sports activities.

Coaching shares with other visual methods, such as modeling, video feedback, pictorial cuing, and peer-mediated procedures, the use of explicit visual cues to assist the individual in acquiring and generalizing social skills across situations. These visual cues help provide children with ASD additional supports made necessary because of their deficits in processing and comprehending verbal instructions. For these reasons coaching, particularly when combined with concept mastery routines, which provide multiple examples of a concept like crossing various streets, show great promise as a teaching procedure (see Laushey, Heflin, Shippen, Alberto, & Frederick, 2009). For a review of research on teaching safety skills to persons with developmental disabilities, the reader is referred to Dixon, Bergstrom, Smith, and Tarbox (2010).

The next section provides examples of various social skills training programs.

Program examples

Theory of mind

OBJECTIVE

Teach the child to understand that others may have thoughts, feelings, and knowledge that are different from his/her own.

PREREQUISITES

The child should have an awareness of facial expressions, body language, and emotion, and the ability to briefly describe his/her current emotions and/or thoughts.

MATERIALS

Various pictures, videos, music.

PROCEDURE

1. Expose the child to some sort of stimulus (e.g. a picture or a video). For example, show the child a video of a tornado destroying homes.

2. After a few minutes, ask the child to describe his/her emotions or thoughts regarding the stimulus. For example, the child may say that he thinks the tornadoes are really cool and that they make him excited.

3. After the child has described his/her thoughts, ask him/her to explain what you (or someone else) probably think/feel about the stimulus. Purposely prepare an answer that is different from the child's opinion of the stimulus. For example, even if you actually are fascinated by tornadoes, be prepared to tell the child that you are scared of them.

4. A correct response involves the child stating that he/she doesn't know how you feel about the stimulus or to guess your feelings based on prior knowledge or your current actions/facial expression. In this case, prompt him/her to ask you how you feel (if he/she hasn't already). Then praise and reward the child for understanding that you may have thoughts/feelings that differ from his/hers.

5. Repeat with other stimuli, several times, until the child understands that his/her thoughts and feelings may differ from others'.

ERROR CORRECTION

If the child states that you feel the same way he/she feels about the stimulus, explain to the child your actual thoughts and feelings. Tell the child a story that may help explain your thoughts on the subject. For example, tell a story about a time when tornadoes blew down a tree in your backyard and it frightened you. If, on the other hand, the child guesses about your feelings or suggests an emotion other than what he/she feels, praise the child for guessing that you may not feel the same way as the child.

GENERALIZATION

Take advantage of natural learning opportunities to teach the child to use these skills in other environments. For example, when the child is playing a game with another child, prompt the child to describe how each player must be feeling (i.e. whoever is winning should be happy, whoever is losing should be disappointed, etc.).

TIPS/SUGGESTIONS

Sometimes have your thoughts/feelings/knowledge the same or similar to the child's so he/she learns that sometimes his/her mind differs from others and sometimes it is similar.

Include tasks that require knowledge of a particular topic, such as knowledge of the location of an object. For example, ask the child to hide something while you step out of the room. When you come back, ask the child to tell you where he/she thinks you will look for the item. Ideally, the child should state that you don't know where to look, or suggest that you will look in an incorrect location. The child should not, however, suggest that you will look in the actual location of the item, as you do not in fact know where the item is located.

TROUBLESHOOTING

If the child has difficulty guessing your thoughts/feelings, try using a textual prompt. Write down your reactions (and have the child write down his/her reactions) to the stimuli. Then compare your written statements one at a time, letting the child read your response. Fade the use of this prompt by waiting a little longer to show the child your response.

OTHER TEACHING METHODS

Prepare two sets of headphones (one for you and one for the child), each with a different sound or type of music playing. After you both listen to your headphones, ask the child what he/she listened to. Then ask him/her what you listened to. The child should say he/she does not know what you listened to, and should not assume that it was the same sounds/music. Be prepared to prompt the child with this task as well, as he/she may not know how to answer correctly. Let him/her listen to your headphones, for example.

FUTURE OBJECTIVES

Expand upon this procedure to help teach the child to empathize with those who may be feeling differently from him/her.

Playing board games

OBJECTIVE

Teach the child to play various board games by the rules of the game.

PREREQUISITES

The skills necessary to play the game depend on which game you are playing. For example, if you are playing Candyland, the child should have learned in a more structured setting to recognize colors, to match, and to count. For example, teach the child to count pennies or other small objects one at a time (as opposed to rote counting where the child simply lists numbers in order).

MATERIALS

Various board games.

PROCEDURE

The important things to remember when teaching the child to play a game include breaking down the steps of the game (i.e. the actual behaviors the child will need to demonstrate) into very small steps that the child can easily master, instructing the child in these steps, modeling, and practicing while providing feedback to the child. The following example demonstrates a way to teach the child to play the game Candyland.

1. To teach the child to play Candyland, start with only you and the child. Do not include other children until the child has learned some basic rules and can sit and play the entire game without attempting to leave.

2. Have the child choose a game piece (generalize color skills by having him/her name the color he/she wants). Show the child where to start.

3. Model the first response for the child by picking up a card, labeling the color, and then moving your piece to the first color space on the path that matches your card.

4. When it's the child's turn, prompt him/her to:

  a) pick up a card

  b) label the color

  c) identify the first space of the same color on the path

  d) move his/her piece to that space

  e) attend to you while waiting for his/her next turn.

5. Reinforce each of the above responses. In the beginning, the child may need tangible or edible reinforcers for each step of his/her turn, for the entire game in order to maintain attention and motivation. This reinforcement schedule can be faded so that you use praise for most steps, and eventually do not need to use any reinforcement, as playing the game will become reward by itself.

6. If the child wins, model "good sport" behavior by telling him/her, "Good job." If you win, prompt the child to show such behavior, and provide a reward for "being a good sport."

Error correction

If the child misses a step, return him/her to the beginning of the turn (i.e. start with picking up the card again). Prompt the child to go through each step, and then deliver praise as the child goes through each step.

Generalization

Once the child has learned the basics of the game, fade prompts and tangible reinforcement for each step, as well as for each turn (continue praising the child for playing the game). Begin to add additional players to the game so the child must learn to wait longer for his/her turn, and to attend to more people.

Tips/suggestions

If the child has difficulty following the path, use a reinforcer (e.g. an M&M) to follow the path in front of the child's piece. Once the child gets to the correct spot on the board he/she can have the reinforcer.

  The child may have difficulty playing games that last longer than a few minutes. Set a timer to go off every 2 to 3 minutes. If the child is attending when the timer beeps, deliver a reinforcer. Whenever the child stops attending, bring him/her back to the game and prompt him/her to continue.

  Consider using picture cues to help the child correctly play the game. Use a picture strip indicating each task involved in the turn and prompt him/her to refer to each picture before engaging in the task.

As difficult as it may be, do not always allow the child to win. The child must learn to maintain attention and focus on the game even if he/she does not win. This will also allow you an opportunity to teach the child how to respond appropriately if he/she loses.

Along the same lines, you may want to teach the child early on to choose different color game pieces and to allow you to go first sometimes. If the child does not learn these skills early on, he/she may have a difficult time when more players are introduced to the game. It may take the child a long time to recover from a battle with another child over a particular color game piece.

TROUBLESHOOTING

It may be necessary to start by teaching the child tasks within the board game, but not while you're playing the game. For example, simply teach the child to pick up one card at a time, and to label the color. Reinforce correct responding. Once the child is able to reliably pick up one card and label the color, reintroduce the board game.

Also, for children who have a hard time attending for the entire game, or for children who have difficulty following the curvy path on the game board, create a mock game board that is much shorter and less curvy. Once the child has learned to play on the mock board, make another that is a bit longer/curvier. Continue until the child is able to play for about 10 minutes or follow curvier paths.

EXAMPLE GAMES

- Barnyard Bingo
- Chutes and Ladders
- Caribou Island
- Scrabble Junior
- Sorry
- Trouble
- Checkers
- Chess.

FUTURE OBJECTIVES

Teach language and social skills involved in game playing. For example, when it's your turn, do nothing. Prompt or have someone else prompt the child to tell you it's your turn. In addition, take the child's turn, prompting him/her to tell you nicely that it's not your turn.

Teach the child other games very soon so that he/she learns to play several common, age-appropriate games. When teaching new games, remember to break down the steps of the game into even smaller steps (the number of steps depends on the child). Do not assume that the child will learn to play the game with vague, verbal instructions as some children might.

If the child can read written instructions, teach him/her to read the instructions to the new games and to then teach you how to play.

Social engagement

OBJECTIVE

Teach the child to engage in various social behaviors.

MATERIALS

Depending on the methods you use to teach your child, you may want access to a video camera or digital recording device as well as note cards and a pen for textual prompting.

PROCEDURE

The following is an example of teaching social skills using coaching. Choose a skill or set of skills to teach the child (see Table 9.2). Be as specific as possible when choosing skills or goals. For example, "Initiate social interactions with peers," is more specific than "Make friends," but "Greet peers and say goodbye" is even better. Use coaching to teach the skill(s) to the child as follows:

1. *Instruction*: Deliver an instruction or rule to the child regarding the skill you are teaching. For example, if teaching the child to maintain eye contact during conversations, you may tell the child, "Look at your friends in the eyes from time to time," using whatever language is appropriate for your child.

2. *Model*: Model the skill by engaging in at least three short social interactions with someone else. If there is no one available, play a short video or television clip demonstrating the skill you are teaching. Talk to the child about the model afterwards, explaining the positive and negative aspects of the social engagement. For example, show a video clip or model someone approaching two people engaged in an intimate conversation, and the appropriate way to interrupt this conversation, if at all.

3. *Practice*: Allow the child the opportunity to practice the skill by engaging in a rehearsal conversation with you or someone else as you watch.

4. *Feedback*: Provide the child with feedback during or after the conversation (e.g. remind him/her of the rules, praise the child for correctly using the skills, etc.). At the end of the conversation, provide specific feedback on what the child did well and ways he/she can improve.

5. *Repeat*, practicing several different scenarios or rehearsal conversations. It is essential that the child have several practice opportunities to really master such difficult skills.

GENERALIZATION

Vary the topics discussed, both in model scenarios and rehearsal conversations. Also, model both successful conversations in which both partners are engaged and exhibiting stellar social skills, as well as less successful conversations in which one partner does not demonstrate appropriate social skills (e.g. one partner begins to bore the other, avoids eye contact, or monopolizes the conversation) so the child can learn how to respond to multiple scenarios.

When you view your child engaged in a social situation throughout the day, provide him/her with feedback afterwards so the child learns what he/she did well and ways that he/she can improve.

TIPS/SUGGESTIONS

During model and practice scenarios, it may help to provide the child with a written list of the rules you are targeting, or pictures representing the rules. Focus on one to four rules at a time, making sure to not overload the child with several rules to remember during a conversation or social situation.

In addition, teaching the child to self-rate his/her skills following a conversation may be helpful in teaching the child to monitor his/her own behavior. You can teach the child to use a rating scale that he/she completes while watching the model as well as following a practice opportunity. Videotaping the child may be a helpful tool to use in the feedback session, especially if the child is self-rating his/her performance.

This approach can also be used to teach your child to follow specific social rules or protocols (e.g. raise your hand before talking in class or don't stand too close to the person in front of you in line).

TROUBLESHOOTING

If the child is having difficulty with a particular social skill, try focusing on only that skill for a while, holding off on teaching several skills at once. Think about other alternatives to the skill. For example, some children may experience anxiety when making eye contact during conversations. You can try to teach the child instead of making direct eye contact to look at the bridge of their partner's nose, or to focus on only one of the person's eyes. Alternatively, consider whether or not the skill is absolutely necessary to teach the child at this time.

OTHER TEACHING METHODS

Some children benefit from social skills classes which typically consist of small groups of same-aged children, led by a professional. Such classes typically use the same approaches outlined here, but there are several model and practice opportunities available, as well as several other children their age to practice with. Just be sure to generalize the skills being practiced in such classes to other environments and situations.

FUTURE OBJECTIVES

Following the acquisition of the targeted social skills, move on to other social skills with which the child may need assistance learning. Use Table 9.2 as a guide for further assistance.

Community outings

OBJECTIVE

Teach the child to complete independently and accurately the steps involved in various community outings.

MATERIALS

Depends on the particular outing.

PROCEDURE

1. Determine the outing or activity you want your child to learn. Start with activities that the child will do with assistance, such as riding the train. Save more difficult outings, such as behaving appropriately at a restaurant, until the child has had success following your coaching during other activities.

2. Once you determine the outing or activity, break down the activity into the small steps that make up that activity. For example, ordering food from a fast food restaurant involves the following steps:

a) standing in line (which can be broken down into numerous steps)

b) approaching the counter when there is an available cashier

c) telling the cashier what you would like to order

d) if teaching money skills, the child can pay the cashier the appropriate amount of money and wait for change

e) wait appropriately for the meal to be ready

f) take the meal and go to a table or leave.

3. The number of steps and the detail involved in the steps will depend upon your child and his/her needs.

4. Reinforce each step with praise or perhaps a token of some sort. You may need to use tangible/edible reinforcers for certain, difficult steps, such as waiting in line. If you do use such reinforcers, try to use them discretely (e.g. slip a piece of candy or a token into the child's hand for every minute he/she waits quietly in line).

ERROR CORRECTION

If the child misses a step, offer a physical or gestural prompt to help the child. Try to minimize verbal prompts, as the child may become dependent on your reminders to get through the task. If your child responds well to verbal prompts, limit them to one reminder, and then do not repeat the reminder again. For example, if the child does not approach the counter when it is his/her turn, say, "Approach the counter," and then wait a few seconds. If the child still does not approach the counter, give a gentle nudge and point to the counter.

GENERALIZATION

Sometimes it helps to teach these skills in a contrived setting (e.g. you create a model fast food restaurant scene). This may be especially helpful if the child tends to engage in some challenging behaviors (e.g. tantrums) in public settings. Teach the child the skills necessary for the outing in the contrived setting. Once the child has mastered the skills, take him/her to small fast food restaurants to practice in the natural environment. Be ready to coach again, even if the child no longer needs coaching in the contrived setting.

TIPS/SUGGESTIONS

Do not use the reinforcers as a bribe (e.g. do not say, "If you come back in line I will give you a cracker.").

Also, it may be very helpful to teach the child the rules of the outing before going. For example, teach the child the rules of waiting in line (e.g. you stand about 1 foot (30 cm) behind the person in front of you, keep your hands to yourself, etc.). Practice some of the rules with the child to be sure he/she understands the rules.

TROUBLESHOOTING

If the child has particular difficulty with a step in an outing, use a highly preferred reinforcer for completing that step. For example, if the child loves suckers, but simply won't sit still in a grocery cart for longer than 2 minutes, give her the sucker once she has sat still in the cart for 1 minute. Each time you go to the store, slowly increase the duration she must sit still before getting the sucker (e.g. by 5 seconds). Try to end the shopping trip before the child becomes upset again. Deliver another reinforcer after the shopping trip is complete, if the child behaved well during the entire trip.

OTHER TEACHING METHODS

A social story may be useful in teaching the rules to the child. For a social story to be effective, be sure to include practice opportunities and reinforce successful practicing. For example, if teaching a child to act appropriately at a restaurant, one of the pages of the social story can say, "I use manners when I am at a restaurant. I act politely by saying 'please,' and 'thank you.' If I act politely for three exchanges I can have dessert (or other reinforcer)." Practice "polite exchanges" with the child before going to the restaurant.

When teaching rules to the child, or using social stories, focus mostly on rules/behaviors with which the child has difficulty. For example, if the child is already polite when in public, do not bother to include that skill in the social story. Instead focus on something the child needs to learn, such as telling the waitress what he/she wants when asked.

FUTURE OBJECTIVES

Continue with more advanced outings that require not only tolerance of the outing, but independence. For example, teach an older child to ride public transportation. For any outing, consider all of the necessary steps involved, including social rules or behaviors, and nonverbal social cues that are important to the outing (e.g. when the waitress turns to you it is your turn to order, even if she doesn't ask you what you want). Remember that some children will need the tasks broken down into much smaller steps than others, and initially each step must be reinforced.

References

Auyeung, B., Wheelwright, S., Allison, C., Atkinson, M., Samarawickrema, N., & Baron-Cohen, S. (2009). The children's empathy quotient and systemizing quotient: Sex differences in typical development and in autism spectrum conditions. *Journal of Autism and Developmental Disorders, 39,* 1509–1521.

Baranek, G., Reinhartsen, D., & Wannamaker, S. (2001). "Play: Engaging young children with autism." In R. Huebner (Ed.), *Autism: A sensorimotor approach to management* (pp. 313–351). Gaithersburg, MD: Aspen.

Baron-Cohen, S., Tager-Flusberg, H., & Cohen, D. J. (Eds.). (2000). *Understanding other minds: Perspectives from autism and development neuroscience* (2nd ed.). Oxford: Oxford University Press.

Bauminger, N. & Kasari, C. (2001). "The experience of loneliness and friendship." In E. Schopler, N. Yirmiya, C. Shulman, & L. Marcus (Eds.), *The research basis for autism intervention* (pp. 151–170). New York, NY: Kluwer Academic/Plenum Publishers.

Bauminger, N., Solomon, M., & Rogers, S. J. (2010). Predicting friendship quality in autism spectrum disorders and typical development. *Journal of Autism and Developmental Disorders, 40,* 751–761.

Beauchamp, M. H. & Anderson, V. (2010). An integrative framework for the development of social skills. *Psychological Bulletin, 136,* 39–64.

Bellini, S. (2008). *Building social relationships: A systematic approach to teaching social interaction to children with autism spectrum disorders and other social difficulties.* Shawnee Mission, KS: Autism Asperger Publishing Co.

Berk, L. E. (2009). *Child development* (8th ed.). Boston, MA: Allyn Bacon.

Blanc, R., Adrien, J. L., Roux, S., & Barthelemy, C. (2005). Dysregulation of pretend play and communication development in children with autism. *Autism, 9,* 229–245.

Charlop-Christy, M. H., Le, L., & Freeman, K. A. (2000). A comparison of video modeling with in vivo modeling for teaching children with autism. *Journal of Autism and Developmental Disorders, 30,* 537–552.

Clifford, S. & Dissanayake, C. (2009). Dyadic and triadic behaviours in infancy as precursors to later social responsiveness in young children with autistic disorder. *Journal of Autism and Developmental Disorders, 39,* 1369–1380.

Cotugno, A. J. (2009). Social competence and social skills training and intervention for children with autism spectrum disorders. *Journal of Autism and Developmental Disorders, 39,* 1268–1277.

David, N., Aumann, C., Bewernick, B. H., Santos, N. S., Lehnhardt, F. G., & Vogeley, K. (2010). Investigation of mentalizing and visuospatial perspective taking for self and other in Asperger syndrome. *Journal of Autism and Developmental Disorders, 40,* 290–299.

Dixon, D. R., Bergstrom, R., Smith, M. N., & Tarbox, J. (2010). A review of research on teaching safety skills to person with developmental disabilities. *Research in Developmental Disabilities, 31,* 985–994.

Flavell, J. H. (1979). Metacognition and cognitive monitoring: A new era of cognitive-developmental inquiry. *American Psychologist, 34,* 906–911.

Frankel, F., Myatt, R., Sugar, C., Whitham, C., Gorospe, C. M., & Laugeson, E. (2010). A randomized controlled study of parent-assisted children's friendship training and children having autism spectrum disorders. *Journal of Autism and Developmental Disorders, 40,* 827–842.

Gillberg, C. & Gillberg, I. C. (1989). Asperger's Syndrome. Some epidemiological considerations: A research note. *Journal of Child Psychology and Psychiatry, 30,* 631–638.

Hobson, R. P. (1993). *Autism and the development of the mind.* Hillsdale, NJ: Erlbaum.

Hobson, R. P. (2005). "Autism and emotion." In F. R. Volkmar, R. Paul, A. Klin, & D. Cohen (Eds.), *Handbook of autism and pervasive developmental disorders: Vol. 1. Diagnosis, development, neurobiology, and behavior* (3rd ed., pp. 406–422). Hoboken, NJ: John Wiley & Sons.

Ingersoll, B. & Dvortcsak, A. (2009). *Teaching social communication to children with autism: A practitioner's guide to parent training and a manual for parents.* New York, NY: Guilford Press.

Koegel, R. L., Vernon, T. W., & Koegel, L. K. (2009). Improving social initiations in young children with autism using reinforcers with embedded social interactions. *Journal of Autism and Developmental Disorders, 39,* 1240–1251.

Koenig, K., De Los Reyes, A., Cicchetti, D., Scahill, L., & Klin, A. (2009). Group intervention to promote social skills in school-age children with pervasive developmental disorders: Reconsidering efficacy. *Journal of Autism and Developmental Disorders, 39,* 1163–1172.

Kokina, A. & Kern, L. (2010). Social story™ interventions for students with autism spectrum disorders: A meta-analysis. *Journal of Autism and Developmental Disorders, 40,* 812–826.

Laushey, K. M., Heflin, L. J., Shippen, M., Alberto, P. A. & Fredrick, L. (2009). Concept mastery routines to teach social skills to elementary children with high functioning autism. *Journal of Autism and Developmental Disorders, 39,* 1435–1448.

Lewis, V. (2003). Play and language in children with autism. *Autism, 7,* 391–399.

Lightfoot, C., Cole, M., & Cole, S. (2009). *The development of children.* Worth, IL: Worth Publishing.

Lind, S. E. & Bowler, D. M. (2009). Delayed self-recognition in children with autism spectrum disorder. *Journal of Autism and Developmental Disorders, 39,* 643–650.

Loveland, K. A., Pearson, D. A., Tunali-Kotoski, B., Ortegon, J., & Gibbs, M. C. (2001). Judgments of social appropriateness by children and adolescents with autism. *Journal of Autism and Developmental Disorders, 31,* 367–376.

Manning, M. M. & Wainwright, L. D. (2010). The role of high level play as a predictor social functioning in autism. *Journal of Autism and Developmental Disorders, 40,* 523–533.

Nikopoulos, C. K. & Keenan, M. (2007). Using video modeling to teach complex social sequences to children with autism. *Journal of Autism and Developmental Disorders, 37,* 678–693.

Rao, P. A., Beidel, D. C., & Murray, M. J. (2008). Social skills interventions for children with Asperger's syndrome or high-functioning autism: A review and recommendations. *Journal of Autism and Developmental Disorders, 38,* 353–361.

Reichow, B. & Volkmar, F. R. (2010). Social skills interventions for individuals with autism: Evaluation for evidence-based practices within a best evidence synthesis framework. *Journal of Autism and Developmental Disorders, 40,* 149–166.

Rogers, S. J., Cook, I., & Meryl, A. (2005). "Imitation and play in autism." In F. R. Volkmar, R. Paul, A. Klin, & D. Cohen (Eds.), *Handbook of autism and pervasive developmental disorders: Vol. 1. Diagnosis, development, neurobiology, and behavior* (3rd ed., pp. 382–405). Hoboken, NJ: John Wiley & Sons.

Russell, J. (1997). "How executive disorders can bring about an inadequate 'theory of mind'." In J. Russell (Ed.), *Autism as an executive disorder* (pp. 256–304). Oxford: Oxford University Press.

Siegel, B. (1996). *The world of the autistic child: Understanding and treating autism spectrum disorders.* New York, NY: Oxford University Press.

Sigman, M. & Capps. L. (1997). *Children with autism: A developmental perspective.* Cambridge, MA: Harvard University Press.

Sigman, M. & McGovern, C. W. (2005). Improvements in cognitive and language skills from preschool to adolescence in autism. *Journal of Autism and Developmental Disorders, 35,* 15–23.

Sigman, M. & Ruskin, E. (1999). Continuity and change in the social competence of children with autism, Down syndrome, and developmental delays. *Monographs of the Society for Research in Child Development, 64* (pp. 1–108) (1, Serial No. 256).

Tager-Flusberg, H., Joseph, R., & Folstein, S. (2001). Current directions in research in autism. *Mental Retardation and Developmental Disabilities Research Reviews, 7,* 21–29.

Whitman, T. L. (2004). *The development of autism: A self-regulatory perspective.* London: Jessica Kingsley Publishers.

Wing, L. & Gould, J. (1979). Severe impairments of social interaction and associated abnormalities in children: Epidemiology and classification. *Journal of Autism and Developmental Disorders, 9,* 11–29.

Yoder, P., Stone, W.L., Walden, T., & Malesa, E. (2009). Predicting social impairment and ASD diagnosis in younger siblings of children with autism spectrum disorder. *Journal of Autism and Developmental Disorders, 39,* 1381–1391.

Further readings

Johnson, S. A., Filliter, J. H., & Murphy, R. R. (2009). Discrepancies between self- and parent-perceptions of autistic traits and empathy in high functioning children and adolescents on the autism spectrum. *Journal of Autism and Developmental Disorders, 39,* 1706–1714.

Scheuermann, B. & Webber, J. (2002). *Autism: Teaching does make a difference.* Belmont, CA: Wadsworth.

Schuler, A. & Wolfberg, P. (2000). "Promoting play and socialization." In A. Wetherby & B. Prizant (Eds.), *Autism spectrum disorders: A transactional developmental perspective* (pp. 251–277). Baltimore, MD: Brookes.

Chapter 10

Self-Regulation Deficiencies

There is an intriguing third set of diagnostic features, in addition to social and language/communication deficiencies. These consist of the repetitive, restricted, and stereotyped interests, activities, and behaviors that characterize individuals with autism. Turner (1999) suggests that the broad range of behaviors in this third symptom category can be subdivided into two subgroups, lower level behaviors in which there is repetition of movement (e.g. stereotyped and repetitive behaviors) and higher level complex responses (e.g. narrow interests and insistence on maintaining sameness). Although stereotyped, repetitive, and restricted behaviors also occur in typically developing children as well as in children with other disorders, such as mental retardation, these behaviors occur with greater frequency in children with autism. Furthermore, there are certain classes of repetitive behavior that appear to be unique to autism (Whitman, 2004).

South, Ozonoff, and McMahon (2005) found that the incidence of four behavior categories (restricted object use, repetitive motor movements, rigid routines, and circumscribed interests) was more pronounced in persons with ASD than in neurotypical individuals, who are more prone to show such behaviors during infancy and early childhood. Individuals with autism were also found to display a higher incidence of certain types of restricted behaviors (object use and rigid routines) than those with Asperger Syndrome. Moreover, Bodfish, Symons, Parker, and Lewis (2000) found that individuals with autism and mental retardation had significantly higher severity ratings for compulsions, stereotypy and self-injury than individuals with only mental retardation. Repetitive behavior severity also predicted severity of autism in this study. These findings raise interesting questions about the role that these types of behaviors play in the cognitive and social development of children with ASD.

Chapter 11 provides several possible explanations regarding the origins of these behaviors. One explanation is that children with ASD learn to regulate unpleasant emotions in challenging situations through their repetitive, restricted, and stereotyped behaviors and that these behaviors are indicative of a poorly developed and immature self-regulatory system (Whitman, 2004; Whitman & Ekas, 2008). This immature coping system, while at least partially successful in that it reduces anxiety, is problematic in that self-regulation is achieved at a great social cost; specifically repetitive, restricted, and stereotyped behaviors make it difficult for children with autism to enter into meaningful interactions with others.

From an intervention perspective, programs directed at reducing repetitive, restricted, and stereotyped behaviors in children with ASD can either focus on reducing the incidence of such behaviors and/or on developing adaptive coping and self-regulatory skills. In the next chapter, strategies for reducing problematic behaviors, including repetitive, restricted, and stereotyped behaviors, are discussed. However, intervention programs that focus on developing self-regulatory skills are preferable; specifically, because once developed such skills allow the child to cope with challenging situations without engaging the aforementioned problem behaviors. The importance of self-regulation in developing social and academic competencies is supported by empirical and anecdotal evidence (Whitman & Ekas, 2008; Zimmerman, 1998).

Although attempts are still emerging to help children with autism to self-regulate their emotions and behaviors more effectively, self-regulatory training programs have been designed and successfully employed with children with other developmental problems, including mental retardation (see Whitman, 1987, 1990). In this chapter, we begin by discussing what self-regulation is and how this process emerges in neurotypical children and children with autism. General intervention strategies for developing self-regulation and promoting independent functioning in children with autism are then proposed. Because many self-regulation training programs emphasize the importance of executive functioning, several components of this system and related self-regulatory processes are discussed along with techniques for developing these processes. Finally, examples of specific self-regulatory training programs are provided.

The nature of self-regulation

Self-regulation is considered to be an essential skill that provides a foundation for a child's development. The manner in which self-regulation evolves in neurotypical children has been actively studied by researchers (see Berk, 2009; Kochanska, Murray, & Harlan, 2000; Lightfoot, Cole, & Cole, 2009). Self-regulation develops during early infancy, progressing from primitive attentional and motor behaviors that regulate arousal and sensory input, to more complex responses that direct cognitive activity, motor behavior, and social interaction. Although children come equipped with a few innate responses for controlling arousal, the development of self-regulation occurs in conjunction with and is closely related to a child's social, cognitive, and language development. As a consequence of this development, children are able to delay gratification, resolve conflict, and adapt to new situations.

Although theoretical perspectives on self-regulation vary, there is general agreement that it involves an action on the part of an individual that results in the self-control of their behavior, emotions, and/or cognitions. Self-regulation has been described by Kopp (1982) as the:

> ability to comply with a request, to initiate and cease activities according to environmental demands, to modulate intensity, frequency, and duration of verbal and motor acts in social and in educational settings, to postpone acting upon a desired object or goal and to generate socially approved behavior in the absence of external monitors. (p. 149)

Within a social-learning framework, more complex forms of self-regulation involve self-monitoring, self-evaluation, and self-reinforcement responses. To self-regulate, children must observe their social and physical environment, as well as their own behavior. Through information gained from self-observation, cognitive strategies are designed or selected to guide behaviors that will help the child obtain a desired goal. Performance standards are also established that allow a child to evaluate whether a desired goal is achieved (Whitman, 1990).

In contrast to a social-learning conceptualization of self-regulation, other cognitive perspectives stress not only the importance of basic cognitive strategies for behavior regulation, but also the interrelationship between metacognitive and lower order cognitive processes. Metacognition involves examining one's self-knowledge, that is the contents of one's mind. For example, in order to self-regulate, a child must examine what he/she knows about a challenging situation that is being confronted, what resources he/she has to meet this challenge, and how these resources can be best utilized. Such an act requires children to understand what is in their minds and sometimes to make guesses about what is in the minds of other people, processes in which children with autism are thought to be deficient (Whitman, 2004).

Thus, self-regulation involves the capacity to change behavior based on past experience, inhibiting responses that have been ineffective and selecting behaviors that have proved useful, in the process anticipating the effects of one's behavior. These capabilities are commonly regarded as functions associated with the prefrontal cortex, an area in the brain in which structural anomalies have been reported in individuals with autism. The ability to be planful, using memories of past experiences to guide new behavior and discarding ineffective response patterns, has been found in animal research to be disrupted by lesions in the frontal part of the cortex and replaced by ineffective perseverative behaviors (see Diamond & Goldman-Rakic, 1989). This type of research lends support to the perspective proposed by Whitman and Ekas (2008) that the ritualistic, compulsive, and stereotyped behaviors found in populations with ASD are symptoms of a poorly developed and defective self-regulatory system.

Self-regulation in children with autism

Due to difficulties in self-regulating their behavior, children with autism often depend on others for guidance or utilize a variety of self-regulatory behaviors that are not adaptive, behaviors that are symptomatic of their disorder. Their unique approaches to dealing with challenging environments include: withdrawing into their private world, physically escaping a situation, restricting their interactions with the environment, engaging in stereotyped motor behaviors, narrowing their attentional focus to small parts of a task, persevering in their response patterns, and developing rigid and ritualistic behaviors (Whitman, 2004).

If autism is viewed as a self-regulatory disorder, children with autism appear to be both undercontrolling and overcontrolling in their self-regulatory style. They are undercontrolled because they do not develop more complex forms of self-regulation, such as executive control processes (e.g. planning and monitoring) or sometimes even simpler forms of self-regulation (soliciting assistance from others). Children with autism share other characteristics in common with undercontrolled children. They often appear impulsive and distractible, seek immediate gratification and are easily influenced by shifting environmental contingencies (Kremen & Block, 1998). Conversely, children with autism appear overcontrolled in that they use primitive self-regulatory techniques to compulsively order their environment. Like overcontrolled children, they have also been described as: obsessive, perseverative, uncomfortable with ambiguities, rigid, temperamentally wary, difficult to soothe, and socially withdrawn (Kremen & Block, 1998).

Research by Gomez and Baird (2005) suggests that children with autism already begin to display difficulties in self-regulation during infancy. They were reported as having more self-regulatory problems at one year than children without disabilities, at a level that is consistent with a diagnosis of a regulatory disorder. In a study of older children, at eight and ten years, Bieberich and Morgan (2004) also found children with autism to have more self-regulation problems than children with Down Syndrome.

Many programs directed at developing self-regulation in children with ASD emphasize the importance of executive functioning (Whitman, 2004). Executive functioning involves components, such as planning, searching, goal and strategy selection, impulse control, and attention shifting; all processes that facilitate flexibility of thought and action. These processes are intentional and conscious in nature rather than automatic and reflexive. Executive control involves active self-control rather than control from the external environment. Control is mental; it is guided by knowledge, goals, ideas, plans, and scripts (see Jordan, 1999). Russell

(1997) refers to executive functioning as "a set of mental processes necessary for the control of action" (p. 258). Actions can be behavioral and/or cognitive in nature.

The reason for teaching children with ASD to self-regulate is to help them to achieve independence. Through self-regulation children with ASD are able to act without external social direction, maintain what they have learned, and generalize learned responses to new situations. Consequently, they are more likely to be able to live in normalized settings. In the next section, general strategies for teaching children to self-regulate are outlined. In subsequent sections, techniques for teaching important components of self-regulation are described. Table 10.1 lists self-regulation behaviors that might be targeted for intervention. In the final section, examples of specific self-regulation training programs are provided.

Table 10.1 Self-regulation behaviors that might be targeted for intervention

Stereotypy, repetitive and restricted behavior, obsessions and compulsions
Impulse control
Flexible action
Verbal control of behavior
    Correspondence (say-do and do-say) training
    Self-instruction
    Rule-governed behavior
Executive functioning and problem-solving
    Task/problem definition, goal setting
    Strategy generation (metacognition, attention shifting, and working memory)
    Strategy selection
    Self-monitoring
    Self-evaluation
    Self-reinforcement

Teaching children with autism to self-regulate

In designing intervention programs for children with autism, their emotional, sensory, motor, cognitive, language, and social delays and impairments must be taken into consideration. Effective self-regulation requires an optimal level of arousal, with both hyperarousal and hypoarousal associated with diminished functioning. The sensory system is critical for self-regulation because it provides information to children about the environment and their behavior. The motor system enables children to engage in rudimentary self-regulation acts, such as thumb sucking and cuddling when distressed, as well as provides a foundation for linguistic and social forms of self-regulation. The cognitive, language, and social interaction systems provide children with essential tools that they need to strategically guide their behavior. In addition, the social environment surrounding the child provides instrumental and emotional supports that gradually allow children to assume control of their thoughts, emotions, and behavior. Research by Bernier, Carlson, and Whipple (2010) suggests that the parent–child relationship plays a pivotal role in the child's development of self-regulation capacities.

Self-regulation in children with autism appears to be particularly influenced by their language and cognitive deficiencies. Russell (1997) suggests that children with autism have difficulty using language/inner speech to direct their actions. Moreover, children with autism do not seem to understand their own capabilities or how to utilize what they have learned as they act in new situations (Whitman, 1990). Consequently, they often perseverate in using ineffective strategies, thereby appearing inflexible. In addition, they do not appear to self-monitor or self-evaluate their actions; and even when they are successful, they do not seem to understand the reasons for their success or experience a sense of self-accomplishment (Millward, Powell, Messer, & Jordan, 2000).

In order to develop self-regulatory skills in children with autism, it is important to recognize how their specific problems and deficiencies may influence how they control their behavior. For example, if a child has anxiety problems, sensory difficulties or motor deficiencies, particularly in the motor structures required for speech, these problems must be addressed. It is especially important to address anxiety and hypersensitivity problems because of their role in producing repetitive, restricted, and stereotyped behaviors. General strategies for addressing emotional, sensory, and motor problems have already been described in Chapters 4, 5, and 6.

Language processes must also be considered in developing effective self-regulation, with considerable emphasis placed on helping children with autism to establish verbal control of their behavior. If, however, language deficiencies are too pronounced, visual control strategies should be considered. Finally, because cognitive processes play a critical role in self-regulation, the focus of intervention programs for children who are higher functioning should be on developing metacognitive and executive-functioning skills. Whether the emphasis is on developing verbal, visual, or cognitive control of behavior, behavioral techniques are typically employed to establish this control.

Two general strategies for developing self-regulation are commonly employed. One strategy involves the use of behavior-focused techniques (e.g. prompts, reinforcement, discrimination training) to develop adaptive behaviors (e.g. self-help, social, or community skills). Once learning occurs, prompts are gradually withdrawn until an individual is able to act autonomously, with responses maintained by natural contingencies in the everyday environment. This approach, which was described in Chapter 2, can be used to help a child act in an independent fashion, teaching specific self-regulatory behaviors.

A second general strategy for developing self-regulation involves teaching specific self-management techniques, such as how to go about solving a problem. This self-management approach focuses on teaching a set of skills which when employed individually or in combination help the child to regulate their behavior (see Table 10.1). Although self-management is a complex process, the skills that are part of this process can be taught like any other skill.

A challenge arises when children with an autism spectrum disorder are unable to maintain skills once external social supports are removed or have difficulty learning specific self-management behaviors. In such instances, children can sometimes be taught to use various video and/or computer technologies that prompt performance and guide an individual in planning and implementing daily activities. For information on teaching students with ASD to use personal digital aids, video modeling aids and other procedures for increasing independence, the reader is referred to articles by Hume, Loftin, and Lantz (2009) and Mechling, Gast, and Seid (2009).

In the next sections, several components of executive functioning and related processes that are critical for developing self-regulation in children with autism spectrum disorders are described. These components include: impulse control, flexible action, verbal control of behavior, and problem-solving. In each section, strategies for helping children with ASD become more self-regulatory are proposed. In the final section specific examples of self-regulation programs are presented.

Impulse control

In contrast to neurotypical children, children with ASD have particular difficulty controlling their impulses. When they want something, they often want it now, with no delay of gratification; they insist that their needs and desires be fulfilled immediately. For example, when they are hungry they want to be fed at once. If another child has a toy that they desire, they insist on having it. If they wish to go swimming, they want to do so immediately. One of the important objectives of early childhood education programs for children with ASD is to get them to wait before satisfying their needs, as well as to sometimes refrain entirely from undesirable activities. Impulse control is an important component in self-regulation and executive functioning.

Intervention perspectives and strategies

Normally, impulse control is taught by either ignoring a child's request for instant gratification, asking him/her to wait, saying no to a request and/or by reinforcing the child for "good waiting." Children with ASD, like neurotypical children, can be taught to control their impulses. Rather than punishing children for impulsive behaviors, the emphasis should be on reinforcing them for demonstrating impulse control. For certain responses, such as waiting, behavior can be shaped by gradually increasing the amount of time the child has to wait. A calendar or a digital clock that counts down can be useful in helping the child understand the concept of time.

It is particularly critical in teaching impulse control that parents do not give in to their children's repeated coercive demands. Parents who give in to children when they make unreasonable demands, in order to avoid the child's whining or temper tantrums, inadvertently reinforce the very impulsive and high intensity behaviors that they want to inhibit. Children are masters of wheedling to get their needs met. Children with ASD are no exception to this rule. Sometimes parents yield to them because they are autistic. This practice is a big mistake. Parents neither do themselves nor their children a favor by giving in to unreasonable demands.

Rules regarding waiting or refraining from an activity must be made clear and consistently enforced. Visual representation of what is not allowed, what is allowed and when it can occur, can be very helpful in promoting understanding of such social rules. For further information on the development of rule-governed behavior the reader is referred to Chapter 9.

Flexibility

Effective self-regulation involves not only impulse control, but also an ability to adjust to changing circumstances. It has been hypothesized that children with ASD lack flexibility in adapting to new situations because of a deficit in their executive control system (Turner, 1997). They have trouble on tasks that require switching responses, such as a discrimination task that initially requires a child to select squares rather than circles, and then subsequently requires the child to select circles, not squares. Children with ASD tend to perseverate on such a task, continuing to select squares even when reinforcement is only given for selecting circles. This perseverative tendency is consistent with the characterization of individuals with autism as acting in a stereotyped, repetitive, and restricted fashion.

Jarrold (1997) suggests that children with autism also have problems with pretend play because of an executive dysfunction; specifically a difficulty inhibiting a dominant response. During pretend play children have to inhibit actions normally elicited by a stimulus; for example in pretending a pencil is a telescope, a make-believe response, (looking through a telescope) has to be imposed in place of an established response (drawing with a pencil).

Turner (1997) hypothesizes that children with autism engage in repetitive behaviors because they are unable to generate alternative ways of acting. They not only lack flexibility, but also are often slow to act or are unresponsive in new situations; conversely sometimes they act in an impulsive mindless fashion. These response styles may be adopted because children with autism are more distractible in new situations, do not monitor their actions, and do not make adjustments based on the feedback they receive. A variety of research suggests that poor mental and behavioral flexibility impact the ability of these children to apply what they learn in new and changing environments (Hume, Loftin, & Lantz, 2009).

Intervention perspectives and strategies

Children with autism when given the choice will do what they typically have done before. Moreover, they often demand that others be perfectly consistent and predictable. Although habits and routines are necessary in everyday living environments, circumstances often warrant that alternative ways of acting are needed. School may be cancelled. Daily schedules may change. Favorite cups to drink from may get broken or lost. Clothes that are typically worn may wear out and have to be replaced. Different routes to the grocery store may need to be taken and the list goes on. Teaching children that schedules are not immutable and that daily routines and habits sometimes need to be altered is an important life lesson. Children with autism especially need to learn this kind of lesson because they tend to lapse into routines and then insist on rigidly adhering to them.

Strategies for teaching flexibility to children with autism differ, but generally focus on varying routines and diversifying the repertoire of responses that are utilized in specific situations. For example, if the cup children drink out of is constantly changed, different clothes to wear are provided each day, television programs that are watched are altered, foods eaten are prepared differently, and books read are varied, children will gradually learn to accept, expect and even embrace change. If visual schedules are used to communicate a daily schedule, these schedules should be changed from day to day. When the routines of children with ASD are not altered, their habits become ingrained and consequently are very difficult to break.

During early development, behavior flexibility can be taught to children with autism in play situations. For example, the specific toys played with should be alternated across days. Pretend play with a specific toy, such as a truck, might involve one day delivering food to a grocery store, on another day transporting cars to an automobile dealership, and on the next day hauling dirt from one location to another. Behavior flexibility can also be encouraged in everyday social situations by varying whom a child plays with and the activities in which the children are engaged. The more change is introduced into their routines, the more likely it is that children with autism will learn to expect and adapt to change, and find satisfaction and delight in doing new things. Research by Brace, Morton, and Munakata (2006) points out the importance of providing children with new experiences, showing and guiding them to do things differently, rather just telling them what they should do differently.

Verbal control of behavior

One of the major tools that children employ to regulate their behavior is language. Because of their language and communication deficiencies, children with autism are less able to control their own actions and those of other people. As a consequence they often use more primitive types of responses, such as restricted behaviors, tantrums, and aggression, to control their environment. However, as they develop language and communication skills, a reduction in these primitive regulation behaviors typically occurs.

Russell (1997) suggests that children with autism have difficulty retaining and utilizing information to guide their behavior because of an inability to use inner speech, a process that has been conceptualized as having its roots in social interaction. A variety of research, including studies by Joseph, Steele, Meyer, and Tager-Flusberg (2005) and Wallace, Silvers, Martin, and Kenworthy (2009), provide evidence of an inner speech deficit in children with ASD. Some theorists emphasize that inner speech or self-verbalization is part of a developmental process in which the interpersonal nature of thought is transferred into an intrapersonal process, that is internalized (Vygotsky, 1978).

The general premise of Vygotsky's developmental theory, elaborated upon by Wertsch (1979), is that development occurs in the context of social interaction. According to these theorists, a child's verbal control over motoric behavior increases with age. During the early stages of human development, adults verbally guide and direct children's behavior. Later, adults gradually relinquish verbal control as the child acquires the capacity for independent action. Whereas adults initially provide considerable and specific assistance to guide children's behavior, children eventually verbally regulate their own behavior, with assistance from the adults given only as needed. As children assume verbal regulatory control over their behavior, this process becomes increasingly covert and "cognitive" in nature.

Because of the problems children with ASD have in their interpersonal relationships, many of which were outlined by Hobson (1993) in his intersubjective theory, it seems likely that the language and internalization processes that assist children in self-regulating their behavior do not develop normally. However, research indicates that some high functioning children with autism sometimes do talk to themselves, particularly when confronted with difficult tasks. When they are able to engage in "self-talk," they are more successful in solving problems (Winsler, Abar, Feder, Schunn, & Rubio, 2007).

Intervention perspectives and strategies

In order to develop verbal regulation of behavior, speech therapy programs directed at increasing receptive and expressive language are essential. Early on during this type of intervention program, it is important to teach children with autism to follow verbal instructions and to make their needs known through verbal requests. Techniques for teaching these core skills are discussed in Chapter 3. Once children acquire these skills, it then becomes important to ensure that their words acquire the ability to control as well as to reflect their actions.

Children with autism often have a disconnect between what they say and what they do. For example, they have difficulty telling others about the types of activities they have engaged in during the day, either resorting to no responses, vague responses, and/or inaccurate reports. These difficulties seem to reflect a broader problem, specifically an inability to monitor their behavior and events in which they are personally involved (Millward, Powell, Messer, & Jordan, 2000). In order to regulate their behavior, children with ASD must first learn to monitor and evaluate their behavior and environment in order to make "course corrections." Language plays a critical role not only in communication, but also in this self-monitoring and self-evaluation process.

Children with ASD have a further important disconnect between their words and actions, in addition to being unable to describe their actions, specifically their words often do not control their actions. During typical development, children first learn to follow directions and then later are able to give directions to others. They also learn how to self-instruct, that is how to verbally guide their own behavior. For example, children intially learn to brush their teeth by being told how to perform a complex sequence of responses. Later they learn to verbalize what they should do, that is they demonstrate that they have acquired specific knowledge. Eventually, they learn to use their verbally expressed knowledge to independently guide their own behavior. In contrast, children with autism have difficulty telling others how to perform an action, such as toothbrushing, and even greater difficulty using verbal knowledge to guide their own actions. If a child's ability to verbally self-regulate does not develop, the probability of covert (cognitive) self-regulation emerging is very low.

In order to develop verbal regulation skills, two procedures are particularly useful: correspondence training and self-instruction. These procedures were initially described in Chapter 2, as well as discussed in Chapters 6 and 9. They are quite similar in that both emphasize teaching children to verbalize what they need to do in a specific situation and then having them actually perform those actions. During self-instructional training, the teacher/parent initially tells a child what to do and then shows the child what to do. Subsequently, the teacher/parent gradually fades control to the child by telling the child what to do, but now having the child follow the teacher/parent's verbal directives. Finally, the teacher/parent further releases control by having the child both verbally state how he/she will perform a particular action and then perform that action. As the instructor gradually cedes control to the child, prompts to correct verbalizations and actions are provided as necessary. Correspondence training involves a similar, albeit, abbreviated protocol (see Chapter 2).

Correspondence and self-instructional training, as pointed out in the last chapter, can be employed to teach children to follow protocols, such as how to cross a street at a traffic signal. Learning to follow such a protocol is an example of rule-governed behavior; children learn a social rule and then to do what the social rule prescribes (see Chapter 9). Although correspondence training and self-instruction are similar in that both are employed to teach children what to say and then to do what they say (i.e. say-do); correspondence training can also be used to teach children self-monitoring, specifically to verbally describe what they have done previously (i.e. do-say). This latter procedure helps teach children to become aware of their behavior. The do-say procedure can also be used to develop truth-telling in children who unintentionally or deliberately misrepresent their actions. The reader is referred to Chapter 2 for further elaboration of these two types of training procedures.

Problem-solving

Individuals with good executive-functioning skills are good problem solvers. In order to become a good problem solver, children must learn to: 1) define the nature of a problem with which they are confronted; 2) examine what they know about solving that problem, that is, possible solutions; 3) make a decision about how to proceed given what they know; 4) initiate the appropriate action; and finally 5) evaluate whether the action solves the problem. If it has not, they must go through these steps again, reviewing what they know and revising the action taken. This is a complex process that requires children to set goals (goal definition), to examine the contents of their mind (metacognition), to draw from their memory specific strategies to guide their actions (working memory), to act and monitor their actions (self-monitoring), and finally to evaluate the success of their actions (self-evaluation) (see Table 10.1).

From an intervention perspective, programs directed at developing problem-solving skills are usually restricted to children on the autism spectrum who have well-developed language skills. Because of the complexity of the problem-solving process, each of the component skills that make up this process can be taught either sequentially or in combination.

Intervention perspectives and strategies

In general, the strategy for teaching these skills involves the instructor/parent first raising questions for children to answer and then providing them, as necessary, with helpful suggestions and possible answers. For example, children who are bored and want to alleviate their boredom might be asked what their goal/problem is (e.g. "What do you want?"), which is to do something that will alleviate their boredom (goal definition phase). Next they are asked to think about activities that might reduce their boredom (generation of possible solutions), then to evaluate each activity in order to determine whether it is feasible for them to pursue that activity, then to choose the activity (e.g. going outside to the playground) that they consider to be the best solution to their problem (boredom) and then to implement that solution (go outside). Finally, the children are asked to evaluate whether going outside to the playground has solved their boredom problem; if not, the process is started all over again.

With adult assistance, in the form of proper questions, verbal prompts, and suggestions, children can be led through this complex process. If employed regularly to solve problems, whether personal, social, or academic, children can learn to be more proficient in making decisions, implementing solutions, and evaluating results. Self-instruction, previously discussed in the last section, can be employed to guide children through this process, with an adult initially going through the entire process and then gradually ceding control to the children, who eventually go through the process by themselves. For children who are less linguistically and cognitively advanced, extremely valuable but less ambitious programs employing visual communication approaches, like the Picture Exchange Program (PECS), should be considered.

In the next section, a variety of program examples for developing components of the self-regulation process described in this chapter are presented.

Program examples

Impulse control: waiting for a desired item or activity

OBJECTIVE

Teach the child to wait for a desired item/activity for a designated period of time.

MATERIALS

A timer may help with this activity, along with items that are preferred by the child.

PROCEDURE

1. Place the reinforcer within eyesight of the child. Once he/she asks for the item/activity, say, "Wait."

2. Immediately start the timer or count quietly for a specific number of seconds/minutes. Consider starting as low as 1 second of wait time.

3. After the time has lapsed, give the child the item, regardless of his/her current behavior (e.g. if she is crying at this point, still give the reinforcer).

4. If the desired item is a tangible reinforcer (e.g. a toy), wait until the child turns away from the item to get it back in your possession. Repeat steps 1 to 3. If the desired item is an activity (e.g. a game), repeat after the activity is complete (i.e. if the child still desires the activity). If the desired item is edible (e.g. candy), give a small amount to the child and repeat after the child has consumed the item.

5. Once the child is able to wait for the specified period of time without engaging in disruptive behavior (e.g. crying, throwing a tantrum, aggression, etc.) for two consecutive sessions, extend the wait time gradually (e.g. by 1 to 5 seconds, depending on the child).

6. Continue to use the above criteria to extend the wait time. This may take several sessions and several days to get to an end goal eventually (e.g. 5 minutes).

7. Practice as often as possible, taking advantage of natural opportunities (e.g. whenever the child is asking for something).

Error correction

There really is no error in this procedure, unless the child is able to get hold of the item before the wait time has lapsed. Try to avoid this from happening by keeping the item out of the child's reach.

Generalization

Once the child has learned this in one setting for an extended wait time (e.g. 3 to 5 minutes), begin using it in other locations. Try it outside the home (e.g. in the backyard). Ask the child's school if they would be willing to use the procedure as well. Eventually try it in public locations (e.g. the grocery store).

If using a timer, do not set the timer for specific amounts of time (e.g. 3 minutes). Instead, set it for ranges (e.g. 2 minutes and 50 seconds to 3 minutes and 10 seconds). In reality, you most likely will not have a timer with you whenever the child requests something, and will therefore not be able to time exact amounts of time. The child must therefore learn that "wait" does not always mean waiting for a specific number of minutes.

Tips/suggestions

If the child typically exhibits severely challenging behaviors when told to wait for a desired item/activity, start this procedure using items that are not highly preferred, but still desired. For example, if the child's favorite food is chips, but she will also accept pretzels, start this procedure using pretzels, and move on to chips once she demonstrates the ability to wait for about 1 minute.

Keep in mind that this procedure is teaching the child to wait for a desired item or activity, and not teaching the child that he/she cannot have the item. Therefore it may be necessary to teach this skill in a more structured setting first, when you have control over the environment. You must give the item or activity to the child contingent on the time lapsing, without fail.

Troubleshooting

If the child continues to engage in disruptive behavior whenever he/she hears the word "wait," consider lowering your initial time limit. If your time limit is already as low as possible (e.g. 1 second), try moving up to 3 to 5 seconds despite the problematic behavior. Stay at the extended time period until he/she stops the disruptive behavior. Continue extending as indicated in the procedure steps above.

Other teaching methods

Some children benefit from the use of visual timers, which help them to see how much more time they must wait. For a visual timer to be effective, however, the child must refer to the timer. If the child is able to tell the time, you can give specific times to the child when using the above procedure. For example, you can tell her that at 12:05 she can have a snack. Even with these alternative approaches, you must be sure to start with a very short wait time, and to gradually extend the wait time in small increments.

FUTURE OBJECTIVES

Continue to extend the wait time, teaching the child to wait for a day or more for some things. A calendar may be helpful for this step, especially if the child is able to cross off days each night before bedtime. Next, teach the child that he/she cannot have certain items or engage in certain activities.

Flexibility

OBJECTIVE

Teach the child to accept and expect changes to daily events.

PROCEDURE

For this procedure, there is not an exact step-by-step protocol. Instead, it is recommended that you change things often right from the very beginning, to avoid inflexibility. It is very important to not give in to demands from the child for routines or rituals. This can be as complex as taking a different route to school every day, so if/when there is a construction detour, the child will not become upset about having to take a different route.

If the child has already established a rigid routine, gradually change that routine and constantly reinforce adherence to the new or changed routine. For example, if the child must switch from a sippy cup to a regular cup, first deliver a reinforcer simply when the child will allow the regular, new cup to be at his/her table setting. For this example, the sippy cup would most likely be a highly effective reinforcer. Move on to requiring the child to touch the new cup, and provide a reinforcer upon doing so. Continue to gradually move on to requiring the child to take a sip from the new cup before giving him/her the sippy cup. Eventually, the child should drink all of the drink from the new cup and no longer have access to the sippy cup. The key is to expect very gradual progress, but continue to push forward.

Tips/suggestions

Do this as soon as possible in your child's development (i.e. before the rigid routines become heavily reinforced) or, if a routine is already established, make change very gradually and be sure to reinforce adherence to change. Use highly preferred reinforcers for such adherence. For some children, a sticker or token chart may help motivate the child to accept change appropriately. Deliver a sticker each time he/she accepts change well. Do not try to reason with the child regarding changes, as this attention may make problems worse.

Other teaching methods

If you use a visual schedule with the child, make sure to change the order of the schedule as often as possible. Every day set up the schedule in a different order. Introduce changes to the schedule throughout the day, as well. For this, you can use a "Change Schedule" card to put in place of the activity that was supposed to come next. For example, if the next thing on the schedule is to do homework, but the child has no homework that day, give the child the Change Schedule card and help him/her remove the homework icon and replace it with the Change Schedule card. Deliver a reinforcer once the child has done this, and then again when the child moves on to the next activity.

Video modeling can help some children learn how to respond in different situations. A good video model will show a child in various situations that require the child to change his/her schedule/routine. The child in the video should model appropriate behavior while making such changes, with adults praising and/or reinforcing such appropriate behavior. Video modeling tends to work well when children attend well to videos and have demonstrated the ability to imitate behavior of others. It may work better when combined with role playing after observing the video.

Self-instruction

Objective

Teach the child to state verbally his/her intended actions and to then demonstrate the stated actions.

Procedure

1. Choose a skill to teach the child (e.g. crossing the street).

2. Verbally state each step as you show the child how to complete the step (e.g. "Stop next to the walk/don't walk sign. Look at the sign across the street.").

3. Fade your model prompts, having the child demonstrate the ability to follow your verbal instructions for each step.

4. Once the child is able to complete step 3, teach the child to tell you each step. Have him/her repeat the steps out loud to you. After he/she states the instruction for each step, the child should then perform the step.

5. Fade your prompts by having the child state the steps without you telling him/her to do so. Use only gestural, physical, or textual prompts.

6. Continue until the child has demonstrated the ability to complete the entire action from start to finish, stating the steps as he/she goes.

Error correction

If the child misses a step, backup one step and have him/her repeat that step. Use increased prompting to help him/her correctly state the previously erred step.

Generalization

If teaching in a structured, simulated setting, eventually graduate to the natural setting where the skill will be useful. Fade your prompts but also fade your presence, so the child learns to complete the skill even in your absence.

Tips/suggestions

Some children may benefit from textual prompts. For example, write down the steps of the instruction for the child to read aloud, rather than having the child repeat your instructions.

   This same procedure can be used to teach the child verbal control of his/her behavior in certain situations. For example, teach the child what to do when he/she becomes upset about something. Using this approach the child can learn to control his/her behavior in such situations. Just be sure that if you first teach this skill in a structured environment that you generalize it by teaching the child to use the learned skills in the actual setting/situation where he/she would need to (e.g. at school when a child takes his/her toy).

Troubleshooting

At the beginning of the procedure, have the child choose a reinforcer to earn. Once the child has completed each step of the task, he/she can have access to the reinforcer. Some children may benefit from reinforcement at each step of the task. For example, after stating where to stop at the crosswalk, deliver a small reinforcer to the child. Then, when he/she states where to look for the crossing sign, deliver another reinforcer. Fade the use of such reinforcement the way you fade prompts so that the child can eventually complete the entire task before receiving a reinforcer.

OTHER TEACHING METHODS

Video modeling can be another way to teach such skills to children. The video should teach the child to repeat the steps out loud to increase correspondence between the child's verbal statements and his/her behavior, thus increasing verbal control over behavior. Practice will still be necessary to ensure that the child can perform the task.

Self-monitoring

OBJECTIVE

Teach the child to monitor his/her own behavior.

MATERIALS

Gather or create some easy-to-use data sheets or self-monitoring sheets. For example, if the child is monitoring his/her toothbrushing behavior, create a calendar where the child can draw a happy face next to AM for each morning he/she brushes, and then a happy face next to PM for each evening he/she brushes. If he/she forgets to brush, have him/her draw a sad face for that day/time.

PROCEDURE

1. Start in a structured setting, perhaps simulating or role playing if necessary.

2. Define the target behavior for the child. Be sure the child can demonstrate instances of the behavior before moving on to self-monitoring. For example, if the child is monitoring instances of yelling, tell him to show you how to yell, and then how to talk nicely so that you can be sure he can discriminate between the two behaviors.

3. Show the child how to complete the monitoring sheet after each instance of behavior.

4. Reinforce instances of self-monitoring.

5. Give the child a goal to strive for (e.g. if you get ten happy faces this week we can go to the movies this weekend). Start with an easily achievable goal. For example, if the child typically only brushes his teeth independently 5 times per week, make the goal 6. Then gradually increase the requirement each week as the child succeeds.

ERROR CORRECTION

If the child does not record an instance of behavior, use prompting to help him/her record the missed instance. Do not record it for the child.

GENERALIZATION

Once the child is regularly performing the behavior at the desired level, make an attempt to remove the self-monitoring log. Continue to require the child to report to you, thus requiring him/her to monitor without using a data sheet. However, if this is too difficult, continue allowing the child to document his/her behavior. Some goals (e.g. calorie counting) can be difficult to track without documenting throughout the day or week. However, other goals (e.g. toothbrushing) should become more of a habit and thus require less documentation.

TIPS/SUGGESTIONS

This procedure will be much easier to teach if the child already knows how to perform the skill that you would like him/her to monitor. For example, if the child does not know how to brush his teeth yet, he may not be ready to monitor his own toothbrushing. Instead teach him to monitor a behavior he can already do independently, such as getting dressed in the morning.

Have the child report to you daily at first, then every other day, eventually reporting weekly or monthly. Goals can also be daily (e.g. eating 1300 to 1500 calories per day), gradually expanding to weekly (e.g. exercising 3 times per week) or monthly.

TROUBLESHOOTING

If the child regularly has difficulty monitoring, check in more frequently. For example, if he is tracking calories per day, check in with him after each meal. Help him determine how many more calories he has left for the day. Gradually decrease your checks, moving to every 12 hours, to every day, then to every week.

In addition, make sure you have a highly preferred reinforcer available to the child for meeting goals, but also reinforce accurate self-monitoring during your checks. However, be careful not to reinforce the behavior itself if the child is monitoring a behavior you are trying to decrease (e.g. yelling). For such behaviors, wait until the child calms down and records the behavior, then deliver a reinforcer for recording. If the child records while he/she is yelling, do not deliver the reinforcer until the child has calmed down. In these instances, be sure that the reinforcer for meeting the goal (e.g. yelling less than 6 times per week) is bigger and better than the reinforcer used for recording. Otherwise the child may engage in the behavior so he/she can record the behavior and thus receive the reinforcer.

OTHER TEACHING METHODS

Some children benefit from having a simple rule about their behavior. For example, if you tell a child he/she must floss after brushing each night, and then reinforce compliance with that rule, some children will progress without having to record such behavior.

✦

Problem-solving

OBJECTIVE

Teach the child to attempt to solve problems and evaluate the success of such attempts using a step-by-step method.

MATERIALS

You may need a pencil and paper for this procedure in order to make lists of possible solutions. Also, depending on the child, visual icons or organizational maps for each step in the problem-solving process may be helpful.

PROCEDURE

1. Teach the child to define the problem. In the beginning, the child will need a lot of help with this complex task. You can do this by asking him/her a question (e.g. "What's wrong?" or "What do you want?") or by writing down the problem and having the child read it aloud. In addition, it will be necessary to reinforce the child's response, even if prompted.

    *   For example, if the child wants to go outside but it is raining out, ask the child, "What's wrong?" Prompt him/her to say, "It's raining and I want to go outside."

2. Help the child set a goal.

    *   An example goal could be that he/she will do something else for an hour and then go outside if it has stopped raining.

3. Next, help the child to generate possible solutions.

   • In this case, the child should consider other activities he/she can do for the next hour. A list is usually helpful, so if the child finishes one activity before the end of the hour he/she can move on to something else from the list. Also, set a timer so the child is aware of how much time is left before he/she should check on the rain.

4. Once the child has generated solutions, have him/her pick the best one and then implement it.

   • If the child chooses to play a board game, help the child to ask others to play with him/her, and then to play the game.

5. After implementing a solution, help the child evaluate the effectiveness of the solution.

   • Once the hour is over, have the child look outside to see if it is still raining. If it is not raining, teach him/her to positively evaluate the problem-solving procedure. If is raining, have the child start over or come up with a new goal or solution (e.g. "I will go outside tomorrow. For tonight I will watch a movie.").

GENERALIZATION

During teaching, use this strategy with multiple problems of all sorts. If necessary, set up situations that are problematic in order to increase the number of learning opportunities. Fade your prompts, including verbal prompts such as asking questions, so that the child can learn to use this procedure to solve problems independently.

TIPS/SUGGESTIONS

Teach the child to verbalize the steps of the problem-solving process. Alternatively, write down the steps on a worksheet so the child can then complete the worksheet or use it as a prompt to complete the steps.

Be sure to reinforce each step of the problem-solving process. Keep in mind that the child may already be upset about the presence of a problem and therefore will need additional motivation to solve the problem without a lot of help.

An evaluation of some sort may be helpful for the child to see that problem-solving can be beneficial. For example, rating scales can be useful when rating boredom before and after problem-solving. This way the child can see a visual representation of how his/her boredom has changed using this procedure. Just be sure to teach the child how to use the rating scale prior to using it in this manner.

Troubleshooting

If the child consistently misses a step, increase your prompts temporarily. Try using textual prompts (e.g. write down the answers) rather than verbal prompts.

References

Berk, L. E. (2009). *Child development* (8th ed.). Boston, MA: Allyn and Bacon.

Bernier, A., Carlson, S. M., & Whipple, N. (2010). From external regulation to self-regulation: Early parenting precursors of young children's executive functioning. *Child Development, 81,* 326–339.

Bieberich, A. A. & Morgan, S. B. (2004). Self-regulation and affective expression during play in children with autism or Down syndrome: A short-term longitudinal study. *Journal of Autism and Developmental Disorders, 34,* 439–448.

Bodfish, J. W., Symons, F. J., Parker, D. E., & Lewis, M. H. (2000). Varieties of repetitive behavior in autism: Comparisons to mental retardation. *Journal of Autism and Developmental Disorders, 30,* 237–243.

Brace, J. J., Morton, J. B., & Munakata, Y. (2006). When actions speak louder than words. *Psychological Science, 17,* 665–669.

Diamond, A. & Goldman-Rakic, P. (1989). Comparison of human infants and rhesus monkeys on Piaget's task: Evidence for dependence on the dorsolateral prefrontal cortex. *Experimental Brain Research, 24,* 24–40.

Gomez, C. R. & Baird, S. (2005). Identifying early indicators for autism in self-regulation difficulties. *Focus on Autism and Other Developmental Disabilities, 20,* 106–116.

Hobson, R. P. (1993). *Autism and the development of the mind.* Hillsdale, NJ: Erlbaum.

Hume, K., Loftin, R., & Lantz, J. (2009). Increasing Independence in autism spectrum disorders: A review of three focused interventions. *Journal of Autism and Developmental Disorders, 39,* 1329–1338.

Jarrold, C. (1997). "Pretend play in autism: Executive explanations." In J. Russell (Ed.), *Autism as an executive disorder* (pp. 101–140). Oxford: Oxford University Press.

Jordan, R. (1999). *Autism spectrum disorders: An introductory handbook for practitioners.* London: David Fulton.

Joseph, R. M., Steele, S. D., Meyer, E., & Tager-Flusberg, H. (2005). Self-ordered pointing in children with autism: Failure to use verbal mediation in the service of working memory? *Neuropsychologia, 43,* 1400–1411.

Kochanska, G., Murray, K., & Harlan, E. T. (2000). Effortful control in early childhood: Continuity and change, antecedents, and implications for social development. *Developmental Psychology, 36,* 220–232.

Kopp, C. B. (1982). Antecedents of self-regulation: A developmental perspective. *Developmental Psychology, 18,* 199–214.

Kremen, A. M. & Block, J. (1998). The roots of ego-control in young adulthood: Links with parenting in early childhood. *Journal of Personality and Social Psychology, 75,* 1062–1075.

Lightfoot, C., Cole, M., & Cole, S. (2009). *The development of children.* Worth, IL: Worth Publishing.

Mechling, L. C., Gast, D. L., & Seid, N. H. (2009). Using a personal digital assistant to increase independent task completion by students with autism spectrum disorder. *Journal of Autism and Developmental Disorders, 39,* 1420–1434.

Millward, C., Powell, S., Messer, D., & Jordan, R. (2000). Recall for self and other in autism: Children's memory for events experienced by themselves and their peers. *Journal of Autism and Developmental Disorders, 30,* 15–28.

Russell, J. (1997). "How executive disorders can bring about an inadequate 'theory of mind.'" In J. Russell (Ed.), *Autism as an executive disorder* (pp. 256–304). Oxford: Oxford University Press.

South, M., Ozonoff, S., & McMahon, W. (2005). Repetitive behavior profiles in Asperger Syndrome and high-functioning autism. *Journal of Autism and Developmental Disorders, 35,* 145–158.

Turner, M. (1997). "Toward an executive dysfunction account of repetitive behavior." In J. Russell (Ed.), *Autism as an executive disorder* (pp. 57–100). Oxford: Oxford University Press.

Turner, M. (1999). Annotation: Repetitive behavior in autism: A review of psychological research. *Journal of Child Psychology and Psychiatry, 40*, 839–849.

Vygotsky, L. S. (1978). *Mind in society: The development of higher psychological processes* (M. Cole, V. John-Steiner, S. Scribner, & E. Souberman, Eds.). Cambridge, MA: Harvard University Press.

Wallace, G. L., Silvers, J. A., Martin, A., & Kenworthy, L. E. (2009). Brief report: Further evidence for inner speech deficits in autism spectrum disorders. *Journal of Autism and Developmental Disorders, 39*, 1735–1739.

Wertsch, J. V. (1979) From social interaction to higher social processes: A clarification and application of Vygotsky's theory. *Human Development, 22*, 1–22.

Whitman, T. L. (1987). Self-instruction, individual differences, and mental retardation. *American Journal of Mental Deficiency, 92*, 213–223.

Whitman, T. L. (1990). Self-regulation and mental retardation. *American Journal on Mental Retardation, 94*, 347–362.

Whitman, T. L. (2004). *The development of autism: A self-regulatory perspective.* London: Jessica Kingsley Publishers.

Whitman, T. L. & Ekas, N. (2008). Theory and research on autism: Do we need a new approach to thinking about and studying this disorder? *International Review of Research in Mental Retardation, 35*, 1–41.

Winsler, A., Abar, B., Feder, M. A., Schunn, C. D., & Rubio, D. A. (2007). Private speech and executive functioning among high-functioning children with autistic spectrum disorders. *Journal of Autism and Developmental Disorders, 37*, 1617–1635.

Zimmerman, B. J. (1998). Academic studying and the development of personal skill: A self-regulatory perspective. *Educational Psychologist, 33*, 73–86.

Further readings

Bronson, M. B. (2000). *Self-regulation in early childhood: Nature and nurture.* New York, NY: Guilford Press.

Luria, A. R. (1961). *The role of speech in the regulation of normal and abnormal behaviors.* New York, NY: Liverright.

Robbins, T. (1997). "Integrating the neurobiological and neuropsychological dimensions of autism." In J. Russell (Ed.), *Autism as an executive disorder* (pp. 21–53). Oxford: Oxford University Press.

Chapter 11

Behavioral Problems, Developmental Challenges, and Medical Issues

Children with autism spectrum disorders (ASD) experience greater challenges in their daily lives than neurotypical children, because of their developmental delays. As a consequence of having less developed coping resources, they sometimes react to these challenges in ways that can have serious adverse personal and social consequences. For example, children with autism may display one or more of the following problems: inattention, hyperactivity, anxiety, depression, obsessive-compulsive behaviors, and aggression. Because of these and other problems, children with ASD often become increasingly isolated from their peers and at increasing risk of being excluded from mainstreamed educational and other community settings. Research indicates that such problems also create greater stress and concern for parents than the social, cognitive, and language delays that are associated diagnostically with autism (Ekas & Whitman, 2010). Without appropriate intervention, these problems often escalate in frequency and intensity over time.

Some of the symptoms observed in individuals with ASD suggest the presence of other disorders (Volker et al., 2010). These symptoms are sometimes thought to be diagnostically indicative of psychiatric conditions, such as depression, anxiety disorders and attention deficit hyperactivity disorders. This chapter begins with a brief discussion of these problems. In the following sections, other socioemotional, behavioral, and developmental problems that frequently occur in this population are described (see Table 11.1). In each section, intervention strategies for dealing with these problems are outlined. In the next to last section of this chapter, possible reasons for the co-occurrence of medical problems and autistic symptoms are discussed. Finally, examples of specific intervention programs that address various behavioral problems are presented.

Table 11.1 Socioemotional, behavioral, and developmental problems that commonly occur in children with autism

Attention deficit and hyperactivity (see Chapter 3)
Anxiety disorders and depression (see Chapter 3)
Repetitive, restricted, and stereotyped behaviors
Self-injurious behaviors
Noncompliance, temper tantrums, and aggression
Self-toileting delays
Eating problems
Sleeping problems

Attention deficit hyperactivity, anxiety, and depression problems

Attention deficit, hyperactivity, anxiety, and depression symptoms are commonly observed in children with autism, often with a greater frequency than occurs in the general population (Pearson et al., 2006). From an intervention perspective, the actual diagnosis of specific disorders is less important than determining whether these behavior problems interfere with the overall development of children in the spectrum and should be addressed as part of a comprehensive intervention program.

Attention deficit hyperactivity problems

About 3 to 5 percent of school-age children in the United States are diagnosed with attention deficit hyperactivity disorder (ADHD), making it the most common psychiatric condition in children (American Psychiatric Association, 2000). ADHD, like many other disorders, is considered to have genetic and environmental factors influencing both its onset and severity. According to Ghaziuddin (2005), individuals with developmental disabilities have a greater risk of ADHD, including children with autism who commonly display symptoms consistent with a diagnosis of ADHD. In the case of autism, it is difficult to determine whether ADHD is really an independent condition or a result of the autistic condition. Treatment for attention and hyperactivity problems in children with ADHD often involves a combination of medications and behavior therapy. Medications fall into two categories: stimulants and non-stimulants (Ghaziuddin, 2005).

The main focus of behavior therapy is to evaluate the role that the environment plays in producing and maintaining attentional problems and hyperactive behaviors. The general strategy employed by most behavior therapists for addressing these problems is to use either behavior techniques exclusively or, if necessary, a combination of behavior and medical interventions. Intervention strategies for dealing with attentional problems are described in Chapter 3. Most commonly, behavior- and environmental-focused interventions are employed for both attention and hyperactivity problems, although emotion- and cognition-focused techniques are being increasingly used. Specific interventions that have been employed include: reinforcement techniques, such as extinction and differential reinforcement, environmental restructuring, desensitization, reciprocal inhibition, and self-instruction (see Chapter 2).

Anxiety problems

Children with autism are also at a higher risk for anxiety problems than neurotypical children. As discussed in Chapter 4, the origins of anxiety responses in this population are complex and include biological factors, sensory, cognitive, and social interaction problems, and poorly developed coping skills. Excessive anxiety leads to both physical and psychological problems if left untreated, and in particular disrupts cognitive and social development. Intervention approaches for dealing with anxiety problems are described at length in Chapters 2 and 4. These approaches emphasize environmental modification, desensitization, and reciprocal inhibition techniques, and adaptive behavior skill development. Furthermore, if necessary, anti-anxiety medications are employed in combination with behavioral approaches.

Depressive disorders

Children with autism are also more likely to suffer from depression than other children. They live in a world without deep and meaningful relationships, where loneliness is common because they lack the cognitive, communication, and social skills necessary to fully enter into and sustain close relationships (Lasgaard, Nielsen, Eriksen, & Goossens, 2010). The risk of depression increases during adolescent years, due to a growing awareness on the part of children that they are different from their neurotypical peers (Stillman, 2005). Depression in turn is sometimes associated with sleep, eating, and other behavior problems.

Although the rate of depression in children with an ASD rises with age, there are no gender differences before puberty, but overall females have higher rates of depression (Ghaziuddin, Ghaziuddin, & Greden, 2002). As with other previously mentioned disorders, a combination of genetic and environmental factors seem to play an important role in the development of depression in this population. Children with an ASD, who have a family history of depression, are more likely to suffer from depression (Ghaziuddin et al., 2002). Moreover, both children with autism with higher IQs and those with Asperger Syndrome have an increased risk of psychopathology, including depression (Pearson et al., 2006). This higher rate of depression in higher IQ children is likely due in part to the fact that depression is more easily diagnosed in individuals who have better developed communication skills.

Similar therapeutic approaches, which include medical and behavioral interventions, are employed in treating depressive disorders in both neurotypical children and children with an ASD. However, whereas cognitive-behavioral techniques are more commonly employed with older neurotypical children, there is a strong focus in intervention programs for children with ASD on increasing social competency through building social skills. The assumption underlying such programs is that depression in this population is precipitated by social interaction deficiencies and a recognition on the part of the child that he or she is being socially excluded. Approaches for building social skills are described in Chapter 9.

Repetitive, restricted, and stereotyped behaviors

Perhaps the most intriguing of the core characteristics used to define autism are those that describe the repetitive, stereotyped and restricted activities, interests, and patterns of behavior of individuals with this disorder. In contrast to social and language/communication deficiencies, this third set of core diagnostic characteristics consists of behaviors that appear unusual and even bizarre in nature; most likely because their origin and function are not well understood. Specific examples of such behaviors include: body rocking, head weaving, object spinning, finger twisting, lining up objects, intense attachment to specific objects, rigid adherence to fixed routines, and obsessive interests.

Considerable attention has been given to the study of stereotyped behavior or stereotypy, sometimes also referred to as self-stimulatory behavior. Although definitions of stereotypy vary, they usually include reference to behaviors that are repetitive, often occurring with high frequency, invariant in topography or pattern, and nonfunctional, in the sense that they do not seem to have an obvious or conventional explanation for their occurrence. Although there are considerable differences in the structure of specific stereotyped behaviors across individuals with autism, there is considerable intra-individual consistency; that is the particular stereotyped responses engaged in by a specific individual are relatively stable.

Stereotyped responses generally do not result in any physical harm. In fact, the lack of injury is an important distinguishing characteristic between stereotypy and self-injurious behavior. Although stereotypies do not threaten personal health and safety, educators and clinicians are concerned with their control and elimination.

The major problem presented by stereotypy is that it interferes with a child's level of attention to environmental stimuli, often limiting the effectiveness of educational programming efforts and learning.

A variety of theories have been proposed to explain the causes of stereotyped repetitive, and restricted behaviors (Whitman, 2004; Whitman & Ekas, 2008). One explanation suggests that there is an optimal level of stimulation necessary for adaptive human functioning. In order to maintain homeostasis, individuals self-activate or seek stimulation when their level of arousal is low or conversely decrease stimulation when their overall level of arousal is high. According to this perspective, repetitive, stereotyped, and restricted behaviors serve a homeostatic function, directed either at increasing stimulation or reducing external stimulation.

A second major, albeit related, explanation for these behaviors is that they serve to reduce tension or anxiety. These responses are activated when an individual becomes stressed or experiences a high level of arousal. Both the homeostatic and the tension/arousal hypotheses suggest that although the external environment plays a role, the critical factor is not what is happening in the environment per se, but what impact the environment has on the state of arousal/activation within the individual.

A third explanation is based on learning theory and the concepts of positive and negative reinforcement (see Chapter 2). From this perspective, stereotyped, repetitive, and restricted behaviors in a child with autism can be increased through negative reinforcement; for example, if parents cease to make demands upon their children when they become upset and engage in repetitive behaviors such as body rocking. Alternatively, these behaviors can also be increased through positive reinforcement; for example if parents provide comfort to children who are distressed and are engaging in rocking behavior.

A number of other explanations for the emergence of stereotyped, repetitive, and restricted behaviors have been proposed. For example, there is some evidence that the dopamine and opiate systems may be involved. It has been suggested that behaviors, like body rocking, produce a pleasant biochemical state that reinforces the individual for engaging in such behaviors. Finally, as discussed in Chapter 10, a cognitive-behavioral explanation for stereotyped, repetitive, and restricted behavior argues that these behaviors are reflective of an immature primitive self-regulatory response system that is sustained over time because of the cognitive and language deficiencies of children with autism.

In addition to the aforementioned stereotyped, repetitive, and restricted behaviors, individuals with ASD frequently engage in a number of other unusual and related behaviors that can be categorized as obsessive and/or compulsive in nature. Obsessions usually relate to "behaviors" that are more cognitive in nature, whereas compulsions typically are nonverbal or motoric in nature. These behaviors appear to be used by the individual to create or maintain order in the environment. Examples of these behaviors include: repetitively writing words or numbers, adhering rigidly to a routine, talking incessantly about a certain topic, and asking repeatedly to engage in a particular activity. These behaviors tend to increase in frequency when an individual is having difficulty adapting to a new environment and/or is under stress. It appears that individuals with autism, like those with obsessive compulsive disorder (OCD), use these behaviors as a way to reduce anxiety (Whitman, 2004). Recent research indicates that individuals diagnosed with OCD also have a higher frequency of autistic symptoms than non-clinical controls (Anholt et al., 2010).

Intervention perspectives and strategies

From an intervention perspective, it is best not to focus on reducing the stereotyped, repetitive, and restricted behaviors of children with autism; specifically because these behaviors, however immature, help children cope with environments that for them are incomprehensible, chaotic, and stressful. Attempts to reduce behaviors, such as stereotypy and restrictive responses, without providing a more adaptive means of self-regulation can leave children with autism defenseless and unable to cope. However, if these behaviors allow children to lapse into their autistic world, interfere with meaningful social interaction, and make learning difficult, some type of behavior reduction program may need to be considered. In such circumstances there are several general intervention strategies that can be employed to address the external and internal circumstances that elicit these behaviors and which can be utilized in conjunction with programs directed at developing more mature forms of self-regulation. These include strategies that are emotion-focused, environment-focused, and behavior-focused.

The assumption underlying the use of emotion-focused strategies is that stereotypy, repetitive, and restricted behaviors occur because children are anxious. Strategies, such as reciprocal inhibition and desensitization, can be utilized to inhibit this anxiety (see Chapter 2). For example, enjoyable activities or stimuli can be introduced to reduce the anxiety that children with autism experience when they are confronted with challenging social interactions or academic tasks. A closely related strategy is environmentally focused and directed toward modifying the structure of the challenging situations in which stereotyped and restricted behaviors occur so as to make these situations less stressful (see Chapter 2). Both strategies are similar in that they attempt to reduce anxiety, either directly or indirectly.

Another set of intervention strategies is behavior focused and directed at the secondary gains that sometimes accrue when children with autism engage in stereotyped, repetitive, and restricted behaviors. More specifically, these behaviors may be reinforced if they gain social attention and/or help a child escape or avoid challenging situations, such as a difficult academic task. Behavior-focused strategies include procedures, such as extinction, in which repetitive and restricted behaviors are ignored, and differential reinforcement, in which constructive engagement with the environment is positively reinforced.

Based on the theories previously reviewed and the general strategies just discussed, one or more of the following intervention procedures might be useful:

- If the child's stereotyped and repetitive behaviors reflect a state of stimulus deprivation and an attempt by the child to obtain a specific type of stimulation, then providing the child an alternative and more acceptable way of obtaining that stimulation should reduce these behaviors. For example, if a child engages in body rocking, because of the stimulation it provides, he/she might be given a rocking chair or access to a trampoline that provides rhythmic stimulation.

  When this strategy is employed, the key to its success is discovering exactly what type or types of stimulation the repetitive response provides and are sought out by a child. Depending on the child, a repetitive behavior might provide auditory, visual, olfactory (smell), gustatory (taste), tactual, and/or proprioceptive feedback that is pleasing.

- If the child's stereotyped, repetitive and/or restrictive behaviors seem to reflect an attempt to ignore or filter out an environment that is too challenging or too stimulating, an environmentally focused strategy directed at altering specific aspects of that environment might be employed. For example, an academic task might be made less stressful by simplifying problem difficulty, reducing the time spent on difficult tasks, and/or intermixing difficult tasks, with easy tasks.

  Alternatively, if an evaluation indicates that a child tends to engage in a high rate of repetitive behavior when his/her surroundings are noisy and/or when adults engage the child in a highly animated way, the following types of procedures could be employed: the noise level could be reduced and the adults could be coached concerning ways that they could reduce their level of animation, such as by slowing their rate of speech and/or decreasing their use of physical gestures.

- If the child's stereotyped, repetitive, and restricted behaviors appear to increase when he/she is anxious, the emotion-focused strategies described in Chapter 2 might be employed to reduce anxiety. For example, a challenging social interaction with a stranger might be introduced into a context which the child finds enjoyable, such as while playing on a computer game or swimming. Alternatively, if a weighted vest appears to calm the child, he/she might be given such a vest to wear when interacting with the stranger.

- If the child's stereotyped, repetitive, and restricted behaviors seem to increase when adults pay attention to these behaviors, these behaviors should be simply ignored, while more appropriate behaviors are reinforced.

- Finally, if the child's stereotyped, repetitive, and restricted behaviors seem to reflect an attempt to escape an unpleasant situation, such as doing homework, the child should not be negatively reinforced; that is, he/she should not be allowed to get out of doing homework. Instead, such escape behaviors should be ignored and the child reinforced for doing homework.

For more information on these and other strategies, the reader is referred to Chapter 2.

Self-injurious behaviors

Another response sometimes classified under stereotypy is self-injurious behavior. Historically, self-injurious behaviors were often observed in custodial institutional settings where little stimulation was provided to residents. Currently, these behaviors have also been found to occur in some individuals with autism (Cohen et al., 2010). Self-injurious behaviors, like stereotyped responses, are often invariant in form, repetitive and can occur with a high frequency. However, self-injurious behaviors differ from other stereotyped responses in that they result in physical harm. Self-injurious behaviors vary considerably in their topography and include such diverse responses as head banging, face slapping, biting, scratching, eye gouging, and hair pulling. Some self-injurious behaviors, like scratching, may not result in an immediate problem, but can cause great harm through their cumulative effects. Estimates of the incidence of self-injurious behaviors in children with autism vary widely; however, what seems clear is that with the introduction of early intervention programs, this type of behavior problem can be effectively dealt with when it does occur.

Explanations regarding the origins of self-injurious behaviors vary considerably, emphasizing, for example, the importance of organic factors, stimulus deprivation, and developmental immaturity (Whitman, 2004). Most of the theories put forth to explain stereotyped behaviors have also been employed to understand the etiology of self-injurious behaviors. In some instances, self-injurious behaviors may evolve from stereotyped responses, such as eye rubbing, that gradually escalate in frequency and intensity, resulting in injury. Researchers acknowledge that environmental factors often play a prominent role in the development and maintenance of self-injurious behaviors.

One learning theory-based hypothesis suggests that children with autism engage in self-injurious behaviors in order to avoid or escape situations that they find aversive; for example a child might scratch himself after his parent asks him to go to bed, something he does not want to do. According to this hypothesis, if the child's self-injurious behavior allows him to escape or avoid an undesirable situation, such as going to bed, then it is being negatively reinforced and as a consequence will increase in frequency. An alternative learning theory-based explanation is that self-injurious behavior becomes a problem if it produces increased attention (positive reinforcement), for example a child being consoled and given loving contact after banging his or her head.

Interventions that involve modifying the reinforcing consequences associated with self-injurious behaviors can be quite effective, especially when employed in conjunction with educational programs directed at developing adaptive behavior. Most of the strategies described in the previous section, including emotion-focused, environment-focused, and behavior-focused, for reducing stereotyped, repetitive, and restricted behaviors can also be employed for reducing self-injurious behaviors. The reader is also referred to Chapter 2 for a description of other response deceleration procedures.

Noncompliance, temper tantrums, and aggression

Noncompliance, temper tantrums, and aggression are all behaviors commonly displayed by children with autism. Noncompliance refers to behaviors that involve ignoring or refusing to respond to the social requests of others. Temper tantrums involve intense and demonstrative behaviors, such as screaming, crying, and physical resistance. Aggression refers to responses directed at the destruction of the physical environment or harming others, such as throwing, pushing, spitting, and hitting. Without intervention all of these behavior problems are likely to increase in frequency and intensity as children grow older.

Aggressive behavior represents one of the most debilitating responses displayed by children with autism (Whitman, 2004). Aggressive responses not only make it difficult to implement intervention programs directed at developing adaptive behavior, but can also result in children being excluded from community settings. Aggressive behavior presents a major obstacle to inclusive education and the development of friendships. Perhaps the most devastating effect of aggressive behavior is the impact it has on other people's perception of individuals who display such behavior. As children with ASD move into adolescence, growing in size and strength, their aggressive behavior elicits not only concern, but also fear in others; which in turn can result in the further isolation of these children who are already isolated because of their social deficiencies.

Noncompliance, tantrums, and aggressive behaviors are dynamically linked in several ways. If untreated, noncompliance may escalate in intensity and in its topography, progressing from noncompliance to tantrums and aggression. All three responses emerge because they assist the child in escaping an undesirable situation and/or allow the child to manipulate a situation so as to get what is desired. Children with ASDs are likely to be at special risk for developing these behavior problems because of their immature self-regulatory system, low frustration tolerance, language and communication deficiencies, poor social skills, and deficits in social cognition (Guttmann-Steinmetz, Gadow, & DeVincent, 2009).

From an intervention perspective, educational programs directed at reducing these behaviors often utilize techniques to increase self-regulatory, social, language, and communication skills, sometimes coupled with behavior reduction and environmental modification programs (see Chapter 2 for a full discussion of behavior reduction techniques). When successful, such interventions are associated with not only a reduction in these behaviors, but also improved adaptive behavior.

Self-toileting delays

One of the early and often most difficult training tasks parents confront is teaching children with autism appropriate toileting behaviors. The reasons for this difficulty relate in part to the autistic characteristics of the children, including their language deficiencies and their desire to maintain existing routines. Parents often defer toilet training until their child is older because they either assume that their child is not able to learn to self-toilet at a younger age or they may decide "not to fight this battle now," instead choosing to fight other battles.

There are, however, a variety of reasons for initiating toilet training during the second or third year. First, the child has less time to establish immature toileting behaviors as a habit, a habit that may be difficult to break. Second, early toilet training reduces the caretaking burden on the family. Finally, it is easier for the toilet-trained child to enter into traditional preschool settings and to be accepted in other social settings.

There are several features that have characterized successful toilet training programs for both typically developing children and children with autism.

- First, the child should be biologically ready to be trained; specifically he/she should show a capacity for remaining dry over night or at least for relatively long periods of time.

- If the child shows a predictable temporal pattern of evacuation/elimination, he/she should be placed on the potty during critical time periods when a response is more likely.

- Another alternative procedure is to place the child on the potty every half hour. While the child is sitting on the toilet, activities he/she enjoys should be pursued.

- Increasing fluids is a good idea because it increases the frequency of urination and thus the possibility of a successful toileting experience.

- Special reinforcers/rewards should be made available to the child for cooperating, sitting on the toilet, as well as for successful evacuations.

- Pants checks should be instituted every half hour and reinforcers/rewards given for dry pants.

- If the child shows signs of needing to go to the bathroom, he/she should be taken immediately. Pants alarms are available commercially that signal the beginning of an urination response. The alarm often interrupts the urination response as well as signals the toilet trainer to bring the child to the bathroom.

- The child should be given a way to communicate when he/she is ready to go to the toilet. If the child does not have words, he/she should be provided a visual toileting card to be given to the person training and taught how to use this card. Reinforcement should be given for this type of communication.

In general, when toilet training is initiated, it is best to dedicate a week for intensive training, incorporating most, if not all of the aforementioned components. Patience on the part of parents is critical, to ensure that the experience is enjoyable for both the parent and child. Once the child begins to urinate appropriately, most of the procedures just listed can be employed for bowel training.

Early eating problems

Estimates of the incidence of early eating problems in the general population vary considerably. These problems are especially prevalent during infancy and early childhood in neurotypical children. Early eating problems appear to occur more often in high-risk populations, especially in children with developmental delays. Based on research and parent report, it is clear that children with ASD frequently have unusual and problematic eating habits.

Early eating problems are often divided into three types: restrictive eating, overeating, and eating non-edible objects (pica). Among children with ASD who have restrictive-eating problems, many foods are a source of anxiety and something to be avoided. Often they have an extremely narrow range of foods that they are willing to accept. In contrast, children with overeating problems compulsively seek out food, in particular foods with a high caloric value. It should be noted that some children are both restrictive in what they eat and are also overeaters. Children with pica have a propensity for eating non-nutritive and inedible substances. Although children with autism display all three of these types of eating problems, restrictive and overeating are particularly prevalent.

The causes of eating problems in children with autism are complex and may be related to medical factors (e.g. allergies, oral-motor problems), autism-related characteristics (e.g. insistence on sameness and routines, specific sensory preferences, and aversions related to the smell, taste, sight, texture, and sound of certain foods) and the social-environment (e.g. parent mismanagement) (Schreck & Williams, 2006). Children with ASD are also likely to be at risk for developing early eating problems because of their lack of attention to the social world and its associated cues that influence eating behaviors, and also because social eating situations are sometimes stressful.

The medical consequences of early eating problems, which can be severe for children with ASD, include: obesity and its associated medical problems, malnutrition, and gastrointestinal problems, including abdominal discomfort, diarrhea, and constipation. Parents of children with autism often turn to medical solutions for these types of problems. Although medical treatments are important for addressing early eating problems that have biological causes and/or medical consequences, the most effective solution to these problems often involves controlling their environmental roots. Environmental intervention includes strategies such as altering: the schedule of feeding, the eating setting, food presentation, and social interaction during meals. This approach makes the assumption that many eating problems are habits that are learned.

Restrictive eating

To expand the repertoire of foods accepted by restrictive eaters, one or more of the following intervention strategies should be considered in cases where there is no clear evidence of biological factors causing the eating problem:

- The range of food choices should be gradually expanded across meals and preferred foods given only after the child has eaten other foods. Initially, only small quantities of less-preferred or non-preferred foods should be offered. If the child chooses not to eat, that is okay, unless medical reasons, such as malnourishment, dictate otherwise.

- Non-preferred foods can be physically blended in a very gradual fashion with preferred foods, with the ratio of non-preferred to preferred foods increasing until preferred foods are eventually faded out.

- A child should not be coerced into eating. Mealtime should be, if possible, accompanied by pleasant activities.

- Healthy non-preferred, but not preferred, foods should be offered as snacks between meals, particularly in conjunction with activities the child enjoys, such as watching a favorite television program. Other members of the family should also eat these snacks, thus serving as role models for the child to emulate.

- If the child becomes upset and demands a certain food, these behaviors should not be reinforced by providing that food. If reinforced, this type of behavior will likely escalate in frequency and intensity, and may result in a more serious eating problem and/or another behavioral problem.

- If the child has difficulty with certain food textures, such textures can be gradually introduced; for example a blender might be used to reduce crunchy foods to a purée, with the texture gradually changed over time to the food's natural state. Other sensory aversions to specific foods can often be handled in a similar way.

Overeating

To address overeating problems the following intervention strategies should be considered:

- A balanced diet should be provided that meets, but does not exceed, recommended daily calorie requirements.

- Between meals, healthy low calorie snacks should be provided.

- If at all possible, the diet of other family members should approximate that given the child. Because overeating and weight problems can be familial in origin, it is important that the child have good role models.

- Treats may be given in small quantities after a healthy meal is eaten, but not as snacks.

- In no instance should a child's unreasonable demands for unhealthy foods be reinforced by giving such foods; because, if reinforced, such demands will only increase over time.

Pica

To reduce pica behavior, the following intervention strategies should be considered:

- The child's environment should be examined and modified as necessary, with inedible objects that a child seeks to eat or might eat removed to the fullest extent possible.

- The child should be provided with desirable, nutritional, food alternatives or non-food objects that can be safely mouthed or sucked.

- Inedible objects that the child seeks to eat should be coated with bitter, sour, or spicy substances, such as lemon and pepper.

- Children should be placed in settings that have high reinforcing value for them. If pica behaviors occur, the child should be removed from this environment.

- For other behavior-reduction methods, the reader is referred to Chapter 2.

In summary, although children with ASD may have a greater tendency to develop eating problems, the solution to such problems is often not a medical one, but rather involves controlling the social and other environmental factors that catalyze these tendencies into an actual eating problem.

Sleeping problems

Estimates of sleep problems in individuals with autism range from 36 to 83 percent (see review by Schreck, 2001). Sleep problems noted in this population include: problems getting to sleep, poor quality of sleep, night waking, sleepwalking, early waking, and irregular sleep patterns (Allik, Larsson, & Smedje, 2006; Arbelle & Ben Zion, 2001). Sleep researchers have documented links between sleep problems and poor behavior regulation, hyperactivity, stereotypy, social skills deficits, anxiety, depression, medical problems, including compromised immune system functioning, decreased alertness and academic problems in both clinical and nonclinical populations (see El-Sheikh, Kelly, Buckhalt, & Hinnant, 2010; Hoffman et al., 2005; Sadeh, Gruber, & Raviv, 2002). Sleep problems in children with autism not only affect the children with the problem, but also their families. Due to children's sleep problems, parents, in particular, also suffer sleep disruptions and as a result have increased stress.

The list of causes and correlates of sleep problems in children with autism is long, and include: age, IQ level, irregular day and bedtime routines, inadequate parental limit-setting practices, environmental disturbances, diet and eating habits, frightening dreams and fear upon awakening, as well as a host of biological problems related to illness, allergies, drugs, and melatonin production (Whitman, 2004). More often than not, sleep problems are related to behavior, lifestyle and social practices and can be addressed without medical interventions. The following intervention strategies can be very helpful in addressing sleep problems in children with ASD:

- A fixed time for going to bed should be established that will allow the child to get 7 to 9 hours of sleep.

- A set schedule of quiet activities that proceed and transition into bedtime should be established. Verbal and/or visual schedules should be provided so that the child is aware of how bedtime fits into his/her schedule. A quiet bedroom activity can be part of that schedule.

- If the child goes to bed without protest, he/she should be praised and given a special reward the next day.

- If the child protests going to bed, he/she should nevertheless be placed gently in bed. Protests and temper tantrums should be ignored. If these behaviors are not ignored and the parents give in to the demand, it is likely that such problem behaviors will increase in frequency and intensity.

- If night awakenings occur, the parents can spend a brief time with child, but then the child should be placed back in bed. Again, protests should be ignored.

- Small night snacks before bed are okay if the child enjoys them.

- When the child goes to bed, the house should be kept reasonably quiet. However, if the child enjoys soft music in the bedroom, it can be provided.

Setting and implementing schedules in a consistent way is critical. Child protests may temporarily increase when such a schedule is put into effect as the child tries to change the rules of the game established by the parents. Such an escalation is normal and to be expected.

Medical issues and autism

Although there is considerable evidence that neurobiological factors play a role in the development of autism, it is less clear what role specific medical factors and conditions commonly associated with autism play in the etiology of this disorder. Barton and Volkmar (1998) review evidence indicating that 10 to 30 percent of persons with autism have a known associated medical condition. Genetic disorders (e.g. Fragile X, Tourette's Syndrome, and Down Syndrome), neurological conditions (e.g. seizure disorders), environmental and infectiously produced diseases (e.g. encephalitis), and prenatal risk factors (e.g. maternal rubella) have been implicated in the development of autism. Barton and Volkmar (1998) suggest, however, that the fundamental relationships may not be between these medical conditions and autism, but between these conditions and intellectual deficiency.

A wide variety of other medical problems have also been linked with autism. Some individuals suggest that these medical problems and the factors that produce them may play a dynamic role in the development of autism. For example, some parents and some parent-related organizations are convinced that immunizations, heavy metals, compromised immune systems, vitamin and other nutritional deficiencies, and gastrointestinal problems play a critical role in the development and treatment of autism as well as its cure. As a consequence of this type of belief, some parents turn to complementary and alternative medicine (CAM), even though most CAM treatments have not been subjected to systematic empirical research (Golnik & Ireland, 2009).

Four possible ways of conceptualizing the relationships between medical problems and autism are described here. One conceptual model asserts that the biological and environmental factors that lead to medical problems in children with autism are different from the biological and environmental factors that produce autism. This model suggests that although children with autism, like all children, sometimes have medical problems, the causal pathways for their autism and their medical problems are independent of one another.

A second conceptual model is similar to the first conceptual model with one fundamental difference. This second model suggests that certain medical problems that children have, such as immune system and gastrointestinal problems, trigger the development of autism. For example, proponents of this conceptualization argue that toxic agents, such as mercury and other heavy metals, in the air, water, or earth or in immunizations produce medical problems that in turn interfere with brain neurochemistry and are instrumental in causing the disorder which is autism.

In contrast, a third conceptual model asserts that medical problems do not cause autism, but rather constitute a biological stressor that merely exacerbates the symptoms associated with autism. Children with autism, not unlike neurotypical children, act differently when they are sick.

Finally, a fourth conceptual model suggests that behaviors associated with autism (e.g. restricted eating habits, sleep problems, pica behaviors, heightened emotional reactivity to environmental stressors), in conjunction with language, cognitive, and social deficiencies, place children at increased risk for developing medical problems, such as dietary deficiencies, immune system problems, and mental retardation. Thus, children with autism are at higher risk for developing certain medical problems because of their autistic and associated risky behaviors.

The clinical implications of each of these models for treating autism is different. Model 1 suggests that children with autism should be treated like neurotypical children when they have medical problems. Model 2 suggests a much more aggressive approach to the treatment of medical conditions that are thought to produce autism, including the use of alternative medicine approaches such as chelation.

In contrast, Model 3 recognizes that medical problems can exacerbate autistic symptoms like other stressors but asserts that such problems do not cause autism. As a consequence the same conventional medical treatments for medical problems that are utilized with neurotypical children are employed with children with autism. Model 4 has implications for preventing medical disorders in children with autism through treating behavior problems that produce such disorders. For example, the probability of developing medical problems can be reduced by changing restrictive eating habits, poor sleep habits, and pica behaviors.

Based on our reading of the literature and consistent with the conceptualizations put forth in Models 1, 3, and 4, we recommend that conventional medicine be applied to children with autism and that behavior-oriented programs be directed toward developing healthy lifestyle behaviors in this population. In contrast, extreme caution should be exercised before employing alternative medical approaches which are often costly, potentially risky, and not empirically validated. More generally, the conceptual models presented here suggest the need for the development of a broader biodevelopmental framework for understanding the antecedents of health and behavior for guiding early childhood policy, including those described by Shonkoff (2010).

Final thoughts

Good educational programs for any child involve hard work. This is particularly true for children with autism. These programs need to be intensive, extensive, and coordinated. At a minimum, they need to be both home-based and school-based. They need to focus on the total child and address sensory, motor, emotional, language/communication, cognitive, and social needs. They should also be directed at helping children to self-regulate and become independent.

Parents, teachers, and other professionals need to coordinate their efforts and have respect for the knowledge and skills that each of them possess. To develop this partnership, social supports need to be put in place to assist families in implementing home-based programs. These supports should not only be directed at teaching new parenting skills, but also at helping parents and siblings cope with the many challenges associated with living with a child with an autism spectrum disorder. Teachers in classrooms also need assistance in developing and delivering education programs for children on the spectrum. Special attention should be given to the provision and training of teacher assistants.

Comprehensive educational and training programs for children with autism are still emerging. Particular emphasis needs to be placed on programs directed at developing cognitive and social skills. In general, based on learning theory and research, we know a lot about how to teach children with autism spectrum disorders. However, more attention needs to be placed on investigating what should be taught. For example, what specific skills are necessary for developing friendships, reading comprehension, and theory of mind. As we learn more about the structure of these complex behaviors and the processes that influence them, programs for teaching these skill sets should be relatively easy to design. Although magic bullets for curing autism are not now available, nor are they likely to be soon, we now know enough, based on theory and empirical research, to alter significantly the developmental trajectory of children with autism spectrum disorders and to help them fulfill their potential. Let us get on with this task.

Program examples

Reducing repetitive behaviors

OBJECTIVE

To reduce the child's stereotyped, repetitive behaviors.

MATERIALS

For this procedure you will need a good data sheet to track the target behavior(s) before, during, and after you implement the procedure(s) below.

PROCEDURE

1. It is first and foremost very important to determine the function of any behavior, even repetitive, stereotyped behaviors. A behavior analyst can assist you with this process. Repetitive, stereotyped behaviors are not always automatically reinforcing, and thus may be maintained by social consequences. For example, a parent may comfort the child who engages in body rocking because the parent assumes the child only does this when he/she is upset. This comfort, in turn, may reinforce the body rocking, and thus maintain the behavior.

2. Once a function is determined, an intervention can begin. There are several different intervention strategies that can be used, but each must be highly individualized. The efficacy of an intervention is determined largely by consistency with program adherence. It is recommended that you seek the help of a certified behavior analyst to implement an actual behavioral intervention. The following list includes descriptions of basic techniques that can be helpful if the behavior is maintained by automatic reinforcement (i.e. not by social consequences).

    a) Replace the behavior with a task that competes with the behavior. For example, if the child is spinning objects, teach the child to do something that will keep his/her hands busy thus decreasing their ability to spin. The child may need prompting to complete this new activity, as well as reinforcement for continuing and completing the activity.

    b) Offer some new reinforcers to the child. Show the child how to engage with each new item. Then place all the items in front of the child and let the child play by him/herself. Keep track of which items the child plays with the longest, as well as which items result in a simultaneous decrease in the target repetitive behavior while the child is engaged with that item. Then use the item(s) that the child plays with the most *and* results in a simultaneous decrease in the target behavior as a reinforcer. Deliver the new reinforcer on a variable time schedule (e.g. about every 5 minutes for 2 to 3 minutes), regardless of what the child is doing (i.e. contingent on time, not behavior). If this is too time intensive, carry out this procedure at a time when the child is most likely to engage in the repetitive behavior.

c) Re-examine the child's day. Consider how much stimulation is in the child's life. Perhaps the child's schedule needs to be revised. Add activities that will help to keep the child engaged and motivated throughout the day. Activity schedules can be very helpful for this purpose.

d) Rotate the toys available to the child. Boredom, or decreased motivation to play with what is available, can sometimes be easily remedied by a daily or weekly toy rotation. Toys that are not always available can have more appeal when they do become available. Remember that some children need help learning how to play with toys, and may need reinforcement for playing appropriately.

e) Give the child a more appropriate means of producing the same stimulation as the repetitive behavior. A child who rocks back and forth throughout the day may be allowed time to rock in a rocking chair once or twice per hour, or upon request. At other times, block or stop the child from rocking and redirect him or her to another activity.

Tips/suggestions

Take data on the frequency, severity, and time of day or location of the behavior before, during and after you attempt any sort of intervention or technique. This way you can see if your intervention is effective, ineffective, or making things worse.

Other teaching methods

If you are concerned about anxiety, consider seeking help with decreasing anxiety. Perhaps desensitization or appropriate coping skills would be effective. Sometimes simply blocking and redirecting the behavior can be effective. For example, if the child is spinning an object, stop the object and redirect the child to another task that does not involve spinning. Keep in mind that this attention may incidentally reinforce the behavior, so do not attend to the behavior any more than is necessary to block the response and redirect (i.e. it is not necessary to tell the child to stop).

Always consider alternative means of communication when decreasing challenging behaviors. What is it that the child is trying to tell you by engaging in this behavior? If it is too loud, teach the child to request that you turn down the music. If the work is too hard, teach the child to request help.

Along the same lines, if the child is engaging in the task only during work time, consider re-evaluating the work tasks. They may need to be broken down into smaller steps, or the child may be missing an important prerequisite skill. Alternatively, increasing the frequency of reinforcement for completing small tasks successfully can go a long way in decreasing challenging behaviors.

Reducing self-injurious behavior

OBJECTIVE

To reduce the child's self-injurious behaviors.

MATERIALS

For this procedure, you will need a good data sheet to track the target behavior(s) before, during, and after you try the procedure(s) below.

PROCEDURE

1. It is essential to first determine the function of the behavior prior to attempting to decrease the behavior. A behavior analyst can assist you with this process. Self-injurious behaviors can be reinforced automatically or through social consequences. For example, a child may poke his eye because of the visual stimulation that occurs when he does so. Or he may poke his eye because when he does, he gets a lot of attention or comfort from people around him. In addition, he could poke himself in the eye because it results in the removal of demands. The effectiveness of the method you choose to decrease the behavior depends mainly upon choosing a method that matches the function of the behavior.

2. Once a function is determined, you can begin attempting to decrease this behavior. There are several different intervention strategies that can be used, but each must be highly individualized. The efficacy of an intervention is determined largely by consistency with program adherence. It is recommended that you seek the help of a certified behavior analyst to implement an actual behavioral intervention. The following list includes descriptions of basic techniques that can be helpful if the behavior is maintained by social consequences (i.e. not by automatic reinforcement).

a) If the function of the behavior is attention (positive or negative) from others, consider the following methods:

i) If the self-injurious behavior is not severe (i.e. does not cause harm) disregard any instance of the behavior. Meanwhile, deliver attention to the child on a consistent, dense schedule (e.g. every 5 minutes for 2 to 3 minutes) to decrease motivation for attention. The attention you provide should be similar to the type of attention that typically follows the self-injurious behavior. For example, if you typically comfort and hug the child when he/she engages in the self-injurious behavior, then provide comfort and hugs on this schedule of reinforcement. However, no longer give the child such attention following the self-injurious behavior.

ii) Use differential reinforcement. Deliver more attention for good behaviors, and less attention for self-injurious behaviors. For example, when you see the child playing nicely, working hard, asking for something appropriately, or any other appropriate behavior deliver a lot of attention.

iii) Teach the child an appropriate way to request attention, or an alternative method of receiving the same attention. Some children prefer reprimands from adults, and thus such reprimands (e.g. "Stop it!") can reinforce any behavior they follow, including self-injurious behavior. Perhaps the child can ask you to play a game of chase with him or her, during which you chase the child saying, "I'm going to get you! Get back here!" in a playful tone. Similarly, a child can learn to request attention by tapping you on the shoulder or asking for a hug. When teaching these alternative forms of communication, reinforce each occurrence of the appropriate communication, and do not reinforce (i.e. attend to) the self-injurious behavior.

b) If the function of the behavior is escape from demands or work situations, consider the following methods:

i) Re-examine work time. Perhaps the tasks are too difficult and the child needs help or needs to learn certain prerequisite skills. On the other hand, perhaps the work is too easy and the child is not stimulated by the work. In this case, consider moving on to new, advanced material, and/or increasing the frequency and different types of reinforcers you deliver.

ii) If the behavior is severe or intense, consider removing demands completely and reintroducing them gradually, one at a time. When reintroducing, do not reinforce self-injurious behavior with escape from the demand. Simultaneously increase reinforcement of compliance with demands as they are reintroduced.

iii) Alternate difficult and easy tasks. Some children do well when an easy task precedes and follows each difficult task, which seems to result in building momentum. For example, if a child can already follow basic instructions, but is still learning to state his/her name, deliver the instructions in this order, "Clap your hands. What's your name? Stomp your feet. Who are you? Arms up." Deliver praise following each easy task, and a highly preferred reinforcer following each difficult or new task.

iv) Teach the child a more appropriate way of communicating the need for a break. Teach this skill when you are in situations in which the child is very likely to engage in the self-injurious behavior. Prior to the occurrence of self-injurious behavior, prompt the child to request a break (e.g. verbally, with PECS, sign language, etc.). Immediately allow the child to take a break. Once the child has learned to reliably request a break when one is needed, start teaching the child to wait for the break. Keep wait times short and gradually build up to longer wait times.

v) Provide frequent breaks from work, prior to the occurrence of any self-injurious behavior. For the most success, time how long the child will work before engaging in the self-injurious behavior. Then deliver the breaks shortly before that time. For example, if a child will work for 1 minute before he hits himself, then work for 30 seconds and give him a break before the self-injurious behavior occurs. Continue, gradually increasing the work time.

TIPS/SUGGESTIONS

Take data on the frequency, severity, and time of day or location of the behavior before, during and after you attempt any sort of intervention or technique. This way you can see if your intervention is effective, ineffective, or making things worse.

If the behavior is severe or harmful to the child, do not attempt to use any intervention without the assistance of a certified or licensed professional.

OTHER TEACHING METHODS

If the self-injurious behaviors are maintained by automatic reinforcement, use methods for reducing such behavior (see program example for Reducing repetitive behaviors).

Increasing compliance (reducing noncompliance)

OBJECTIVE

To increase a child's compliance with instructions.

MATERIALS

For this procedure, you will need a good data sheet to track the target behavior(s) before, during, and after you try the procedure(s) below.

PROCEDURE

1. Deliver an instruction to the child (e.g. "Throw away your napkin.").

2. Wait 3 to 5 seconds for the child to comply or begin the task.

3. If the child does not comply within 3 to 5 seconds, repeat the instruction and use a gestural prompt (e.g. point to the napkin and then the trash can).

4. If the child does not comply within 3 to 5 seconds, repeat the instruction and use physical guidance to help the child complete the task (e.g. put your hand over the child's hand, use the child's hand to pick up the napkin and then throw it in the trash).

5. Use differential reinforcement to reinforce compliance at the various stages of prompting.

   a) If the child complies the first time you deliver the instruction deliver the most highly preferred reinforcer (e.g. 10 minutes of computer time) and enthusiastic praise.

   b) If the child complies after a gestural prompt deliver a preferred reinforcer, but not necessarily the best one, or for a shorter period of time (e.g. 5 minutes of computer time).

   c) If the child requires physical guidance to complete the step, deliver praise and no tangible reinforcer, or for early learners a very small or less preferred reinforcer (e.g. 1 minute of computer time, or a small snack).

TIPS/SUGGESTIONS

If the child is an early learner, you may have to also teach him/her to follow basic instructions with a more structured program (see Chapter 3). Along the same lines, be sure that the child understands the instructions. Deliver instructions in a very simple, straightforward manner. For example, when asking a child to clean his room, say, "Put your trains in this blue bucket," rather than, "Clean your room."

OTHER TEACHING METHODS

If the child is resistant to physical guidance and/or tends to engage in aggressive behavior, you may not be able to implement the above procedure. Instead, categorize instructions into high probability (i.e. the child is very likely to comply with this instruction), medium probability (i.e. the child may comply), and low probability (i.e. the child is unlikely to comply) instructions, based on how the child is likely to respond to the instruction. For example, a high probability instruction may be, "Eat this piece of candy." A medium probability instruction may be, "Go down the slide." And a low probability instruction may be, "Sit down in the chair." Such categorization will be different for each child.

Once you have categorized the instructions, begin the above procedure with high probability instructions. Reinforce compliance with such instructions. Occasionally, sandwich a medium probability instruction in between two high probability instructions, increasing the number, frequency, or time with the reinforcer for compliance with medium probability instructions. Continue in this pattern, eventually building up to low probability instructions. Again, increase the number, frequency, or time with the reinforcer for compliance with low probability instructions. This method can be highly effective when used in conjunction with the procedure outlined above.

Toilet training

OBJECTIVE

To teach the child to use the toilet to urinate.

MATERIALS

For this procedure, you will need highly preferred beverages (e.g. juice), preferred food and toys, a timer, a picture of a toilet (if the child uses PECS), and ideally a urine alarm.

Procedure

1. When beginning toilet training, be sure you can devote a substantial portion of time to training (e.g. 3 to 5 days). You must be ready and available to catch accidents before they happen or while they are happening.

2. On the first day, make sure the child is drinking a preferred beverage very frequently in order to increase the number of opportunities he/she will have for urination. Stop giving the child as much to drink toward the end of the day so that the child will not have accidents in the evening or overnight.

3. Before putting the child on the toilet, prompt him/her to say or sign, "Potty," or give you the icon for "potty." Do not simply tell the child it's time to go potty. This will help the child learn to initiate going to the bathroom when he/she needs to go.

4. Place the child on the toilet using a sit schedule. Begin with a very dense schedule (e.g. 5 minutes on the toilet, 5 minutes off the toilet). Increase the schedule gradually (e.g. 5 minutes on, 10 minutes off) once an hour for the first 4 to 6 hours.

5. Use differential reinforcement:

    a) If the child urinates in the toilet, deliver highly enthusiastic praise and highly preferred food, toys, or other reinforcers. Ideally these reinforcers should be used only for successfully urinating in the toilet and not for any other behaviors until the child has completed toilet training. Let the child get off the toilet and go play.

    b) If the child has an accident, immediately take the child to the toilet. Have him/her request potty and then sit the child on the toilet. If he/she finishes on the toilet, deliver reinforcers as in step a) above. If he/she does not finish urinating in the toilet, do not deliver a reinforcer.

6. Continue fading the sit schedule, as the child succeeds.

Tips/suggestions

Prior to toilet training, teach toileting behaviors. For example, do not change the child's diaper in the living room; instead always take the child into the bathroom and have him/her sit down on the toilet. Teach the child to wash his/her hands every time he/she leaves the bathroom. Also, your child should be able to stay dry for at least 30 minutes prior to beginning this procedure.

It may be helpful to use a portable DVD player to play the child's favorite videos while he/she is sitting. Or try singing songs and playing with the child.

A urine alarm can be a helpful way to catch accidents quickly. The alarm will also startle the child, thus making him/her more aware of the accident. Once you start this procedure, you shouldn't place your child in diapers again except during bedtime or long car trips.

Consider the consequence of an accident that is not completed in the toilet. In addition to withholding the reinforcer, you may need to widen the distinction between successes and failures when it comes to toileting by adding a negative consequence. Positive practice is one method commonly used in toilet training, in which the child must return to the scene of the accident, request potty, then walk back to the toilet, sit down and then stand immediately backup and repeat the sequence 3 to 5 times. Sometimes positive practice is also paired with a firm reminder of the rule, "We go potty on the toilet, not in our pants," or something similar.

OTHER TEACHING METHODS

Conduct pants checks and record data every 15 minutes as to whether your child is wet or dry. Once you have collected consistent data for 1 to 2 weeks, analyze the data and determine if the child goes at approximately the same time each day, or in relation to the last time he/she ate or drank something. Use this data to schedule toilet sits for your child around the time you expect him/her to urinate. This will maximize success in the toilet. However, you will still need to use differential reinforcement to increase toilet successes and decrease accidents.

Restrictive eating

OBJECTIVE

Teach the child to eat a wider variety of foods.

MATERIALS

For this procedure, you will need highly preferred foods and beverages as well as a range of non-preferred foods. Cut all the foods into very small (e.g. dime sized or smaller) pieces.

Note: This procedure should be completed under the supervision of a certified behavior analyst, speech pathologist, or feeding expert. Any attempts to increase or change eating habits could incidentally lead to decreased eating in general, which can have severe health effects.

PROCEDURE

1. Assess the preference of the child's non-preferred foods. Start with the food that the child resisted the least out of all the non-preferred foods.

2. Place a small piece of the non-preferred food in front of the child.

   a) Immediately deliver a preferred food to the child.

   b) Repeat until the child does not exhibit any escape behavior (e.g. attempting to leave the table, yelling, pushing the food away, etc.) for three consecutive trials.

3. Next, ask the child to touch the food. Model the response for the child. The child can use one finger or the whole hand as long as he/she briefly touches the food.

   a) Immediately deliver a preferred food to the child contingent on this behavior.

   b) Repeat until the child does not exhibit any escape behavior (e.g. attempting to leave the table, yelling, pushing the food away, etc.) for three consecutive trials.

4. Ask the child to pick up the food. If appropriate, use a utensil to do so.

   a) Immediately deliver a preferred food to the child contingent on this behavior.

   b) Repeat until the child does not exhibit any escape behavior (e.g. attempting to leave the table, yelling, pushing the food away, etc.) for three consecutive trials.

5. Tell the child to smell the food.

   a) Immediately deliver a preferred food to the child contingent on this behavior.

   b) Repeat until the child does not exhibit any escape behavior (e.g. attempting to leave the table, yelling, pushing the food away, etc.) for three consecutive trials.

6. Ask the child to then taste the food with his/her tongue.

   a) Immediately deliver a preferred food to the child contingent on this behavior.

   b) Repeat until the child does not exhibit any escape behavior (e.g. attempting to leave the table, yelling, pushing the food away, etc.) for three consecutive trials.

7. Then instruct the child to take a bite. For this stage, the child must put the food into his/her mouth.

   a) Immediately deliver a preferred food to the child contingent on this behavior.

   b) Repeat until the child does not exhibit any escape behavior (e.g. attempting to leave the table, yelling, pushing the food away, etc.) for three consecutive trials.

8. Tell the child to swallow the food.

   a) Immediately deliver a preferred food to the child contingent on this behavior.

   b) Repeat until the child does not exhibit any escape behavior (e.g. attempting to leave the table, yelling, pushing the food away, etc.) for three consecutive trials.

9. Increase the number of food bites, or the size of the food the child must eat.

Tips/suggestions

Do not force the child to stay at the table or to move forward in the procedure before he/she is ready. Alternatively, do not remove the non-preferred food contingent on him/her engaging in inappropriate behavior. If at any time the child gags or vomits end the procedure. Start this procedure at a time the child is likely to be hungry (e.g. lunchtime).

For step 7, provide the child with a "no thank you" cup that he/she can spit the item into if the child decides that it is not desired. This is a more appropriate way of refusing the item than perhaps throwing the food or swiping it off the table. Also, you can count or use a timer to help the child understand how long he/she must keep the food in his/her mouth before he/she can spit it out. At some point very soon after reaching this step, however, the child will need to be instructed to move on to step 8.

For swallowing, some children may understand better if you instruct them to "make the food disappear" or "go away." Use better reinforcers for this stage.

If the child is stuck at stage 6 or 7 for more than 4 to 5 days, consider giving up on this particular food. Some people simply do not enjoy the taste of certain foods and should not be forced to eat them. Instead, find alternatives. For example, if the child needs to eat more vegetables, think of foods she already likes. If she likes to eat crunchy foods, choose raw vegetables, such as carrots. Similarly, try adding preferred foods to non-preferred foods. For example, dip strawberries in chocolate, put peanut butter on apples, and so on.

Sleeping problems

OBJECTIVE

To reduce the child's sleep problems.

PROCEDURE

1. First, if your child is having sleeping difficulties, seek a complete medical assessment from your pediatrician to ensure that there are no medical reasons for the child's sleep problems.

2. If there are no medical problems, set up a regular nighttime routine.

    a) Choose a strict, consistent bedtime.

    b) Do not allow naps prior to bedtime.

    c) Pick an activity or series of activities to precede bedtime. For example, brush teeth, take a warm bath, read a story, sing a song. Keep the routine pretty consistent each night.

    d) Leave the child's room. Do not reenter the room, despite crying.

    e) If the child gets out of bed, place him/her back in bed without saying anything to the child. Then leave the room again. Repeat as necessary.

3. Use a reward system to reinforce appropriate bedtime behavior. Consider a sticker chart or deliver a special breakfast treat each time the child goes to bed the night before without any problems.

TIPS/SUGGESTIONS

Take data on the number of times the child gets out of bed each night to see if this procedure is effective. As difficult as it is, the less attention you give to the child for leaving his/her bed, the quicker the child will learn to stay in bed. Do not allow the child to sleep in your bed and/or do not sleep in the bed with the child. These are very difficult habits to break. Use the above procedure to break such habits, but be prepared for the procedure to take longer and for the child to become a bit distressed temporarily. Do something noisy to preoccupy yourself during the first few hours of bedtime, such as the laundry, so that you will not be tempted to retrieve your child when you hear him/her crying. Keep a video monitor in the child's room so you can keep an eye on him/her without having to open the door.

OTHER TEACHING METHODS

If a child consistently wakes early, despite the bedtime or number of hours slept, consider teaching the child to remain in his/her room and/or engage in a safe task until a certain time. For example, teach the child to put on a DVD, or read a book in bed until a certain time. Use an alarm clock to cue the child as to when he/she can leave the room and go wake up others.

Playing music or giving massages can also be great methods to help your child relax before bedtime. Also, despite your child's preferences, lights may actually prevent your child from falling asleep. If your child insists on sleeping with a light, consider a night light, or turn the light off after he/she falls asleep.

References

Allik, H., Larsson, J. O., & Smedje, H. (2006). Sleep patterns of school-age children with Asperger syndrome or high-functioning autism. *Journal of Autism and Developmental Disorders, 36,* 585–595.

American Psychiatric Association (2000). *Diagnostic and statistical manual of mental disorders* (4th ed.) (*DSM-IV-TR*™). Washington, DC: American Psychiatric Association.

Anholt, G. E., Cath, D. C., van Oppen, P., Eikelenboom, M., Smit, J. H., van Megen, H., & van Balkom, A. J. L. M. (2010). Autism and ADHD symptoms in patients with OCD: Are they associated with specific OC symptom dimensions or OC symptom severity? *Journal of Autism and Developmental Disorders, 40,* 580–589.

Arbelle, S. & Ben-Zion, I. (2001). "Sleep problems in autism." In E. Schopler, N. Yirmuja, C., Shulman, & L. Marcus (Eds.), *The research basis for autism intervention* (pp. 219–228). New York, NY: Kluwer Academic Plenum.

Barton, M. & Volkmar, F. (1998). How commonly are known medical conditions associated with autism? *Journal of Autism and Developmental Disorders, 28,* 273–278.

Cohen, I. L., Tsiouris, J. A., Flory, M. J., Kim, S. Y., Freedland, R., Heaney, G., Pettinger, J., & Brown, W. T. (2010). A large scale study of the psychometric characteristics of the IBR modified overt aggression scale: Findings and evidence for increased self-destructive behaviors in adult females with autism spectrum disorder. *Journal of Autism and Developmental Disorders, 40,* 599–609.

Ekas, N. & Whitman, T. L. (2010). Autism symptom topography and maternal socioemotional functioning. *Journal of Intellectual and Developmental Disabilities, 115,* 234–244.

El-Sheikh, M., Kelly, R. J., Buckhalt, J. A., & Hinnant, J. B. (2010). Children's sleep and adjustment over time: The role of socioeconomic context. *Child Development, 81,* 870–883.

Ghaziuddin, M. (2005). A family history study of Asperger syndrome. *Journal of Autism and Developmental Disorders, 35,* 177–182.

Ghaziuddin, M., Ghaziuddin, N., & Greden, J. (2002). Depression in persons with autism: Implications for research and clinical care. *Journal of Autism and Developmental Disorders, 32,* 299–306.

Golnik, A.E. & Ireland, M. (2009). Complementary alternative medicine for children with autism: A physician survey. *Journal of Autism and Developmental Disorders, 39,* 996–1005.

Guttmann-Steinmetz, S., Gadow, K. D., & DeVincent, C. J. (2009). Oppositional defiant and conduct disorder behaviors in boys with autism spectrum disorder with and without attention-deficit hyperactivity disorder versus several comparison samples. *Journal of Autism and Developmental Disorders, 39,* 975–985.

Hoffman, C. D., Sweeney, D. P., Gilliam, J. E., Apodaca, D. D., Lopez-Wagner, M. C., & Castillo, M. M. (2005). Sleep problems and symptomology in children with autism. *Focus on Autism and Other Developmental Disabilities, 20,* 194–200.

Lasgaard, M., Nielsen, A., Eriksen, M. E. & Goossens, L. (2010). Loneliness and social support in adolescent boys with autism spectrum disorders. *Journal of Autism and Developmental Disorders, 40,* 218–226.

Pearson, D. A., Loveland, K. A., Lachar, D., Lane, D. M., Reddoch, S. L., Mansour, R., & Cleveland, L. A. (2006). A comparison of behavioral and emotional functioning in children and adolescents with autistic disorder and PDD-NOS. *Child Neuropsychology, 12,* 321–333.

Sadeh, A., Gruber, R., & Raviv, A. (2002). Sleep, neurobehavioral functioning and behavior problems in school-age children. *Child Development, 73,* 405–417.

Schreck, K. (2001). Behavioral treatments for sleep problems in autism: Empirically supported or just universally accepted. *Behavioral Interventions, 16,* 265–278.

Schreck, K. A. & Williams, K. (2006). Food preferences and factors influencing food selectivity for children with autism spectrum disorders. *Research in Developmental Disabilities, 27,* 353–363.

Shonkoff, J. P. (2010). Building a new biodevelopmental framework to guide the future of early childhood policy. *Child Development, 81,* 357–367.

Stillman, W. (2005). *The everything parent's guide to children with Asperger's Syndrome: Help, hope and guidance.* Avon, MA: Adams Media.

Volker, M. A., Lopata, C., Smerbeck, A. M., Knoll, V. A., Thomeer, M. L., Toomey, J. A., & Rodgers, J. D. (2010). BASC-2 PRS profiles for students with high-functioning autism spectrum disorders. *Journal of Autism and Developmental Disorders, 40,* 188–199.

Whitman, T. L. (2004). *The development of autism: A self-regulatory perspective.* London: Jessica Kingsley Publishers.

Whitman, T. L. & Ekas, N. (2008). Theory and research on autism: Do we need a new way of thinking about and studying this disorder? *International Review of Research in Mental Retardation, 35,* 1–41.

About the Authors

Tom Whitman is a professor of Psychology at the University of Notre Dame. His research and scholarship have centered on the investigation of biological and social factors that place children at risk for physical, cognitive, and socioemotional problems. He is the author of over a hundred research articles and chapters, as well as five books including *The Development of Autism: A Self-Regulatory Perspective*. His current research and publications focus on stress and coping in mothers of children with autism spectrum disorders. He is the co-director of the Notre Dame Research Training Program on Intellectual and Developmental Disabilities. He has been the recipient of numerous federal research and training grants, including two current projects funded by the National Institutes of Health. Finally, he has been teaching courses in the area of developmental disabilities and autism during most of his professional career.

Nicole DeWitt's educational background is in the area of psychology. She received a master's degree in psychology and behavior analysis from Western Michigan University. She is a certified behavior analyst who has trained graduate and undergraduate college students in the principles and application of learning-based education programs for children with disabilities. She has served as a director of home-based services for children with autism and their families. In her current position at the Sonya Ansari Regional Center for Autism she is involved in developing and evaluating intervention and education programs for children with autism in family, school, and other community settings.

Subject Index

Author Index